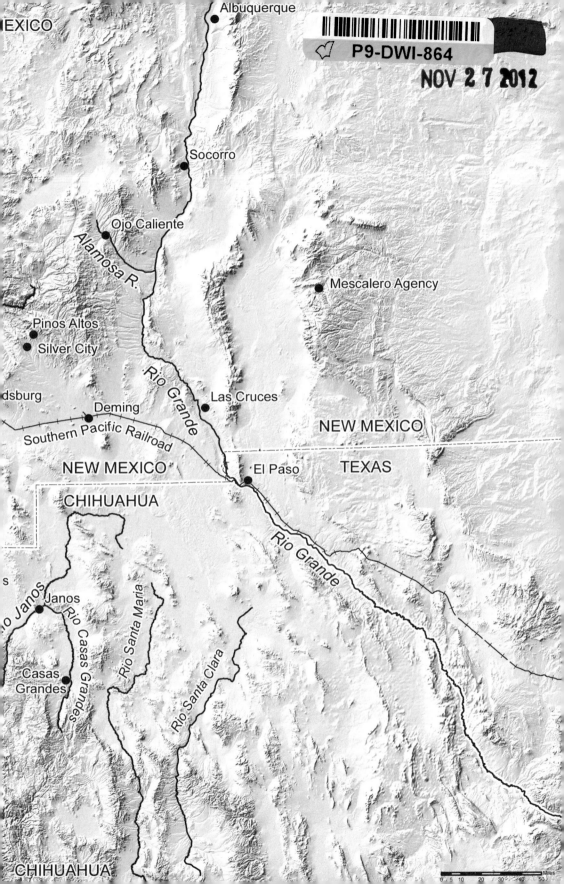

MEXICO

Albuquerque

Socorro

Ojo Caliente

Alamosa R.

Mescalero Agency

Pinos Altos

Silver City

Rio Grande

Las Cruces

dsburg

Deming

NEW MEXICO

Southern Pacific Railroad

NEW MEXICO

TEXAS

El Paso

CHIHUAHUA

Rio Grande

s

Rio Janos

Janos

Rio Casas Grandes

Rio Santa Maria

Casas
Grandes

Rio Santa Clara

CHIHUAHUA

Miles
0 5 10   20   30   40   50

GERONIMO

Recent Titles

Furs and Frontiers in the Far North: The Contest among Native and Foreign Nations for the Bering Strait Fur Trade, by John R. Bockstoce
War of a Thousand Deserts: Indian Raids and the U.S.–Mexican War, by Brian DeLay
Defying the Odds: The Tule River Tribe's Struggle for Sovereignty in Three Centuries, by Gelya Frank and Carole Goldberg
The Bourgeois Frontier: French Towns, French Traders, and American Expansion, by Jay Gitlin
"Liberty to the Downtrodden": Thomas L. Kane, Romantic Reformer, by Matthew J. Grow
The Comanche Empire, by Pekka Hämäläinen
Hell on the Range: A Story of Honor, Conscience, and the American West, by Daniel Herman
William Clark's World: Describing America in an Age of Unknowns, by Peter Kastor
The Jeffersons at Shadwell, by Susan Kern
The American Far West in the Twentieth Century, by Earl Pomeroy
Borderlines in Borderlands: James Madison and the Spanish-American Frontier, 1776–1821, by J. C. A. Stagg

Forthcoming Titles

Welcome to Wonderland: Promoting Tourism in the Rocky Mountain West, by Peter Blodgett
The Shapes of Power: Frontiers, Borderlands, Middle Grounds, and Empires of North America, by Pekka Hämäläinen
Bold Spirits, by Monica Rico
Chosen Land: The Legal Creation of White Manhood on the Eighteenth-Century Kentucky Frontier, by Honor Sachs

GERONIMO

ROBERT M. UTLEY

Yale UNIVERSITY PRESS/NEW HAVEN & LONDON

Yale University Press books may be purchased in quantity for educational, business, or
promotional use. For information, please e-mail sales.press@yale.edu (U.S. office) or sales@
yaleup.co.uk (U.K. office).

Designed by Mary Valencia.
Set in Adobe Garamond type by Westchester Book Group.
Printed in the United States of America.

Library of Congress Cataloging-in-Publication Data

Utley, Robert Marshall, 1929–
Geronimo / Robert M. Utley.
p. cm. — (Lamar series in western history)
Includes bibliographical references and index.
ISBN 978-0-300-12638-9 (clothbound : alk. paper)
1. Geronimo, 1829–1909. 2. Apache Indians—Kings and rulers—Biography. 3. Apache
Indians—Wars, 1883–1886. 4. Apache Indians—History. I. Title.
E99.A6G3276 2012
979.004'972560092—dc23
[B]
2012019521
A catalogue record for this book is available from the British Library.

This paper meets the requirements of ANSI/NISO Z39.48–1992 (Permanence of Paper).
10 9 8 7 6 5 4 3 2 1

For Ed Sweeney,
master of Chiricahua sources and friend and colleague.
This book rests heavily on his pioneering work.

CONTENTS

Illustrations follow page 156

PREFACE

GERONIMO!

A shouted or muted code word for a range of uses from World War II paratroopers to Osama bin Laden's Pakistani compound. Why Geronimo? Why does the name stand out more prominently than other North American Indian leaders? Why has Geronimo been the Indian name that has lodged more deeply in the public mind than any other since the early 1880s? The name of this Apache leader has cast a shadow over Indian chiefs ranging from Tecumseh and Pontiac to Crazy Horse and Chief Joseph. None comes close to challenging the dominance of Geronimo. His name is the best known of all North American Indian leaders.

Yet Geronimo was not a chief. Sometimes he led parts or all of the Chiricahua Apache tribe; at other times he commanded only a personal following of about thirty in his extended family. Sometimes he executed brilliant strategy and tactics; at other times he neglected the most elementary techniques of Apache warfare. He was not, as legend asserts, the hero leading his people in a last stand to retain their homeland.

If not, who was he? What persona resides beneath the legend?

With Geronimo, to penetrate the layers of legend is to engage in the detective work of a great mystery. He was fifty-four years old before his name came to the notice of white people. Before that, only his flawed autobiography and a few other Indian sources cast light on his life. After that, many whites and Indians stated their opinions of who he was. They are so contradictory that they define Geronimo *as* a personality of many contradictions.

Once before, in *The Lance and the Shield: The Life and Times of Sitting Bull* (Henry Holt, 1993), I attempted to understand a significant person from another culture. The Lakota Sioux chief Sitting Bull has also achieved legendary status, although not as prominently as Geronimo. I steeped myself in Sitting Bull's culture and tried to interpret his life's path within his context.

Multiple reliable sources, both Indian and white, chronicle his life's path, from birth to death. Unlike Geronimo, Sitting Bull consistently acted as his culture prescribed. Culture, dedication to the welfare of the Lakota, a consistent resistance to the encroachments of the white people, and an unflinching devotion to his people narrowed the quest for the real person obscured by the legend.

For Geronimo, the task is infinitely harder. The real person beneath the legend is more of a ghost. One can master his culture, but unlike Sitting Bull he did not rigidly adhere to it. Much of his early life remains shrouded in mystery. Much of his later life must be inferred from both white and Indian sources. They tell where he was and what he did, but rarely why he did it. The context of Geronimo's life is much wider than Sitting Bull's.

Furthermore, Geronimo exhibits essentially two personae. When he came to white public notice, he was a Chiricahua Apache leader, often fighting the Americans, often accommodating to them. The newspapers carried frequent accounts of his activities—usually embellished or even false. To the newspapers he owes his prominence, for the stories that clogged them planted his name in the public mind. After his surrender, he evolved into a different person, but no less prominent and no less contradictory. For nearly thirty years, in these incarnations, he fascinated the public. By then, the fascination had gained such momentum that it rolled unabated into the twenty-first century and in 2011 demonstrated its continuing appeal in the Pakistani compound of the current world's most malevolent terrorist.

Geronimo's life's path is far rockier than Sitting Bull's, but it is a path worth exploring.

The path has been explored many times, in books, articles, motion pictures, and museums. The standard biography since 1976 has been Angie Debo, *Geronimo: The Man, His Time, His Place* (University of Oklahoma Press, 1976). Why, then, with a sound biography followed by countless unsound books and articles, explore the path again? I have undertaken this project because of much new material, published and unpublished, becoming available since 1976. Also, not to denigrate Angie Debo, my research leads me to different interpretations than hers. Thus my exploration has added another entry to the Geronimo bibliography.

I have tried to present various episodes from both the Apache and the white perspectives, instead of using what award-winning author T. J. Stiles

terms the usual historian's "omniscient overview." Thus what the Indians per-
ceived is set down without including vital information they did not know.
This is followed by the white perspective, what they knew and reported. The
change of perspective is signaled by space breaks and transitional sentences in
the body of the book.

Military installations in the Southwest were named either camp or fort.
This can be confusing, especially since many camps later became forts. I have
avoided this confusion by naming all these places forts. Thus Camp Bowie,
later Fort Bowie, is Fort Bowie from the first mention.

According to the only reliable source, compiled by Gillette Griswold at Fort
Sill in 1958–61, Geronimo had eight wives over his lifetime, all but one of
whom is named. I have attempted to place these eight at the appropriate places
in Geronimo's lifetime. (A ninth marriage was quickly terminated.) Unfortu-
nately, several additional wives, not named, turn up in the sources as shot
or taken captive. I cannot account for them but include them as the sources
dictate.

I wish to acknowledge those whose interest and aid have contributed importantly to this book. Topping the list is Edwin R. Sweeney, whose biographies of Mangas Coloradas and Cochise and history of the Chiricahuas from
Cochise to Geronimo proved indispensable. Sweeney probed Mexican
sources—archives, papers, newspapers—as no one else has. Geronimo and his
cohorts cannot be followed through their Mexican adventures without resort
to Sweeney's work. Moreover, Ed has become a close friend and adviser who
often pointed the way for me as I struggled with questions about Apache life
south of the border. He has also exploited numerous archives in the United
States that I have been unable to reach and provided me with photocopies of
critical sources. I am deeply grateful for Ed's generosity and counsel.

This is the fourth book for which I have worked with cultural geographer
Peter Dana of Georgetown, Texas, to create shaded relief maps to illustrate
my text. This project has proved very difficult because it ventured into Mexico
and involved the most tangled mountains on the continent. Thanks, Peter.

Never have I submitted a manuscript that my wife, Melody Webb, has not
thoroughly vetted. Her comments are always relevant and valued, and almost
all result in correction and revision. Thanks again, Melody.

Longtime friend H. David Evans of Tucson, Arizona, is intimately familiar
both with the literature of Geronimo and the Chiricahuas and the geography

of the land they roamed. I asked him to review and comment on all the text. Dave graciously consented, and his comments and editing have proved extremely valuable.

I owe a debt of gratitude, as usual, to my longtime agent, Carl Brandt of Brandt and Hochman in New York, and to my valued editor at Yale University Press, Christopher Rogers. In fact, I chose Yale because I wanted to work with Chris. He provided the most thorough and thoughtful evaluation of my manuscript in my experience and offered many suggestions that have led to major revisions. The book is much different and much better than the original because of Chris Rogers. Yale's Laura Jones Dooley deserves special gratitude for the exellent copyediting.

Others whose help has been beneficial include Towana Spivey, director of the Fort Sill Museum; Senior Historian Richard Sommers at the US Army Military History Institute at Carlisle Barracks, Pennsylvania; Gatewood biographer Louis Kraft; Henrietta Stockel; Katherine Reeve of the Arizona Historical Society; and, for crucial help with illustrations, Roy Marcot, Jay Van Orden, and Mark Sublette. Historian T. J. Stiles offered valuable advice in presenting the text. To all: thank you.

PROLOGUE

NOT UNTIL THE AGE of fifty-three did Geronimo come to the attention of the American people. For thirty years he had raided and made war on Mexicans, whom he detested, and occasionally raided in the American Southwest. Apache raids typically ranged from simply stealing stock and other plunder to killing and mutilating or capturing victims. Geronimo practiced all forms of raiding and accumulated a record of brutality that matched that of any of his comrades.

In 1876 Geronimo grew careless and boldly demanded government rations from the agent at the Ojo Caliente agency in New Mexico. He used this place as a base for raids into Arizona while insisting on rations for the time he had been absent. A government agent from Arizona's White Mountain Reservation caught up with him, tricked him into opening himself to seizure by Apache police, took him, shackled in irons, to the White Mountain Reservation, and threw him in the jailhouse, still shackled. Here he endured a humiliating four-month ordeal until released. Here he began his checkered career as a reservation Apache.

A muscular, squat, fierce-looking man, Geronimo had mastered the skills of an Apache fighting man. He possessed the strength and endurance to travel long distances rapidly, even without food or water. He came to know every feature of the Apache landscape—mountains, canyons, deserts, water holes, natural food sources, and above all the virtually inaccessible canyons and heights of Mexico's Sierra Madre. He could "read" signs on the landscape from a broken twig to an upturned stone, and he could travel without leaving his own trail. Bow and arrow, knife, lance, rifle, and pistol were his weapons, and he used them to great effect.

Geronimo was not a chief. Only about thirty Apaches counted him their leader, but a superb leader he was in raid and war. Therefore, he frequently led larger numbers than his own following. On the reservation, he aroused contradictory opinions. "Thoroughly vicious, intractable, and treacherous,"

1

pronounced one army officer. "Schemer and liar," declared another. But still another found him "friendly and good natured." His own Chiricahua tribe had mixed feelings, but they stood in awe of one attribute that either intimidated or impressed them: the Apache cultural concept of "Power." Geronimo possessed, or was thought to possess, this surreal potency that could be applied for harm or help. His Power included high achievement as a shaman, or medicine man, with healing qualities. Even so, some who knew him well agreed with the harsher army officers. "I have known Geronimo all my life up to his death and have never known anything good about him," said one Apache.

The government reservation provided a comfortable environment for Geronimo only in one sense: government rations, and those were often inadequate or not forthcoming at all. His true home lay in both southern New Mexico and Arizona, but more often he stayed in the peaks, gorges, canyons, and ridges of the Sierra Madre of Mexico. There he could hide from Mexican or American soldiers and launch raids against ranchers, villagers, and travelers in both Chihuahua and Sonora. Three times after 1876 Geronimo broke free of the reservation, eluded the soldiers who took his trail, and returned to the Sierra Madre.

Illustrating Geronimo's qualities of leadership in war was an ambush he and his fellow leader Juh arranged in Chihuahua. Juan Mata Ortíz had led a massacre of Apaches who had come to negotiate. In Apache culture, such an act demanded revenge. Mata Ortíz kept a ranch near Galeana. Geronimo and Juh led about 130 fighting men from their Sierra Madre sanctuary down to Galeana and struck Mata Ortíz's ranch. On November 14, 1882, Ortiz collected a force of twenty-two citizens and led them to retaliate. The Chiricahuas had prepared an ambush in Chocolate Pass. Mata Ortiz avoided the trap and had his men dig in on a high hill. Geronimo and Juh gathered their men and attacked up the slope against a heavy fire and overwhelmed the enemy in hand-to-hand fighting. Mata Ortíz and all but one of his men perished. As the lone survivor galloped away on a horse, Geronimo shouted to let him go. He would bring more Mexicans to be slaughtered.

Geronimo demonstrated his raiding technique on April 27, 1886. It occurred during his last raid into Arizona. He led a small party of raiders down the Santa Cruz River and, ten miles north of the border, rode into Hell's Gate Canyon. Here they discovered a ranch house. Approaching, one man climbed a rail fence around a corral and sat. Dogs began barking. A young girl came out to investigate, then ran back inside. A woman rushed out, a baby in her arms. The Apache shot her, picked up her baby, and dashed the baby's head against an adobe wall. Fifteen raiders entered the house and ransacked it. They discovered a young girl, whom Geronimo saved and took captive. From a ridge the Apaches spotted two men working with cattle. They had heard the shots and mounted. Bullets killed one and downed the other's horse, throwing him to the ground and knocking him senseless. Apaches roused him with rifle butts, stripped off his boots and clothing, and took him before Geronimo. For an unknown reason, Geronimo told the man he was free to go and then led the raiders away. The man, Artisan Peck, walked back to his house and saw what had been done to his wife and child and his home. He had seen his wife's niece, a captive, mounted behind Geronimo's son Chappo.

The raiding party killed men both before and after this raid but quickly returned to Mexico when US cavalry got on their trail. The raid exemplified only one of hundreds Geronimo had led both in Mexico and the American Southwest for thirty years.

Geronimo's career in raid and war and on the reservation ended on September 3, 1886.

While Geronimo's legacy in history is undying, he emerges essentially as a not very likable man—neither the "thug" of some accounts nor the great leader fighting to save his homeland of other narratives. The latter image, encompassing all American Indians, seized the American imagination in the late twentieth century and the early twenty-first. It still prevails, largely the result of the remarkable success of Dee Brown's *Bury My Heart at Wounded Knee* and Vine DeLoria's *Custer Died for Your Sins*. Not only motion pictures but popular and some scholarly literature, and the Indians themselves, embraced the new vision, which was a return to the "Noble Savage" era of American history. Crazy Horse, Sitting Bull, Quanah Parker, Satanta, Chief Joseph, Tecumseh, Pontiac, and of course Geronimo crowd the heroic mold. Indians were heroes, culturally pure innocent victims of American expansion. For Geronimo, my book rejects both extremes—thug and hero—and reveals that, within the constraints of Apache culture, he was a human being with many strengths and many flaws.

The public, however, continues to look on Geronimo as an Apache leader fighting to save his homeland from takeover by the westward-moving white people. The image persists even though demonstrably untrue. Geronimo and his fellow leaders passed much of their adult lives in Mexico, raiding and plundering Mexicans or eluding Mexican and American military units trying to catch them. Mexico was not their homeland. The Chiricahua tribe, to which Geronimo belonged, could lay claim to southern New Mexico and Arizona, and a band of the tribe to a slice of northern Mexico. Here they rarely fought the army or the more efficient Apache scouts but here, too, either raided and plundered or resided on a reservation. None of this remotely resembles fighting for their homeland.

So deeply entrenched is the image of hero fighting for his homeland that this book, though strongly revisionist, is unlikely to purge it from the collective memory. The legendary Geronimo promises to live on in the American mind because it gives comfort to a public, both white and Indian, that for almost half a century has been full of remorse over the fate of the victims of American expansion.

ONE

APACHE YOUTH

GERONIMO'S LAWLESS BAND EL PASO, Texas, May 15.—W. J. Glenn, who has just arrived here from the State of Sonora, Mexico, gives a truthful account of the terrible atrocities of *Geronimo* and his band of Apaches in Sonora and Southern Arizona. He asserts that the Indians seem encouraged, and are more bloodthirsty than for several months, and Mexicans and their families, as well as Americans, are indiscriminately butchered when found. Three surveyors who recently went into the mountains have disappeared, and no trace of them can be found. There is no doubt they were butchered. Mr. Glenn said that Northern Sonora is terribly excited over the report that a body of Mexicans numbering 50 men have been surrounded in the mountains, and are in danger of being massacred.

—*New York Times,* May 15, 1886

HISTORY WOULD AWARD THE youth born sixty-three years earlier with hundreds of such articles in newspapers all over the United States. Some were mere rumors or fabrications, but the stories were bad enough to brand this man a bloody butcher who shot, lanced, or knifed dozens of victims throughout his adult life. His name induced fear and horror in settlers in Arizona and New Mexico as well as the Mexican states of Chihuahua and Sonora. And the public at large knew the name to stand for terrible atrocities. His youth featured nothing that portended such a record.

He first glimpsed daylight in a broad river valley, yellow grass waving in the breeze, bordered by towering mountains capped in green. This was the homeland of his people, the Bedonkohe (Bee-*don*-ko-hee) band of the Chiricahua (Cheer-i-*ca*-wah) Apache tribe. His father, Taslishim, The Gray One, and his mother, remembered only by her Mexican name, Juana, named their son Goyahkla, The One Who Yawns. Like his mother, in manhood he would also be known by his Mexican name and emerge as the most famous North American Indian of all time—Geronimo.

The year was 1823, the place the upper Gila (*Hee*-la) River Valley where it flows south from the Mogollon (Mug-ee-*yone*) Mountains in the modern state of New Mexico. The river then describes a southward bend and runs west across the line that would mark the border of the future state of Arizona. Eighty years later, Geronimo would recall his birth year as 1829 and his birthplace as the Gila River in Arizona just west of the boundary with New Mexico. His memory—or his interpreter—played him false. The year 1823 fits with other known events, and the New Mexico site his own description of the country.[1]

The Mogollon Mountains played a prominent role in the life of Geronimo, both as refuge from pursing soldiers and as base for murderous raids on white farmers and miners below. The highest and most rugged range in New Mexico, the Mogollons rise above eight thousand feet, with more than five peaks soaring above ten thousand. Deep, precipitous canyons snake around the peaks, and steep, rocky ridges climb one on the other toward the summit. Douglas fir and aspen, golden in autumn, cover the high areas, with juniper, oak, and cactus crawling down the lower slopes. Storms of rain and snow sweep the jagged heights. Only the hardiest and most knowledgeable, such as the Apaches, could summon these tortuous mountains to their purposes.

Taslishim was the son of a great chief, Mahco. Goyahkla never saw his grandfather, but his father described him as a man of great size, strength, and sagacity, as well as a man of peace. Mahco's chieftainship coincided with a long period of relative peace between the wars that periodically occurred with the Spanish people far to the south. This period began about 1790 and continued into Goyahkla's youth, by which time Spanish rule had been overthrown, and the people to the south called themselves Mexicans. Even so, Mahco was also remembered as a great fighter, and his grandson heard war stores from his father that related to the few episodes of war that occurred during Mahco's tenure. Well into adulthood, when other loyalties developed, Goyahkla venerated the memory of his grandfather.[2]

Geronimo said he had three brothers and four sisters. Actually, he had only one sibling, a sister named Nah-dos-te, four years his senior. The rest were grandchildren of Mahco and his second wife, whose name is not known to have been written down. The Apache language made no distinction between cousins and siblings. Except for one true sister, the others Geronimo referred to were all cousins. His favorite "sister," Ishton, was two years younger and the daughter of one of Mahco's sons or daughters.[3]

After Mahco's death, the Bedonkohe chieftainship fell not to Taslishim but to a Bedonkohe named Teboka, which explains why Geronimo never became a chief. Already, however, another chief had largely inherited the role filled by the great Mahco, and Teboka generally followed this chief. He was then known as Fuerte (Spanish for strong), but within a decade Mexicans would provide his lasting name, Mangas Coloradas (Red Sleeves).[4]

Three other Chiricahua bands adjoined the Bedonkohe. To the east, extending almost to the Rio Grande, lived the Chihenne (Chee-*hen*-ee) band, which translates to Red Paint People. To the southwest ranged a Chiricahua band that in later years took the name of the most prominent subdivision, Chokonen (Cho-*ko*-nen). These people occupied the Chiricahua and Dragoon Mountains and the intervening valleys of southeastern Arizona. South of this band, below the line that would divide the United States and Mexico, the Nednhi (*Ned*-nee) band lived among North America's most rugged and inaccessible mountains, the Sierra Madre.

No single chief guided the Chiricahua tribe or its bands. Each band divided into local groups—extended families and any others who wished to belong. Each local group had one or more chiefs. All the bands included local groups of more or less size and influence that rose and fell. For example, the Warm Springs (or Ojo Caliente: Oho Cal-*yent*-tay) is the best known of several Chihenne local groups.

All the Chiricahua bands shared a virtually identical language, culture, and life-way. Their neighbors to the west, the White Mountain Apaches, bore close resemblance to the Chiricahuas in band and local group organization and in language and culture. Tensions sometimes unsettled Chiricahua and White Mountain Apache relationships, but in general they coexisted

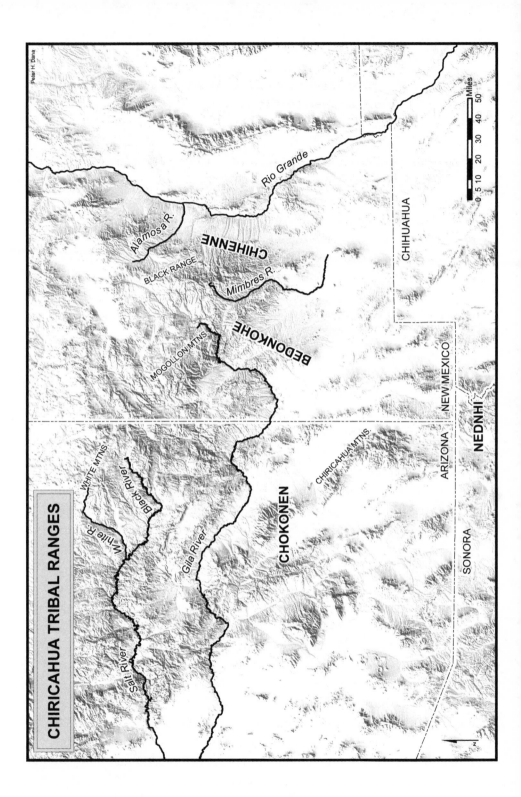

CHIRICAHUA TRIBAL RANGES

Peter H. Dana

Miles
0 5 10   20   30   40   50

Rio Grande

Alamosa R.

CHIHENNE

BLACK RANGE

Mimbres R.

BEDONKOHE

MOGOLLON MTNS.

WHITE MTNS.

Black River

White R.

Gila River

Salt River

CHIRICAHUA MTNS.

CHOKONEN

CHIHUAHUA

ARIZONA   NEW MEXICO

NEDNHI

SONORA

N

amicably. The White Mountain Apaches were the largest division of the Western Apaches, which on their south and west also included Cibicue (Sib-i-*que*), San Carlos, and Northern and Southern Tontos. East of the Rio Grande, in the Sierra Blanca of southern New Mexico, the Mescalero Apaches shared much of the Chiricahua language and culture and friendly if sporadic relations. The Jicarilla (Hick-a-*ree*-a) tribe lived in northern New Mexico, Kiowa-Apaches in Oklahoma, and Lipan Apaches in Texas, but they did not interact with the Chiricahuas. (See Appendix.)

During Geronimo's heyday, the entire Chiricahua tribe numbered about three thousand people, so in the relatively small local groups most people tended to know one another. By 1886, when Geronimo surrendered, the tribe had declined by about 80 percent, mainly the result of warfare.[5]

During his maturing years, Geronimo's most influential mentor was his fellow Bedonkohe, Mangas Coloradas. By the 1850s, Mangas Coloradas excelled all other Chiricahua leaders in almost every way. Physically, he was a giant, six and a half feet tall, muscular, with an expansive chest and shoulders, brawny legs, and posture "straight as a reed from which his arrows were made." Black eyes flashed from beneath a high and wide forehead. A massive jaw and prominent cheekbones completed a physique unusual by every Apache standard. His character featured the trait most admired by Apaches, courage. In battle he fought with vigor, and after war resumed with Mexicans in the 1830s, he frequently demonstrated his bravery by aggressive moves against Mexican troop formations and in hand-to-hand combat. His hatred of the Mexican state of Sonora knew no bounds, but his attitude toward the state of Chihuahua was less belligerent. Yet as the years passed and his influence remained supreme, he increasingly wanted to cultivate crops in peace on the prairies where the upper Gila River emerged from the Mogollon Mountains. His superb leadership talents included a political instinct for uniting both tribes and bands behind his policies.[6]

Born about 1790 (killed 1863), Mangas married about 1810 into a mixed Bedonkohe-Chihenne group living near Santa Lucía Springs, located in the foothills of the Burro Mountains bordering on the south the large southward arc of the upper Gila River in southwestern New Mexico. (See the map of the homeland of Geronimo and Mangas Coloradas.) Consistent with Chiricahua custom, Mangas went to live with his wife's family. Santa Lucía Springs remained his home base for the rest of his life and the center of a growing hybrid local group that drew on all the Chihenne local groups, the Bedonkohes, and even some of the Chokonens. By the time Geronimo had reached manhood and taken the name Geronimo, the Bedonkohes looked on Mangas Coloradas as having filled the leadership void left by the death of Chief Mahco. Over several decades, the hybrid group turned essentially into the Bedonkohe Chiricahua band. As an admiring protégé, Geronimo firmly linked himself to Mangas Coloradas until his death.

In old age Geronimo remembered rolling on the dirt floor of the family dwelling and being bundled in his cradle board fastened to his mother's back or swinging from a tree limb. When scarcely out of the cradle board, his instruction began. His mother taught him the origins, traditions, customs, beliefs, and ceremonies of his people. His father regaled him with stories of war and tales of hunting the animals on which much of the people's subsistence depended.[7]

From his mother, the boy learned of Usen, Life-Giver, and the all-knowing, all-seeing deity that governed Apache life. She taught him to pray to Usen for strength, health, wisdom, and protection. She told of White Painted Woman, Child of the Water, and the Mountain Spirits. All had their role in the beginnings of the people; all had many, not always consistent, stories handed down of their place in the mists of antiquity; all except Usen had ceremonies of celebration or propitiation.

Rituals abounded. Geronimo learned them and practiced them. They defined the proper path through life, from which one strayed at his peril. For example, an elaborate ceremony conducted by a shaman attended the construction and first use of the cradle board. The process climaxed with a shaman raising the cradle to the four directions three times, after which the infant was placed in it. "Putting on the Moccasins" celebrated release from the cradle board and first steps. It, too, featured a shaman as well as much feasting. Certain men and women knew how to conduct the ceremony. This power came to them through the culture hero Child of the Water. This ceremony, as one old Apache related, "is done to keep the child healthy and strong, and because Child of the Water, when he started to walk, had a ceremony like this one." As in all Indian tribes, the number four was sacred and governed all ceremonies, which customarily lasted four days. Many others drew Geronimo along life's path.[8]

The most critical personal attribute Geronimo's mother conveyed was "Power." Every Apache sought or received Power. Power derived from both the animate and the inanimate—an animal, a bird, even an insect, or simply a spiritual revelation, perhaps from Usen. Power featured a wide variety of expressions, for both good and evil. Controlling the weather, such as bringing rain or redirecting lightning, are examples of good. Most notably, shamans and healing dominated the uses of Power. As he grew into manhood, Geronimo acquired a wide range of Power that impressed his people, including healing the sick through incantations.

Apache culture provided many occasions for social gatherings, including all the ceremonies. Simply a consensus that the people wanted to assemble for a good time was excuse enough. They told stories, danced, feasted, and drank a mild beverage fermented from corn called tiswin. Only when ample supplies of corn could be obtained as rations or by theft or cultivation, however, could the beverage be prepared. Women made tiswin. Some acquired distinction as tiswin brewers. As early as age fourteen, adolescents could drink tiswin.

Because tiswin soured several days after being made, an entire supply had to be consumed during a social affair. Increasingly, its alcoholic effect induced men to fast for several days before an event and then drink themselves into oblivion. Often, mayhem and even death occurred during a tiswin drunk. Not all, or even most, social affairs were tiswin drunks, but custom made them common.[9]

Tiswin bears more of the blame for Apache intoxication than warranted. Much stronger drink could be made from the agave (or century) plant, including mescal, tequila, and pulque. Ultimately whiskey could be obtained by purchase or theft. So powerful was the addiction to alcohol in any form that it led to drinking parties that often featured violence, mayhem, and even murder. Worse, time and again it overcame experience and common sense to entice groups to expose themselves to massacre by Mexicans. By adulthood, many Apaches had become addicted.

Such would be Geronimo's fate, but for young Geronimo, all was not study and learning. He played with his brothers and sisters. Hide-and-seek was a perennial favorite. Also, they played at war. Imitating fighting men, they crept up on an object or playmate designated the enemy and, reenacting the stories they had been told of adult deeds, "performed the feats of war." A difficult and competitive game, hoop-and-pole, tested their emerging skills.

As the youth grew taller and stronger, he joined other young people in helping their parents till the soil. They cultivated corn, beans, melons, and pumpkins. The boys also joined with the women and their daughters to gather berries and nuts when ripe. Not until adolescence, after mastering horsemanship, did they begin to hunt the animals that provided a major source of sustenance.[10]

As soon as the boy entered adolescence, Taslishim began to prepare his son for the novice period, the years when the boy learned, experienced, and ultimately mastered the demanding trials that ended in formal admission to adulthood and fighting status. Most men had qualified because the culture demanded fighters. Chiricahuas distinguished between raid and war. Raids aimed at replenishing provisions or stock running low, with every possible measure, including spiritual, undertaken to avoid casualties. War, much larger and more formal, was strictly for revenge of an earlier death or injury at the hands of the foe. Mexicans bore the brunt of both raid and war.

Taslishim and a shaman helped Geronimo construct a powerful and sacred bow and arrows and learn to use them accurately. Taslishim subjected his son to the beginnings of rigorous physical training, designed to build strength and endurance and tolerate deprivation of water and food for long periods. The boy exercised to toughen muscles throughout the body, but the challenge repeated almost daily was a long, fast run over rough terrain, usually up a steep slope and back down. To demonstrate that he had done his breathing through his nose, he carried a small stone in his mouth and showed it to his mentor on return. As the boy progressed yearly toward the novitiate, the runs became longer and harder.

Taslishim died when his son was ten, several years before the onset of novitiate. Someone else had to continue the training. Taslishim lingered in illness long before death, so he may have designated a man to take responsibility. An uncle often undertook this task. Taslishim had no brother, so his successor may have been an uncle who was born of Mahco's second wife or even some other willing member of the Bedonkohe band.[11]

Horsemanship and skill in hunting were part of the preparation. Geronimo began serious hunting at the age of ten, about the time his father died. The prairies at the foot of the Mogollon Mountains abounded in deer, antelope, elk, and buffalo. Geronimo found buffalo the easiest to kill, using both bow and arrow and spear. Deer were the hardest. They had to be stealthily approached from downwind. "Frequently we would spend hours in stealing upon grazing deer." Once within range, the boys could often bring several down before the rest stampeded. The deer provided both meat and hide. "Perhaps no other animal was more valuable to us than the deer." Apache taboos barred eating the flesh of the fish swarming in the streams and the bears roaming the forests.

Special techniques applied to wild turkeys and rabbits. The hunters drove the turkeys from the woods into the open and pursued them slowly until they tired. Then the boys prodded their mounts and dashed on the birds, sweeping them from the ground with a hand. If a bird took to flight, they raced their horses beneath and struck with a hunting club. Rabbits posed a contest in speed, as the horses galloped after a fleeing animal and the rider either scooped it up by hand or threw the hunting club to strike it down. "This was great sport when we were boys, but as warriors we seldom hunted small game."[12]

The novitiate that ended in formal acceptance as an adult and fighter required participation in four war expeditions. When the youth felt ready, he volunteered. How long the process took depended on how many war expeditions occurred, as well as how many for which he volunteered. It could last several years or as little as one year or even less. Geronimo completed the trial at the age of seventeen, but he revealed nothing about his experiences or when he first volunteered.[13]

A "bow shaman," endowed with powers to locate and defeat an enemy and grant invulnerability from harm, instructed one or more youths in the host of rituals and taboos that governed their conduct throughout a raid or war expedition. He made the jacket, hat, and other appurtenances that protect a man in battle. He told of the hardships and dangers and the behavior expected by full fighters. He imparted the special warpath vocabulary that must be used, in which eighty or more words were substituted for the usual conversation. A special drinking tube attached to a skin scratcher, ornamented with special designs, was presented to each novice and required to be used throughout the experience and returned to the shaman afterward. For violations of each of the prescribed rites, bad luck resulted, and for some, permanent impairments of character.

One or more shamans accompanied most raiding or war expeditions to ensure their sacred character and to advise on strategy and tactics. They gave particular attention to the novices. More important, each novice had a mentor to guide him through the process and whom he served as a personal attendant. Novices had to perform all the usual chores of camping, such as carrying water, gathering wood, building and maintaining fires, cooking, erecting shelters, and performing quickly any task any man might assign. Novices above all had to display courage, although mentors usually held them aside or sent them to the rear in actual combat. The death or injury of a novice reflected badly on their leadership.

Not all novices passed the test. "If a boy is unreliable and doesn't show improvement," disclosed an informant, "they don't take him out any more. They just drop him." But after the fourth expedition, if the novice had performed satisfactorily, he was admitted to the status of fighting man. He was free to join future expeditions as a full fighter, to marry, and in camp to think and behave as he pleased.

Geronimo absorbed and practiced the traditions, rituals, and taboos imparted by his mother. As an adolescent, he aspired above all else to become a fighter and be accepted by others as a brave and capable leader and follower. He followed all the rules of the novitiate and gained full approval of the council.

As Geronimo recalled in old age, on completion of the novitiate, "I was very happy, for I could go wherever I wanted and do whatever I liked." Since his father's death, he had been under no one's control. On the contrary, he had assumed full responsibility for his mother's support; she had never remarried. Now, however, he could go on the warpath. "This would be glorious. I hoped soon to serve my people in battle. I had long desired to fight with our warriors."[14]

TWO

Apache Manhood

EVERY ADULT WHO PASSED the required tests and grew to manhood had been trained to be a fighter. It was a way of life mandated by Apache culture. Now that he was a man, Geronimo could join other men in expeditions as he had long desired. First, however, he had another mission: marriage.

He had long admired a young woman he called "the fair Alope." He described her as slender and delicate and long a "lover," although the term likely does not connote sexual relations. Her Bedonkohe father, No-po-so, demanded many ponies in return for her hand. Geronimo returned "in several days" with many ponies. The several days were probably several weeks as he participated in his first raid as a fighter and gathered them at some Mexican ranch or town. He delivered the animals at the lodge of No-po-so and departed with Alope. With no other ceremony prescribed, Geronimo erected a wickiup of buffalo hide near his mother's dwelling, carpeted it with robes and hides, and moved in with Alope and his arsenal of bows, arrows, spears, knives, and shields. Alope completed the decoration with beads and wall paintings.

"She was a good wife, but she was never strong. We followed the traditions of our fathers and were happy. Three children came to us—children that played, loitered, and worked as I had done."[1]

While still a youth, possibly while Geronimo was undergoing novitiate training, a Nednhi youth came up from the Sierra Madre for a visit with the Bedonkohes. His name was Juh (Hoo, although other variants are common),

15

and the two became friends. With a playful disposition, Juh and other boys often hid themselves in the woods and teased girls gathering acorns. They waited until the girls had accumulated a supply and then confiscated them. This came to the attention of Chief Mahco's widow, who instructed Geronimo and some of his friends to ambush Juh and his cohorts and give them a sound punishment. The teasing ended.

Juh lived with the Bedonkohes long enough to grow to adulthood, possibly taking his novitiate with the band. Like Geronimo, Juh sought an admired young woman for a wife. He married Ishton, Geronimo's favorite "sister," one of his youthful victims. Ultimately Juh took Ishton back to his homeland in the Sierra Madre, where he rose to become the most powerful Nednhi chief.

In white-man terms, Juh would be considered a military genius. He exercised absolute control over his people and maneuvered his fighters expertly in both defensive and offensive conflicts. Stocky, muscular, like Mangas Coloradas tall by Apache standards, well over six feet. When excited, he stuttered so badly that in battle he had to use hand signals to communicate. Even so, he could sing lustily without stuttering.[2]

Roughly the same age, related through Juh's marriage into Geronimo's family, the two would be intimate comrades until Juh's death.

The long period of relative peace with Mexicans that permitted Chief Mahco to be remembered as a man of peace depended largely on Mexico's intermittent policy of maintaining "feeding stations" in northern Chihuahua. Here Apaches could draw rations as the price of remaining at peace. Parts of some Chiricahua bands settled near towns such as Janos (*Han*-os), Corralitos (Core-a-*lee*-tos), and Galeana (Gal-e-*ana*), where authorities occasionally issued rations. Since raids, as contrasted with war, aimed at replenishing provisions, the feeding stations helped offset the need for raids. Sonoran authorities, always more belligerent than Chihuahuan, rarely rationed Apaches, and Sonora therefore suffered the consequences.

Relations had begun to deteriorate in the late 1820s because of diminishing rations. They collapsed altogether in 1831, when Mexico, no longer able to afford the cost, abruptly terminated the feeding stations. Although some Chiricahuas continued to reside near the stations in hope of their revival, all the Chiricahua bands resumed the old pattern of plundering raids. Now and then Mexico doled out enough rations to encourage some of the Apaches to remain in Chihuahuan camps, but throughout the 1830s raiding gained

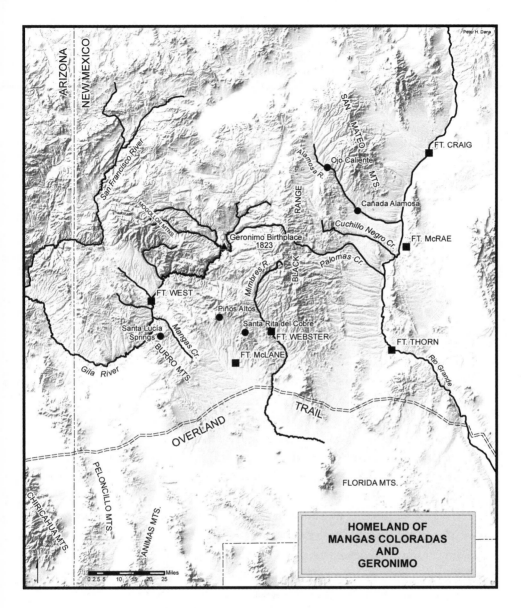

momentum. With some of the bands still hoping for peace and rations, the Chiricahuas broke into war and peace factions. Mangas Coloradas headed the war faction of all the Chiricahua bands. Geronimo grew to manhood during these years, his Bedonkohes firmly anchored to Mangas Coloradas. Geronimo participated in some of the raids as part of his novitiate training.[3]

Raids gave way to full-scale war in 1837. Sonoran officials recruited an Anglo trader named John Johnson to launch a war of extermination against the Chiricahuas, his recompense half the stock and plunder he gained. With seventeen mercenaries, Johnson accidently came across a party of Nednhis with a few Chokonens and Chihennes in the Animas Mountains of southwestern New Mexico. Mangas Coloradas and some of his followers had come down from their winter camps in the Mogollons and joined the Nednhis. The Indians knew Johnson as a trader, and for two days they traded amicably with him and his men. On the third day, April 22, 1837, as the Apaches approached Johnson's camp, a small cannon loaded with scrap metal blasted them, and his men opened fire with musketry. More than twenty Apaches fell dead, including a Nednhi chief. Mangas escaped, but two of his four wives died. The Johnson massacre put the Apaches on notice that Sonora had declared war, and that demanded revenge. For the growing war factions of the Chiricahuas, war rather than raids became the norm. It stoked the fury of Mangas Coloradas toward Sonora.[4]

Chihuahuan authorities soon followed the lead of Sonora. In December 1839, Chihuahua enlisted an Indian trader named James Kirker to raise a band of thugs and wage war on the Apaches. Like Johnson, Kirker would keep half the plunder and establish his claim through scalp bounties—pesos for Apache scalps. His campaign was ruthless and profitable, so successful that some of the Chiricahuas still living in Mexico put out peace overtures. As they negotiated with Chihuahuan authorities, Mangas Coloradas continued his war expeditions, which doubtless now included the newly ordained fighting man Geronimo.[5]

On July 4, 1842, Chihuahuan authorities at Janos finally signed a treaty with leaders of the Chihenne and Chokonen peace factions. The state resumed issuing rations, and depredations in Chihuahua declined dramatically. Early in 1843, influenced by the peace faction and the overtures of Mexican officers, even Mangas Coloradas cautiously accepted the treaty and drew rations.[6]

The ration rolls at Corralitos dated August 13, 1843, bear the name Geronimo. By this time, twenty years old, he had assumed the name Geronimo among the Mexicans and even his own people. He had been a full-fledged fighting man for three years and had ridden in many raids and battles that established his stature. Students debate how he came to acquire this name, but it seems to have emerged simply as a common Mexican name, the equivalent of the English Jerome. Whatever the origin, Geronimo bore that name for the rest of his life.[7]

From early adulthood to middle age, Geronimo's life is almost impossible to follow. An occasional event is documented, but rarely supporting more than the fact that he was there. His autobiography, however, recounts raid after raid into Mexico, with cattle, horses, and other plunder the objective, as well as the lives of their owners. Combat with Mexican troops also figures prominently. The details of these expeditions are too explicit to be ignored, although the years specified are plainly wrong. If the traditional distinction between raid and war governed his actions, he either ignored or applied a highly elastic standard of need for raids. War, on the other hand, could always find a reason for revenge. He tells of receiving eight wounds, describing how and where inflicted. As for the victims, "I have killed many Mexicans; I do not know how many, for frequently I did not count them. Some of them were not worth counting." If he were young again, he declared, "and followed the warpath, it would lead into Old Mexico."[8]

Sonorans had long been convinced that the Apaches ravaging Sonora came from the supposedly peaceful camps around Janos and Corralitos and that they traded the plunder from their Sonoran raids in the Chihuahuan towns. Some probably did, but most rode from the north under Mangas Coloradas and a rising Chokonen leader, Cochise, drawn into alliance with Mangas by marriage to his daughter.

Cochise proved a powerful ally—and friend as well as son-in-law. Born about 1810 and thus twenty years younger than Mangas and thirteen older than Geronimo, he swiftly evolved into a superior fighter and leader. Like Mangas and Juh, Cochise was unusually tall for an Apache, and his shoulder-length black hair, high forehead, Roman nose, prominent cheekbones, and slender, powerful physique made him a conspicuous presence among the Chokonens. He lacked Mangas's political skills and did not pursue alliances, although he frequently fought in concert with other Chiricahua bands. By the 1840s, he gave evidence of ultimately rising to the stature of his father-in-law.[9]

As Geronimo matured into his twenties, he evolved into an accomplished fighter. Thick, squat, of medium height, muscular, with a grimly assertive face, he was coached by Mangas Coloradas in the skills of the fighter. He possessed the Apache virtues of courage, endurance, energy, cunning, ruthlessness, stealth, and mastery of bow and arrow, knife, and lance. He enhanced the Apache ability of living, traveling, and fighting in a landscape of deserts, rocks, and mountains. He could mobilize every harsh feature of this land as weapons in raid and war. He had led his own raids against Mexicans—some successful, some not—and he rode in war expeditions with Mangas Coloradas.

The Sonoran military commander Colonel Elías González resolved to smash the culprits suspected of the raids in Sonora. Without consulting or even alerting Chihuahuan officials, González led an army of about six hundred men across the Sierra Madre and on August 23, 1844, struck the rancherías—the Apache term for village—at Janos and Corralitos. About sixty-five Chiricahuas died, mostly women and children, and twenty-five fell captive. The survivors fled north to their homelands.[10]

With the ration program lapsing and the Apaches resuming raiding from the north, in the autumn of 1845 Chihuahua again declared war. James Kirker went back on the payroll and began rampaging across Apache country, seeking scalps for the promised bounty. Geronimo's Bedonkohes remained aloof in their Mogollon and Burro mountain refuges.

Kirker, however, engineered another disaster that would reverberate among all Chiricahuas. In the summer of 1846 Chokonens and Nednhis came to Galeana under a truce. The Mexicans invited them to a feast in town and got them drunk. Early in the morning of July 7, Kirker swept into town and fell on the helpless Chiricahuas, slaughtering 130 men, women, and children as the men lay in drunken stupor. Preceded by the governor and a priest, Kirker's little army marched into Chihuahua City to public acclaim. They bore poles adorned with scalps to be exchanged for the scalp bounty. The massacre united Chiricahua war and peace parties and unleashed unremitting war on both Chihuahua and Sonora.[11]

The Kirker massacre mandated a revenge expedition. Chihenne chief Cuchillo Negro (Coo-*chi*-yo *Na*-gro) took the lead in calling together an alliance. Both Mangas Coloradas and Cochise with their followers united with the Chihennes. In November 1846, about 175 Apaches, Geronimo included, clashed with Mexican soldiers and civilian defenders at Galeana, quickly defeating and routing them in a savage fight. As recounted by Jason Betzinez, "The whole tribe were tremendously proud of their fighting men and for years thereafter loved to hear the stories of the battle retold. Among those who increased their reputations in the battle were Cochise, Mangas

Coloradas, Benito, my cousin Goyakla (Geronimo), and my grandfather." In the revenge raid on Galeana, to be singled out by his people as a man of special distinction, together with Mangas Coloradas and Cochise, was a high Apache tribute to Geronimo's fighting qualities.[12]

Critical to any successful Chiricahua was Power. When and what Powers came to or were sought by Geronimo is not clear. Geronimo told no one of his Powers, simply demonstrating enough to lead his followers to believe that he was highly endowed. A successful medicine man he undoubtedly became, for he performed curing ceremonies in plain view of anyone who wished to watch.

One Power for which he became most noted was a revelation that no bullet or other projectile would ever kill him. As Juh's son Daklugie explained this attribute, "Geronimo did not tell them he could not be hurt by a bullet but their imagination made them think he could not be hit. But he was meat and bones just like any other man, only he had more courage than the others."[13]

Perico, one of Geronimo's most loyal followers, explained another widely held perception:

Many medicine men can make it rain or stop raining. Geronimo had strong power. He could make it rain, and he could even make night last longer. To make it rain, he sang, without using pollen. He even remained seated. He sang about water, and it rained in an hour. When on the warpath Geronimo fixed it so that morning couldn't come so soon. He did it by singing. They were going to a certain place, and Geronimo didn't want it to be dawn before he reached his objective. He saw the enemy while they were in a level place and he didn't want the enemy to spy on them. He wanted the morning to break after they had climbed over a mountain, so that the enemy couldn't see them. So Geronimo sang, and the night remained two or three hours longer. I saw this personally.[14]

To which the anthropologist Morris Opler added, in a discussion of cultural and personal determinism: "Shamanism is an important part of Apache religion, but the use of Geronimo's ceremony in this context was particularly crucial because it happened to be a ritual considered useful for locating the enemy, hiding from him, or confounding him. Geronimo's ability to command a following was likewise due to a combination of cultural and personal attributes."[15]

All the great chiefs possessed a variety of Powers. Geronimo's followers ascribed these and other Powers to him, and they accounted for much of his influence.

Geronimo also lived a happy family life. Alope bore him three children (their gender was not recorded). The couple reared them in accord with Chiricahua tradition and the commands of Usen.

At the early age of forty, Geronimo appeared to have the potential to become an outstanding leader, if not as great as Mangas Coloradas or Cochise, still at least the accomplished head of a Bedonkohe local group. As Mangas's biographer concludes, "Geronimo, although he enjoyed a reputation for supernatural power and was a fighter nonpareil, did not demonstrate the other leadership abilities to attract more than an intimately devoted band of followers, most of whom were related by either blood or marriage."[16]

THREE

BATTLE AND MASSACRE

AS THE 1850S OPENED, Chihuahua and Sonora continued to divide the Chiricahuas. Many, up to half the Chihennes and some Nednhis, succumbed to the lure of Janos, with its prospect of rations and trade. The largest of a cluster of communities in northwestern Chihuahua, about fifty miles below the US boundary, Janos had been a center of Chiricahua attention for a generation, a place to trade plunder from raids in Sonora and to draw rations when the government wanted peace. By the end of 1850 Chihuahua had treaties in place at Janos and issued rations. The rest of the Chihennes, together with the Bedonkohe and Chokonen followers of Mangas Coloradas and Cochise, including Geronimo, opposed the peace overtures. As throughout the 1840s, chiefs continued to waver between the attractions of Janos and the plunder of Sonora.

Even with treaties concluded at Janos, in January 1851 the war faction of the Chihennes, Bedonkohes, and Chokonens organized a formidable expedition against Sonoran towns and ranches. It advanced in two forces of about 150 fighters. With Mangas about sixty years old, the more vigorous Cochise employed superior war skills. But the stature of Mangas ensured his dominant influence, and as always he fought fiercely in the vanguard of any combat. Geronimo, at twenty-eight a highly regarded fighter, was a prominent presence, and his friend Juh had come over from Janos with some treaty Nednhis.[1]

23

Mangas and Cochise thrust far down the Sonora River to the southwest as far as Hermosillo. The other division of the war faction rode closer to the western foothills of the Sierra Madre, along the Bavispe River and south as far as Sahuaripa (Sow-ah-*reepa*). Ranches, haciendas, villages, and travelers fell prey to the warriors, losing lives, horses, mules, cattle, and other booty. Both groups then turned back north, generally up the Nacozari River midway between their downward sweeps along the Sonora and Bavispe Rivers.

As ordained by Apache war culture and inflamed by their hatred of Sonora, the men ruthlessly cut down any Mexican who strayed into their path and made off with any stock or booty that appealed to them. An expedition of this magnitude provided an opportunity for Geronimo to demonstrate his raiding skills and to cement his bond to Mangas Coloradas and Cochise, his mentors.

The raiders encountered little of the organized resistance that confronted earlier Sonoran raids. Unknown to them, their old nemesis, Colonel Elías González, Sonora's leading military figure since the 1830s, who would have deployed such troops as his little garrisons allowed, had fallen casualty to Mexican politics. His successor, Colonel José María Carrasco, a fierce, arrogant advocate of war of extermination, had yet to arrive in Sonora. Even so, Governor José de Aguilar organized a force to cut off the raiders as they returned northward. Under his orders, fifty national guardsmen under Captain Ignacio Pesqueira moved from Arizpe eastward to unite with another fifty under Captain Manuel Martínez marching west from Bocoachi. They came together amid some rolling hills twelve miles northeast of the upper Nacozari River. Then, when scouts brought word of a dust cloud approaching from the south, Pesqueira and Martínez set up an ambush in a beautiful, mountain-girt valley containing the well-known "Stinking Springs," or Pozo Hediondo. The date was January 20, 1851.

The dust rose from the war expedition of Mangas Coloradas and Cochise returning to their home country. Ahead of the main force rode a small party driving 350 head of stock. Behind, Mangas drove a herd of about one thousand horses in his front. The advance party triggered the ambush, which took the Apaches by surprise. Although badly outnumbered, the men abandoned their stock, withdrew into defensive positions in the hills, and fought fiercely. The Mexicans assailed these defenses, overran them, and routed the Apaches.

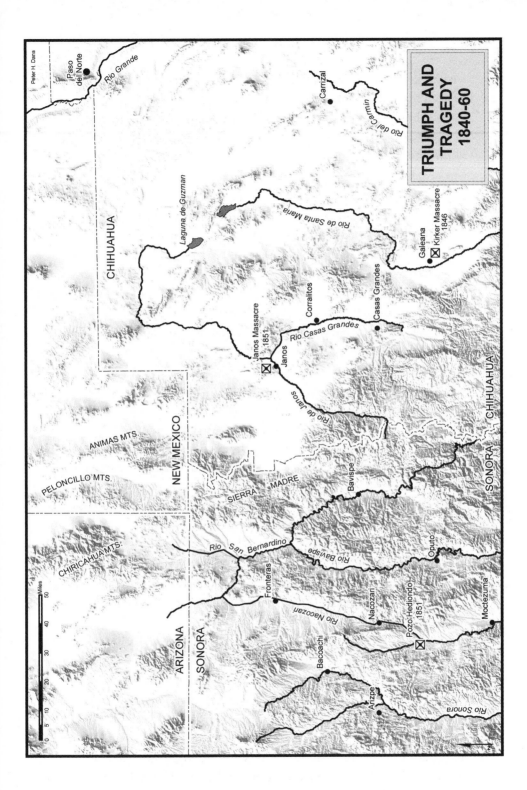

TRIUMPH AND TRAGEDY 1840-60

Peter H. Dana

Paso del Norte
Rio Grande

Carrizal

Rio del Carmin

Laguna de Guzman

Rio de Santa Maria

CHIHUAHUA

Galeana
Kirker Massacre 1846

Janos Massacre 1851

Corralitos

Casas Grandes

Rio Casas Grandes

Janos

Rio de Janos

ANIMAS MTS.

PELONCILLO MTS.

NEW MEXICO

SIERRA MADRE

Bavispe

SONORA CHIHUAHUA

CHIRICAHUA MTS.

Rio San Bernardino

Rio Bavispe

Oputo

ARIZONA

SONORA

Fronteras

Rio Nacozari

Nacozari

Pozo Hediondo 1851

Moctezuma

Bacoachi

Arizpe

Rio Sonora

Miles
0 5 10 20 30 40 50

Although also surprised, Mangas and his men quickly recovered. The Mexican ambush had misfired and led them into an Apache ambush. They now faced half again as many as their own number. The Apaches charged to the rescue of their brethren and collided with the foe. A savage conflict, lasting three hours and featuring hand-to-hand encounters, drove the Mexicans from one hilltop defense to another, with heavy losses. Geronimo recalled that "I fought with fury. Many fell by my hand, and constantly I led the advance. Many braves were killed." At the end, "over the bloody field, covered with the bodies of Mexicans, rang the fierce Apache war-whoop."[2]

Contributing to this outcome, by late afternoon, the second war expedition, mainly Chokonens working their way north, reached the scene and threw about a hundred men into the fight. Skirmishing continued until dark, but the Mexicans had been devastatingly defeated. All the officers had been killed or wounded. Mexican casualties amounted to twenty-six killed and forty-six wounded, nearly three-fourths of the command. Apache casualties are unknown.

Pozo Hediondo stood as the greatest victory Apaches had ever won over Mexican military forces. As the biographer of Mangas Coloradas notes, his importance at Pozo Hediondo "rested on his ability to draw together the coalition of bands and to infuse them with a confidence—perhaps even bordering on arrogance—that they were invincible to Sonoran firepower, which resulted in the rout and annihilation of Pesqueira's command." Geronimo fought fiercely, as did Cochise, Juh, and others. But to Mangas Coloradas belonged the laurels.[3]

That Apache culture mandated wars of revenge is ironic in light of the revenge motive that powered the response of the new Sonoran commander, Colonel José María Carrasco. The catastrophe at Pozo Hediondo demanded savage reprisal.

Mangas Coloradas and others who participated in the war expedition, including Geronimo, withdrew to their homes, Mangas and the Bedonkohes to the Burro Mountains. Fearing Sonoran retaliation for Pozo Hediondo and aware of the peace and rations enjoyed by many Chiricahuas at Janos, Mangas put out peace feelers to see if he and his people could receive similar benefits. He did not want to relocate to Janos but wished to move to more secure havens in the Animas Mountains about seventy-five miles northwest of Janos, in New Mexico. Following up on these overtures, he and many of his people, including Geronimo, journeyed to Janos to discuss the issue with the authorities. Like other Apaches settled near Janos, Mangas and his people camped outside town. Each day the men went into the town to trade, bargaining with loot taken in the recent war expedition into Sonora and freely partaking of the intoxicants available there. They produced a quicker and stronger effect than tiswin.[4]

Meantime, Colonel Carrasco and about four hundred guardsmen and militia crossed the Sierra Madre from Sonora into Chihuahua and crept up on Janos without discovery by either the Apaches or the Janos authorities. On March 5, 1851, he struck, destroying several of the Apache rancherías. Carrasco reported killing sixteen men and five women and taking sixty-two captives. Fifty-six of these were women and children, herded off with his command to be sold into slavery. Carrasco's count of women and children likely fell short of the actual number. Most of the victims were Chokonens and Nednhis, although Mangas's Bedonkohes, including Geronimo, temporarily at Janos on a peace mission, suffered also.

As Geronimo recounted his own experience:

> Late one afternoon when returning from town we were met by a few women and children, who told us that Mexican troops from some other town had attacked our camp, killed all the warriors of the guard, captured all our ponies, secured our arms, destroyed our supplies, and killed many of our women and children. Quickly we separated, concealing ourselves as best we could until nightfall, when we assembled at our appointed place of rendezvous—a thicket by the river. Silently we stole in one by one: sentinels were placed, and, when all were counted, I found that my aged mother, my young wife, and my three small children were among the slain. There were no lights in camp, so without being noticed I silently turned away and stood by the river. How long I stood there I do not know, but when I saw the warriors arranging for a council I took my place.[5]

Geronimo leaves unsaid whether he actually saw or recognized the bodies of his family, although in old age he told artist E. A. Burbank that he found them lying in a pool of blood.[6] He may have seen them; more likely, since no lights were lit, he did not. For all he knew, they were among the captives taken into slavery. Uncontested, however, is that Carrasco had wiped out Geronimo's entire family. "I had lost all," he lamented. "I was never again contented in our quiet home. True, I could visit my father's grave, but I had vowed vengeance upon the Mexican troopers who had wronged me, and whenever I came near his grave or saw anything to remind me of former happy days my heart would ache for revenge against Mexico."

As Geronimo testified, the Carrasco massacre planted in him a bitter hatred of all Mexicans that lasted until the end of his life. At twenty-eight, this landmark event shaped the man and marked out his life's pathway.

FOUR

"AMERICANS"

WHILE LAUNCHING RAIDS AND conducting war against Mexicans, Chiricahuas knew about other white people approaching from the north and east. The newcomers called themselves "Americans." As early as the 1820s, these white people had appeared in Mangas Coloradas's country. They were American fur trappers, and they began to base themselves at Santa Rita del Cobre for westward expeditions into the Gila country. Located about thirty-five miles east of Santa Lucía Springs, at the southern edge of the Pinos Altos Range of southwestern New Mexico, they lay within the homeland of Mangas Coloradas and his Bedonkohe and Chihenne followers. The Santa Rita copper mines were first exploited by the Spanish in 1803 and then the Mexicans. The Spanish had built a presidio and other adobe structures to work the mines. Both Spanish and Mexicans also had used the copper mines as a military base both for making war and peace with the resident Apaches. Mangas extended friendship to the Americans and often conferred with them; Geronimo was almost certainly nearby. They proved no threat and merely wished to pass through his domain.[1]

The Americans next appeared in 1846, when they had declared war on Mexico. An American general, Stephen Watts Kearny, led an expedition of dragoons by way of the copper mines and Santa Lucía Springs toward California to claim it for the United States. He needed mules. He and Mangas Coloradas established a wary friendship, and Kearny got his mules.

29

In the years following the friendly meeting between Mangas Coloradas and the American general, the Chihennes and Bedonkohes largely concentrated on their ongoing war-and-peace relations with Chihuahua and Sonora. The revenge raid for the Janos massacre, in which Geronimo lost his family, had to be plotted and carried out. At the same time, the Chiricahuas noted the creeping advance of American soldiers down the Rio Grande and the few undermanned forts they built.

As early as 1848, some of the Chihennes, the Chiricahua band closest to the Americans, had even stirred up the soldiers. The Rio Grande flowed south from New Mexico through the Pass of the North, after passing the Mexican towns of Mesilla and, nearby to the north, Doña Ana. The soldiers had stationed themselves at Doña Ana. On December 12, 1848, a small party of Apaches approached Doña Ana and shouted that they wanted to talk. When a detachment rode out, the Apaches opened fire and drove them back. This may have been the first hostile encounter with American soldiers.[2]

The Chiricahuas occasionally raided around the Rio Grande settlements of Mesilla, El Paso, and Doña Ana and carried off many mules. In August 1849 about one hundred raiders, probably Bedonkohes led by Mangas and probably Geronimo, killed citizens near El Paso and hurried home with a big herd of mules. Soldiers from Doña Ana pursued and caught up near the copper mines. In a two-hour battle, the soldiers routed the Apaches, captured and destroyed their camp with all its contents, and recovered some of the stolen mules. From the Apache viewpoint, they had done nothing wrong. Although in country now claimed by the Americans, almost all the victims were Mexicans, still fair game. Mangas had made clear to Kearny himself that the Chiricahuas would always war on Mexicans. The American claim to the land, moreover, meant nothing to the Apaches. After this encounter, although Mangas was still inclined to trust the Americans, for many Chiricahuas Americans as well as Mexicans became enemies.[3]

Both Apaches and Americans wavered between war and peace. American civil authorities, based in Santa Fe, New Mexico, consistently sought peace. The army, also headquartered in Santa Fe, seemed to pursue both war and peace at the same time. Officials closest to the scene had a better feel for the disposition of the Apaches at any given time than those in distant Santa Fe.

The senior military officer in southern New Mexico, one of the army's best, was Captain Enoch Steen, who commanded a squadron of the First Dragoons at Doña Ana. He had led the pursuit in August 1849 that destroyed the

Bedonkohe camp near the Santa Rita copper mines. Yet in August 1850 he led sixty dragoons to the copper mines to try to discuss peace. For six days he and Mangas Coloradas talked. Other chiefs participated, including some of the major Chihenne chiefs, still residing in their homeland closer to the Rio Grande. All said they wanted peace, but with Mexicans it was "war to the knife." Steen concluded that if a civil agent of the Bureau of Indian Affairs established himself at the copper mines within the next six weeks, he could conclude a lasting peace.[4]

That did not happen because Colonel Edwin V. Sumner, a tough old dragoon who commanded the army in New Mexico, did not want peace. In January 1852 he established Fort Webster at the copper mines, but moved it nine months later fourteen miles to the east, on the Mimbres River, Chihenne country. The colonel had hoped that Fort Webster would control the resident Apaches, but in his mind control meant military power rather than peaceful accommodation. And with good reason. The Bedonkohes and Chihennes had never stopped raiding the Rio Grande settlements. Sumner considered them at war and sent weak military columns into their country. And the Apaches did consider themselves at war, since the soldiers clearly invaded their country with hostile intent. Sumner blamed the civil authorities for the failure of peace initiatives. In truth, they had lacked both money and officials to extend their reach into the Chiricahua country.[5]

Ironically, even before Sumner had fully organized his offensive, in June 1852 word reached Santa Fe that the Chihennes and Bedonkohes wanted to make peace. The leading chiefs had achieved triumph at Pozo Hediondo and suffered defeat at the Janos disaster and now wanted to be friends with the Americans. With Mangas Coloradas, they had even started north to meet with the officials. John Griener, acting as superintendent of Indian affairs, and Colonel Sumner set forth to negotiate a treaty. On July 11, 1852, at Ácoma Pueblo, Mangas Coloradas and the other chiefs placed their marks on a treaty of peace and friendship. It ceded no country and promised issues of rations and other items. Mangas vigorously rejected articles requiring an end to raiding in Mexico and the return of Mexican captives, but signed anyway. Now he could go back to the Santa Lucía country and resume life as normal, warring with Mexico and farming at home. He had signed the only treaty he ever would sign with the United States.[6]

Griener and a new governor, William Carr Lane, followed up on the Ácoma treaty. A new agent, Edward H. Wingfield, arrived at Fort Webster in

December 1852, to find the veteran Captain Enoch Steen commanding the post. Together, they spent the winter trying to round up the Chiricahua chiefs and launch a farming enterprise among the Mimbres local group of the Chihennes on the Mimbres River. At the same time, however, small raiding parties struck the Mexican settlements along the Rio Grande, undermining the prospects for peace. In the spring of 1853, Governor Lane himself journeyed to Fort Webster and worked with Wingfield and Steen to gather enough chiefs to negotiate a compact supplementing the Ácoma treaty. Since it still took no land and promised rations, the chiefs signed. Mangas Coloradas, raiding in Sonora with Chokonens, did not show up until May 18 to give his "cordial assent." Lane even traveled west of the copper mines to inspect Santa Lucía Springs. He concluded that this country would make an ideal reservation and agency for the Chihennes and Bedonkohes.[7]

As so often would happen in the unhappy relations between the Chiricahuas and US officialdom, Lane's compact met with disapproval. He had to advise Wingfield of a "chilling frost" in Washington and instruct him to reduce rations to the lowest level possible and tell the Indians to hunt and collect desert food.[8]

The "chilling frost" lasted nearly two years. For Mangas and his followers, the small handouts at Fort Webster hardly warranted the effort to go there, although in September 1853 he had a brief talk with the agent. Besides, Mangas and his people felt secure in their homes on the upper Gila and in the Mogollons. Also, in part reflecting disappointment over the broken promises of the Lane compact, they turned their attention to Mexico. Both provisions and revenge could be gained there. During 1853–54, Mangas and his son-in-law Cochise repeatedly led savage forays into Sonora. The raids distracted Mangas's attention from what the Americans and the Chihenne chiefs were up to. Cochise, his Chokonen homeland remote from American officials, did not care. Geronimo, the loss of his family still heavy in his mind, probably welcomed the opportunity to kill more Mexicans.

Not until the summer of 1854 did Mangas begin to think about the Americans, with whom he continued to desire good relations. He found that Fort Webster had been abandoned in December 1853 and the soldiers and the Indian agent relocated on the Rio Grande. The army named the new station Fort Thorn. A new agent had appeared and reestablished the old agency at Doña Ana, and he was doling out rations and other issues to the Chihennes. With the Janos massacre amply revenged by the bloody incursions into Sonora, Mangas turned his attention back to the Americans. Nothing is known of Geronimo's part in any of these events. He either remained close to Mangas Coloradas or carried out his own raiding in Mexico.[9]

None of the Chiricahua chiefs or their followers, including Mangas Coloradas, knew anything of the changes taking place in Washington and Santa Fe. Nor would they have understood had they known. The governmental structure of the Americans, so different from Apache organization, remained a mystery for decades to come. What motivated the baffling fluctuations in American policy and action remained equally unknown. Somehow, a remote and vague "Great Father" determined relations with the Apaches.

In March 1853 a new "Great Father" had taken office in Washington. President Franklin Pierce, following the usual practice, replaced the appointees of President Millard Fillmore with his own loyal followers. That meant a new secretary of the interior, a new commissioner of Indian affairs, and a new governor and superintendent of Indian affairs for New Mexico. A veteran fur trapper, David Meriwether, replaced William Carr Lane in Santa Fe. He in turn repudiated most of Lane's program and named new Indian agents. Fortuitously for harmonious relations in Santa Fe, "Bull" Sumner yielded the New Mexico military command. Meriwether sought to negotiate treaties with all the tribes of New Mexico. He succeeded, although only a few Mimbres represented the Chiricahuas. The Senate ratified none of the Meriwether treaties.

On July 6, 1854, a new agent arrived at Doña Ana. He was a Pennsylvania physician with proper political credentials, Dr. Michael Steck, and he turned out to be the best Indian agent in New Mexico, certainly the best the Chiricahuas had ever had or would have. Governor Meriwether instructed Steck to move his agency up the Rio Grande from Doña Ana to the vicinity of Fort Thorn, and he issued the September annuities there. By October Steck had toured all the Chihenne and Bedonkohe country under his jurisdiction and met with as many chiefs as he could find—except Mangas Coloradas.[10]

Late in October the chiefs and their people began to gather around Fort Thorn for the next ration issue. On October 27 Mangas Coloradas came in with two other chiefs and ninety people, probably including Geronimo. Mangas met with Steck, the first meeting between the two. They quickly established a rapport that, as Mangas came in for the monthly issues, ripened into a genuine friendship and mutual respect. For the balance of the

1850s, each supported the other and established an increasingly close relationship.[11]

Michael Steck saw the Mimbres as only a small part of his mission. The Mimbres River could not sustain even the Mimbres, much less other Chihennes. In August 1857 he urged that a new reservation be set aside on the upper Gila River with a military post of at least four companies and an agent to get them started farming and see to their immediate wants.[12]

Steck did not yield his vision, even though it had already been severely undermined. A Bedonkohe had murdered a Navajo Indian agent, which led to a major military offensive against both Chiricahuas and White Mountains. Colonel Benjamin L. E. Bonneville thrust far down the Gila River and assaulted a White Mountain village. The campaign sent shock waves through all the Apaches.[13]

Bonneville's invasion predictably alarmed the Chiricahuas, and they began to draw off to the south and contemplate overtures to Janos for rations. Mangas's hybrid following began to fall apart as he aged and younger chiefs asserted leadership of their respective local groups. His influence weakening and his country swarming with soldiers, Mangas turned to his son-in-law Cochise, now the leading chief of the Chokonens to the west. He remained with him until the Bonneville campaign had run its course.[14]

Back at Santa Lucía Springs for the October 1858 issue of government provisions, Mangas and Geronimo took their provisions and again moved to Cochise's country, from which they intended to launch raids into Sonora. About December 1, 1858, both Mangas and Cochise, with about a hundred Bedonkohe and Chokonen warriors, struck into Sonora. Geronimo accompanied Mangas. Cochise had returned with much stock by the end of December, when he met the energetic Michael Steck and received government issues for the first time. Mangas and Geronimo returned from Sonora in the middle of February 1859, also with many horses, mules, and other booty, leaving behind the usual scenes of devastation. With their Mexican plunder, they went back to the upper Gila and settled into farming near Santa Lucía.[15]

By 1860, Geronimo was thirty-seven and a tough, seasoned fighter with a long record of raid and war in Sonora and Chihuahua. He had risen in stature to gain the respect and admiration of Mangas Coloradas. Mangas often took him on forays into Sonora as a trusted lieutenant, and he enjoyed the admiration of the Bedonkohes and Chihennes. He had also cemented relations with

Cochise and often mixed with the Chokonens in the Chiricahua Mountains and used them as a springboard for incursions into Mexico. His home, however, remained the Gila country near his birthplace in New Mexico.

That he lived there drew motivation from two sources: first, the nearby home of his mentor, Mangas Coloradas, at Santa Lucía Springs; second, his evolving role as a family man. Shortly after losing his mother, his wife, Alope, and his three children in the Carrasco massacre of 1851, Geronimo had married Chee-hash-kish, a Bedonkohe, and would later sire a son and a daughter. Soon afterward, he took still another wife, his third, Nana-tha-thtithl, another Bedonkohe. Together, they had one child. The family probably traveled occasionally with Geronimo but most of the time remained on the upper Gila.[16]

As a well-known Bedonkohe fighting man and a close associate of both Mangas Coloradas and Cochise, by 1860 Geronimo had become a prominent figure not only among Bedonkohes but Chihennes, Chokonens, and even Nednhis.

Three developments interrupted the favorable prospects of Steck's alliance with Mangas Coloradas. First was the discovery of gold in the Pinos Altos Range twenty-five miles east of Santa Lucía and the gold rush this set off in 1860. Second was a grievous wrong to Cochise inflicted by a young army officer bereft of experience and judgment. Third was the outbreak of the Civil War.

FIVE

War with the Americans

GOLD!

Beginning with the great California discovery in 1848, the cry of "Gold!" invariably brought swarms of unruly American prospectors in search of elusive riches. It occurred repeatedly throughout the mountain West in the decades following the California strike of 1848. Always, gold-seekers encountered resident Indians, shouldered them aside, ignored any government effort to protect them, and treated any who resisted with violence and death. Tribe after tribe lost their lands, some their lives. Apaches enjoyed no immunity from the ruling American conviction that mineral extraction prevailed over all other forms of land use.

Mexican lessees who mined at the Santa Rita copper mines intruded little on the Chiricahua world, nor did the few prospectors who probed the surrounding mountains for gold in late 1859 and early 1860. But on May 18, 1860, a party out of Mesilla made a big strike in the Pinos Altos Range northwest of the copper mines. By California standards, the influx of rough-hewn Americans set off by this discovery was minor, but by August 1860 seven hundred prospectors spread up the creeks from the new town of Pinos Altos. Mangas told his people to avoid the miners if possible, which was difficult.[1]

Because of the activity centered on the mining town of Pinos Altos, Geronimo was often drawn to these forested ridges and peaks. They rose to above eight thousand feet but did not offer the tangled terrain that made the Mogollon Mountains to the north so secure a haven for him. The Pinos Altos (Tall Pine) Range lay west of Geronimo's birthplace and tapered down to the prairies that bore most of the human traffic west and east. They figured frequently in Geronimo's life so long as miners continued to antagonize the Chiricahuas.

In May 1860 Agent Michael Steck, on leave in Washington, reached agreement with the commissioner of Indian affairs to establish a reservation on the upper Gila for the Mimbres and Bedonkohe Apaches. The reservation formed a square, fifteen miles on each side, anchored on the southeast corner by Santa Lucía Springs. The commissioner requested the US General Land Office to instruct the surveyor general of New Mexico to run the new boundaries.[2]

By July 1860, the New Mexico superintendent of Indian affairs, James L. Collins, worried that the new reservation would conflict with the invading miners. He looked to a new military post to be established at the foot of the Burro Mountains to guard the Indians against the miners. (A rude collection of cabins christened Fort Floyd soon sprang up, later to be renamed Fort McLane; it lasted only three years.) Collins's worries quickly took form when a party of Americans settled on the Gila within the reservation intent on founding a town and cultivating the soil to sell food to the miners. Committed to the reservation, the government refused to honor the claim and instructed Collins to remove the interlopers.[3]

The world of Geronimo and his people verged on great change. Unknown to him, in November 1860 Americans had elected a new Great Father, Abraham Lincoln. Almost at once some of the southern states began to secede from the American union. More would follow, and in April 1861 civil war would break out between North and South. Though far distant from the homeland of the Chiricahuas, they would experience consequences of Americans fighting one another.

Since 1849, Americans had flowed in increasing numbers across the southern route to California. The overland trail brushed the southern edge of Mangas's country but did not seriously disturb the Apaches. Westward, it climbed to a pass named for a prominent mountain headland, Stein's Peak (named in honor of Captain Enoch Steen, pronounced *Steen* although misspelled). The Stein's Peak Range of wrinkled brown desert mountains, pierced by Stein's Pass, was shouldered on the south by the Peloncillo Range, a long series of mountains snaking northwest from Mexico across southwestern New Mexico and into Arizona's Gila country. These mountain chains would play a continuing role in Chiricahua history.

After surmounting Stein's Pass, the immigrant trail descended a long incline into the flat San Simon Valley, with the forested rocky up thrust of the Chiricahua Mountains rising against the western horizon. The trail then climbed into the Chiricahua Mountains. A large open gap lay to their north, but it was waterless, which forced all since Spanish times to cross the mountains through Apache Pass. Apache Springs (and several others nearby) provided the necessary water. On the north of the pass, the Dos Cabezos (Two Heads) reared their rocky knobs. On the south lay the peaks, forests, and rocky spires of the Chiricahua Mountains.

Much longer and more tortuous than Stein's Pass, Apache Pass opened on the west to the Sulphur Springs Valley, separating the Chiricahua from the Dragoon Mountains. This broad valley, rich with nutritious grama grasses, proved ideal cattle country—once the Indian threat moderated.

These mountains and valleys formed the homeland of Cochise's Chokonens. "Cochise's Stronghold," hidden among immense piles of boulders in the Dragoon Mountains, provided a virtually inaccessible base for the chief, but he frequently could be found in Apache Pass.

In 1858 the Butterfield Overland Mail began running stagecoaches from Saint Louis to San Francisco. The coaches had to labor through Apache Pass on the overland trail. The company established a relay station in the pass, and Cochise quickly made friends with the attendants, even supplying them with firewood. Apache Pass would loom in relations between Americans and Chiricahuas for twenty-six years after 1860.

The Chiricahua Mountains provided Cochise and his Chokonens with the equivalent of Geronimo's Mogollon Mountains—a secure refuge against any intruders. Rimmed on east and west by two broad valleys, dry but grassy, the Chiricahuas rose to almost ten thousand feet at their highest peak. Twisting canyons drained the summits, providing ideal campsites, well-watered and rich with grass, the walls forming barriers against the incessant wind and the storms of snow and rain that swept the mountains in winter and summer. Ponderosa pine carpeted the heights with green. A forest of rock spires rose from a depression below a high ridge at the northern end. More than a refuge, the Chiricahuas provided the Chokonens with an abundance of game animals and edible plants. Apache Pass at the northern edge was more important to travelers than to the Chokonen residents.

"Cut the Tent," the Apaches called it. The Bascom Affair, white students have called it ever since 1861. "Cut the Tent" turned Cochise into an unforgiving foe of Americans and set off a war against them that lasted more than a decade. It also alienated Mangas Coloradas and Geronimo from the Americans because they participated, although defense of their homeland from Pinos Altos miners remained their highest priority.[4]

In January 1861, Cochise returned to the Apache Pass area from a raid into Mexico. In his absence Mangas Coloradas, Geronimo, and some of their men, angry over the miners at Pinos Altos and other disturbances at home, had journeyed to the Chokonen country, then embarked on their own raid into Sonora. They had not returned when "Cut the Tent" began.

As February 1861 opened, Chokonen scouts brought word to Cochise, his people secure in winter lodges in a mountain canyon, of a column of mule-mounted soldiers approaching from the west. That was routine news. Soldiers often threaded Apache Pass, destined for the two forts to the west or to the supply bases on the Rio Grande.

On February 3 Cochise received word that the soldiers had camped near the Butterfield station in Apache Pass and that the officer wished to talk with him. Prodded by another messenger the next day, he arrived shortly before noon at the soldier camp, a line of tents near the Butterfield mail station. Sensing no danger, he had some of his family with him—his brother Coyuntura, two nephews, his wife, and two of his children. The officer, flanked by a few soldiers with muskets, exchanged greetings with Cochise, as the troops began their noon-hour lunch, and invited him into his tent at the end of the soldier line. Cochise and Coyuntura entered the tent and ate.

With a white man interpreting, the officer began to question Cochise. The questions actually amounted to an accusation. Cochise, the officer said, had led a raid that seized the young stepson of the interpreter and some of his oxen. The soldiers had come to retrieve them. Cochise vehemently denied the charge, although he knew about the raid. The raiders had not been Chokonens, he explained, but other Apaches. Given a week, Cochise thought he could regain the boy and restore him to his father.

Through the interpreter, the officer informed Cochise that he and his companions would be held prisoners until the boy was turned over. Furious that an American soldier would treat an Apache chief so insolently, Cochise instantly drew his knife, slashed the canvas wall of the tent, and bolted up the slope of a steep hill behind the line of soldier tents. The interpreter managed to fire a pistol round before the soldiers could even load their muskets. Swiftly Cochise gained the edge of a broad ravine and disappeared. Before he could follow, soldiers seized Coyuntura, as well as the rest of Cochise's family. As Geronimo recalled years later, Cochise escaped by "cutting through the tent."[5]

An hour after his escape, Cochise came to a hilltop and shouted, asking to see Coyuntura. The soldiers answered with a blast of musketry. Cochise replied to this affront by raising his hand and, through the interpreter, denouncing the soldiers for wrongly accusing him of theft. He swore revenge, then vanished behind the hills.

Early the next morning, February 5, Cochise dispatched a group of men to approach the stage station, where the troops now had barricaded themselves in the corrals. The Indians bore a white flag. A single Apache advanced to declare that Cochise wanted to talk between the lines. As the officer, interpreter, and two soldiers ventured out, so did Cochise and three comrades. Cochise tried to convince the officer that he did not have the boy and pleaded for the return of his family. The officer's only response was a promise to release the family once the captive boy had been delivered.

With these talks under way, one of the station attendants, a friend of Cochise's, set forth to try to make his own peace. As he tipped over the crest of a ravine, Apaches seized him. As they struggled, the officer and his group raced back to the station. The Indians opened fire, knocking one down with a bullet in his back. The others made it to the corral, where the barricaded soldiers returned the Apache fire. Now Cochise had his own prisoner to bargain with.

At this point Mangas Coloradas reached the scene. He and Geronimo and their Bedonkohe warriors had returned from the raid in Sonora and joined Cochise in grappling with the crisis. Cochise retained leadership, but Geronimo took part as directed by Cochise.

The following day, February 6, Cochise watched from the hills as soldiers cautiously led mules to water in Apache Springs. Still hoping to end the affair peacefully, he refrained from ambushing them on the trail twisting down a ravine to the springs. Instead, he appeared on a slope above the mail station leading the Butterfield employee seized the day before. He had bound the man's hands behind his back and looped a rope around his neck. He offered to exchange the prisoner and sixteen mules for his family. Again the officer refused. Only the release of the captive boy would end the stalemate.

A few hours later Cochise gained more hostages for bargaining. A freight train of five wagons entered Apache Pass from the west. Cochise had followed its approach across the Sulphur Springs Valley. Near the summit he sprang the trap. Geronimo strongly implies that he participated in this atrocity. They surrounded the train, seized the mules, and took the teamsters prisoner. Of the nine men, they spared the three Americans but bound the six Mexicans to the wagon wheels, tortured them, and set the wagons afire. Geronimo's hatred for Mexicans would have given him particular pleasure in slicing, then incinerating the Mexicans.

Even though he now held four American captives, Cochise thought more could be taken from the eastbound stagecoach approaching in the hours of darkness after midnight. At the summit he opened fire from the hills on all sides. His men hit two of the mules and the driver. A passenger jumped from the coach, cut out the fallen mules, mounted the box, and whipped the remaining mules into a gallop, the Apaches in pursuit. They had destroyed a rude stone bridge that carried the road across a steep ravine. The mules hurtled across the ravine and, spurred by the momentum of the coach, clawed their way back to the road. The chase continued three miles to the stage station. Cochise still held but four hostages.

Sending his people back to their winter homes, Cochise resolved on one last effort to regain his family. On February 8 Chokonens and Bedonkohes attacked another detachment leading mules to the springs for water. This resulted in a desperate conflict with reinforcements sent from the stage station, but as the Apaches drew off, they stampeded all the mules and left the soldiers on foot.

The stalemate, however, had ended. Cochise gave up the fight and with some Chokonens embarked on a raid into Sonora. Mangas Coloradas, with Geronimo and the Bedonkohes, turned east toward their home on the upper Gila. Before parting, however, they tortured, killed, and mutilated their prisoners and left their remains near the summit of the pass.

Reinforcements arrived for the soldiers, who remained for more than a week scouring the country for Apaches. Finding none, they marched away on February 19, pausing at the summit of Apache Pass to hang Cochise's brother and two nephews from the limbs of oak trees. (The wife and children were liberated.)

The standoff with the officer had been bad enough, but nothing could have stoked Cochise's fury more than the wanton hanging of his family as the soldiers left.

None of the Apaches knew the officer or much of what animated the military in conducting this mission. The officer was Second Lieutenant

George N. Bascom, and part of his regiment, the Seventh Infantry, garrisoned Fort Buchanan.

The Gadsden Purchase, ratified in 1854, had added southern Arizona to the Territory of New Mexico. With Americans already in the little adobe town of Tucson and prospecting for gold farther up the Santa Cruz River, the New Mexico civil and military systems had to be projected into Arizona. Late in 1856 Major Enoch Steen led two squadrons of the First Dragoons through Stein's Pass and marched to Tucson. Finding it unsuited for a military post, early in 1857 Steen moved fifty miles to the southeast and established Fort Buchanan in the verdant Sonoita Valley. Michael Steck showed up to try to cement relations with the Apaches to the north and west. To the east, Chiricahuas gave little trouble, but others, chiefly Aravaipas, brought on dragoon campaigns that accomplished little. By 1860 a sister post, Fort Breckinridge, had risen on the lower San Pedro River to help guard the Butterfield coaches that began to appear in 1859. West of Cochise's country, therefore, two forts established American military presence in southern Arizona, Forts Buchanan and Breckinridge.[6]

On January 27, 1861, Aravaipa Apaches raided the ranch of John Ward in the Sonoita Valley near Fort Buchanan. They ran off some oxen and took captive Ward's stepson, mixed-blood offspring of an Apache and Ward's Mexican wife, a former captive of the Apaches. (Sold to and reared by the White Mountain Apaches, the boy grew up to figure prominently in Apache history as Mickey Free, an interpreter widely distrusted by the Chiricahuas.) Ward trailed the raiders only as far as the San Pedro, then hastened to Fort Buchanan to tell his story to Lieutenant Colonel Pitcairn Morrison. The trail, Ward contended, showed that the culprits were Cochise's Chiricahuas in Apache Pass.

Morrison assigned a company of the Seventh Infantry to take the field and try to recover the boy. With the company's captain and first lieutenant absent, the mission fell to Second Lieutenant Bascom. Morrison instructed Bascom to march to Apache Pass and take any measures he thought needed, including force, to recover the boy. Leading fifty-four infantrymen on mules and accompanied by John Ward to act as interpreter, Bascom set forth for Apache Pass. His arrival on February 3 led to the "Cut the Tent" sequence that so infuriated Cochise.[7]

On his return to Fort Buchanan, Lieutenant Bascom submitted a self-serving report that by omission and commission portrayed his role in the fiasco as an exercise in sound judgment and competent command. Colonel Morrison, possibly aware of his own culpability in sending an inexperienced young officer lacking in judgment to act in any way his judgment dictated, accepted the report at face value.

Bascom gained a commendation from the department commander and, with the outbreak of the Civil War, rose rapidly to captain. He was killed in the Battle of Valverde in 1862 and honored in the name of a short-lived military post, Fort Bascom.

Arizona paid a heavy price for Bascom's blunder.

"After this trouble," Geronimo recalled, "all the Indians agreed not to be friendly with the white men any more."[8]

Although a significant understatement, the agreement did take place. It occurred after Mangas Coloradas, Geronimo, and the Bedonkohes had returned to their homes on the upper Gila following the "Cut the Tent" affair. They found conditions no better than when they had left, the Pinos Altos miners still making trouble for everyone—Apaches, the army at nearby Fort McLane, and freighters on the overland trail. The Bedonkohes began raiding far and wide. In April 1861 Mangas journeyed to Apache Pass for the war council with Cochise that Geronimo recalled.

The leaders agreed to strike in two groups of about sixty men each, Cochise in the area west of Stein's Peak, Mangas the whites at Pinos Altos, the Santa Rita copper mines, and the Mimbres River. Freighters on the overland trail fell prey to the raiders and lost many mules. Farmers and ranchers on the Mimbres River fled their homes. Miners began to abandon Pinos Altos.

The Bedonkohes and Chihennes not only watched their victims yielding to their raids. They witnessed other strange happenings. For one, the Butterfield coaches disappeared from their accustomed passage on the overland trail. Even stranger, the soldiers began to march away from their forts, headed east. In New Mexico, the garrison of Fort McLane abandoned the post; in Arizona, the same occurred at Forts Buchanan and Breckinridge. They gathered at Fort Fillmore near Mesilla. Both Cochise and Mangas concluded they had driven the soldiers out of the country.

All that remained was to rid their homeland of all whites, and the war they agreed to in April continued through the summer into the fall without letup. The townsmen still clinging to Pinos Altos offered an especially tempting target.

Gradually, the Apaches learned that the soldiers had departed not because of Apache aggressions but because war had erupted in the East between North and South, and the soldiers in the West left to join in the fight of brother against brother. Some of these soldiers united with their southern brothers. Most remained in their blue uniforms to fight with their northern brothers.

A new era had dawned in the Apaches' fight with the white people.[9]

RETURN OF THE BLUECOATS

AS MANGAS COLORADAS AND Cochise plotted further war on the Americans during the summer of 1861, they could not have been ignorant of events that drew more white men into the Chiricahua domain. They doubtless knew nothing of the conventions assembled in Mesilla and Tucson in March 1861 that voted to create a Confederate Territory of Arizona in southern New Mexico and Arizona. But they surely watched the military force that reached Mesilla from the south in July. They wore gray rather than blue uniforms (if they wore uniforms at all), and they forced the surrender of the bluecoats gathered from the abandoned posts at Fort Fillmore. These events did not affect the chiefs' resolve to assail the closer enemies still living in Pinos Altos.

Geronimo took no part in these events. Increasingly he followed his own instincts rather than consistently join in the movements of Mangas Coloradas. During the summer of 1861, Geronimo set off with some Bedonkohes for a raid into Chihuahua in the vicinity of Casas Grandes. In a fierce battle with Mexican soldiers, he suffered a serious wound. His comrades treated him and withdrew to the Santa Rita Mountains in Arizona, near Tucson, where they camped with their families as he healed. But Mexican troops had followed. In September, with many men absent hunting, the soldiers launched a surprise dawn attack. Geronimo succeeded in escaping with Chee-hash-kish, his second wife. But his third wife, Nana-tha-thithl, and their child died in the deadly fire that killed most of the women. The troops burned the camp and returned to Mexico with four women captives. Now Geronimo had lost two wives, four children, and his mother to Mexican troops. His rage at Mexicans is easily understood.[1]

As Geronimo fled the massacre of his people by Mexican soldiers far to the west, Cochise and Mangas assembled a large alliance of Chiricahuas to attack Pinos Altos. The force, several hundred strong, consisted of their own Bedonkohes and Chokonens as well as Chihennes. At daybreak on September 27 they surrounded the town and its satellite mining camps and attacked from all sides. The startled miners, isolated in scattered defenses, could not mount effective resistance. The battle raged all morning, with heavy casualties on both sides. Unknown to the Apaches, a small Confederate detachment was camped in the town. The officer organized his own men and the miners into a fighting force. Around noon they fired a small cannon filled with nails at the Apaches, then counterattacked. The Apaches gave way and fled the scene.[2]

The alliance attacked several freight trains on the overland road, but they found themselves now facing fresh soldiers. Mangas was now more than seventy years old; he tired easily and increasingly wanted peace. The younger Cochise, full of vigor, took the more active role in the warfare of the alliance. By the end of 1861 the two chiefs had parted, Cochise to strike into Mexico, Mangas to withdraw to his accustomed sanctuary on the upper Gila. Secure in his refuge, he may not have been fully aware of the actions of the new officers and troops at Mesilla. In February 1862 they sent a column west to take possession of Tucson. Also in the spring they sent more soldiers to occupy and defend Pinos Altos, and they tried to wage a war of extermination on the Chihennes.

The newcomers at Mesilla were a Texas regiment of Confederate troops under Lieutenant Colonel John R. Baylor. In February 1862 he sent a detachment under Captain Sherod Hunter to occupy Tucson. Soon a formidable brigade of Confederate Texans under Brigadier General Henry H. Sibley marched up the Rio Grande with the mission of conquering New Mexico and even Colorado for the Confederacy. While Baylor remained in Mesilla, Sibley defeated Union troops under Colonel Edward R. S. Canby in the Battle of Valverde, south of Socorro. Not until after seizing Santa Fe and advancing up the Santa Fe Trail toward Colorado did Sibley meet defeat. On March 26–28, 1862, at the Battle of Glorieta Pass, Colorado Volunteers turned back the Confederate invasion.

As Sibley's battered, demoralized troops straggled down the Rio Grande and back to Texas, Baylor remained in Mesilla. He pursued a relentless campaign against the Chihennes. Alerted to the approach of a large Union force from the west, Baylor ordered Captain Hunter to withdraw his small force from Tucson. Cochise attacked them while they camped at Dragoon Springs, killed four men, and ran off thirty mules and twenty-five horses. Unmolested, the rest of the soldiers continued through Apache Pass and reached the Rio Grande in safety.

Cochise had also learned of the large column of bluecoats approaching Tucson from the west, marching across the desert in separate contingents because of the distance between water holes. He knew they entered Tucson and that some marched to reoccupy abandoned Forts Buchanan and Breckinridge. They then began to move eastward, again in separate detachments, toward the heart of Cochise's homeland.

On June 25, 1862, Cochise looked down from the hills as 140 American soldiers camped at the abandoned Butterfield station in Apache Pass. With the execution of his brother and nephews by American soldiers still fresh in his memory, he did not greet these soldiers in friendship. From above Apache Springs, his men fired down at the troops watering their horses. They stopped, however, when a white flag appeared below. An hour later, backed by seventy-five men, Cochise ventured down to talk with the American officer. He assured the chief that they came in peace and wanted to be friends. He then handed over presents of tobacco and pemmican. After the meeting ended, the officer discovered that three of his soldiers had been shot, lanced, and stripped. A frantic pursuit of the culprits revealed only mocking Apaches watching from high hills and ridges. The soldiers moved two miles farther east and camped. During the night Apaches fired into the camp, wounding a soldier and killing a horse. The next morning the column formed and hastened east on the trail. The Apaches let them go.

From the officer's revelations, Cochise quickly concluded that these American newcomers foreshadowed a fresh offensive into his country and that they numbered too many for him to contest without help. He sent out an appeal for another great alliance. Mangas Coloradas and his Bedonkohes responded. So did Chihennes of Victorio and Nana, and even Juh with a few Nednhis. Within hardly more than a week, they gathered at Apache Pass.

Victorio was a chief of the Warm Springs, or Ojo Caliente, local group of the Chihennes. Born about 1820, he rapidly became a conspicuous fighter.

Shorter than Mangas Coloradas, he nevertheless boasted the usual powerful Apache physique and a potential for leadership that elevated him to chief. The less warlike Loco, also competent and respected, inherited a chieftainship at the same time as Victorio. When Chihenne war parties took the field, however, Victorio rather than Loco rode in the lead. Thus his speedy response to Cochise's call for help at Apache Pass.[3]

Nana, a tall Warm Springs Chihenne with a decided limp, never attained a chieftainship. But he rode as a highly effective war leader for decades. He married Geronimo's sister, Nah-dos-te (his one full sister, not a cousin). Staunchly loyal to Victorio, he could usually be found in any war expedition led by Victorio, such as the impending conflict at Apache Pass in 1862.[4]

Whether Geronimo and his followers, who had been struck by Mexicans in September 1861, participated in Cochise's effort to fight off the return of the Americans is unrecorded. He dictated nothing of these significant events for his autobiography. Never, in fact, would he talk to whites about conflict with white soldiers. But he had participated in every previous important occasion that brought Mangas and Cochise together for war or raid, and so formidable and organized was the enterprise at Apache Pass that he must be assumed to have taken part.[5]

Late on July 14, 1862, Mangas and Cochise spotted a large dust cloud rising from Dragoon Springs, forty miles west of Apache Pass. From what Cochise had learned in his recent talk with the soldier chief at Apache Springs, they knew that another force of American soldiers advanced on the old stage road. They would march all night and into the next day, reaching Apache Pass exhausted and in dire want of water. The chiefs hid fighting men on the slopes shouldering both sides of the trail as it approached the abandoned stage station.

Aware of how the sweltering heat of July 15 would affect the soldiers, Mangas and Cochise let them straggle down the trail. Horsemen arrived at the stage station about noon and began to unsaddle. The footmen soon followed. Twenty men and two supply wagons, with two wheeled vehicles that the Apaches later called "wagon guns," brought up the rear. The chiefs signaled the attack. From the hillsides, a deadly fusillade tore into these men, killing a soldier and wounding a teamster. From the rear, the Apaches then descended in force and charged the outnumbered rear guard. Soldiers from the station hastened back to the fray, fighting in hand-to-hand combat until the Apaches withdrew into the hills, hastened by rounds from the "wagon guns" bursting among them.

The soldiers still had not reached Apache Springs, some six hundred yards beyond the station in a narrow gorge dominated by steep, rock-strewn slopes on both sides. The Apaches had already studded the slopes with rock breastworks and commanded a field of fire that could sweep the springs below.

Even so, the soldiers had to have water. In the afternoon they deployed and worked carefully up the ravine toward the water. The barricaded Apaches opened fire, secure behind breastworks from any return fire. They had not reckoned, however, on the wagon guns. The soldiers sought to bombard them in their improvised forts. Bursting rounds, however, sprayed the deadly fragments of iron not on them but on the other side of the ridge. Soldiers fanned out in skirmish lines and charged up the slopes. Even though unharmed by the exploding shells, they frightened the defenders into hastily scattering from their defenses.

Amid the confusion, six horsemen galloped west up the trail. Mangas and about twenty men took up the chase. Beyond the summit of the pass, they caught up with the soldiers, wounded one, and hit two horses. One soldier had paused to rest his horse and found himself cut off. Quickly mounting, he expertly maneuvered his horse and avoided the Apaches closing in. He had a repeating carbine, which may have taken them off guard. One of his shots struck Mangas Coloradas in the chest and knocked him from his horse. Quickly his men bore their wounded chieftain to safety, and the soldier escaped.

As the Bedonkohes carried Mangas south to Janos for medical treatment, Cochise and the Chokonens, and any other warriors who had not yet left, reoccupied the breastworks above Apache Springs. Late that afternoon the soldiers marched out of the pass to the west but returned the next morning, July 16, with even more men. At the springs they formed on horseback and foot and advanced with military precision. The wagon guns barked again, the soldiers fired their weapons at the defenders, and then charged. Cochise's men again scattered as the shells burst above them.

The Apaches had lost the two-day battle, and the soldiers commanded the springs.

Many more soldiers than Cochise had confronted were on the way. California had responded vigorously to the outbreak of the Civil War, raising more volunteer regiments than any other western state or territory. A full brigade of

California Volunteers, more than two thousand strong, set forth in early 1862 to span the Southwest and help Colonel Canby fend off the invasion of New Mexico by Confederate general Sibley. Colonel James H. Carleton raised the force, receiving a brigadier's star while en route. Part of his command defeated some of Captain Sherod Hunter's Confederates in a brief skirmish at Picacho Peak, north of Tucson, and hastened his return to New Mexico.

A tough, dogmatic veteran of the prewar regular army, Carleton imposed firm discipline, possessed unbounded self-confidence, and had no tolerance for opposition. An experienced Indian fighter, he intended to sweep aside any Indians who interfered with his mission.

By early June 1862 Carleton and most of the California Column had arrived in Tucson. Seeking to open communication with Canby, he dispatched Lieutenant Colonel Edward E. Eyre and 140 cavalrymen to scout the overland trail as far as Mesilla. At Apache Pass on June 25, Eyre talked with Cochise and lost three men before proceeding on to Mesilla. By the time Eyre reached the Rio Grande and learned of Sibley's defeat and retreat, Baylor had left for Texas and the last of his troops were evacuating Mesilla.

Meanwhile, Carleton planned to move the California Column in stages to the Rio Grande. The first contingent left Tucson on July 10 under Captain Thomas L. Roberts. It consisted of a mixed force of 126 infantry and cavalry, twenty-two teams, and 242 head of cattle. Two howitzers rumbled in the rear, manned by infantry. (Howitzers were cannon designed not for direct fire but for lobbing rounds into the air to descend on the target.) Depositing wagonloads of supplies on the San Pedro River for the next detachment, Roberts left an escort for the train and cattle to follow and, with sixty infantrymen, eight cavalrymen, and the howitzers, continued to Dragoon Springs. Resting here for two days, on the afternoon of July 14 he resumed the march across the Sulphur Springs Valley. The dust cloud raised by his column alerted Cochise and Mangas Coloradas that it would reach Apache Pass the next day, July 15.

The two-day Battle of Apache Pass ensued. Roberts proved a superior leader, expertly deploying his troops and his artillery. Both on July 15 and again on the next day, his howitzers proved the decisive factor in the victory, even though the shells burst over the reverse slope instead of above the Apaches.[6]

Captain Roberts had not only won an important victory. Even more significant, when General Carleton arrived at the pass on July 27, Roberts strongly recommended that a military post be erected on the top of the hill overlooking the springs. Otherwise, he argued, every command that attempted to pass would have to fight for water. Carleton readily agreed.

Fort Bowie, named for one of the California colonels, rose on this site. Later moved a short distance to the east, Fort Bowie would prove a festering sore in the heart of the Chiricahua domain for the remaining decades of Apache warfare. Not until eight years after the collapse of Apache resistance did the troops march away.[7]

Carleton reached Fort Thorn on the Rio Grande early in August 1862 and proceeded at once to Santa Fe. Canby had gained promotion to brigadier and a transfer to the East. Carleton inherited his command of the Department of New Mexico, over which he reigned tyrannically for the rest of the Civil War years. Confronted on his journey across the Southwest with evidence of the ferocity of Apache hostilities, he had left most of the California Column in southern New Mexico under his blustery second-in-command, Colonel Joseph R. West. Elevated to brigadier general in October 1862, West turned to the Apaches with the same venom as his Confederate predecessor, John R. Baylor.[8]

By mid-August 1862, Mangas and his followers who had fought at Apache Pass in July had returned to their home country. In Janos, his men had forced a Mexican doctor to dig the ball received in the battle out of their chief's chest. Despite his age, he healed quickly enough to travel back to the upper Gila and the Mogollons. He wanted nothing more than to make peace with the Americans and resume farming at Santa Lucía.

Only about thirty families still lived in Pinos Altos, although a contingent of men formerly in Confederate service helped bolster their defenses. Mangas journeyed north to Ácoma to send an appeal for peace to the new general in Santa Fe. Receiving no answer, he went back home to try bargaining with the people at Pinos Altos. He found them receptive. In council in the town itself, he talked with a tall man, who promised to issue beef, blankets, and other provisions if he would bring all his people in. The tall man was Jack Swilling, a former Confederate militia officer. Mangas agreed to come back in two weeks.[9]

As so often in the past, Mangas trusted the Americans. After the meeting in Pinos Altos, he gathered the Bedonkohes south of Stein's Peak in the Peloncillo Mountains for a council to decide the next move. Mangas described his hopes for the future: peace with the Americans and a life of undisturbed farming at Santa Lucía. He wished to lead the Bedonkohes to Pinos Altos and deliver this message. Few of the Bedonkohe leaders, including Geronimo, trusted the Americans or thought this a good idea, and they expressed their disapproval. But Mangas still projected the magnetism of old, and all consented to a compromise. Half the band would return to Pinos Altos under Mangas and learn whether the Americans acted in good faith. The other half would remain in Arizona to await word of how the Americans had reacted. In another indication of Geronimo's increasing independence, he stayed in Arizona.

Before again heading for Pinos Altos, Mangas conferred with the Chihenne leaders Victorio and Nana. Both agreed with the Bedonkohes who waited in Arizona. The Americans could not be trusted. Even so, Victorio and some Chihennes joined Bedonkohes to act as a bodyguard for Mangas as he approached Pinos Altos.

Late in the morning of January 17, 1863, Mangas and his escort arrived within 150 yards of the town, walking slowly. The same tall man who had previously greeted Mangas, Jack Swilling, came forward from the men lined up behind him. When the two met, exchanging words in broken Spanish, Swilling looked back, and suddenly his men leveled their rifles. He informed Mangas that he now would remain as a hostage for the good behavior of his men. As the two started back to the town, the body guard advanced, too. Swilling informed Mangas that they would not be needed. As Mangas dismissed them, he stoically comprehended that he had been betrayed and would probably be killed. At an earlier stage of life, his cunning might have worked an escape. Now past seventy, he understood such an attempt to be futile.

At the edge of town, soldiers emerged from hiding in shacks and chaparral, although Swilling did not turn Mangas over to them. Geronimo, Victorio, Nana, and others who counseled against taking the Americans at their word had been right. Their chief should not have undertaken so risky a move. They knew the Americans could not be trusted.

The next day, the soldiers formed and, accompanied by Swilling with his own men and his prisoner, rode toward the old army post of Fort McLane. Although burned by the Apaches when abandoned, its ruins had been reoccupied by troops. Here Swilling turned Mangas over to an American general. He was Joseph H. West, a pompous little officer Carleton had left to war against the Apaches in southern New Mexico. Now aware of his impending fate, Mangas denied the general's accusations that he had led all the bloody raids of the past few years in southern New Mexico and Arizona.

Warned that any attempt to escape would cost him his life, Mangas entered the shells of one of the fallen adobe buildings with two guards. The soldiers ordered him to the ground, gave him a single blanket, and built a fire nearby for themselves. As the night of January 18 turned bitterly cold, the chief bore the torment under the single blanket. At midnight four more soldiers replaced his two-man guard. One soldier walked sentry on half the building's perimeter, a second on the other half. The two remaining with Mangas heated their bayonets in the fire and several times pressed them against his legs and feet. Mangas shifted from one side to another and tried to tighten the blanket around him. About an hour after the new guards took station, now January 19, 1863, Mangas raised on one elbow and loudly protested this treatment. Both soldiers raised their muskets and fired into the chief's chest. He fell back on the ground. Another soldier advanced to fire a revolver into Mangas's skull. If he was not already dead, he was now. The old man, now about seventy-three, had paid the price for his trust in the Americans.

General West himself had arranged for Mangas's death. He personally instructed the guard detail before they took station beside Mangas at midnight: "Men, that old murderer has got away from every soldier command and has left a trail of blood for five hundred miles on the old stage line. I want him dead or alive tomorrow morning, do you understand? I want him dead."

The next morning, January 19, 1863, West got what he wanted. His official report, contrived less for a sympathetic Carleton than for public consumption, explained that Mangas had been shot on his third attempt to escape. Hung together by one fabrication after another, the report concluded that "the good faith of the U.S. Military authorities was in no way compromised."[10]

General West had not finished with the Apaches, as Geronimo would soon learn. But he had decisively ended a long and significant era in the history of all the Chiricahua bands. His treachery, backed by General Carleton, would forever blacken the record of American relations with the Apaches.

Although a Bedonkohe, Mangas Coloradas had towered over the history of all the Chiricahua bands for more than thirty years. Other influential chiefs of the bands and local groups had come and gone. Mangas reigned supreme. No other chief rivaled him in influence or stature. Cochise came close but had not attained this distinction by the time of the perfidious slaying of his friend and father-in-law.

Geronimo, Mangas's most important protégé, had already begun to drift toward Cochise. He surely mourned his mentor's death, but it freed him from the magnetism that had bound him to the old chief for twenty years. He would excel Mangas Coloradas in only one way: his name would resonate around the world as the best-known of all Indian leaders. In no other way, however, did Geronimo approach the significance of Mangas Coloradas.

Mangas Coloradas was simply the greatest of all Apache chiefs.

SEVEN

COCHISE: *War and Peace, 1863–72*

DEMORALIZED BY THE MURDER of their venerable chief Mangas Coloradas and fearful of aggressive campaigning by the soldiers, the Bedonkohes abandoned the headwaters of the Gila River and moved west. As Geronimo recalled, "We retreated into the mountains near Apache Pass." This was Cochise country, and as Geronimo noted, Cochise "took command of both divisions." The Chokonen chief assumed the mantle of Mangas Coloradas, although he lacked the qualities to bind the Bedonkohes as solidly to his leadership.

Neither the Chokonens nor Bedonkohes remained quietly in the Chiricahua Mountains around Apache Pass. The killing of Mangas Coloradas demanded revenge. On March 22, 1863, a raiding party struck a newly built military post in the Pinos Altos Mountains and ran off with sixty horses. They fled westward into Arizona and paused on the Rio Bonita, a southern tributary of the Gila, at a place favored by Cochise. Pursing soldiers found them. A surprise attack took twenty-five lives in twenty minutes and scattered the rest.[1]

Revenge raids continued throughout 1864 and into 1865, both in New Mexico and Arizona. Soldiers proved unrelenting in tracking down raiding parties and exacting many lives in sudden surprise attacks while suffering few casualties themselves. Their victories fueled the need for more vengeance, hence more raiding parties. They ran off much military stock, killed a few soldiers, but only seemed to stir them to further offensives. Rarely had the Chiricahuas engaged an enemy in so many open conflicts or suffered such damaging losses.

As the conflict escalated, Indian families remained relatively secure, tucked away in mountain recesses in the Chiricahua and neighboring mountain ranges. Among the women and children was Geronimo's family. It consisted of his second wife, Chee-hash-kish, who in 1864 gave birth to a son, Chappo (not to be confused with Chatto, another Chiricahua). Lulu would follow in 1865. Geronimo's third wife, Nana-tha-thithl, and her child had been killed by Mexican soldiers in 1861. Geronimo would soon take another wife, a Chiricahua-Nednhi whose name is lost but who was the sister of a close relative of Cochise and his second son, Naiche.[2]

Deprived of the strong leadership of Mangas Coloradas, in the three years after his death the Bedonkohes fractured into three groups. Illustrating the hybrid composition of Mangas's following, some joined with Victorio's Chihennes in New Mexico, ultimately to seek peace with the Americans; by the early 1870s, they would be fully absorbed by the Chihennes. Others drifted under the influence of Cochise and Juh. Given his friendship and family tie with Juh since youth, Geronimo and his following joined Juh. The bond linking the two grew ever stronger by the year.[3]

The treacherous murder of Mangas Coloradas in January 1863 should have alerted the Chiricahuas that they faced a new breed of soldiers. Brigadier General James H. Carleton, the military potentate in Santa Fe, set the tone: ruthless, energetic, persistent, demanding, determined that his men keep in the field until they had accomplished their mission. In southern New Mexico, the task fell to Brigadier General Joseph R. West. He wholeheartedly subscribed to Carleton's mind-set, as demonstrated by his personal order to kill the captive Mangas Coloradas. He expected no less from the able captains who so aggressively kept to the trail of raiding parties and inflicted heavy casualties; nor from the troops themselves, consisting of hardy California gold miners anxious to sweep aside the Indians and, as Carleton encouraged, exploit the mines of southern New Mexico. From 1863 to 1865, the California Volunteers conducted rigorous campaigns that cost Chiricahua lives but did not conquer them.[4]

In his annual report for 1866, Major General Irvin McDowell reported from division headquarters in San Francisco that the regular Fourteenth Infantry and First Cavalry had replaced all the Volunteers in the District of

Arizona. They were warring successfully against the Apaches and letting them know they could have peace by settling at Fort Goodwin, a post erected on the Gila River by the Volunteers. But they could not be kept there. The army could not feed them, and they did not want to settle with other Apache groups with which they had long been at enmity. In 1866, therefore, the US Regular Army opened a new era in the Apache wars.[5]

What part Geronimo played in Cochise's battles with the California Volunteers for the three years after the death of Mangas Coloradas in 1863 can only be speculated. Consistent with his growing drift away from Mangas in the years before his death, as the Bedonkohes gradually fragmented Geronimo aligned himself with the local group that adhered only partly to Cochise. Sometimes they followed him into battle. Sometimes they raided and fought on their own. Equally as often, they could be found with Juh's Nednhis in Sonora. There, Geronimo and Juh grew ever closer in raids and warfare, on both sides of the border. Both against the California Volunteers and in the intense warfare with the regulars after 1866, Geronimo and Juh came and went between Mexico and Arizona. Although more independent than Chokonens, Geronimo and Juh still honored the power of Cochise's leadership and fought closely for and with him.

The name Geronimo surfaced in Mexican records in 1843 and occasionally in American records in the 1860s. Not until the 1870s, however, in his fifties, did Geronimo appear to any whites in both name and person. His autobiography links him to numerous fights and raids throughout the period when Mangas and Cochise battled Mexicans and Americans, but placing him definitely in all but a few is impossible. That in the middle and late 1860s his Bedonkohe local group bonded as closely with Juh's Nednhis as with Cochise's Chokonens suggests that Geronimo passed much of these years in Sonora and Chihuahua. His family probably remained hidden in the Sierra Madre most of the time. Sometime in the years after 1865, Geronimo added to his family of four wives and three children a fifth and a sixth wife. His fifth was a Bedonkohe named Shit-sha-she, his sixth a Nednhi named Zi-yeh. Since the two children of Geronimo and Zi-yeh, Fenton and Eva, were not born until 1882 and 1889, respectively, the sixth marriage probably occurred in the middle or late 1870s.[6]

As the Chiricahuas learned of the end of the white man's Civil War, they watched anxiously as Arizona and New Mexico began to fill with miners, cattlemen, and farmers. They provided tempting targets, and Apache depredations increased. Many of the newcomers lost life and possessions. Travelers on the overland route, especially the mail coaches, proved especially vulnerable. Cochise had not forgotten the Bascom Affair, and the years 1869 and 1870 featured the fiercest fighting of the Chiricahua wars. Fort Bowie, in the heart of Cochise's homeland, played a central role in the fighting, its patrols tracking and defeating the chief's raiding parties time and again.[7]

In his ten-year war of revenge for the senseless atrocity inflicted on his family by Lieutenant Bascom, Cochise had killed many white people and fought many battles with the white soldiers. He had made southern Arizona dangerous for travelers and settlers. But the conflicts with soldiers, both California Volunteers and US regulars, had cost many fighters. His women and children never felt secure from a sudden attack. They never had enough food and feared to search widely for it. He grew increasingly alarmed at his shrinking population and personally weary of always being forced to fight, whether offensively or defensively. Sixty or more years old by the early 1870s and in failing health, Cochise began to think seriously of peace.[8]

To the east, the Warm Springs Chihennes had the same thoughts. Their homeland centered at Ojo Caliente, the sacred springs that fed the Alamosa River, which flowed southeast into the Rio Grande. Downstream lay the Mexican village of Cañada Alamosa, where the Warm Springs people traded. In 1869 hunger had driven them to seek peace and rations from the officer at Fort McRae assigned as their agent. Within a year they were holding peace talks at Cañada Alamosa, although the government's sparse rations had done little to abate their hunger. During one of the many talks, in December 1869, Chief Loco disclosed that Cochise had said he would bring his people in as soon as a treaty was made. But he wanted to be satisfied that it involved no treachery.[9]

Only a month earlier, although raids continued unabated, Cochise had sent a peace messenger, perhaps his wife, to a new military post to the north, where the White Mountain Apaches lived. He himself followed on August 30 and told the officer in charge that he wanted peace. But, uncomfortable among the alien tribe of White Mountains, he returned to his own country. His Chokonen followers refused to go there ostensibly for the same reason. More likely, they had heard of the promising talks between the Chihenne chiefs and government agents at Cañada Alamosa.[10]

On October 20, 1870, at Cañada Alamosa, a government emissary from Santa Fe parleyed with Warm Springs chiefs Victorio and Loco. The next day, as Loco had predicted, Cochise rode in with thirty-four men, including captains and headmen with their families, ninety-six in all. On October 22, he conferred for several hours with the official and explained that since 1860 he had been at war and had lost many men. Now he had more women and children than he could care for and still fight. He wanted peace so that he would not have to hide his women and children and could travel the roads in safety. The official said the Great Father wanted peace, too, and would provide rations. Cochise promised to try to bring his people to Cañada Alamosa and keep them quiet. He returned with some in December, but learning now that the government intended to move them all to the Mescalero Reservation near Fort Stanton, east of the Rio Grande, he led his people back home. Cochise had made clear that he wanted peace, and he intended, if the government called off the plan to move to Mescalero, to take his people back to Cañada Alamosa. But the war continued, as the troops chased him all over his homeland, allowing him "no rest, no peace."[11]

In fact, the government had not established a reservation for the Chihennes but argued over several proposals. Loco and his fellow chiefs made it clear that they wanted a reservation only in the Ojo Caliente country and would accept no other.

On June 16, 1871, on a spur of the Dragoon Mountains, Cochise received an emissary from Cañada Alamosa, one Cochise had met there the previous October. Cochise liked him and named him "Stagalito," Red Beard—a fitting sobriquet for the big man with red hair and beard. (Thomas J. Jeffords, a trader; earlier he had scouted for General Carleton and briefly operated a mail and stage line between Santa Fe and Tucson.) Now Stagalito told Cochise that the highest government official in New Mexico asked him to bring his people and settle near Cañada Alamosa, where he would receive rations and protection and an invitation to visit Washington. Cochise replied that he would like to settle there, but he could not expose his people to the soldiers swarming in the country. If they were withdrawn, he would come.[12]

Finally, in September 1871, Cochise summoned the resolve to gather some of his people and move to Cañada Alamosa. They arrived on September 28—thirty men and about two hundred others. Still another big chief hastened down from Santa Fe and joined with the new agent to meet with

Cochise. Meantime, more people arrived, bringing the number of his followers close to 250. In the council with the white officials early in October, Cochise promised to remain at peace and send runners to bring in other Chokonens. He thought that most of the groups still out would come, but not all. He could not be held responsible for them. Specifically, the Nednhis under Juh and Geronimo would fight to the last.[13]

Thus Cochise himself confirmed the activities and attitude of Geronimo. Teamed with Juh and the Nednhis since 1865, he remained wedded to continuing raid and war against both Americans and Mexicans. Even though Cochise wanted peace, Geronimo remained in good health and determined to take life and property as long as he pleased. Peace formed no part of his thinking. With Juh, he ranged between Mexico and Arizona, murdering and depredating at will.

Having finally settled Cochise at Cañada Alamosa, the government again blundered. No reservation existed here, and another touring special agent judged it unsuited for a reservation. He decreed that all the Chihennes be moved to a high, cold, sterile, and unhealthy mountain location seventy miles to the northwest in the Tularosa Valley, a tributary of the San Francisco River. This enraged them. They looked on the Alamosa Valley and the Ojo Caliente at its head as their sacred homeland. All resisted such a move, and as the controversy played out Cochise gathered his people and, at the end of March 1872, returned to their Arizona homeland. For the government and Cochise, peace remained as elusive as ever.[14]

Rejecting Tularosa and giving up on Cañada Alamosa, Cochise turned to Janos in hopes of a treaty and rations from the Mexicans. Also in the vicinity were Juh and Geronimo with the Nednhis, who had been hounded out of Sonora by aggressive Mexican offensives and also sought succor at Janos. Cochise remained near Janos until late July 1872, when he concluded that the Mexicans would not respond. He therefore returned to his favored stronghold in Arizona's Dragoon Mountains.[15]

EIGHT

COCHISE: *Peace at Last, 1872*

ALTHOUGH THE CHIRICAHUA MOUNTAINS remained the homeland of the Chokonens, Cochise passed much time in his two strongholds, east and west, in the Dragoon Mountains, a lesser range forty miles west of the Chiricahuas. The base of the mountains consisted of pile on pile of huge boulders, and the strongholds could be reached only by intricate pathways. The strongholds provided open spaces for councils, with wood and water surrounded by rock walls and accessible only to Apaches. Between the two mountain ranges lay the flat, grassy Sulphur Springs Valley. Anyone approaching the Dragoons from the east could not avoid being seen from the mountains.

Late in September 1872 Cochise's lookouts, posted on the summit of the Dragoons, spotted the approach across the Sulphur Springs Valley of a group of five men. The sentinels reported to Cochise and kept close watch. Early on the morning of September 30 the party entered a defile that accessed a path to Cochise's West Stronghold. At the same time, signal smokes announced that the men came in peace. One of the five, who clearly knew the way in, went ahead to take word to Cochise. His name was Chie (ironically, the son of Coyuntera, Cochise's brother hanged at Apache Pass by Lieutenant Bascom). Word reached Cochise that the party consisted of two other old friends, Ponce and Red Beard Jeffords, and two army officers, one a bearded general who had only one arm. They came, Cochise was told, to talk peace. Two boys went down to lead these men up the steep, winding trail across the Dragoon Mountains to Cochise's West Stronghold.

61

A group of Chiricahuas camped here, but not Cochise. He would come the next morning. Early on October 1 he appeared, preceded by his brother Juan and accompanied by his sister, his youngest wife, and his youngest son, a teenager named Naiche. Juan rushed to embrace Red Beard, as did Cochise when he dismounted. "This is the man," Jeffords said to the older American officer. Cochise turned to shake his one hand, noting that the sleeve of his other arm, severed at the elbow, was tied to a button on the front of his shirt. "Buenos Días, Señor," Cochise said. After warmly greeting Chie and the other Apache, Ponce, Cochise shook hands with the other officer. Jeffords named them as General Howard and Captain Sladen.[1]

A blanket had been spread in the shade of a big oak. As a growing circle of women and children crowded toward the blanket, Cochise bid his guests to sit. Cochise, Ponce, and Jeffords all spoke rudimentary Spanish, and the conversation proceeded entirely in Spanish; but what Howard and Cochise expressed emerged clearly. After a long conversation in Apache with Chie and Ponce, Cochise turned to Howard and asked why he had come. Through Jeffords, Howard replied that he had come from Washington to meet Cochise and his people and make peace, that he would stay as long as necessary. Cochise responded that he too wanted peace, that he had done no harm since returning from Cañada Alamosa, that he was poor and could have relieved his distress by raiding traffic on the Tucson road but had not done it.[2]

Howard then went directly to the point of his visit. He wanted Cochise and the Chokonens to move to Cañada Alamosa and live with the Chihennes. Although he had twice tried to settle there, Cochise now replied that he himself would go, but all his people would not follow. His band of Chokonen Chiricahuas would be broken. He had already said as much to white officials, especially singling out the Nednhis of Juh and Geronimo. Neither they nor some of the Chokonen groups would give up their free life for a reservation.

Abruptly, Cochise also went directly to the point: Why not give him Apache Pass? Give him that and he would protect all the roads. He would see that nobody's property was taken by Indians.

Howard answered by conceding that this might be possible but went on to extol the virtues of the Cañada Alamosa country.

Without further argument, Cochise asked how long the general would stay. Would he wait for all the subchiefs to be summoned for a formal council? This would take ten days. Howard repeated that he would stay as long as necessary. At once Cochise dispatched runners on this mission.

He also expressed apprehension that his captains would encounter patrols of soldiers while converging on his stronghold. Howard offered to send Captain Sladen to Fort Bowie with orders to initiate a cease-fire and to telegraph this message to all other forts. Cochise objected. Sladen was only a "teniente," while Howard was a "Grande," whom the soldiers were certain to obey. Howard agreed to accompany Sladen, but Cochise insisted that only Chie go with him; Sladen and Jeffords would remain in the Apache camp.[3]

In Howard's absence, some of Cochise's men came in and reported slaying four soldiers a few days earlier. Certain that pursuing soldiers could not find his stronghold, he nonetheless abandoned it and led his people to a steep mountainside that could easily be defended. From here, the next morning, they spotted the approach of Howard's party across the plain below. In a mountain pass, they welcomed the "Grande" back to the Dragoons. He had with him three white men, one of whom drove a spring wagon drawn by four mules and loaded with provisions. By early morning on October 4 all had returned to the original camp.

One after another Chokonen captain brought his people to the stronghold. To Cochise's disappointment, his eldest son, Taza, had not come; he was raiding deep in Sonora. During the wait, Howard and Cochise continued to argue over the solution—Cañada Alamosa or Cochise's traditional homeland. One of the white men who had arrived with Howard was a Spanish interpreter; he spoke no Apache. So again the dialogue proceeded in Spanish.[4]

By October 10 all had come who could be expected, ten, all men of influence. Cochise decided to proceed with a formal council, which he regarded as of great significance. He and his ten captains sat in the center of a shaded circle, with Howard, Jeffords, Sladen, and Howard's Spanish interpreter. Cochise wanted his own Spanish interpreter, and he too seated himself next to the chief. Circle after circle of people—men, women, and children—crowded as close as possible to try to hear what transpired.

The issue was the general's proposition that all the Chiricahuas move to a reservation, yet to be selected, and be fed and cared for by the government. Actually, Howard had already given in. Even so, formal agreement had to be reached. Cochise spoke in Apache to his interpreter, who translated into Spanish for the general's interpreter, who translated into English for him.

The talks amounted to a formal ratification of what had already been decided. Instead of moving to Cañada Alamosa, as Howard had wanted, Cochise could have a reservation in his own homeland, with Red Beard Jeffords as agent. In return, his people would cease all raiding and warfare and keep the roads open and safe.

Cochise wanted the officers at Fort Bowie to know what had been decided and asked the general to summon them to a council at Sulphur Springs the next day, October 12. Four officers appeared there after a nighttime ride, and again, for their benefit, the terms of the agreement were set forth—again, from Apache to Spanish to English.

Geronimo claimed in his autobiography to have been at the Howard peace conference, and one of the officers at Sulphur Springs backed his claim.[5]

Without much effort, Cochise had got his way from the American general, who did not argue very forcefully for his way or against Cochise's way. Both Jeffords and Cochise were pleased with the outcome, although neither foresaw the immense trouble it would cause the Chiricahuas in only a few years.

Unknown to Cochise—or Geronimo—General Howard's mission was but part of a comprehensive government effort to concentrate all the Apaches of Arizona and New Mexico on reservations, either by diplomacy or by military force. For Howard, diplomacy had worked.

In Washington, in March 1869, a new Great Father had taken office. He was Ulysses S. Grant, the Union Army's most famous general in the Civil War. Under his auspices, a new policy toward the Indians had taken shape. Labeled Grant's Peace Policy, it sought to approach the Indians by peaceful means, not military force: "conquest by kindness." As part of the reform package, an act of Congress had authorized creation of a Board of Indian Commissioners, composed of eminent humanitarians, to advise the Interior Department on policy and ensure the proper expenditure of funds appropriated for the Indians. Under its oversight, moreover, Protestant religious bodies were to nominate agents to gather roaming Indians on reservations and see to their care and "civilization."

With Arizona and New Mexico swept by Apache depredations, no part of the West demanded quicker action. The outraged governor of New Mexico, William A. Pile, had journeyed to the southwestern counties of the territory and compiled a list of depredations between November 25, 1869, and May 21,

1871. For each of the fifty-four entries, he specified the loss in cows, horses, mules, burros, sheep, and other stock, together with the dollar value of each. He named ten men killed and two wounded. Governor Anson Safford of Arizona also complained of depredations in a letter published in the San Francisco *Alta California*. Between September 15 and October 24, 1871, he listed and described ten. Both governors and settlers ensured that Washington knew of their distress.[6]

The grievances of the citizens had to be addressed. The secretary of the Board of Indian Commissioners, a man of colossal ego named Vincent Colyer, received instructions directly from the president to travel to New Mexico and Arizona and collect all roaming Apaches on a reservation to be set aside at Cañada Alamosa. En route, Colyer succeeded in getting his powers enlarged to place the Indians not just at Cañada Alamosa but at any reservations he might designate. The army received orders to aid Colyer in any way he asked. He arrived in New Mexico in August 1871.[7]

To collect even all the Chihenne Chiricahuas at Cañada Alamosa, much less all the Apache tribes, dramatizes how ignorant of Apaches and their country the Washington policy-makers were. When Colyer got to Cañada Alamosa, he found only a few Indians; most had left because of a rumored impending attack by miners. Worse yet, he judged it unsuitable for a reservation. The Mexican improvements in their village would have to be purchased; why incur that expense when so much unoccupied land lay nearby? Also, he believed that Cañada Alamosa afforded insufficient land once Cochise and his people settled there. So, aided by the superintendent of Indian affairs and the local agent, he chose another reservation. It lay in the Tularosa Valley about seventy miles to the northwest. Colyer pronounced it remote from whites and surrounded by mountains and arable land, with plenty of wood, water, and grass. When they returned to Cañada Alamosa, the Chihennes did not want to go to Tularosa: it was too high, too cold, and swampy, and it lacked good farming grounds; above all, they loved their sacred homeland. Not until April 1872 did the movement begin, and then only 350 people could be found. Already, all Apaches not at Tularosa or still at Cañada Alamosa had been declared hostile and subject to military action.[8]

Understanding that Cochise would settle his people at Cañada Alamosa (that is, now Tularosa), Colyer proceeded to Arizona to deal with the other Apache tribes. Here he entered another military jurisdiction. In 1870 the military District of Arizona had been elevated to the Department of Arizona, a part of the Division of the Pacific. Colonel George Stoneman had been named commander. Ensconced in comfortable headquarters in distant Los Angeles, he designated certain forts as "feeding stations," where Indians could be safe and receive rations. He proved unable, however, to quell the bloody depredations sweeping the territory, including many by Cochise's men. The governor and territorial press demanded aggressive military action instead of "feeding stations."

On June 4, 1871, a new commander relieved Stoneman. Lieutenant Colonel George Crook had achieved outstanding success against the tribes of the Pacific Northwest. Ignoring both Secretary of War William W. Belknap and General-in-Chief William T. Sherman and the claims of many officers of superior rank, President Grant assigned Crook to command the Department of Arizona in his brevet grade of major general. A taciturn, aggressive field commander, the militarily unorthodox Crook set forth at once to learn how to deal with and fight Apaches. With five troops of cavalry, he made a grand sweep of eastern Arizona, by way of Forts Bowie, McDowell, Apache, and Verde. Finding no Apaches to fight, he turned to establish headquarters at Whipple Barracks in Prescott.[9]

En route, while contemplating the organization of a multipronged offensive against all the warring Apaches, Crook learned from a newspaper of Vincent Colyer's mission. Although his own chain of command had not withdrawn authorization to round up the Apaches by force, he had little choice but to suspend operations. He believed "Vincent the Good" a tool of the "Indian Ring" and abject failure the certain result of his efforts. As he had in New Mexico, however, Colyer sketched out a complex of reservations for all but the Chiricahuas and left the army's post commanders in charge until the Indian Bureau could take responsibility. Reports from post commanders declared that as soon as Colyer had left each group, the Apaches had resumed their marauding ways.[10]

On February 7, 1872, Crook issued orders that after February 16 any Indians not within the boundaries of the reservations defined by Colyer would be regarded as hostile and subject to military action. He immediately began preparing his long-deferred offensive against all such roamers, including those of Cochise. This set off alarm bells in Washington, which desperately wanted to preserve the peace thought to have been concluded by Vincent Colyer. To head off an Apache war, another peace commissioner vested with the full powers Colyer had enjoyed set forth early in March 1872.

He was Brigadier General Oliver O. Howard, the one-armed "Christian general" known throughout the army for his deep piety. His recent assignment as head of the Freedmen's Bureau, caring for freed slaves, had hardly covered him with glory. Yet he later told Crook "that he thought the Creator had placed him on earth to be the Moses to the Negro. Having accomplished that mission, he felt satisfied his next mission was with the Indians." Howard's main accomplishment during the four months he toured Arizona and conferred with Indians was to force Crook, once again, to call off military action against the Apaches. Back in Washington by June, Howard reported extensively on his peace efforts, which he viewed with as much optimism as had Colyer. He conceded, however, that he had not dealt with New Mexico or with Cochise and believed he should return and carry out that task.[11]

After conferring with the Navajos early in August 1872, Howard proceeded to Fort Apache, where he made some unsuccessful efforts to contact Cochise, then turned back to Fort Tularosa. There he found fewer than three hundred Indians, although more, including the principal chiefs, camped nearby. From various sources, both Indian and white, Howard had learned that the only white man who could take him to Cochise was Thomas J. Jeffords, then an Indian trader at Cañada Alamosa. Sent for, Jeffords arrived at Tularosa on September 7. He bluntly informed the general that Cochise would not come for talks, that Howard, accompanied only by his aide, Jeffords, and two Indian guides, would have to journey to Cochise and talk there. Howard agreed. The party was later enlarged to include a Spanish interpreter, a mule packer, and a cook.

Meantime, while awaiting Jeffords, Howard had been talking with Chihenne chiefs Victorio, Loco, Nana, and Chiva. All, especially Victorio and Nana, impressed the general. They poured forth their complaints about the awful conditions at Tularosa, the appeal of their home country, and the government's betrayal in making them move after they thought the government would give them a reservation at Cañada Alamosa. Howard not only sympathized with the chiefs but had in mind the larger scheme of persuading Cochise to move his people to Cañada Alamosa and gathering all other Chiricahuas there. On September 12, with the agent and New Mexico superintendent of Indian affairs Nathaniel Pope sitting in, Howard and the chiefs met in a formal council that simply repeated the arguments already stated. The council ended with an agreement to inspect the Cañada Alamosa area. This occurred on September 16, when Howard promised the chiefs to recommend to the president that the Tularosa Reservation be abolished and the people there returned to their home in the Alamosa Valley below Ojo Caliente. So certain was he of the success of his larger plan that he appointed Tom Jeffords agent of the new "Cochise Reservation."[12]

In his autobiography, Howard narrates his long journey across New Mexico and into Arizona as if fraught with high risk. Accompanied by Jeffords, Ponce, and Chie, however, and with Jeffords having already learned directly from Cochise of his desire for peace, the danger was considerably diminished. Howard did heed advice to reduce his party and sent his ambulance and driver, interpreter, and cook to wait at Fort Bowie. Nor does Howard hint of the earlier talks with Cochise or of his efforts to settle at Cañada Alamosa. Not that the mission lacked risk, and Howard did accomplish a significant feat in persuading Cochise to settle peaceably on the reservation of his own choice. Because of his autobiography, however, and the mythology that developed around Jeffords as he aged, history has tended to credit General Howard with a larger achievement than the facts warrant.

Because of his companions, Howard readily gained admission to the Dragoon Mountains and sat with Cochise in the West Stronghold. Although arguing for a "Cochise Reservation" in the Alamosa Valley around Ojo Caliente and Cañada Alamosa, he did not push this scheme very hard and easily acquiesced in Cochise's demand for a reservation in his homeland. Yielding to his insistence that Tom Jeffords be appointed his agent posed no problem, since Howard had already appointed him agent of the "Cochise Reservation" at Cañada Alamosa. Omitted from any consideration was the understanding of Victorio and the other Chihenne chiefs that Tularosa would be abandoned and they could return to their homes around Ojo Caliente. In Howard's mind, this depended on persuading Cochise to move there and make it a genuine "Cochise Reservation." If he stated or implied such a condition to the Chihenne chiefs, they certainly gained no impression of it. Not surprisingly, they felt grievously betrayed when Tularosa remained in place and the government continued to argue over whether the reservation should be there or at Cañada Alamosa. Howard thus contributed to the mix that within seven years would lead to the bloody Victorio War.

At the formal councils on October 10 in the stronghold and the next day at Sulphur Springs, none of the whites knew or cared who Cochise's Spanish interpreter was. Lieutenent Sladen, however, left compelling clues in his journal. Even though Geronimo was not yet known to the white world,

Sladen's description accurately portrays the man who would soon become known to the white world, an

> old looking [nearly fifty], very dark complexioned, unprepossessing appearing Indian, who had returned to camp only the day before. His sensual, cruel, crafty face, as well as his dissatisfied manner had prejudiced me against him from the start. . . . He was short and stout, exceedingly dirty, and wore a white man's shirt, loose like a blouse, and with little else beyond the usual breech cloth and moccasins. I thought nothing strange about this at first but, later, my interest was aroused in the garment by several unusual things about it.

For one thing, despite its filth, the shirt betrayed its origins as of white manufacture: eyelets substituted for buttons, which meant that it came from no trader's store but had been purchased in the East. Mainly, however, Sladen got close enough to read a name embroidered on the shirt flap: "Cushing." One of the army's most aggressive Indian fighters, Lieutenant Howard B. Cushing had been slain in the Whetstone Mountains on May 5, 1871, a year and a half earlier. Sladen believed that this Indian had probably either killed Cushing or been a member of the war party.

The leader of the war party that had killed Cushing was recognized on a hilltop as Juh. Since Geronimo and Juh often rode and fought together, Geronimo may well have been the wearer of Cushing's shirt. Moreover, at this time Geronimo and Juh camped with the Nednhis near Janos. Geronimo had come in the day before, according to Sladen. And he brought his people into the new reservation early in November 1872. The factors of time and distance are not inconsistent with his identity as the interpreter. Sladen continued:

> I . . . had conceived the utmost dislike and repugnance of him. It was not entirely the incident of the shirt, though this intensified it much. But his crafty, cruel, vindictive looks; his seeming disinclination to treat with us at all made him an object of extreme dislike and suspicion to myself and others of our party. I think the General was inclined to share this dislike, but he thought him a man of importance in these consultations and attempted to win him over by every reasonable means in his power.[13]

In 1872 Sladen knew no more than the name Geronimo, and probably not even that. Neither did Captain Samuel Sumner, who was present at the Sulphur Springs council; but Sumner knew Geronimo later and recognized him as present at the Howard peace conference. Although the identity of Cochise's interpreter cannot be proven, Sladen's observations raise a strong presumption that he was Geronimo.

However flawed Howard's agreement turned out to be, it left the Chiricahuas with a lasting memory of a rare friend among the military. As Geronimo would recall thirty years later, "He always kept his word with us and treated us as brothers. We never had so good a friend among the United States officers as General Howard. . . . If there is any pure, honest white man in the United States army, that man is General Howard." No other American officer earned such an accolade. That Geronimo remembered his brief experience with Howard more than thirty years later reinforces the possibility that he was indeed Cochise's interpreter.[14]

Howard's peace mission had insulated Cochise from Crook's military operations. Crook had launched small striking commands, composed of cavalry and Indian scouts, to follow and destroy the other Apache groups that had resumed old habits after Vincent Colyer had made peace with them. His tactics proved both innovative and effective and by the end of 1872 had subdued most of the recalcitrants. By February 1873, he had concentrated thirteen troops of cavalry near the new Cochise Reservation to enforce the general order that required all reservation Indians to submit to a daily roll call. He then learned that Howard had promised Cochise that no soldiers would go near the new reservation. "The whole peace system among the Apaches here has been a fraud," he had declared. Now he wanted a copy of the treaty Howard had concluded with Cochise, only to discover that nothing had been set to paper.

The Apaches did not expect a paper and had never been asked to sign one. Howard had promised the reservation, and therefore the reservation existed. Howard had promised that no soldiers would go near the reservation, and the Apaches expected to see none except those at Fort Bowie. From the white perspective, these promises should have been committed to paper, whether called a treaty or something else. How else for all to understand commitments both sides had made? Howard never explained why he failed this elementary requirement, the more important since he knew that Crook eagerly waited for him to leave so that the long-contemplated offensive could be launched. The incident dramatically illustrated the clash of the oral with the written, the Apaches' concept and the whites' concept.

By April 1873 Crook could issue a general order announcing the end of his Tonto Basin campaign and the surrender of all the Tonto, Pinal, and other Apache groups against which he had been campaigning.[15]

On October 29, 1873, President Grant again intervened in army affairs. Jumping all the colonels and senior lieutenant colonels, he promoted Lieutenant Colonel George Crook to brigadier general in the regular army.

NINE

THE CHIRICAHUA RESERVATION, 1872–76

WHETHER OR NOT GERONIMO acted as Cochise's Spanish interpreter at the councils with General Howard in October 1872, he was present and observed what happened. He promptly returned to his ranchería near Janos, Chihuahua, where he had been living with Juh's Nednhis since military forces drove them out of Sonora the previous summer. They hoped the Janos authorities could be persuaded to issue rations. On Geronimo's heels, runners arrived bearing Cochise's invitation to Juh and others near Janos to settle on the new reservation. Cochise's Chokonens were already there, since it was their home country. If Juh had any doubts, Geronimo could have overcome them with appealing words about what he had seen and heard at the peace council, especially the promise of the rations, which the Janos authorities had not granted them. Moreover, both would have instantly appreciated the advantages of a secure base in the United States for raiding across the border into Mexico. Late in November 1872, Juh, Geronimo, and other leaders led several hundred Nednhis and Bedonkohes to Pinery Canyon, in the Chiricahua Mountains about fifteen miles south of Fort Bowie. There they met and conferred with Cochise and Agent Tom Jeffords, and there they settled their people on the new reservation.[1]

Red Beard Jeffords pursued a relaxed management style. Every week or two he distributed the rations and supplies Howard had promised and let the Apaches come and go as they pleased. Cochise kept his promise to Howard to restrain his young men from committing any depredations in Arizona.

Travelers on the overland trail proceeded in complete safety. Ranchers and farmers worked their lands secure from the threat of an Indian attack.

Not so the Sonorans. The southern boundary of the Cochise Reservation coincided with the boundary between Arizona and Sonora. Now secure from retaliation, bands of raiders crossed repeatedly into Mexico and spread havoc across both Mexican states. Cochise himself never participated, but neither he nor Jeffords did much to interfere with plundering expeditions. Geronimo and Juh both indulged old habits repeatedly. In the months following the establishment of the reservation, Sonora suffered as grievously as in previous years.[2]

Word of the Chiricahua Reservation quickly spread to other Apache groups. Jeffords's easygoing oversight contrasted with the strict agents elsewhere. Also, he issued the visitors rations the same as the resident Indians. A few White Mountain Apaches from the north appeared, together with a scattering of others from farther south. But the largest influx came from Tularosa, ever a hotbed of discontent. Some arrived in February 1873 and said more would be coming.

There were. With Tularosa as usual in an uproar, in May 1873 about two hundred Chihennes and Bedonkohes, led by Nana, Chie, and Gordo, a rising Bedonkohe subchief, left Tularosa and traveled to the new reservation. They had learned of a massive impending raid into Mexico, and some wanted to take part. Others simply wanted to visit with old friends.

All the Chiricahua bands—Cochise's Chokonens, Juh's Nednhis, Geronimo's Bedonkohes, and many of the fugitives from Tularosa—joined in the foray into Mexico. For a month they ravaged the settlements of both Chihuahua and Sonora, returning in mid-June.

While scourging Chihuahua, Geronimo seized a young boy and took him as prisoner back to the reservation. Cochise disapproved, and Jeffords tried to get the boy back. For an Apache, however, a captive was valuable property, to be ransomed, traded, or reared as a member of the band. Mexican captives had even higher value, for the Mexicans held so many Apache captives. Now fifty, Geronimo had nurtured the independent streak that began with the death of Mangas Coloradas. He defiantly turned down Jeffords's request even at the risk of offending Cochise. At a stormy council, other tribesmen backed Geronimo but eventually agreed to turn over the boy if a Chokonen captive seized by Mexicans more than a year earlier were freed. Jeffords promised to investigate, but he also presented a small gift to Geronimo. Even though investigation held almost no promise and the gift amounted to empty appeasement, further resistance could alienate Cochise. Geronimo turned the boy over to the agent. A month later, Jeffords discovered that the boy's parents were then living in New Mexico. He put the boy on a stage, and the contentious dispute faded.[3]

Although the raids involving both Chokonens and Tularosa Indians continued throughout the summer of 1873, both Cochise and Jeffords suddenly began to try to stop the forays. The people would not be persuaded; they hated the Mexicans too intensely, and they afforded a source of valuable plunder. In October an important government officer from Washington, Indian inspector William Vandever, arrived to talk with Cochise, who came in from his Dragoon Mountain stronghold. They met at Sulphur Springs, in the Sulphur Springs Valley west of Fort Bowie. The talk centered on the continuing depredations in Mexico. Cochise declared that in making peace with the Americans, he had not made peace with Mexico. He himself wanted peace with everyone and contended that his people crossed into Mexico without his knowledge or approval. He also asked that the Tularosa Indians on his reservation, drawing rations from Jeffords, be sent back home; they might get his own people into trouble. Vandever strongly urged Jeffords to quit feeding these people and send them back home, which Jeffords promised to do.[4]

By August 1873, Jeffords had convinced Cochise that he must intervene to prevent the raids. Cochise made a few half-hearted gestures to demonstrate that he understood. He did not. In October Jeffords flatly informed him that unless the raids ceased, the reservation itself stood in jeopardy. It could well be abolished and Jeffords relieved. Cochise had a hard time believing that the Americans would break General Howard's promises, but he finally took decisive action. In November, with the agency in the process of being relocated to Pinery Canyon in the Chiricahua Mountains south of Fort Bowie, he summoned all his headmen to a formal council. There he declared that he ruled this country and that all who wanted to remain must quit their incursions into Mexico or leave the reservation altogether.

Geronimo and Juh promptly gathered their people and moved back to Mexico. Raiding was their way of life.[5]

Cochise must have sensed that outside pressures pushed Jeffords into his increasingly firm leadership, especially his insistence that raiding in Mexico stop. Neither he nor any Apaches, however, could have been remotely aware of the complexity and confusion of the Great Father's "Peace Policy" in Arizona and New Mexico.

They could not have known, for example, that their own reservation enjoyed a special status compared with the others laid out by Vincent Colyer and later revised by General Howard. Howard had exempted the Chiricahuas from any military action and little civilian oversight except for their agent, Tom Jeffords. By contrast, the Chihenne "reservation" Colyer defined at Tularosa was never officially established, although a new military installation, Fort Tularosa, rose nearby.

Most important for the future of the Chiricahuas, among the changes made by Howard, was the expansion of the White Mountain Reservation south to embrace the Gila River. It was established mainly for the Aravaipa and Pinal Apaches of the Camp Grant Reservation, which Howard had abolished. These and other smaller groups of Apaches gradually merged into what came to be known as the San Carlos Apaches. The reservation remained the White Mountain Reservation, administered by the San Carlos Agency, on the Gila River at the mouth of the San Carlos River (see the map of the White Mountain Reservation).[6]

Discovering no document that recorded the establishment of the Chiricahua Reservation, General Crook felt that he had no choice but to leave it free of military interference.[7] Probably unknown to Crook, a presidential executive order of December 14, 1872, established and precisely defined the reservation—essentially the lands embracing the Chiricahua and Dragoon Mountains as far east as the New Mexico boundary. Howard had undoubtedly dictated these boundaries for the president's signature.[8]

Even so, Crook believed that the Chiricahua Reservation would cause constant trouble so long as Cochise was allowed to occupy it. Other reservations could easily accommodate the Chiricahuas, and they ought to be forced to move there. Crook's opinion, shared by his chain of command, found agreement with the commissioner of Indian affairs, who received the same advice from Inspector Vandever, who visited the reservation and talked with Cochise in October 1873.[9] Worse, the commissioner bore constant complaint from the State Department of the repeated demands of Mexico that the raids from the American sanctuary be halted. The commissioner's pressure on Agent Jeffords explained his increasingly firm stance with Cochise.

In demanding that Cochise take decisive action or face the abolition of the reservation altogether, Jeffords anticipated the future actions of his superiors. At the council in Pinery Canyon in November 1873, Cochise ordered the raids stopped and decreed that all who would not comply leave the reservation. Geronimo and Juh left. Only a month later the expected order arrived from the commissioner. The army had demanded that the reservation be turned over to Crook. Unless depredations ceased, the request would be honored.[10]

Even though the raids had tapered off, Jeffords doubted that they would cease altogether. In May 1874 he officially conceded as much. General Howard, he thought, had made concessions to Cochise in the belief that the Chiricahuas would have to be moved elsewhere in the future, after they had learned how well the government treated them. Jeffords had tried and failed to stop the depredations. He did not believe they could be stopped as long as the Indians roamed freely. He thought that if confronted with orders to move elsewhere, about half would go and the rest remain.[11]

When Jeffords penned these words, he knew that Cochise lay dying in his Dragoon Mountain stronghold, probably of stomach cancer. His oldest son, Taza, had already begun to exert leadership over the reservation. Taza had been prepared for the chieftainship, but Jeffords knew he could never exert the strong governance of his father. He could not enforce the ban on raiding in Mexico and thus lift the peril to the Chiricahua Reservation.

The commissioner of Indian affairs instructed New Mexico's superintendent of Indian affairs, Levi Dudley, to go to the Chiricahua Reservation and see if Cochise would agree to move his people back to New Mexico. With Jeffords, Dudley met with Cochise twice late in May 1874 but found him exhausted and barely rational. He did convey that for his part he preferred Arizona but would leave the final decision on New Mexico to his son Taza.[12]

On June 8, 1874, Cochise died in his East Stronghold.[13]

The venerable chief's death left the reservation on the brink of turmoil, as several strong leaders resented the chieftainship falling to Taza, his tall, muscular eldest son who had been specially groomed by Cochise for leadership. At first they pledged loyalty, but within a few months they began to splinter into rival groups. Skinya, an older and experienced man with an outstanding war record, emerged as the most prominent, powerful, and demanding. Only about half of Cochise's old following of Chokonens remained loyal to Taza, who in his mid-thirties was the youngest of the contenders. Juh and

Geronimo with the Nednhis had been driven by Sonoran troops back onto the reservation, and Chihennes from Tularosa came and went or lived there. Without Cochise's restraining influence, they all resumed raiding in Mexico. Geronimo and Juh, based in Mexico since rejecting Cochise's demand for an end to raiding, had never ceased.[14]

In 1874 the government finally yielded to the demands of the Chihennes at Tularosa to be returned to Cañada Alamosa. Many had already gone anyway, and in September 1874 the agent at Tularosa moved the agency to Cañada Alamosa. The army gladly abandoned Fort Tularosa; it had proved a logistical nightmare because of its distance from transportation routes. Chihennes on the Chiricahua Reservation returned to their old homes, seven hundred square miles designated the "Hot Springs Reservation" but commonly known as the Ojo Caliente Reservation.[15]

The government still hoped to concentrate the Chihennes and Chokonens at Ojo Caliente, as General Howard had first proposed, and thus be rid of the Chiricahua Reservation. On April 16, 1875, Levi Dudley, now a special commissioner working out of Washington, conferred with the various leaders of the fractured band at the Chiricahua Agency, now located in Pinery Canyon, and proposed the move. None would have any part of it; they would fight rather than go there.[16]

By Dudley's authority, on May 14, 1875, Jeffords moved the agency once more, this time to Apache Pass, near Fort Bowie. He reasoned that Pinery Canyon was too far from the traveled road for him to oversee relations between his charges and the whites and Mexicans who used the road. A lively trade had sprung up, the Apaches exchanging horses and mules for whiskey and guns and ammunition. Jeffords conceded that the trade tempted the Indians to steal but stopped short of admitting that it also disclosed the resumption of raids into Mexico.[17]

In the aftermath of Cochise's death, the threat of the commissioner of Indian affairs to turn the Chiricahua Reservation over to General Crook if raids into Mexico did not stop held equal validity, for the raids had now resumed. But General Crook no longer commanded in Arizona; he had been moved north to command the Department of the Platte.

On March 22, 1875, Colonel August V. Kautz assumed command of the Department of Arizona in his brevet grade of major general. A stolid German with a mediocre record and no understanding of Indians, he found himself at once embroiled with an infuriatingly bombastic young man of immense self-importance and limitless certitude. He was John P. Clum, agent at the White Mountain Reservation, enlarged by General Howard in 1872. On August 8, 1874, at the age of twenty-two, Clum took office at the San Carlos Agency of the White Mountain Reservation.

The government's original plan for the Chiricahuas aimed at concentrating all the Chiricahuas at Cañada Alamosa, thus freeing the Chiricahua Reservation for return to the public domain. All the other Arizona Apaches, who had been living on the Colyer-Howard reservations under the jurisdiction of Crook's officers pending appointment of civilian agents, would be concentrated on the White Mountain Reservation.

Clum detested the army and feuded with its officers incessantly. He recruited his own Indian police force, captained by former army scout Clay Beauford, to avoid calling for military help in moving the Apaches. By the middle of 1875 Clum had completed the removal, although only part of the White Mountain Apaches succumbed to his bullying and moved south to the Gila.[18]

Early in 1876, the Chiricahua Reservation boiled with unrest. Taza still stirred resentment from leaders who thought they should be the Chokonen chief. Skinya, backed by his turbulent half-brother Pionsenay, grew bolder in his opposition to Taza, who was backed by his younger brother Naiche, only twenty. Skinya and Pionsenay had settled about sixty Chokonens in the Dragoon Mountains. Tension rose when Taza and Naiche also took up residence in the Dragoons with about 180 Chokonens. Skinya tried to persuade Naiche, his son-in-law, to free himself of Taza and lead their followers in a breakout to Mexico. Naiche refused.

Unlike other Apache agents, Jeffords had never tried to ban tiswin, and both resident and visiting Chiricahuas often participated in tiswin drunks. During one such drunk, the inevitable quarrel broke out. The exchange of fire killed a man of each group as well as Cochise's grandchild. Taza immediately moved his people back to Apache Pass.[19]

Geronimo, a Bedonkohe with close ties to the Nednhis, held aloof from the Chokonen conflicts. Since driven back to the reservation by Sonoran troops, he kept a ranchería at the western base of the Chiricahua Mountains but raided widely, both in Mexico and New Mexico.

As Skinya's people grew ever more confident and successful in raids into Mexico, in March 1876 they learned that Nicholas Rogers, who ranched and maintained the mail station at Sulphur Springs, had bought a keg of whiskey in Tucson and installed it at his ranch. On April 6 Pionesenay and a companion rode to Rogers's ranch and, with gold dust stolen in Mexico, bought several bottles for ten dollars each. The next day Pionsenay returned with his nephew and bought more whiskey. Back in the Dragoons, drunk, he picked a fight with Skinya. When their two sisters tried to interpose, Pionesenay shot and killed both women. He and his nephew promptly left for Sulphur Springs, where they found Rogers and his partner, Orizoba Spence, sitting in chairs in front of their ranch. Pionsenay demanded more whiskey. Rogers refused. Both he and his partner died in a hail of gunfire. The two Indians ransacked the house and left for the Dragoons leading a horse laden with whiskey, cartridges, and food.[20]

Alarmed by Pionsenay's actions, Skinya sent a runner to alert Taza. Jeffords asked for a troop of cavalry from Fort Bowie to take up the trail. Taza accompanied it as guide. Lieutenant Austin Henely commanded. They bivouacked that night, April 8, at Sulphur Springs. The next morning a messenger reported that Pionsenay and his companion had killed a man, Gideon Lewis, and committed other depredations on the San Pedro River west of the Dragoons. Back in the Dragoons, Pionsenay took refuge with Skinya, who immediately led his people south toward Mexico. Henely caught up, but the Apaches barricaded themselves behind rocks high in the mountains. After an exchange of gunfire, Henely wisely concluded the defenses so impregnable that, rejecting Taza's urgings, he withdrew his troop to Fort Bowie.[21]

As so often happened, the Tucson newspaper used vague reports of the disturbances on the reservation to stoke Arizonans' fears by proclaiming a full-scale Chiricahua uprising. Reflecting public opinion, the editor wrote:

> We heard a man say today, and he was of the opinion that he was endorsed by 999 out of 1000 people that the kind of war needed against the Chiricahuas was steady, unrelenting, hopeless and undiscriminating war slaying men, women, and children . . . and no relenting until every valley and crest and crag and fastness shall send to the high heavens the grateful incense of festering and rotting Chiricahua Indians, down to the last one of the guilty and their elders and abettors.[22]

Stirred by such news but motivated by the murder of Rogers, Spence, and Lewis, Washington reacted differently to the need of the hour. On May 1, 1876, Congress enacted legislation mandating the removal of the Indians on the Chiricahua Reservation to the White Mountain Reservation.

On June 5, 1876, John P. Clum, backed by General Kautz and half a regiment of the cavalry Clum so detested, arrived at Apache Pass to carry out the intent of Congress.

By executive order of October 30, 1876, the Chiricahua Reservation reverted to the public domain.

REMOVAL TO THE GILA RIVER

WITH GENERAL KAUTZ'S TROOPS strategically placed to head off trouble, John P. Clum's removal of the Chiricahuas from their reservation went relatively smoothly despite the monthlong rift between Taza and Skinya. All the reservation leaders had vowed to die rather than move, but they either fled or accommodated.

Most of Cochise's people had remained loyal to Taza. But Skinya formed a militant group under his own leadership and late in 1875 took sixty Chokonens to settle in the Dragoon Mountains. They included fourteen men, of whom one was his notorious half-brother Pionsenay.

Early in 1876 word reached the Indians that smallpox had appeared among whites in New Mexico. To escape the scourge, Juh (and probably Geronimo) led a raiding party of Nednhis and Bedonkohes into Chihuahua, while Taza and Naiche moved their 180 Chokonens back to the Dragoons.

Skinya and his men were raiding in Mexico. They returned to the Dragoons with ample spoils and in high spirits, only to find Taza and his people there, too. Skinya approached Naiche, his son-in-law, with a proposal that all unite in a breakout to Mexico and resume hostilities. If Naiche agreed, Skinya knew Taza would follow. On his deathbed, however, Cochise had admonished his sons to remain at peace and obey Jeffords, and they flatly refused Skinya's idea.

During a tiswin drunk a quarrel broke out. The exchange of fire killed one man on each side and left a grandson of Cochise dead. Taza and Naiche

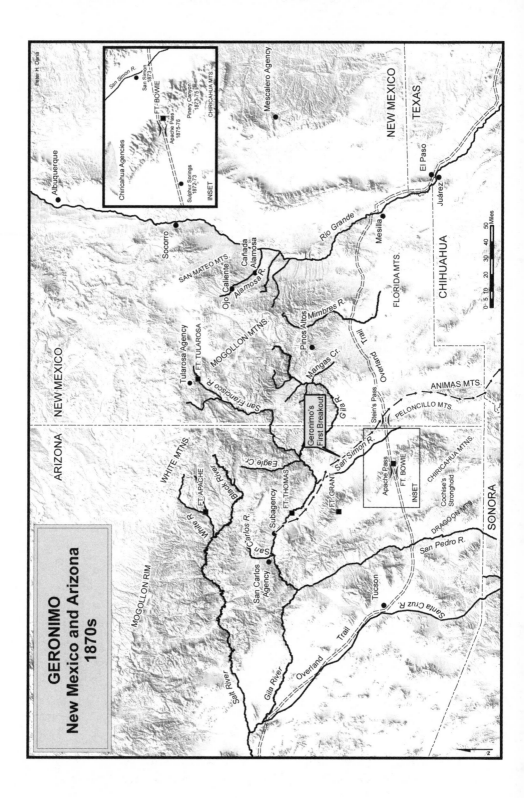

GERONIMO
New Mexico and Arizona
1870s

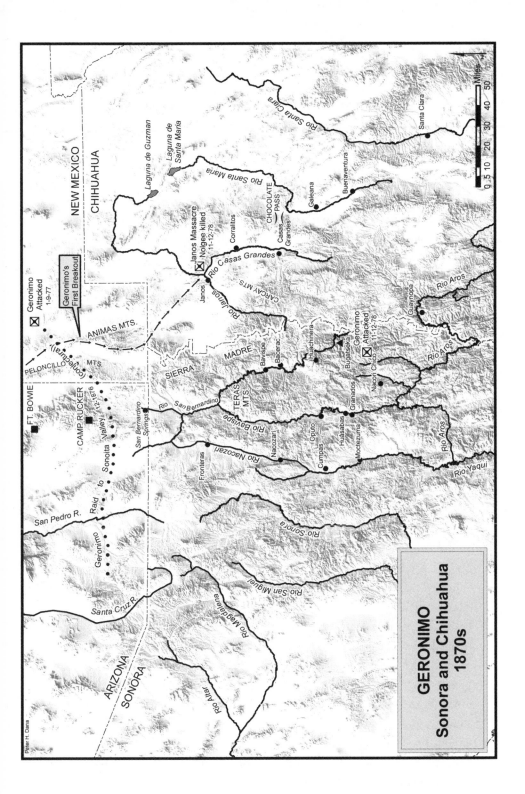

Peter H. Dana

GERONIMO
Sonora and Chihuahua
1870s

Miles
0 5 10 20 30 40 50

NEW MEXICO
CHIHUAHUA

ARIZONA
SONORA

Santa Clara
Rio Santa Clara

Laguna de Guzman
Laguna de Santa Maria

Buenaventura
Galeana
Rio Santa Maria

CHOCOLATE PASS

Janos Massacre
Nolgee killed
11-12-78

Corralitos
Casas Grandes
Rio Casas Grandes

Geronimo Attacked
1-9-77

Geronimo's First Breakout

ANIMAS MTS.

PELONCILLO MTS (Cordilleran)

FT. BOWIE
CAMP RUCKER 12-16-76

San Bernardino Springs
Rio San Bernardino

Janos
Rio Janos
CARCAY MTS

SIERRA MADRE

Huachinera
Bacerac
Bavispe

Rio Bavispe

TERAS MTS

Bugatseka
Geronimo Attacked
11-12-78
Nacori Chico
Granados
Huasabas

Guaynopa
Rio Aros
Rio Aros

Rio Aros

Rio Aros

San Pedro R.
Raid to Sonoita Valley

Geronimo

Santa Cruz R.

Rio San Bernardino

Fronteras
Nacozari
Rio Nacozari

Oputo
Cumpas
Moctezuma

Rio Sonora

Rio San Miguel

Rio Magdalena

Rio Altar

Rio Yaqui

at once took their people back to Apache Pass. To keep them distant from Skinya, Jeffords moved them to the eastern side of Apache Pass.

Skinya's group still lived in the Dragoon Mountains in April 1876, when Pionsenay and his comrade murdered Rogers and Spence and committed depredations on the San Pedro. Lieutenant Henely's pursuit and exchange of gunfire with Skinya's barricaded fighters followed. Wild talk of a general Indian war rolled across Arizona, and rumors of impending abolition of the Chiricahua Reservation further disturbed the Apaches.

Alarmed by the uncertainties, particularly that the army might seek to capture Pionsenay, Skinya decided that his followers would be safer near Taza. Early in May he approached Jeffords to talk over the matter. The talks ended abruptly when Pionsenay and his backers sought to kill Jeffords but were prevented by Skinya. The next day Skinya and his people appeared at the agency, without Pionsenay and his friends, and said he and his people would place themselves under Taza's leadership. Jeffords located them near Taza's ranchería in Bonita Canyon on the eastern side of the mountains.[1]

As Skinya may have feared, the murder of Rogers, Spence, and Lewis set off the chain of events that led to the appearance of John Clum on June 5 with a telegram ordering him to move the Chiricahuas to the Gila. He showed it to Jeffords, who had heard rumors of the impending move but received no official word.

About an hour before midnight on the day before Clum's arrival, another disaster had further ruptured the Chiricahuas. Upset over the convergence of soldiers on Apache Pass, Skinya had entered Taza's camp with Pionsenay and about a dozen of his most committed followers. With the rancor that had boiled between Skinya and Taza for months inflaming both groups, Skinya exhorted Taza to join him in a breakout of all the Chiricahuas in a flight to Mexico. Faithful to his father's dying admonition to keep the peace, Taza refused. The volatile Skinya pushed the issue until a melee broke out. Both sides opened fire. The young Naiche, only twenty, raised his rifle and aimed at Skinya. The bullet hit Skinya in the head and killed him, removing from Chokonen chaos the leading agitator. At the same time, Taza singled out Pionsenay, the second-ranking agitator. A second bullet lodged in Pionsenay's shoulder joint, inflicting a wound severe enough to convince him that he would die. The encounter ended as Skinya's people scattered. Jeffords and a troop of cavalry rode out to bring Taza and his remaining people to the Chiricahua Agency in Apache Pass. They arrived just before Clum on June 5.[2]

In a parley with Clum at the agency on June 6, Taza consented to take those people camped with him to the new reservation. None of the Chiricahuas wanted to go, and Taza could not bind all of them. In fact, most of the leaders had said they would fight rather than move. Taza agreed only because he had promised his father always to obey Jeffords, who counseled him not to resist.

Not content with having the Chokonen chief Taza talk for them, the Nednhis and Bedonkohes had insisted on their own parley with Clum. On June 8 three came in: Juh, Geronimo, and a rising Nednhi chief named Nolgee. Geronimo spoke for the others, probably because he was the only one who had been present at the Howard councils in 1872, and in part because Juh stuttered badly. His people and the Nednhis had joined in the Howard treaty, he said, and now that the rest of the reservation people had agreed to go with Clum, the Nednhis and Bedonkohes would go, too. But they would need twenty days to round up their people and bring them in. Although suspicious, Clum granted four days. The next day an emissary from Skinya's old camp came in and said that Pionsenay wanted to come in "to die of his wounds." A detachment of Clum's police accompanied the man back to camp and brought in the wounded Pionsenay, together with an old man and thirty-eight women and children.

But the police also reported that the Nednhi rancherías, only ten miles from the agency, had been hastily abandoned. Once more, when perceiving a threat, Geronimo had heeded his own instincts—get back to Mexico. He got there before General Kautz's soldiers could catch him.

On June 12 a caravan of army wagons, loaded with three hundred Chokonens and twenty-two Bedonkohes, left Apache Pass. Only forty-two men rode the wagons, the rest women and children. Among the leaders were Taza, Naiche, and Chihuahua, who had his own band of Chokonens separate from Taza's. Jeffords accompanied Clum and his fifty-four Apache policemen, all escorted by three troops of cavalry. Twenty men and their families of Taza's following had remained behind, scattering into Mexico or heading for New Mexico. People who had moved from Ojo Caliente to Jeffords's reservation, about two hundred Chihennes and Bedonkohes, had already gone back.

The Fort Bowie surgeon had dressed Pionsenay's wound, and Clum intended to turn him over to Tucson civil officials to be tried for the murder of Rogers and Spence. En route, however, the sheriff and a deputy from Tucson met the caravan and relieved Clum of Pionsenay. Although securely bound in the bed of a wagon, as the lawmen drove toward Tucson he freed himself and vanished without even alerting them. He snuck into Clum's procession and persuaded two men, four women, and a boy to leave for Mexico with him. Pionsenay had not ceased to make trouble for the Chiricahuas.[3]

On June 18, 1876, the procession reached the Gila. Taza had agreed to locate on the Gila about two miles below abandoned Fort Goodwin. The Indians crawled from the wagons at their new home on the Gila River extension of the White Mountain Reservation.[4]

It probably was the only choice offered. This extension of the reservation, however, tortured anyone who lived there. Summer sun scorched the desert valley, spotted with cactus and crawling with spiders, tarantulas, scorpions, centipedes, Gila monsters, and a variety of other unfriendly creatures. Where water gathered in stagnant pools, mosquitoes swarmed to infect humans with malaria. The Gila Valley lay at the southern base of the forested ridges rising to the White Mountains, a friendly land and climate that the White Mountain Apaches called home.

Geronimo and Juh would have nothing to do with this environment—yet. They and their people had escaped safely into Mexico. The canyons and caverns of the Sierra Madre afforded the only place Juh ever felt safe. But unless rationed, they had to rely on raids for subsistence.

Scarcely a month after the Chokonens had been settled near the San Carlos Agency, Juh sent Geronimo to scout the Ojo Caliente Reservation as a possible refuge. He discovered the agent scared of his charges and virtually powerless to do more than issue rations to them or any others on the reservation. Geronimo also had relatives at Ojo Caliente, and the place appealed to him. He could settle his family and his Bedonkohes here, draw rations, and use the reservation as a base for further raiding. Others who had fled the Chiricahua Reservation rather than move to San Carlos did the same. Returning to Mexico, Geronimo made his case to Juh. The Nednhi chief could not be persuaded.[5]

By November 1876 Geronimo had resolved to part with Juh and return to the United States—not to Ojo Caliente but to a small group of Chihennes and Bedonkohes who had been living in the Florida (Flor-ee-da) and Animas Mountains of southwestern New Mexico. In the summer of 1876 war parties from these people had carried out some minor depredations on ranches to the north as well as in Chihuahua. Both white posses and US cavalry pursued and skirmished with them. But they remained in their mountain hideaways. Geronimo and his family and small following took up residence with them.[6]

Geronimo lost no time reverting to old patterns. As early as December 1876, he had led a small party of Bedonkohes on a raid across southern Arizona to the Sonoita Valley, southeast of Tucson. Besides depredations earlier inflicted by Pionsenay, still living in Mexico and recovered from his gunshot wound, the Apaches had once more stirred up southern Arizona.

Geronimo and his followers and some Chokonens established a winter camp of sixteen lodges on the northern tip of the Animas Mountains, a range close to the territorial boundary on the New Mexico side. It numbered about thirty-five men with their families. At daybreak of January 9, 1877, the men were making their way back to their wickiups from an all-night dance when a burst of gunfire caught them by surprise. They raced to the nearest rocks and returned a brisk fire at their attackers. After two hours of firing, attacks came from two directions. The people hastily abandoned their stock and possessions and fled, leaving the bodies of ten men dead and fighting a stubborn rearguard action.

What surprised the Apaches almost as much as the attack was the attackers. Apache Indian scouts outnumbered the cavalry troopers. Even though recognized as White Mountain Apaches, for the first time Chiricahuas had been struck by a force composed of Apaches in alliance with soldiers.[7]

After this setback, angry and burning for revenge, Geronimo led his people to the Ojo Caliente Reservation. As he recalled, Victorio welcomed him and his people warmly and shared food with them. Not all the Warm Springs people thought this a good idea. The always peaceful Loco and old Nana warned Victorio that Geronimo's presence, with loot from his raids, would inevitably cause trouble. Victorio's response: "These people are not bothering us."[8]

These people would soon bother Victorio. Geronimo remained only a short time before organizing an expedition to avenge his rout by the soldiers and their Apache scouts. He persuaded Gordo to join him with about forty or fifty Bedonkohe, Chihenne, and Chokonen raiders for a sweep through southern Arizona. Detouring through Mexico, where they picked up reinforcements under Juh and Pionsenay, they entered Arizona early in February 1877. Marauding through the Sonoita and Santa Cruz Valleys south of Tucson, in two days they killed nine men and captured about one hundred head of horses before quickly slipping back into Mexico.[9]

Back at Ojo Caliente with the stolen horses, Geronimo appeared on ration day to draw issues for the period he had been absent raiding in Arizona. The agent refused. Although angry, Geronimo remained near the agency as others left for thieving raids. On subsequent ration days, he received handouts for himself and his followers.

April 21, 1877, was ration day, and as Geronimo made ready to ride into the agency, he received a message inviting him to come for a talk with a government official. At daybreak, he and about fifty of his people arrived at the agency. Other Bedonkohes, including Gordo and his followers, accompanied the influx. Gathering his men in front of the agency porch, Geronimo faced San Carlos Agent John P. Clum, whom he had last met at Apache Pass during the Chiricahua removal. Twenty White Mountain Apache policemen backed him up. As soon as the Apaches had assembled, Clum gave a signal and eighty more Indian police, arms at the ready, filed out of the adjacent commissary building and surrounded them. Clum singled out Geronimo and accused him of breaking his promise, at Apache Pass, to take his people with Taza to San Carlos. Clum ordered him, together with recent raiders Gordo and Ponce, escorted to the blacksmith shop and placed in irons. Clum descended the steps and, after a few tense moments as Geronimo considered his predicament, took his rifle from him and several others. Next a policeman pulled Geronimo's knife from his belt. He had reluctantly concluded that resistance was futile; the police would gun him down instantly.

The next day, April 22, confined with the other prisoners in the agency jail, he observed cavalry arrive at the agency and later all the Indians called to a council. He may have suspected or been told that these Indians were to be removed to San Carlos. They were. By April 30, most of the Ojo Caliente Reservation Indians had been assembled and begun the journey to San Carlos. Clum's seventeen prisoners, with Geronimo and three others in irons, climbed aboard army wagons and, escorted by cavalry, set forth on the road to the west. On May 20 they reached the San Carlos Agency, and Geronimo, still shackled, found himself once more behind bars.

The events of 1876–77 leading to Geronimo's shackled removal to the Gila showed the civil and military establishments of Arizona at both their best and their worst. Their worst highlighted the perennial conflict between San Carlos Agent John P. Clum and General August Kautz. The best landed Geronimo in the San Carlos jail.

Clum's animosity for all things military, and for Kautz in particular, spilled over into constant public feuding. It intensified as Clum enlisted Governor Anson P. K. Safford in his hostility to Kautz and succeeded in getting him to urge the War Department to relieve Kautz. Clum also fed venomous articles to Tucson newspapers attacking Kautz personally and extolling his own brilliance. In the autumn of 1876 Tucson merchants complained loudly of constant Apache raiding in the San Pedro and Sonoita Valleys, attributable to the Chokonens and Nednhis who had refused to move to San Carlos with Taza. Kautz sent commands under reliable officers to verify the complaints, but they discovered no evidence of trouble anywhere in the valleys southeast of Tucson. Their reports failed to still the charges of Kautz's incompetence spewing from Tucson. Kautz attributed them to the anger of the "Tucson Ring" over his refusal to move the Department of Arizona headquarters from Prescott to Tucson.[10]

In December 1876, however, Geronimo's raid as far west as the Sonoita Valley seemed to confirm the wrath of the Tucson citizens. Kautz took prompt action. He set high value on the White Mountain Apache scout companies General Crook had organized and employed so effectively in the Tonto Basin campaign. An exceptionally able cavalry officer, Lieutenant John A. (Tony) Rucker, commanded a company of scouts stationed at Fort Bowie. He promptly took the field with ten cavalrymen and thirty-four scouts. In the Sonoita Valley he picked up Geronimo's trail leading east with a herd of stolen horses and followed it 130 miles to the Stein's Peak Range on the New Mexico border. His animals and supplies exhausted, he returned to Fort Bowie to refit.[11]

On January 4, 1877, Rucker turned back to Stein's Peak with his scouts, seventeen troopers, and a mule pack train. Here the trail veered to the southeast. Rucker sent Chief of Scouts Jack Dunn with the scouts to follow the trail, while he proceeded twenty miles farther and bivouacked. A courier from Dunn announced that he had found evidence of the Indians and asked Rucker to come forward. They met about 3:00 a.m. on January 9, 1877. Dunn indicated an Apache ranchería about four miles farther. Leaving the horses under guard, Rucker led the command to the objective. He sent Dunn to hide the scouts on a ridge line about 150 yards west of the camp, while he and the troopers headed for a hill about three hundred yards north of the camp. Both units were to attack at daybreak. The cavalry had not even reached their hill when Dunn's Apaches opened fire and rushed the ranchería. The cavalry began firing at once, taking the enemy from the reverse direction. Dashing from their wickiups to rocky defenses, the surprised Chiricahuas opened such a brisk fire that they drove the scouts back twice. After exchanging fire with them for about two hours, Rucker and Dunn simultaneously charged into the ranchería and sent the occupants scattering.

Rucker counted sixteen lodges and estimated the foe at about thirty-five fighting men. Ten lay dead in the village, together with a large stock of weapons and ammunition and winter food provisions. The scouts captured forty-six horses. Although Rucker did not know whose camp he had struck, a small boy found in the village was later identified as a nephew of Geronimo.[12]

Rucker received high praise from General Kautz and could take satisfaction in achieving a rare surprise attack on a Chiricahua ranchería.

During February 1877 depredations once more scourged southern Arizona. Lieutenant Rucker again took the field, heading directly east this time. He failed to overtake the raiders but noted that their trail led toward the Ojo Caliente Reservation. General Kautz had other reports that the culprits were mainly Chiricahuas and Nednhis, refugees from the old Chiricahua Reservation, based at Ojo Caliente and led by Geronimo, Juh, Nolgee, and Gordo. Furthermore, Victorio's men often joined in these forays.[13]

Kautz therefore dispatched a command from Fort Bowie to reconnoiter the Rio Grande country and ascertain the validity of the reports. Lieutenant Austin Henely, another able young officer and brother-in-law of Rucker, led the scouting party. Near Ojo Caliente Henely observed a raiding party driving a herd of stolen horses and recognized one of the men as Geronimo. A few days later, at the agency, he again spotted Geronimo, incensed at the agent because he could not draw rations for the period of his absence. The lieutenant concluded that the Ojo Caliente Reservation provided shelter and rations for unruly Apaches from elsewhere who used the cover of Victorio for sporadic raiding.[14]

Henely's report of sighting Geronimo led to uncharacteristically swift decision in Washington. Alerted by the War Department, the commissioner of Indian affairs on March 20, 1877, telegraphed Agent Clum: "If practicable take Indian police and arrest renegade Chiricahuas at Southern Apache Agency. Seize stolen horses in their possession. Restore property to rightful owners. Remove renegades to San Carlos and hold them in confinement for murder and robbery. Call on military for aid if needed."[15]

Clum lost little time in responding. His police captain, Clay Beauford, was in Tucson with eighty police. Clum took twenty-two of the San Carlos police and arranged for Beauford to meet him at Fort Bayard, New Mexico, near Silver City, with the other eighty. Relying on a trivial pretext, Clum had refused to ask General Kautz for military support but instead arranged for cavalry from New Mexico to arrive on April 21. On April 20 the police approached the reservation. Clum left Beauford and his men about ten miles out and proceeded with his small contingent to the agency. During the night Beauford quietly moved his police into the agency and concealed them in a storehouse next to agency headquarters.

Early on April 21, even though the New Mexico cavalry had been delayed a day, Clum summoned Geronimo and other chiefs with about one hundred people for a talk. The small number of police visible appeared to pose no threat, so they came. As Clum confronted Geronimo, Beauford led his police from concealment and surrounded the Apaches. The showdown between the agent and a defiant Geronimo proceeded tensely but ended quietly because of the overwhelming strength of Beauford's police. He took Geronimo and two "renegades" into custody and had them escorted to the blacksmith shop, where they were ironed, then jailed. By the end of the day Clum had seventeen prisoners in the guardhouse, four of them shackled.[16]

Clum dispatched Beauford and his police back to Arizona, and the next day, April 22, Major James F. Wade arrived with three troops of the Ninth Cavalry. Already, on April 15, Clum had wired the commissioner of Indian affairs from Fort Bayard advising that all the Ojo Caliente Indians be moved to the San Carlos Agency so that the Ojo Caliente Reservation, like the Chiricahua Reservation, could be abolished. Two days later he received permission, provided the military agreed. Wiring Major Wade of his intent, on April 24 Clum called together the principal reservation chiefs, and after a "short talk" they all agreed to move to San Carlos. Doubtless Wade's cavalry and Clum's San Carlos police had a bearing on their ready consent.

On April 30, under charge of Clum's chief clerk, a cavalcade of 435 reservation Indians got under way, cavalry escorting. Clum and the seventeen prisoners boarded army wagons and traveled by road to unite with the others at Silver City. The procession numbered about 300 Chihennes and 153 Bedonkohes and Chokonens. Reluctantly, Victorio went, too, although about 150 Chokonens and Nednhis slipped away. Clum's new charges reached San Carlos on May 20, and Geronimo, still ironed, was locked in the agency guardhouse.[17]

San Carlos would be Geronimo's home for two years, until again Mexico beckoned.

ELEVEN

GERONIMO'S FIRST BREAKOUT, 1878

ON MAY 20, 1877, the day Agent John P. Clum reached San Carlos Agency with the people from Ojo Caliente, the shackled Geronimo and his "renegade" cohorts had been thrown in the agency jail. There they remained week after week. Years later Geronimo recalled only that he was tried or perhaps only heard that he was tried. More likely, he picked up occasional tidings of the administrative turmoil afflicting San Carlos, the departure of Clum, and the long-delayed arrival of a new agent. After three months of this infuriating humiliation, the prisoners were set free and, without explanation, walked out to become reservation Indians. Clum had notified the sheriff in Tucson to come get Geronimo, but he had not. So he had been released. He joined Taza's Chokonens fifteen miles up the Gila from the agency, where Clum had placed them more than a year earlier. He discovered, if he did not already know, that a major change had occurred in the Chokonen leadership.

Clum was to blame. Shortly after locating Taza's Chokonens in the Gila lowlands upriver from San Carlos, he had decided to take a leave of absence and travel to Ohio, where a young lady waited to wed him. He had the temerity to request the Indian Bureau to pay his way, which met with blunt refusal. Clum therefore conceived the scheme of organizing a band of Apache "thespians" to stage dramas at large cities en route displaying the wild ways of the Apaches. Bankrolled by some friends, he organized a troupe of twenty-two, mostly Chokonens, and including Taza. On July 29, 1876, little more than a month after the Chokonen removal, the entourage loaded on three wagons and set forth for the nearest railroad depot, a monthlong journey to El Moro, Colorado.

Three performances in Saint Louis in early September convinced the theater owner, if not the impresario, that the Apaches failed as "thespians." Clum took the delegation on to Washington, DC, where he treated them to the usual attractions of the capital. After a violent rainstorm, however, Taza fell ill with pneumonia and on September 26 died. In the medical efforts to save the chief, together with an impressive burial in the congressional cemetery—General Howard attended—the irrepressible agent discerned a bright side: "They afforded the Indians of our party an opportunity to observe the civilized methods and customs of caring for the sick and preparing the dead for burial, as well as our funeral rites and ceremonies."[1]

The commissioner of Indian affairs paid the fare for the Apache delegation to return to San Carlos. Clum tarried in the East for his wedding and did not reach San Carlos until late December 1876.

The young chief's tragic death elevated his younger brother Naiche to the chieftainship. Tall, handsome, and well liked by all, he lacked even the leadership skills of Taza. He had not been schooled by his father in the duties of the chieftainship. This was the change in leadership Geronimo noted when released from jail.

Clum had returned triumphantly from Ojo Caliente with his "renegades" and as many of the Chihennes as he could round up, including Victorio. The day after his arrival, May 21, 1876, Lieutenant Lemuel A. Abbott appeared with a detachment of soldiers, sent by General Kautz, he explained, to inspect agency issues to ensure their honesty. Although San Carlos had reeked with the corruption of contractors and agency employees from the beginning, Clum had tried to conduct an honest administration. His lengthy absences, however, made that impossible. Confronting an army inspector at San Carlos, Clum erupted with protest and refused to have anything to do with him. Finally, making no headway in Washington, he launched a proposal: raise his salary, give him two more companies of Indian police, and he would manage all the Indians of Arizona, allowing the army to withdraw altogether. When the Indian Bureau rejected this wild scheme, Clum resigned and on July 1 rode away from San Carlos.[2]

Indian inspector William Vandever had been at San Carlos most of the summer of 1876. With Clum's departure, he informally took over the agency, although he elevated the agency clerk, Martin Sweeney, to acting agent pending the arrival of a new agent. Throughout the summer, beginning with Clum's return from Ojo Caliente, angry disputes flared between the civil officials and Lieutenant Abbott, backed vociferously by General Kautz. Abbott's reports persuasively indict Vandever of swindling the Indians, whose ration issues fell so precipitously that they had to take to the mountains to look for subsistence.[3]

Vandever did understand the resentments caused by the continued incarceration of Geronimo and the others in the agency jail. Since the sheriff in Tucson had failed to come for Geronimo, late in July Vandever sought permission to release the prisoners. Mortified and burning with a hatred of whites that would last for years, Geronimo and his friends walked free.[4] He joined the Chokonens upriver from San Carlos and, with Taza dead, immediately attached himself to Naiche. Always respectful, he nonetheless quietly counseled the new chief. The two remained close for the rest of their lives.

A new era appeared to dawn with the arrival on August 21, 1877, of Agent Henry L. Hart. He immediately moved to repair the damage with the military as well as the restless Indians. He sought to clean out the rot long burrowed in the contracting system and, with the departure of Vandever, the fraudulent conduct of agency employees. As it turned out, Hart would prove the most corrupt agent in San Carlos history, his tenure culminating in a scandal that brought down the commissioner of Indian affairs himself.

The new agent had to deal with Apaches made uneasy by the concentration policy, which mixed so many tribes of Apaches that had long been at enmity, and by the summer-long shortage of rations. Worse, only ten days after taking control, he suddenly confronted two crises. On September 1, the always fractious Pionsenay, who had never settled at San Carlos, entered the Chokonen subagency and persuaded several men and their families to flee with him to Mexico.[5]

Probably coincidentally, on September 3 Victorio launched his long-planned breakout. He and Loco fled the reservation with about three hundred Chihennes and headed east for their home country. Cavalry and Indian police skirmished with them, but they made good their escape. In New Mexico they ran into the Ninth Cavalry, which pushed them northward to ultimate surrender at Fort Wingate. The army could think of no better solution than to place them at Ojo Caliente as prisoners of war until the government decided what to do with them. Victorio and his people greeted this move joyously—they were back in their homeland.[6]

Geronimo held fast with Naiche and the Chokonens, despite the temptations of Pionsenay and Victorio—and despite the fact that about 150 Chokonens and Bedonkohes who had refused to move to San Carlos raided in New Mexico and Arizona. Taza had agreed with Clum to settle in the Gila bottomlands east of San Carlos, where a subagency took care of them. The army erected Fort Thomas upstream from the subagency. Officials reported the Chokonens well satisfied. They may have said so, but these were mountain Apaches planted in a desert environment seared by the sun and swept by wind, sand, and dust. Worse, a nearby spring created a swamp that bred mosquitoes, and malaria would soon begin to strike down the people. Geronimo cannot have been any more satisfied here than the rest of the Chokonens, but he had been chastened by the weeks spent in irons behind bars.

Meantime, Juh had returned to Mexico late in 1876 and remained for more than a year raiding and fighting Sonorans. By late 1877 he and the other Apaches who had not moved to San Carlos with Taza, about 250 Chokonens, Nednhis, and Bedonkohes, had begun to concentrate near Janos in another bid to make peace. A Sonoran force took the trail of a group leading stolen cattle toward Janos. The camp stampeded before the Mexicans could attack, but they confronted a force of fifty to sixty fighters under Juh, Pionsenay, and Nolgee riding from Janos to help their comrades. In an exchange of fire, Pionsenay met his death.[7]

Back at San Carlos, Geronimo found himself labeled a "bad Indian" by none other than Victorio. When the Chihennes surrendered after their breakout from San Carlos, Victorio explained the motivation as the influence of "bad Indians." These were about 145 Chokonens, Bedonkohes, and a few Chihennes who had been moved from Ojo Caliente by Clum in April 1877 and had chosen to remain with Naiche's Chokonens rather than go with Victorio. Although they bore no direct blame for the breakout, Victorio correctly held them responsible for the removal by using Ojo Caliente as a base for raiding and thus bringing the wrath of the government down on all the agency people. In fact, Loco had opposed the outlaws using Ojo Caliente as a base, while Victorio had refused to condemn them. Geronimo was the most prominent of the "bad Indians" living with Naiche. On September 23, 1877, Agent Hart held a council with Naiche and the other Chokonen chiefs at their subagency. He appointed Geronimo "captain" of the Chiricahuas Clum had moved from Ojo Caliente. Together with Naiche and the

Chokonen chiefs, Geronimo promised the agent that he would remain on the reservation.[8]

Affairs at San Carlos remained uneasy into the summer of 1878. The scarcity and uncertainty of ration issues caused anxiety and threatened hostilities. Appropriations failed to provide for the full amounts. Contractors proved consistently late in delivery. Graft continued to take its toll. Several times, emergencies forced the army to "lend" the Indian Bureau flour and the secretary of the interior to authorize purchases of beef and flour on the open market. At times Apaches took to the mountains to supply their own wants. Some committed depredations outside the reservation. General Kautz kept patrols ranging the country, which helped dampen the impulse to break out.

On March 7, 1878, Colonel Orlando B. Willcox took over from Kautz, serving in his brevet grade of major general. He continued Kautz's operations. The Chokonen subagent used various words to describe the temper of his charges, including "sulky." He believed that sooner or later they would flee.[9]

Two developments in 1878 contributed to the next stage of Geronimo's life. In the spring, for the first time, malaria struck Naiche's Chokonens with particular vehemence. Some fifty to sixty people died of the "shaking sickness." Availing themselves of Agent Hart's permission to augment their scarce rations by hunting and gathering in the mountains, many also sought to escape the malarial scourge by fleeing to the mountains.

Either by trade or as part of their scant rations, the Chiricahuas had acquired corn. Except for Tom Jeffords, agents as far back as Michael Steck in the 1850s had tried to end the manufacture of tiswin. Clum had used his police to break up tiswin stills wherever found. Now, without any police or other officials watching, Naiche's Chokonens and Geronimo's Chokonen and Bedonkohe followers resumed making tiswin.

On the night of August 1, 1878, Geronimo and some of his people staged a tiswin drunk. Well into the evening, with most of the group intoxicated, Geronimo began to berate his nephew (name unknown), "for no reason at all," as Jason Betzinez recalled. In some manner, however, the youth offended Geronimo, probably a remark or behavior induced by tiswin. Mortified by the great Geronimo's scolding, the nephew killed himself. While rare, suicide occurred among the Apaches, but for reasons more substantive than the nephew's offense. Shamed—a common Apache characteristic—

and vividly remembering his weeks in the San Carlos jail, Geronimo and his immediate family, three wives and two children, packed their gear and fled to the east. That no men went with him persuaded the agent acting in Hart's absence that Geronimo would return when the affair blew over. He did not. He and his family kept going, south through the Peloncillo Mountains and into Chihuahua. Near Janos he teamed up once more with his old friend Juh.[10]

As in the past, when a real or imagined threat took shape in Geronimo's mind, he reacted in the same way—Mexico. He had broken his promise to Agent Hart to remain with Naiche at San Carlos. He made no more such promises, and his breakout of 1878 would not be his last.

TWELVE

BACK TO SAN CARLOS, 1878–79

GERONIMO AND JUH HAD been close friends since youth and became close allies in the 1860s. Even before Cochise began to lose strength and journey frequently to Ojo Caliente in search of a satisfactory peace, Geronimo and Juh were tightly aligned. Mangas Coloradas had been a mentor more than a comrade. Cochise had been an admired leader of the Chokonens, whom Geronimo followed at times. But even before Cochise's death in 1874, Juh and Geronimo had become true comrades, in war and peace.

Many thought Geronimo a Nednhi. Although he remained a Bedonkohe by heritage, by the 1870s his Bedonkohe band had largely taken up residence with the Chihennes, the Chokonens, or the Nednhis. At San Carlos, where Geronimo had settled with Naiche's Chokonens in August 1877, he had been appointed "captain" of the combined group of Bedonkohes and Chokonens who had been moved from Ojo Caliente but had been labeled "bad Indians" by Victorio before he broke from San Carlos in 1877. None had followed the "captain" to Mexico after the tiswin drunk of August 1, 1878; for all its faults, San Carlos remained preferable to the uncertainties of Mexico. Geronimo now integrated with Juh's Nednhis.

At Janos, Juh, Geronimo, and the Nednhi subchief Nolgee had been negotiating with Chihuahuan authorities for peace and rations, as Juh had done periodically since the 1850s. Now, however, Chihuahua demanded impossible conditions: relocate all the Nednhis at Ojinaga, a town far down on the Rio Grande, and stay there. Insulted, on September 26, 1878, the Nednhis retaliated by ambushing a wagon train in Chocolate Pass, southeast of Casas Grandes, and killing all the occupants—twenty-five men, women, and children.[1]

With Sonoran troops in the field, the Nednhis then split into three groups. Nolgee returned to Janos to try to revive the talks. Geronimo took refuge about one hundred miles to the south. Juh hid in mountains even farther south. In October 1878 the two groups began moving north again, raiding as they came. Emissaries sent to scout conditions at San Carlos returned with reports of short rations and the "shaking sickness." The three leaders preferred to take their chances in Mexico.

On November 12, 1878, disaster struck twice. At Janos Nolgee let his guard down and fell for the old Mexican stratagem of gathering the Indians to trade, getting them drunk, then falling on the helpless victims. Mexican federal troops surrounded them and wiped out two-thirds of the group, twenty-six women and children and nine men, including Nolgee. On the same day a Sonoran force fell on Geronimo's group of about forty people in the mountains east of Nácori Chico. "I do not know how they were able to find our camp," Geronimo later related, "but they were shooting at us before we knew they were near. We were in the timber. We kept behind rocks and trees until we came within ten yards of their line, then we stood up and both sides shot until all the Mexicans were killed. We lost twelve warriors in this battle." (Geronimo did, but they did not kill all the Mexicans.)[2]

These disasters, especially the death of the prominent Nolgee, prompted Juh and Geronimo to give some thought to escaping the Mexican troops and gaining rations by returning to San Carlos. But for now, the adverse reports on conditions at San Carlos kept them in Mexico, raiding in Chihuahua and Sonora and occasionally in New Mexico and Arizona, in the usual way.

Victorio may well have joined them now and then. He and Juh disliked each other, but they could partner in raiding. After the Chihenne breakout from San Carlos in September 1877 and their surrender at Fort Wingate, the army sensibly held them as prisoners of war at Ojo Caliente until the government made up its mind. But the government could not make up its mind. Ojo Caliente was clearly the best place; leaving them in their homeland would almost certainly keep them peacefully happy. The Indian Bureau, however, was obsessed with removal back to San Carlos. As the argument dragged on month after month, Victorio alternated between pleading with officials at Ojo Caliente and raiding in New Mexico and Sonora.

Although Victorio had vowed to die rather than go back to San Carlos, he left the peace chief Loco to deal with the threat. In July 1878 the government resolved to take the Ojo Caliente Chihennes back to San Carlos. Both chiefs argued vehemently against the move, but by October they knew the government would use force if they resisted further. When the military escort took over, Victorio had vanished, leaving leadership to Loco. The grueling trek took a month, slowed by a mountainous trail and constant cold, rain, sleet, and snow. On November 25, 1878, Loco and 172 Chihennes arrived at San Carlos. The number included only twenty men.[3]

For the first half of 1879, the sometime negotiations with Victorio had focused on trying to get him to settle on the Mescalero Reservation, in the Sierra Blanca east of the Rio Grande, where Nana had already taken refuge to avoid the coming explosion. The Indian Bureau even started moving the Chihenne families from San Carlos to Mescalero. Confusingly, in July 1879 some high officials had proposed placing the Chihennes where they had belonged all along, at Ojo Caliente.

It was too late. Exasperated, Victorio had already taken his people into the San Mateo Mountains north of the Alamosa Valley. In September 1879, he declared war by seizing the entire horse herd of the troop of cavalry at Ojo Caliente. (Juh participated in this event.) The Victorio War lasted more than a year, pitting the entire Ninth Cavalry against the elusive Chihennes. Ranchers lost lives and stock, and the black troopers contended doggedly against the fugitives. On October 27, 1879, in rugged terrain a few miles south of the border in Chihuahua, Juh and Geronimo joined Victorio in a hard-fought battle with pursuing cavalry. Leaving the exhausted troops behind, the Apaches turned east and, with Juh and Geronimo participating, inflicted two massacres on the citizens of Carrizal, Chihuahua. The two then returned to their refuges to the west.

The Victorio War ended on October 15, 1880, at Tres Castillos, Chihuahua, when Mexican troops surrounded and all but annihilated Victorio's following. The chief himself died, supposedly by his own hand. Old Nana and a remnant of Victorio's force escaped the carnage and took refuge back in the Sierra Madre. In revenge, in the summer of 1881 he ravaged New Mexico in a classic operation called "Nana's Raid."[4]

By late November 1879, Juh and Geronimo had parted with Victorio and headed west to their base camp in the Carcay Mountains near Janos, raiding and plundering along a tortuous path to their destination. The Carcay

Mountains, south of Janos in the angle formed by the Janos and Casas Grandes Rivers, had long been a favorite refuge of Juh and often of Geronimo. Rising five thousand feet and covered by shrub, they offered hiding places while affording easy access to Janos.

At their base camp in the Carcay Mountains, Juh and Geronimo confronted surprising news. In their absence, Chiricahuas from San Carlos had arrived bearing peace feelers, from their own people as well as from the military authorities. They wanted Juh and Geronimo to bring the Nednhis to San Carlos and settle on the reservation. Juh and Geronimo knew the emissaries well: the Bedonkohe subchief Gordo and Ah-Dis, a survivor of Nolgee's slaughtered Nednhis who had taken refuge with Naiche's people. Both had friends and relatives among the Nednhis.

In the absence of their leaders, the men in the camp could make no commitment. Two Nednhis with their wives and three children, however, agreed to accompany Gordo and Ah-Dis to a military post in the Chiricahua Mountains south of Fort Bowie and meet with an army officer there. When Juh and Geronimo came back to camp, they hoped serious talks could be held.

Juh reacted instantly and emphatically to Gordo's proposal. "I am not going in, for anybody." He got his gun out. "If they get me they kill me."

Gordo placated Juh enough to get him to listen. "You got lots of children, girl children, and I don't see why you run like a wild man—no sleep and food, no water. Why, you stay when you go back to white man's village. Nobody kill you. They give you food and you not going to starve. Little children—you carry them around and get them killed and like the coyote, crow eat you. Now you got a good finish. Nobody going to hang you." Gordo made sense, at least enough in Juh's mind to keep the talks going all night. Despite the adverse reports from San Carlos, Juh gradually weakened. By morning, Gordo had prevailed. "You take me back over there," said Juh.[5]

He would go, but not that simply. Both Juh and Geronimo distrusted the whites and remained deeply skeptical, suspicious, and unsettled by Gordo's assurances. To coax them in would require infinite patience, skilled diplomacy, and weeks of frustration.

The patient diplomat was the officer waiting at Camp Rucker, in the southern Chiricahua Mountains. He was Lieutenant Harry L. Haskell, aide-de-camp to the department commander, Brevet Major General Orlando B. Willcox. In July 1878 Haskell had been assigned the seemingly impossible task of persuading Juh and Geronimo to return to the reservation. After months of burgeoning scandal at San Carlos, the Indian Bureau had assented to the detail of an army officer as acting agent. Captain Adna R. Chaffee proved a highly competent and efficient administrator, and he restored honesty and order to the governance of the reservation. Through the Department of Arizona's chief scout, Archie McIntosh, Chaffee had sounded out Naiche's Chokonens about the possibility of inducing Juh and Geronimo to bring the Nednhis in Mexico to live among them at San Carlos. Chaffee's favorable report led General Willcox to select Lieutenant Haskell for this delicate mission.[6]

Seeking out Tom Jeffords, Haskell obtained his consent to help by modeling the venture after Jeffords's role in General Howard's successful peace effort with Cochise in 1872. In September 1879, among Naiche's people, Haskell found the chief and his leaders in a cooperative frame of mind. Haskell formed his peace party, consisting of Archie McIntosh, Gordo, Ah-Dis, San Carlos police sergeant Atzebee, possibly Chief Chihuahua, and George, an influential Chokonen who had close friends among the Nednhis. By September 20 Haskell had established his base at Camp Rucker, where he met Tom Jeffords prospecting nearby. Haskell promptly sent Gordo and Ah-Dis on their mission into Mexico. Not until mid-October did they locate Juh's stronghold in the Carcay Mountains near Janos. Finding Juh and Geronimo absent (fighting with Victorio), they persuaded the seven Nednhis to journey to Camp Rucker. Sergeant Atzebee met them at the border and led them to Rucker.[7]

The wait at Camp Rucker proved long and frustrating. Discouraged, Haskell himself set out with a small party, including the two Nednhis, to probe south in the Guadalupe Mountains into Mexico. In the Guadalupes he teamed up with an Indian scout company under Lieutenant Augustus P. Blocksom. At San Bernardino Springs on December 12, a runner arrived in the camp and said that the Nednhi leaders wanted to meet with Haskell but that he should come alone, without soldiers. Accompanied by the runner and Blocksom's interpreter, Haskell journeyed to the Nednhi camp. It lay in the Guadalupe Mountains, about forty miles east of Camp Rucker. The Indians had also sent a runner to Camp Rucker, and Archie McIntosh reached the camp a few hours before Haskell.[8]

The lieutenant confronted his last test. Unknown to him, a few days earlier the Nednhi leaders had held a council to talk more about the proposal of Gordo and Ah-Dis that Juh had already consented to. All but one of the leaders agreed to surrender. The discussion grew angry, and Geronimo ended it by drawing his pistol and killing the dissident.[9]

About eighty Nednhis scattered around the floor of the canyon. Haskell told them that General Willcox would treat them well as long as they were "good Indians," that he had sent Haskell to meet with them, and that he would tell the general what they had said. With what trepidation Juh and Geronimo greeted Haskell's assurances is suggested by his description of them as "suspicious" and "very wild." Yet they allowed themselves to be escorted to Camp Rucker.

By the end of December, with more Nednhis in tow, Haskell had reached Fort Bowie and had a "big talk" with them. Tom Jeffords participated. The chiefs greeted him warmly and said all their people had now joined. Because of Juh's stutter, Geronimo did most of the talking. Haskell wired Willcox that he had 102 "renegades" and eighteen agency Indians and that he expected to arrive at San Carlos in eight days.[10]

On January 7, 1880, the cavalcade reached the Nednhi camp near the San Carlos subagency. They erected their wickiups at a site near Naiche's Chokonens designated by Captain Chaffee, still the acting agent. They had their new homes.

The Haskell episode ended one era in Geronimo's life and began another. He had made his first breakout from San Carlos and returned once again to take up agency life. The second era would end only when he faced General Nelson A. Miles on September 3, 1886.

THIRTEEN

GERONIMO'S SECOND BREAKOUT, 1881

IN JANUARY 1880 GERONIMO and his personal following, mainly Bedonko-hes, settled in with Juh and his Nednhis at the site designated by Captain Chaffee near the subagency on the north bank of the Gila, about fifteen miles upstream from the San Carlos Agency. The Chokonen camp of Naiche spread out nearby.

Naiche's camp included not only the Cochise Chokonens but also the fol-lowers of Chief Chihuahua, a superior leader and a fierce fighting man who maintained his separate group among the Chokonens. Although shorter, lighter, and paler than Mangas and Cochise, he possessed the typical Apache physical attributes. About the same age as Geronimo, Chihuahua com-manded greater admiration and respect. He followed no leader but himself. During 1880 and 1881, however, he was rarely present with Naiche's people because he enlisted as an army scout at Fort Apache and served faithfully in the military operations against Victorio in 1879–80 and Nana in 1881.[1]

Other Indians drew rations at the subagency. The White Mountain Apaches, moved from the mountains to the north by John Clum in 1875, camped nearby. They followed the lead of two chiefs, George and Bonito. The latter was born a White Mountain Apache but had married into the Chiricahuas and lived now and then with them. But his life-way remained White Mountain, and so he considered himself. Clum had failed to move all the White Mountain Apaches, and many remained in their home ranges near Fort Apache.

The Chokonens and Nednhis were not the only Chiricahuas at San Carlos during 1880–81. The Chihennes of Loco, driven out of their Ojo Caliente Reservation in 1878 and forced to live at San Carlos, had erected their wickiups on the north bank of the Gila on a rise just across the San Carlos River from the agency. The agent placed them here so the police could keep an eye on them. They drew rations at the agency and made the best of the new life in the burning sands of San Carlos, accommodating to the reality that the government would never let them go back to their beloved home in New Mexico. With Victorio dead at Tres Castillos in October 1880, the peace chief Loco exercised the sole role of leadership.

The months after Geronimo and Juh came to San Carlos in January 1880 brought Geronimo conspicuously to the attention of officialdom and the public beyond Arizona for the first time. Physically, he was described in almost the same terms that Lieutenant Sladen used to characterize Cochise's interpreter at the Howard peace council of 1872: erect, deep-chested, about five feet, nine inches in height, square shoulders, muscular, a face locked in a perpetual scowl. Hardly anyone thought well of him. "Thoroughly vicious, intractable, and treacherous," pronounced one army officer. "Schemer and liar," declared another. Feared, distrusted, disliked by his own people, said another. His personal following numbered scarcely thirty, but most of the Chiricahuas believed in his immense Power. He displayed these mysterious, surreal attributes often enough to convince the people of the strength of his Power. Also, he had ranged every mountain, desert, river, and trail in Apachería all his adult life, and he knew the country and how to live with and exploit it.[2]

The white man who knew Geronimo better than any other was George Wrattan, official interpreter, who traded and lived with the Chiricahuas for decades. According to Wrattan, "Geronimo came into prominence, *not* from his prowess in battle or personal bravery but from the great powers he was thought to have. He would prophecy victory in battle meeting soldiers defeating them, then getting something else; these prophecies which came true so often that his true word could become law. His own people were afraid of him."[3]

The opinions of white observers found agreement in statements of many Chiricahuas, but not all. One of the rising leaders among Naiche's people was Chatto (not to be confused with Geronimo's son Chappo), who late in life would declare, "I have known Geronimo all my life up to his death and have never known anything good about him."[4]

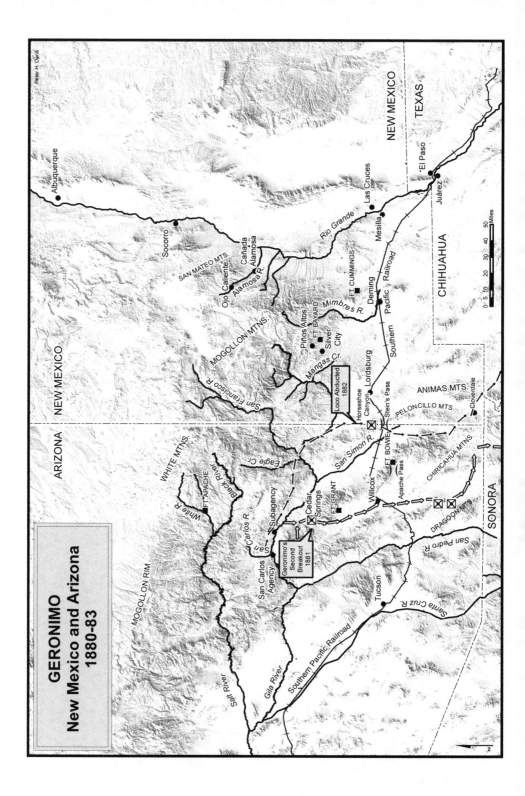

GERONIMO
New Mexico and Arizona
1880-83

Peter H. Dana

NEW MEXICO
TEXAS

ARIZONA
NEW MEXICO

CHIHUAHUA

SONORA

Albuquerque

Socorro

El Paso

Juárez

Las Cruces

Mesilla

Rio Grande

SAN MATEO MTS.

Cañada
Alamosa

Ojo Caliente

Alamosa R.

FT. CUMMINGS

Deming

Southern

Pacific

Railroad

MOGOLLON MTNS.

Piños Altos

FT. BAYARD

Silver
City

Mimbres R.

San Francisco R.

Mangas Cr.

Loco Abducted
1882

Horseshoe
Canyon

Lordsburg

Stein's Pass

ANIMAS MTS.

PELONCILLO MTS.

Cloverdale

WHITE MTNS.

FT. APACHE

Black River

White R.

Eagle Cr.

San Carlos R.

Subagency

San Carlos
Agency

Cedar
Springs

FT. GRANT

Geronimo's
Second
Breakout
1881

San Simon R.

FT. BOWIE

Willcox

Apache Pass

CHIRICAHUA MTNS.

DRAGOON MTS.

San Pedro R.

Tucson

Santa Cruz R.

MOGOLLON RIM

Salt River

Gila River

Southern Pacific Railroad

Miles
0 5 10   20   30   40   50

N

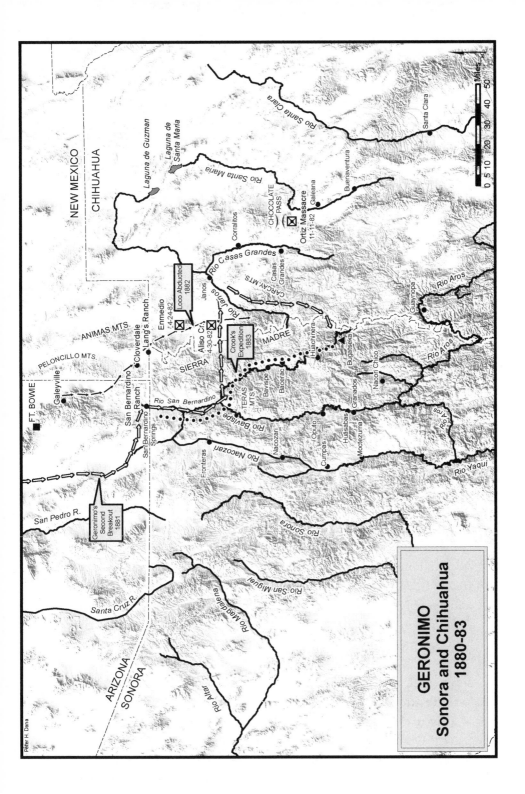

GERONIMO
Sonora and Chihuahua
1880-83

Peter H. Dana

As Geronimo emerged as a public figure, therefore, the record reveals ample condemnation by white officials who observed him closely. His prominence, however, silenced critics among the Chiricahuas, many of whom belittled him after his surrender.

Although Geronimo maintained his close but subordinate role with Juh, he also drew nearer to Naiche. Geronimo had long since sized up the impressionable young chief, tall, handsome, and likable but at twenty-three not an effective leader. His people knew it, too, but respected his hereditary status as Cochise's son. Geronimo edged into the vacuum in leadership and, always deferential, counseled Naiche.[5]

Neither Geronimo nor Juh had "surrendered" to Lieutenant Haskell. They had simply agreed to give up the warpath in Mexico and settle at San Carlos. Nothing in Geronimo's attitude toward the whites, especially white oversight, had changed. The ordeal to which John Clum had subjected him in 1877 strengthened the already dominant suspicion, distrust, fear, and hatred that had prevailed since his years with Mangas Coloradas. At San Carlos both he and Juh remained alert to any sign of official perfidy, coiled to stampede to Mexico at the slightest provocation, real or imagined.

Throughout 1880 and most of 1881, however, the Chiricahuas, according to many observers, lived "contented" and "happy." That overstated their temperament because periodic rumors portrayed Juh as dissatisfied and planning an outbreak. Moreover, the spring of 1880 brought another wave of "shaking sickness," which greatly disturbed Naiche. They received regular rations, however, and seemed unlikely to make trouble.

Even the appeal of mysterious events among the White Mountain Apaches failed to lure the Chiricahuas from their apparent complacency. The Cibicue group of the White Mountains obtained a pass from the agent to spend the summer of 1881 on Cibicue Creek, forty-five miles northwest of Fort Apache. During the summer the Chiricahuas near the subagency learned of a chief and holy man on Cibicue Creek claiming powers to raise three dead chiefs to life. His name was Nakadoklini, and his dances and ceremonies at first aroused only casual notice from the authorities. Hardly any Chiricahuas, probably foreseeing trouble, heeded invitations to join with the Cibicue people.[6]

They made the right decision, because trouble did explode with a vengeance. During August 1881, civil and military officials grew alarmed at rumors that Nakadoklini plotted an uprising. Both the San Carlos agent, Joseph C. Tiffany, and the Department of Arizona commander, Brevet Major

General Orlando Willcox, finally convinced themselves that the chief and holy man must be arrested. Orders went out from department headquarters instructing Colonel Eugene A. Carr, commanding Fort Apache, to take Nakadoklini into custody. With two troops of cavalry and a company of Indian scouts—ominously, including thirteen of Nakdoklini's own Cibicue people—Carr arrived at the village on Cibicue Creek on August 30.

Whether the Cibicue Apaches adroitly set up an ambush or were harmless victims of a misconceived interference in their spiritual life is still debated. Nakadoklini surrendered, but his fighting men swarmed over Carr's camp and set off a vicious battle. The Apache scouts mutinied and joined their brethren in the attack. Troopers shot Nakadoklini twice, killing him. Carr sustained casualties of one officer and six troopers killed and two wounded. He beat a hasty retreat out of the valley and marched overnight to reach Fort Apache in the afternoon of August 31.[7]

The Cibicue Indians, joined by other White Mountains, attacked Fort Apache itself but were readily driven off. They also killed and robbed white travelers and ranchers where they could be found. General Willcox, certain that he had a full-scale Indian uprising to contend with, appealed for fresh troops from other departments. They began arriving early in September, and their hurried movements in the Gila Valley distressed the Chokonens at the subagency. They knew of Cibicue, but they did not know the purpose of all the soldiers. Agent Tiffany's reassurance failed to quiet the suspicion of Geronimo and Juh.

Meantime, General Willcox established his headquarters at Fort Thomas, up the Gila from the subagency, and set about organizing a massive three-pronged offensive against an enemy that had long since scattered to hiding places in the mountains or come to San Carlos to surrender. Willcox also wanted to arrest the White Mountain chiefs George and Bonito. He and the subagent, however, differed on the means of their surrender. They shuffled the two chiefs back and forth between Fort Thomas and the subagency. Finally, losing patience, Willcox ordered a large force of cavalry to descend on the subagency and arrest them. That triggered the flight of the two chiefs. On the night of September 30, 1881, George and Bonito stormed into the Chiricahua camp and proclaimed that the soldiers were coming to arrest and shackle the chiefs and kill all the people.

Alarmed by Chief George, the Chiricahua chiefs at once met in council. Juh and Geronimo, camped with the Nednhis nearby, came over to participate.

As Chatto later recalled, "Geronimo was just like a wild animal. Troops made him nervous."[8] The alarm created by George and Bonito made Geronimo more wild than nervous. It made Juh "very much excited." Juh and Geronimo dominated the council. Although reluctant to leave, Naiche and Chihuahua both deferred. Chatto fell in with the majority. One chief dissented but was ignored.[9]

At 10:30 p.m. on September 30 Juh, Geronimo, Naiche, Chatto, and Chihuahua, with seventy four-men and their families—two hundred Chokonens, eighty-nine Bedonkohes, and eighty-six Nednhis—stole quietly away from their camp and headed south. Half the subagency people remained in camp. George, who had stirred up the fuss, at the last minute refused to join the outbreak. Bonito and his band of Chokonens, Bedonkohes, and a few White Mountains went along.[10]

The usual Chiricahua route to Mexico lay northeast to Eagle Creek, down to the Gila, then southeast into the Peloncillo Range all the way to Mexico. Shrewdly, the Chiricahuas did not choose this path. They knew the country to the east swarmed with troops, looking for hostile White Mountains. So they struck directly south, more dangerous because of open valleys but presumably not yet full of soldiers.

Soldiers would soon be on their trail, the leaders knew. About twelve miles up the Gila, they turned abruptly south and, to confuse any pursuers, broke into four groups, headed by Juh, Naiche, Chatto, and Bonito. As chief of the Nednhis, Juh led the group that included Geronimo, who took charge of his Bedonkohes. Circling widely, the leaders arranged to come together again at Black Rock, a prominent landmark in the northern foothills of the Santa Teresa Mountains.

En route, Geronimo took a raiding party that hit two freight trains and a ranch and made off with fifty horses and mules. He rejoined the exodus at Black Rock.

South from Black Rock, the united groups camped the night of August 1 in the eastern foothills of the Santa Teresa Mountains. The next day the breakouts took to the road pointing south to Fort Grant and Willcox, which with the arrival of the Southern Pacific Railroad had become a major shipping point for freight destined for the forts and agencies to the north. The men followed the road, while the women and children threaded the foothills of the Pinaleño Mountains to the east. Cavalry and Apache scouts out of Fort Thomas pushed down the road behind them, but not close enough to prevent depredations. A number of travelers met death, but the worst disaster befell a Mexican freight train headed for San Carlos—twelve wagons, 108 mules, fourteen thousand pounds of goods, and the teamsters. The Chiricahua fighters pounced on the train, slew all the teamsters, and made off with much of the contents. A volley from a nearby hill signaled troops approaching, so the Apaches beat a hasty retreat to the south.

Soon they spotted four soldiers repairing the telegraph line to Fort Grant. After killing them and plundering their bodies, the Apaches, aware of the close pursuit, drew into the Pinaleño foothills to the east, where the women and children were traveling, and prepared an ambush. As the cavalry halted and dismounted to examine the bodies, the Chiricahuas loosed a deadly volley and set off a six-hour exchange of gunfire—the Battle of Cedar Springs.

Needing to get their families to safety, the leaders launched a vigorous flank attack that ended the battle. They then left the road and hastened the people around the battlefield on the south and into the Aravaipa Valley to the west. On the night of October 2, they made camp in an open valley in the shadow of the Galiuro Mountains. The next day, October 3, the men fanned out across the valley, stealing horses from the Hooker ranch, while the families moved among the foothills of the Galiuro and Winchester Mountains. They made camp that night at Point of Mountains, the southern flank of the Winchesters, just north of Willcox.

Since putting the Cedar Springs fight behind them, the Chiricahuas, even though in open country, appeared to have an unopposed flight south through the Sulphur Springs Valley, thence across the border into Mexico. No forts barred the way. Skirting Willcox on the west, the Apaches entered familiar territory—their old home country of the Sulphur Springs Valley and Dragoon Mountains. By midmorning they came on a herd of cattle near Cochise's East Stronghold and stopped to butcher meat. The women began to set up camp. Suddenly a burst of gunfire startled everyone; believing they were safe, they had let their guard down. Actually, the gunfire was a premature volley from Indian scouts, and it ruined a surprise attack by three troops of cavalry. Even so, the troopers soon charged the Chiricahuas, and three troops of the veterans of Cedar Creek joined the fray. The Apaches had failed to spot them because they had climbed aboard railroad cars at Willcox. At the summit of Dragoon Pass, they had debarked and turned back into the valley to pick up the Chiricahua trail.

At the first blast of gunfire, the Apaches stampeded, abandoning their camp with all its stock and contents and skirmishing south among the southern foothills on the Dragoon Mountains. Finally, the men chose a canyon defensive position and stopped the attacking soldiers. The troopers pulled back and bivouacked for the night. The morning of October 5 revealed the Indians all gone. During the night, they had traveled swiftly across the Sulphur Springs Valley, threaded a pass in the Swisshelm Mountains, and made good their escape into Mexico by way of the old Peloncillo route.[11]

The four-day flight had been masterfully conducted by tough and seasoned leaders—even Naiche rising to new strength—and had successfully brought the people into Mexico. As slightly subordinate to Juh, Geronimo supported his friend in decision-making and fighting. His particular adventures remain unrecorded, but his ferocity as a fighter undoubtedly placed him in the forefront of the fights at Cedar Springs and the Dragoon Mountains.

When the Apaches started, most of the soldiers were to their north and east, preoccupied with the White Mountain Apaches, but the military adapted quickly and soon had ample strength deployed behind and, finally, in front of them. It was to no avail. The fugitives easily evaded them and slipped across the border.

The Southwest again confronted the specter of a renewal of the old outrages committed by Apaches based in Mexico.[12]

FOURTEEN

GERONIMO ABDUCTS LOCO, 1882

HAVING THROWN OFF ALL the army could mobilize against them and found safety in Mexico, the Apaches moved directly to Juh's old refuge in the Carcay Mountains, near Janos. Shortly afterward, they teamed up with Nana. After his summer raid into New Mexico to avenge Victorio, he and his Warm Springs Chihennes returned to the Sierra Madre. Juh and his cohorts lost no time in linking with Nana and reaching agreement to cooperate, which they cemented with a nighttime feast and dance. Combined, the followers of Nana and Juh numbered between 425 and 450 people.[1]

The chiefs talked over their future course. They resolved to approach Chihuahuan authorities and once again open peace talks. They carried out this initiative, but in practice they alternated between talking with Mexicans and extensive raiding. Juh led his fighters up and down the east side of the Sierra Madre, while Geronimo, propelled by his usual hatred of Sonora, ravaged the west side of the mountains. Nothing came of the peace talks with Chihuahua.

Another topic, however, engaged the early councils—the continued presence at San Carlos of the Warm Springs Chihennes following the lead of the peace chief Loco. Except for Loco's people and some Chokonens and Bedonkohes who had remained behind, all the Chiricahuas had now based themselves in Mexico. Should Loco be there, too? Why? Adding more women and children to the numbers to be fed seemed to make little sense. But some resented the supposedly well-fed "contentment" with which the

Warm Springs Chihennes lived at San Carlos. Others simply wanted to be reunited with kinfolk. Geronimo declared that he needed Loco's men to strengthen the Apaches in their battles with the growing number of Mexican troops—a thin rationalization since only thirty-two unarmed men lived with Loco. As one of the most belligerent of the leaders, Geronimo also savored the thought of a massive descent on San Carlos to force Loco to break away. That also appealed to many of the young fighting men.[2]

Geronimo organized and led the expedition. That he attracted sixty-three men to what must have seemed a risky and futile venture testifies to his persuasive powers; they loom even larger in the array of outstanding leaders he enlisted: Naiche, Chatto, Kayatena (a Chihenne chief who had fought with Victorio to the last), Mangas (son of Mangas Coloradas), Sánchez (an influential Chihenne), Bonito, and even the normally thoughtful Chihuahua. Significantly, Juh chose to remain behind.

Nor did Geronimo contemplate a surprise attack. In mid-December 1881, scarcely two and a half months after the escape into Mexico, the chiefs decided to let Loco know they were coming. They selected Bonito, who had left thirty of his people behind in the breakout, to carry the word. With seven men, Bonito easily crept into the White Mountain Reservation. Late in January 1882, he entered Loco's lodge and informed him that within forty days a Chiricahua force would come to take him and all his people to Mexico. Any who refused would be killed. In coming weeks two other delegations followed Bonito to deliver the same message.

Loco did not want to go, and each time he made sure the authorities knew of the threat. Thus alerted, both the agent and General Willcox reacted. Expecting the attack sometime in February 1882, they deployed both police and roving military patrols to screen all the southern and eastern approaches to the reservation. When nothing happened in February or March, they relaxed their vigilance. Three policemen remained posted south of the reservation, but the army units returned to their respective posts. Eighty days after Bonito's warning, April 19, 1882, the blow fell.[3]

"Just as the sun was beginning to shine," remembered Jason Betzinez, a young man in Loco's camp, "we heard shouts along the river. Running out of our tepee we saw a line of Apache warriors spread out along the west side of our camp coming our way with guns in their hands. . . . One of their leaders [Geronimo] was shouting, 'Take them all! No one is to be left in the camp. Shoot down anyone who refuses to go with us!' "[4]

The raiders rousted the Chihennes from their beds, tore down their dwellings, and hastened them all east along the north bank of the Gila. Loco tried to argue, but Chatto leveled a rifle at his chest and threatened to kill him. Chihuahua and some of his men stayed behind at Loco's camp. They fired two shots. As expected, that alerted the agency and brought police chief Albert Sterling and his sergeant galloping across the San Carlos River to the scene. Men at once shot down Sterling, a competent former army scout disliked for enforcing the tiswin ban. The sergeant raced back to the agency and returned with more police. He was killed, and the demoralized police retreated.

Including the Chokonens who had not broken out in October and Geronimo's sixty-three raiders, the cavalcade that made its way up the Gila on April 19, 1882, numbered about four hundred. While the army sought to organize a pursuing force, White Mountain Apaches seized the initiative. The Chiricahuas had made off with a White Mountain horse herd. Behind these Apaches straggled the agency police under the post trader and cavalry units hastily assembled at Fort Thomas.

All day Geronimo pushed the procession hard, turning northeast into the Gila Mountains and briefly pausing to rest at a spring. Aware that cavalry had taken up the trail, the Apaches pressed on in the darkness. Before dawn on April 20, having come down from the Gila Mountains, they stopped at Eagle Creek to rest. At daybreak a troop of cavalry attacked, setting off a brief skirmish before the Indians withdrew. The soldiers followed a few miles but then bivouacked. Indian scouts returned with word that the Apaches had scattered, and the soldiers turned back to Fort Thomas.[5]

The Apaches had scattered, but in small groups to raid ranches on both sides of the Gila in both Arizona and New Mexico. They needed horses and provisions. Once supplied, they could rendezvous and take the usual Apache route down the Peloncillo Range into Mexico. The roving groups killed ranchers, scooped up herds of horses and mules, and loaded themselves with plunder.

Jason Betzinez had observed the discipline with which the Chiricahua leaders conducted the trek to Mexico, and he particularly admired the leadership of Geronimo: "Geronimo was pretty much the main leader although he was not the born chief of any band and there were several Apaches with us, like Naiche, Chatto, and Loco, who were recognized chiefs. But Geronimo seemed to be the most intelligent and resourceful as well as the most vigorous and farsighted. In times of danger he was a man to be relied upon."[6]

Stein's Peak had been set as the rendezvous for the various groups, and on April 23 they began converging on a tangled, rocky canyon four miles north of the peak. It took the name of Horseshoe Canyon. They had made camp on the canyon floor to greet the returning groups. Nearly all the fighting men had gathered, about one hundred counting Loco's men. Lookouts posted on the canyon rims spotted a small group of horsemen cautiously threading its way up the narrow access to the wider canyon floor where the Apaches camped. They quickly doused their cooking fires and backed out, posting themselves on the canyon slopes to ambush any who came this far.

As the Chiricahuas well knew, southern New Mexico and Arizona teemed with troops, mobilized from all the forts and reinforced by units from other departments. Those of the most danger to the Apaches began reaching the Southern Pacific Railroad at the telegraph office at Separ, New Mexico, on April 19, the day of the outbreak. Lieutenant Colonel George A. Forsyth commanded. Forsyth shuttled troops back and forth on the railroad looking for where the Indians may have crossed. Scouts, however, could only find trails pointing north, which Forsyth erroneously assumed represented groups coming from Mexico to help their comrades. In fact, they were his quarry hastening to the rendezvous. Setting San Carlos as his destination, Forsyth gathered five troops of his regiment, the Fourth Cavalry, and headed north. He also sent Lieutenant David N. McDonald with a soldier and six Indian scouts to reconnoiter the Stein's Peak area.

McDonald and his party ventured into the narrow access gorges to Horseshoe Canyon and spotted a faint pall of smoke in the distance, the residue of the cooking fires so hastily extinguished. Only one of his scouts, the legendary Yuma Bill, would accompany the officer in further reconnoitering, although the rest grew shamed and came up. As McDonald came close enough to spot the smoldering campfires, the Apaches sprang the ambush, killing Yuma Bill and sending all the rest hastily to the rear. McDonald sent one of the scouts on the regiment's fastest horse to summon Forsyth, while he and the remaining scouts dug rifle pits. The lieutenant himself crawled forward and saw Apaches dancing around the body of Yuma Bill and several other scouts killed in the ambush. One spotted McDonald and rode toward him. He set his sights at five hundred yards and fired, killing the Apache.[7]

McDonald's messenger found Forsyth and the main command about sixteen miles distant. The colonel swiftly turned the column around and took up the gallop, one that did not lessen until he reached McDonald with the horses verging on collapse. Organizing his five troops into two battalions, Forsyth advanced into the canyon and encountered the Apaches posted on the rocky slopes.

Although the battalions maneuvered and attacked, perhaps in less orderly battle formation than Forsyth described, essentially the fight unfolded as Betzinez recounted:

> When the soldiers had reached a point about a mile from our hiding place our warriors stripped off their shirts and prepared for action. I heard our leaders calling all the able-bodied men to assemble for battle. . . . Soon we saw our warriors moving down toward a deep U-shaped ravine. The soldiers were approaching up the canyon while our men were on the rim. The fighting began. Three of our men were wounded and were carried back up the mountainside. . . . The firing grew very heavy, almost continuous. The soldiers fired ferocious volleys. Those of us who were watching were shivering with excitement as our men slowly withdrew under this fire. Finally toward sunset our whole band moved to the southwest side of the mountain and the fire died out. I don't think we ever found out how much damage we did to the troops.[8]

Not much: one man killed and five wounded. Forsyth reported two Indians killed and blood on the ground suggesting more, although the Apaches admitted to only one killed, the one shot by McDonald. The colonel liked to think he had won a great victory, but all he did was scatter the Indians without slowing their race toward Mexican sanctuary. Curiously, he did not even pursue; still convinced that he had fought "renegades" from Mexico hastening to help their brethren, he pointed his column north, toward the Gila and San Carlos, leaving his true objective behind to continue their flight to Mexico.[9]

Geronimo continued to lead them in the flight. Their story is a saga of skill and tragedy.

After the battle in Horseshoe Canyon, Geronimo waited for nightfall, and then slipped out into the San Simon Valley to the west. By dawn of April 24 the people had reached a spring in the Chiricahua Mountains about fifteen miles southeast of Fort Bowie. Resting here briefly, they proceeded to another spring to the south, near the little mining community of Galeyville. By this time, Loco's people had accepted the reality of their forced removal and knew they had become part of the "hostiles." They followed the lead of Geronimo. Betzinez, in fact, proudly boasted of being designated "an apprentice or helper to Geronimo."[10]

As the people rested most of the day, a few men stole some horses at Galeyville and killed two men at another mining camp to the west. But in the afternoon they spotted a dust cloud approaching across the San Simon Valley. (The truth had finally dawned on Colonel Forsyth.) They quickly gathered their possessions and embarked on a long, hard night march, back across the San Simon Valley to the southeast. They traveled through the next day, across the Peloncillos, and after another night march dropped into Mexico southeast of Cloverdale, New Mexico. The day was April 26, 1882, only a week since their descent on San Carlos.[11]

Under Geronimo's leadership, the Chiricahuas had achieved a masterly raid and withdrawal, encountering only one force of soldiers despite the many searching for them. They had incorporated Loco and his people into their ranks, and he reluctantly assumed the mantle of a "hostile" chief. Now nearly all the Chiricahuas had reached the safety of Mexico and deserved a rest. After crossing the Espuelas Mountains, they descended into a valley near the eastern face of the Enmedio Mountains, about seventeen miles south of the protective border. They settled into camp for two nights of feasting and dancing, April 26 and 27. So confident were they that on the second night they failed even to post lookouts.

Before daybreak on April 28, as the adults ended the night's dances and crawled into their bedding, three women and a man edged out into the darkness to the east to check a pit in which mescal roasted. As they approached, a shot rang out and the youngest of the women fell dead. The others ran back to the camp. Immediately after the single shot, a volley of shots from the same area swept the Indian camp. Startled Apaches emerged from their wickiups and raced to a rocky defensive butte to the south. Jason Betzinez had already gone there to get his mule for the day's move. He turned to see two troops of cavalry charging the camp, one from the northwest, the other from the southwest. The Apaches, well positioned, made a stubborn stand against the attacking troops, aiming a fire so heavy it forced the troopers to stop and dismount.

Sam Hauzous told his story, although he confused this fight with a later one against Mexicans. Eliminating that confusion, he described the scene accurately: "Geronimo he holler, he call the men—his fighting men—so there's soldiers on the west side. . . . There's [more] American white man soldiers in that side. . . . Then on the east side, Indian scouts that way, that's the way they hold us right there so we can't get away." Troops had seized the horse herd and kept up the exchange of fire until near noon, the Indian scouts, as Hauzous recounted, blocking the escape into the Enmedio Mountains behind them. But some daring men got behind the scouts and opened fire. Also, the scouts had nearly run out of ammunition. With the scouts' attention distracted, the chiefs led the people out of their defenses and escaped into the Enmedio Mountains. The surprise attack had left five men and three women dead on the battlefield, including Loco's son. Most of the horse herd had also been seized. Thinking they were safe in Mexico, the Chiricahuas had suffered a disaster when American soldiers and scouts unlawfully ignored the boundary.[12]

Driven now by the likelihood of pursuit by the US troops who attacked them at Enmedio, the Chiricahuas prepared for another night march in the effort to reach the safety of Juh's stronghold in the Carcay Mountains. Exhausted by hard travel and little sleep since Horseshoe Canyon, on the night of the battle they emerged from the Enmedio Mountains and struck south across a sandy plain cut by shallow ravines. They formed a long procession: an advance guard of fifteen men, including Chatto, Naiche, and Kayatena; Loco and his people, mostly women and children, strung out a mile behind; and two miles farther back a rear guard of most of the fighting men under Geronimo and Chihuahua prepared to fight off any attack by pursuing American soldiers. Thirty or forty horses captured by the Americans had been recovered, but most of the people shuffled along slowly on foot.[13]

The advance guard had ranged far forward, perhaps an hour in advance of Loco and his people. At dawn they entered a shallow ravine that contained the dry streambed of Alisos Creek, which ran southeast to the Rio de Janos, here almost dry. The foothills of the mountains lay only a mile beyond the creek. The advance guard had already left the ravine and aimed for the foothills. As Loco's people turned into the creek bed, however, a hail of bullets swept through them. They had walked into a Mexican ambush.

Betzinez, with his mother and sister, lagged behind the main body. He saw what happened:

Almost immediately Mexicans were right among us all, shooting down [and bayoneting] women and children right and left. Here and there a few Indian warriors were trying to protect us while the rest of the band were running in all directions. It was [a] dreadful, pitiful sight, one that I will never forget. People were falling and bleeding, and dying, on all sides of us. Whole families were slaughtered on the spot, wholly unable to defend themselves.

Or as Sam Hauzous remembered the chaotic scene, "just fighting, fighting, fighting."[14]

Geronimo and his rear guard, thirty-two well-armed and mounted men, charged into the fray and drove the Mexicans back. The men gathered such women and children as they could in a steep arroyo and repulsed a second Mexican charge. The women began scooping rifle pits out of the sides of the draw. Geronimo, Chihuahua, and Loco were all present. Chatto, Naiche, and Kayatena, part of the advance guard, had stopped to rest and have a smoke. Unaccountably, they remained where they had stopped and took no part in the fighting. The Mexicans had let the advance guard pass unharmed to allow the main body to walk into the trap.

The two sides exchanged heavy gunfire until midmorning, when the beleaguered Apaches saw a formation of Mexican soldiers charging with fixed bayonets. Before they reached their objective, however, the commander fell dead, shot by Geronimo himself, he insisted. The soldiers quickly turned back. The firing continued for another hour, with both sides running low on ammunition. Sporadic firing continued all afternoon.

At dusk, the Apaches began to steal out of the arroyo in small groups. After nightfall, someone proposed that the mothers strangle their babies to prevent their crying, but no one accepted the proposition. Various individuals in the always factionalized Apache society named Geronimo as the instigator of this tactic and further accused him of cowardice during the arroyo fighting. The controversy continues, but the evidence is not strong enough to verify the charge.[15]

In fact, Geronimo had performed at his best in taking Loco's people by surprise at San Carlos, then leading them in the flight toward Mexico. Since he had planned and carried out the operation, he must have fought with distinction at Horseshoe Canyon. He also fought effectively in the arroyo at Alisos Creek. As Betzinez declared, "In times of danger he was a man to be relied upon."

But the ambush at Alisos Creek had dealt the Chiricahuas a shattering defeat. Seventy-eight people lost their lives, nearly all women and children of

Loco's Chihennes. The Mexicans also bore off thirty-three captive women and children, including Loco's daughter. But the survivors of the slaughter made good their escape. Climbing into the Carcay Mountains, they united with Juh and Nana. Now 650 Chiricahuas, nearly all the tribe, had lodged themselves in the Sierra Madre.

The Carcays are mere foothills of the soaring Sierra Madre, long providing haunts for Apaches from the north and resident Tarahumari Indians. The Sierra Madre consists of two north-south ranges enclosing the great central plateau of Mexico. The Sierra Madre Oriental faces Chihuahua and parallels the Gulf of Mexico for seven hundred miles. The Sierra Madre Occidental, farther north, curves through Sonora facing the Pacific Ocean for a thousand miles. A few peaks are permanently snow-covered. A dominant characteristic of the mountains is plunging, steep-sided canyons called *barrancas*. Chaparral covers the canyon cliffs. Oak and pine forests rose from the tortured landscape between five and ten thousand feet. (Logging has denuded them in modern times.) The slopes facing east and west are humid and thickly vegetated while the inner slopes are nearly barren. Winters are mild and summers humid and rainy. Wolves, bears, deer, and other animals roam the forests. Snakes, including three species of rattlesnake, share the land with a wide variety of insects, some venomous.

The Apaches knew how to hide and live in these lofty mountains. The canyons, with many tributary canyons, pocked with rocky gouges and ledges, offered secure refuges for the Apaches. Game animals provided food, and ramshackle Mexican villages and ranches in the river valleys afforded food and plunder when game proved scarce. Both Mexican and American troops found the Sierra Madre virtually impossible to penetrate, and therefore impossible for military operations.

Not for the first time, the Chiricahua survivors of Alisos Creek found refuge in the impenetrable fortress of the Sierra Madre.

Despite the disasters at Enmedio and Alisos Creek, the Apaches had conducted their flight more skillfully than the army had conducted the pursuit. The pursuit ended in failure. For one thing, the Chiricahua retreat ranged across two military jurisdictions, Arizona and New Mexico. Confusion of command complicated planning for heading off the outbreak. As Colonel Forsyth pursued his course, therefore, reporting to Colonel Ranald S. Mackenzie in Santa Fe. General Willcox, headquartered at Fort Whipple in

Prescott, conceived his own strategy for heading off the Chiricahuas. He had assigned command of all his troops in southeastern Arizona to Major David Perry, based on the railroad in Willcox, Arizona.

As soon as he learned of the outbreak, Major Perry had units of the Sixth Cavalry, accompanied by Indian scouts, probing for the Chiricahuas all the way from Fort Thomas to the New Mexican line and south to the railroad. But he could get no reliable information of where the Apaches were. On April 24 one of his units, a troop of cavalry and a company of Indian scouts under Captain Tullius C. Tupper, were at San Simon Station of the Southern Pacific preparing to patrol the railroad. At nightfall a citizen from Galeyville galloped in and reported large numbers of Indians around his town, near the northern end of the Chiricahua Mountains. Perry at once telegraphed Tupper to hasten to Galeyville, where he would be joined by another troop and scout company under Captain William A. Rafferty, coming from Fort Bowie.

At 3:00 a.m. on April 25 Tupper reached Galeyville and found the citizen's report correct. His scouts discovered the Indian trail pointing southeast across the San Simon Valley. Shortly after daybreak Captain Rafferty with his troop and company of scouts arrived after a night march from Fort Bowie. As senior captain, Tupper took command. At once the battalion moved out on the trail—unaware that Forsyth had fought the Indians two days earlier in Horseshoe Canyon and was also looking for them. Reaching the Mexican boundary where the Chiricahuas had crossed, Tupper continued on the trail. Chief of Scouts Al Sieber accompanied the command, and on the night of April 27, as the Apaches danced through their second night of celebration west of the Enmedio Mountains, he and some of the scouts found the camp.

Tupper and Rafferty worked out a plan for surprising the festive ranchería at dawn on April 28. They would post the two troops of cavalry in the foothills of the Espuelas Mountains west of the objective and the two companies of Indian scouts in the valley on the east to block any attempt to escape into the Enmedio Mountains. When all the units reached their positions, the scouts would open fire, signaling the cavalry on the other side to open fire also.

The plan went awry when the sergeant of scouts took it on himself to shoot the young woman who ventured out to the mescal pit early in the morning of April 24. The cavalry had not yet reached their positions, but the battle had begun. Tupper mounted his two troops and charged from northwest and southwest toward the camp. Had the scout not precipitated the fight prematurely, Tupper may well have seized or destroyed the entire camp. Because not yet positioned, however, the troops had to cover too great a distance and then, confronted with heavy fire from the Apaches in their new defensive positions, dismount and settle into a long-distance exchange of fire that lasted all morning. When a few Apaches turned the flank of the scouts, the people slipped out into the Enmedio Mountains.

Almost out of ammunition and awaiting the arrival of an expected pack train, Tupper withdrew to the north eleven miles, back into New Mexico. Here to his astonishment he met Colonel Forsyth and his command. As Tupper declared, he had no idea any troops were closer than a hundred miles. His battalion at once came under Forsyth's command.[16]

On April 30 Forsyth moved out on the Indian trail with his entire command and Tupper's units. They paused at the Enmedio battlefield and then continued on the trail for two miles until they came across Lieutenant Colonel Lorenzo García of the Sixth Mexican Infantry. García and his adjutant crossed the Alisos Creek bed and met the American officer. García demanded to know why US troops had violated the boundary. Forsyth lamely responded that he had been pursuing the Indians, and later in the day he wrote a letter to the colonel explaining his motives and actions and agreeing to return at once to the American side of the boundary.

García informed Forsyth that the day before he had met and crushed the retreating Apaches, and he gave Forsyth and his officers a tour of the battlefield. The bloodied dead of both Apaches and soldiers shocked the Americans. With fewer than 250 Mexican infantrymen, García had smashed the Apaches, who left seventy-eight dead on the field and lost thirty-three women and children as captives. García conceded his loss as two officers and nineteen men killed and three officers and thirteen men wounded. His command had no medical officers, and Forsyth offered his own to tend to the Mexican wounded. This allowed more time for the Americans to tour the battlefield.

Late in the morning Forsyth turned his command around and marched back north. By May 2 he was back in the United States, released Tupper and Rafferty to return to their Arizona posts, and continued the march back to his New Mexico stations.[17]

The Loco campaign did not display the US Army at its finest. The efforts to find, much less intercept, the fleeing Chiricahuas proved fumbling at best, both from Arizona and New Mexico. Forsyth mismanaged the battle at Horseshoe Canyon and allowed the Indians to escape unharmed. The blunder of a single Apache scout cost Tupper the complete victory at Enmedio that lay within his grasp. Only the García ambush at Alisos Creek cut off and almost destroyed the quarry. Then the army suffered the embarrassment of intruding unlawfully on Mexican territory, which brought diplomatic protests to the State Department.

In Arizona, General Willcox had played little part in the campaign, leaving operations to Major Perry. For weeks after the escape, on Willcox's initiative all the generals, up the chain of command to General Sherman, burdened the official record with petty quibbling over where Geronimo entered the United States, Arizona or New Mexico—that is, the Department of Arizona or the District of New Mexico. At the same time, Willcox and Colonel Eugene A. Carr carried on a highly visible feud, both official and public, over where the blame for Cibicue belonged. Offended by an order issued by General Sherman, Willcox even went around the entire chain of command and complained to the president. Failing to get satisfaction, he went political.

In July 1882 Willcox received notice from the War Department that he would be relieved of command of the Department of Arizona. On September 4, 1882, Brigadier General George Crook assumed command.

FIFTEEN

MEXICO: *Massacres and Raids, 1882–83*

DESPITE THE EFFORTS OF some rivals to portray Geronimo as a coward at Alisos Creek, he had emerged from the massacre with enhanced reputation. He had proved the ablest leader and fighter in the bloody combat in the ravine, and he had steered the pathetic survivors out of the trap. In the aftermath of Alisos Creek, he continued to provide strong leadership in guiding the survivors through the Carcay and other mountains to the south. After Alisos Creek, no one questioned his role as the dominant leader. Finally, traveling forty laborious miles, about May 5 they reached Juh's camp in a secluded stronghold on the western slope of the Sierra Madre, at the head of the Bavispe River in Sonora. The Apaches called the hideout Bugatseka. Geronimo now, as in the past, shared leadership with Juh.

Geronimo's achievements in 1882 are especially notable because of family distractions. Among the captives seized by the Mexicans at Alisos Creek was Chee-hash-kish, his second wife. They had been married since about 1852, shortly after the massacre of his first family by Mexicans. She was the mother of Chappo and Lulu, born in 1864 and 1865, respectively. In Mexico, after her capture, Chee-hash-kish married another Chiricahua captive and never saw Geronimo again.

In 1880 Geronimo had taken a fifth wife, Zi-yeh, a Nednhi, who in 1882 gave birth to a son, Fenton. Eva would follow in 1889. Like all Apaches, Geronimo loved his family, and the loss of a wife and the gain of a son occurred at the same time as he employed his most brilliant leadership.[1]

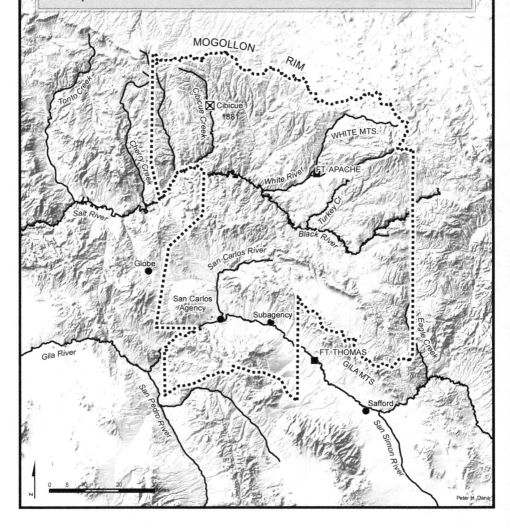

WHITE MOUNTAIN INDIAN RESERVATION
1881

Created in 1871 by Vincent Colyer and enlarged in 1872 by General
O. O. Howard, the White Mountain Reservation was home to the
White Mountains, Cibicue, San Carlos, Tonto, and until 1886
Chiricahua Apaches, as well as Yumas and Mojaves. Although
commonly called the San Carlos Reservation, the entire area was
White Mountain. San Carlos Agency administered the reservation.
Reflecting pressures of white settlers, three times during the 1870s
portions of the reservation were restored to the public domain and
the reservation shrunken. In 1896 it was divided into the Fort
Apache Reservation and the San Carlos Reservation.

MOGOLLON RIM

Tonto Creek

Cibicue Creek

⊠ Cibicue
1881

Cherry Creek

WHITE MTS.

White River

FT. APACHE

Turkey Cr.

Salt River

Black River

Globe

San Carlos River

San Carlos
Agency

Subagency

Gila River

FT. THOMAS

GILA MTS

Eagle Creek

San Pedro River

Safford

San Simon River

0   5   10   20   30 Miles

N

Peter H. Dana

Bugatseka afforded an ideal refuge for the Chiricahuas to rest, hunt, dance, and renew old friendships. Hundreds of people from several bands had gathered, and they could muster about seventy-five fighting men. Never content to remain long in one place, however, they began to grow restless and quarrelsome. The thoughts of their leaders, especially Juh and Geronimo, turned to a course of action that had proved fatal numerous times in the past.[2]

Chihuahuan towns such as Janos, Corralitos, and Casas Grandes repeatedly attracted the Apaches under the guise of seeking peace and rations from Mexican officials. Apaches never trusted or eased their hatred of Mexicans. Juh and Geronimo were particularly hostile. But Mexican authorities encouraged the Indians to come in and trade, make a treaty, and above all gain access to whiskey. Such visits had usually proved fruitless in concluding a treaty and on occasion had led to the massacre of inebriated Apaches. In 1851, near Janos, Geronimo had lost his entire family to such wanton treachery. Juh had just returned from Casas Grandes. Now he and Geronimo led about 200 to 250 of their people across the Sierra Madre and set up a base camp four miles southwest of Casas Grandes. Mexican authorities and merchants welcomed them.

Throughout April 1882, while Geronimo raided and fought south from San Carlos with Loco and his people, Juh had traded at Casas Grandes. His motive seems to have been strong drink. Increasingly, as often as not, he was drunk. The new initiative that took him and Geronimo with their people to Casas Grandes, supposedly to make peace with the Mexicans, may have had similar origins in Juh.

On May 18, 1882, Geronimo and Juh met with officials in Casas Grandes. "We shook hands and promised to be brothers," recalled Geronimo. "Then we began to trade, and the Mexicans gave us mescal. Soon nearly all the Indians were drunk." For a week people circulated between their camp and the town. More Chiricahuas came down from the mountains, until the camp contained families from groups not only of Geronimo and Juh but also of Naiche, Zele, and Chatto. Geronimo and Juh, ever suspicious, made sure both did not enter the town at the same time, and the talks continued while the people continued to trade and get drunk.[3]

On the morning of May 24, city officials sent two wagons to the Chiricahua camp. One contained bottles of whiskey, the other shelled corn, the prime ingredient of tiswin. That should have been warning enough, but

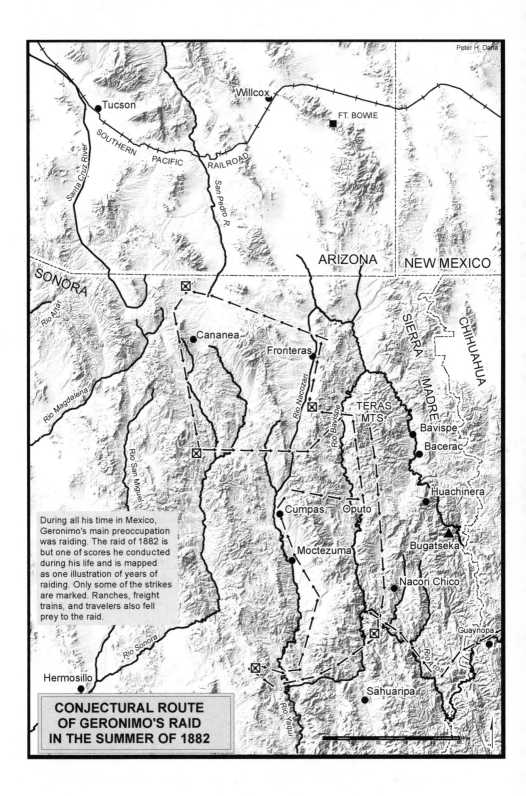

Peter H. Dana

Tucson

Willcox

FT. BOWIE

SOUTHERN PACIFIC RAILROAD

Santa Cruz River

San Pedro R.

ARIZONA

NEW MEXICO

SONORA

Rio Altar

Cananea

Fronteras

SIERRA

CHIHUAHUA

Rio Magdalena

Rio Nacozari

Rio Bavispe

TERAS MTS

MADRE

Bavispe

Bacerac

Rio San Miguel

Huachinera

During all his time in Mexico, Geronimo's main preoccupation was raiding. The raid of 1882 is but one of scores he conducted during his life and is mapped as one illustration of years of raiding. Only some of the strikes are marked. Ranches, freight trains, and travelers also fell prey to the raid.

Cumpas

Oputo

Bugatseka

Moctezuma

Nacori Chico

Guaynopa

Rio Sonora

Rio Aros

Hermosillo

Sahuaripa

Rio Yaqui

CONJECTURAL ROUTE OF GERONIMO'S RAID IN THE SUMMER OF 1882

throughout the day and all night the Indians staged a glorious binge. Jason Betzinez had the good sense to spend the night at a distance from the main camp. "During the night I could hear the drunken Indians in their camp, howling and dancing," he remembered. As early as 2:00 p.m., recalled Sam Hauzous, "the whole camp—everybody singing away and just running around. All—they seem like very happy. But they don't know what's coming to them."[4]

They didn't. An hour before dawn on May 25 a volley of shots shattered the darkness. Juh, Geronimo, and others not too drunk to rouse themselves gathered the women and children and, abandoning their horses, fled the camp. In fact, some soldiers had fired before other elements were in place, and a well-planned attack from four directions failed. Nonetheless, soldiers swarmed into the camp and fell on all who had been too intoxicated to escape, killing ten and capturing thirty-seven. Geronimo and Juh rallied the men who had escaped and fought off the soldiers until they gave up the pursuit.[5]

Watching from a distance, Hauzous saw the soldiers load the captives in three wagons and haul them into town. More soldiers arrived. One was Lieutenant Colonel Lorenzo García, who had taken such heavy casualties at Alisos Creek. Twenty-five of the captives fell into his hands, and he had them slaughtered. The Chiricahuas returned to their original camp, gathered their belongings, and journeyed back to the Sierra Madre to Juh's favorite stronghold in rugged terrain north of the Aros River, across from the village of Guaynopa, in Chihuahua near the Sonora boundary. They took unassailable positions on the heights above what Betzinez termed a "Great Canyon."[6]

One of the motives for seeking peace at Casas Grandes lay in the increasing concentration of Mexican troops in both Chihuahua and Sonora. Part of these troops, of course, inflicted the disaster at the Chiricahua base camp near Casas Grandes. In Juh's stronghold at the Guaynopa Great Canyon, the leaders worried about being trailed by soldiers, as in fact they were. Juh and Geronimo decided to launch a savage raid to the west, toward the Yaqui River in Sonora. After the first day's journey through a series of difficult canyons, they sent a party forward to scout several targets that had been contemplated. The scouts returned to report units of soldiers moving around Sonora. Undaunted, Geronimo resolved to continue to raid. More cautious, Juh wanted to withdraw to secure mountain refuges. The two decided to divide. Juh turned around with about five hundred people, including Loco, Nana, Naiche, Chatto, and Bonito. Thirty men and teenage boys capable of bearing arms elected to follow Geronimo, supported by Chihuahua and Kayatena. The separation occurred in late June 1882. For the next four months, Geronimo would rip up and plunder one Sonoran village or ranch after another, one freight-laden pack or wagon train after another, waylay and kill one luckless traveler after another. He hated all Mexicans.[7]

Geronimo had been raiding in Sonora and Chihuahua all his adult life. Other Chiricahuas raided, too, but Geronimo brought special vehemence to raids in Mexico because of the massacre of his first family by Mexicans in 1851. *Raid* seems an inadequate word to describe what happened when a town, ranch, freight train, or traveler was victimized. Besides plunder, raiders butchered people, often in the most brutal fashion. Thirty years of such barbaric slaughter, often involving torture and mutilation, form a major characteristic of Geronimo's persona. Barbarous as raiding was, however, Apaches almost never scalped or raped.

Raids in Mexico and New Mexico and Arizona had become a way of life, blurring the distinction between raid and war. Chiricahua culture held raids to be for provisions and subsistence, war for revenge. Raiding was constant, justified by need but not always confined to need. It could also be rationalized as war, since hostilities provided constant justification for revenge. Clearly, for Geronimo the motivation for raids did not stamp him as a hero fighting for his homeland. No part of Mexico formed his homeland. North of the border, the upper Gila River and Mogollon Mountains comprised his actual homeland, but it could be broadened into southwestern New Mexico and southeastern Arizona.

Sonoran troops tracked the raiding parties and occasionally skirmished with them. The soldiers posed a constant threat that worried the Chiricahuas, but not enough to stop the raids. Finally, however, in September Geronimo again demonstrated his Power, as described by Betzinez:

> That night Geronimo told us that Mexican soldiers were on our trail. He prophesied as to the exact moment they would appear. The next morning the women and children were, as usual, on the mountain top while the men were watching the back trail. Sure enough, just as Geronimo had predicted Mexican soldiers appeared in the very place and at the exact

time that Geronimo had foretold. The Mexicans went on to the creek then retraced their steps toward Oputo. Our warriors followed and attacked them about sunset. Our men captured all the enemy's horses and did considerable other damage.[8]

This encounter persuaded Geronimo to reunite with Juh, and early in October 1882 his raiders reached the Great Canyon near Guaynopa.

Juh and his followers had hardly been inactive. Throughout the summer, they too had conducted devastating raids, though not on the scale of Geronimo's party. They had also fought with Mexican troops, once decisively. Jason Betzinez learned the details from participants. After two days of fighting and nearly out of ammunition, the Apaches could not shake the enemy. So Juh resorted to a stratagem:

> The Indians made a plain zig-zag trail up a steep mountain to a point just below the summit where the trail ran parallel to the ridge line. . . . [Juh] had the men roll a line of big rocks into place along the trail, ready to be dislodged down the mountainside. The warriors took their positions as the enemy appeared on a ridge across the ravine. The Indians were well concealed with brush, grass, and leaves. They lay there motionless but impatient for the Mexicans to get within the danger zone. The latter confidently marched up the zig-zag trail. When they reached the summit the Apache warriors sprang out and attacked them. The Mexicans started to withdraw down the mountainside whereupon at Juh's command the Indians began rolling the great boulders on them. Some of those rocks were so big that they knocked down pine trees. Many soldiers were crushed by the tumbling boulders and falling trees. Not many escaped.[9]

Together once again, Geronimo and Juh discussed their next venture. They knew the names of the two leading officers who had massacred many of their people near Casas Grandes in May. They had negotiated with them in the town. They also knew where one, Juan Mata Ortíz, kept a ranch, near Galeana, on the Rio Santa María southeast of Janos, Chihuahua. They conceived a scheme for luring the officers and any troops they could muster into an ambush in nearby Chocolate Pass, scene of earlier ambushes. Abandoning Guaynopa late in October, the entire body moved to the northeast and in early November camped about thirty miles from Galeana. The fighting men numbered between 130 and 140.

Raiders struck twice in the vicinity but could decoy no pursuers into Chocolate Pass. The third raid hit the ranch of Mata Ortíz himself. Infuriated, he assembled twenty-two citizens from Galeana and on November 14, 1882, trailed the raiders to Chocolate Pass. The entire Chiricahua fighting force lay in wait, arranged in two groups designed to spring a trap from in front and the rear. The trap misfired when Mata Ortíz encountered the first contingent and led his men to a high hill and dug in. Even so, Geronimo and Juh brought all their men to bear on the position. They stormed up the slope in the face of intense fire and swarmed among the defenders, fighting hand to hand. Mata Ortíz and all but one of his men perished. As the sole survivor fled on a horse, Geronimo shouted to let him go. He would bring more Mexicans to be slaughtered.[10]

Back in their mountain refuge of Bugatseka, Sonora, the people settled into camps among ridges and canyons so treacherous they doubted that Mexican troops could penetrate. Juh, however, grew nervous and led about 350 people, including Naiche, Chatto, Bonito, and Loco, into more rugged country to the south, near the Aros River. Geronimo and Chihuahua, with about 250 people, stayed at Bugatseka. Here they maintained their base camp for the first six months of 1883. Throughout January 1883 Geronimo and Chihuahua led a raiding party west to villages along the Bavispe and Yaqui Rivers and returned with ample plunder and fresh herds of stock.[11]

Juh had likewise launched some devastating raids in Sonora during December 1882 and January 1883. Still more fearful of Mexican troops than Geronimo, after the raids he decided to relocate his winter camp from Guaynopa to another mountain hideout about twenty-five miles to the west, in Sonora. On January 24, 1883, Mexican troops, most of them deadly Tarahumari Indians on the Mexican payroll, found him. They launched a surprise dawn attack, sweeping through the ranchería. Juh's young son Daklugie, awakened by a blazing brush arbor, emerged from his wickiup to see charging horsemen. "They dashed through the camp, firing as they came." The people grabbed their children and ran from the camp. Once secured, the men returned to battle the Mexicans but failed to drive them out. The Chiricahuas lost fourteen dead, and the Mexicans took away thirty-seven captives. The dead included Juh's wife and son-in-law and Bonito's wife and child. Among the captives were Chatto's wife and two children and two wives and two children of Geronimo's (one must have been the nameless

Chiricahua/Nednhi who later appears under the name Mañanita, the other Shitsha-she). Among Juh's personal following only four fighters still lived.[12]

Juh had never sustained such a devastating defeat or such a huge personal loss. He never regained his stature as a tribal leader or his own self-esteem. The destitute survivors straggled into Geronimo's stronghold at Bugatseka. Geronimo was now clearly the supreme leader, even though Juh pretended that he retained his former influence.

With provisions and rifles and ammunition running low, the Chiricahuas at Bugatseka plotted two raids to remedy the shortages. Geronimo and Chihuahua led seventy-five to eighty men in a sweep through towns along the Sonora River, their objective to obtain stock and provisions. Chatto and Bonito led twenty-six men in a raid through southern Arizona to gather weapons and cartridges.[13]

Not since Geronimo had descended on San Carlos and spirited Loco and his people back to Mexico in April 1882 had any depredations fallen on southern Arizona. All the Chiricahua plunders until Chatto's raid in late March 1883 had fallen on Chihuahua and Sonora. Taken by surprise, army units in Arizona and New Mexico scrambled in futile search for the Chiricahuas.[14]

Chatto's raiders crossed the boundary near the Huachuca Mountains and swept east across southern Arizona and into New Mexico. They killed anyone they encountered and struck at any target likely to yield arms and ammunition. In six days they traveled four hundred miles, killed eleven whites, lost one man and another who deserted to return to San Carlos, and slipped back into Mexico with stolen stock and large quantities of arms and ammunition. Not a soldier had seen them.

Geronimo and Chihuahua and Chatto and Bonito had vastly surpassed their purpose. The triumphant raids in Sonora, combined with those in Arizona and New Mexico, provided all the Chiricahuas in Bugatseka needed, and more. Euphoric, they celebrated with dances, feasts, and ceremonies.

Little did they know of the forces gathering in Arizona that would drown their euphoria.

SIXTEEN

GERONIMO CONFRONTS CROOK
IN THE SIERRA MADRE, 1883

THE GENERAL WHO REPLACED Orlando Willcox as commander of the Department of Arizona on September 4, 1882, brought a fresh and unorthodox persona back to Arizona, after a five-year absence. Making extensive use of Indian scouts and pack trains, in 1872–73 Brigadier General George Crook had defeated and rounded up all the Apaches but the Chiricahuas, who had remained safe on the Chiricahua Reservation established by General O. O. Howard.

Unlike other generals, Crook believed that only an Apache could catch an Apache, so he placed more confidence in Apache scouts than regular troops. He also regarded pack mules rather than wagon trains as the key to mobility; mules could go anywhere, wagons could not. Unorthodoxy likewise dominated his character and appearance. He closely held his own counsel, rarely sharing his views and plans even with his staff. He rode a mule and carried a shotgun. As a lieutenant assigned to Fort Apache in 1884 recalled in retirement: "Crook was not particular in dress. He loved being in the field but then delighted in accompanying the pack train, dressing as the packers did, in a dirty brown canvas suit, with his flowing beard in two braids, wrapped in red tape. He slept and ate with the packers."

Young officers did not particularly like Crook, according to this source. A story made the rounds that Crook had once said of officers just out of West Point that he "had more use for a good pack mule than a second lieutenant."

Yet he relied heavily on bright junior officers who demonstrated insight into Indian culture, and he knew how to command their respect.[1]

Crook parted with almost all who dealt with Apaches in sympathizing with their mistreatment by the government. After touring the White Mountain Reservation shortly after taking command, he wrote that only after a second visit could he get his old enemies to talk frankly with him. "The simple story of their wrongs," he reported, "as told by the various representatives of their bands, under circumstances that convinced me they were speaking the truth, satisfied me that the Apaches had not only the best of reasons for complaining, but had displayed remarkable forbearance in remaining at peace." He added, "They have been openly plundered of the supplies provided them by the Government and they spoke with bitterness of nearly every one of their agents."[2]

Crook chose two enterprising junior officers to command Indian scouts: Captain Emmet Crawford at San Carlos and Lieutenant Charles B. Gatewood at Fort Apache. He instructed them to discharge all the scouts and recruit new companies to oversee conditions on the reservations. When not actually in the field, they were to live with their native groups, the better to keep them under observation. Crawford and Gatewood were to report directly to Crook.[3]

Emmet Crawford would play a vital role in Crook's operations for three years. Tall, dedicated to his profession, smart, and physically imposing, he enjoyed the confidence and respect of his men. Duty above all ruled his actions, and he could not be deflected from what he considered his duty.[4]

Gatewood, "tall, spare, of extraordinary endurance, patient and fearless," had commanded an Apache scout company since the Victorio War. He knew Apaches better than any other officer. They liked and respected him. Often in ill health, he strove so hard to protect the reservation from white encroachments that he became entangled in civil litigation. His frequent absence performing what were the civil agent's responsibilities and fighting lawsuits alienated General Crook.[5]

Crook's most challenging problem lay not with the reservation Indians but with the Chiricahuas in Mexico. They had to be dug out of the Sierra Madre and returned to the reservation. Even before Chatto's devastating raid sparked outrage in Arizona and New Mexico, Crook had begun to put in place his plan for accomplishing that mission.

A stroke of good fortune awarded Crook a reliable guide into the Chiricahua strongholds. On March 31, 1883, Lieutenant Britton Davis, another
bright young officer trusted by Crook, arrested the Chiricahua (a White
Mountain married to a Chiricahua) who had slipped away from the Chatto-
Bonito raiding party and made his way to San Carlos. He was Tzoe, but his
light complexion led whites to name him "Peaches." Tzoe knew the Sierra
Madre intimately, and he knew where the Chiricahuas most likely would be
found. He agreed to serve as Crook's guide.[6]

Other priorities challenged Crook as he based himself in Willcox and began to assemble his expedition. He had orders from General Sherman to ignore departmental and national boundaries. The United States and Mexico
had concluded a treaty providing for the troops of both nations to cross the
border when "in hot pursuit." Clearly, Crook would not be in hot pursuit
when he crossed the border. He therefore visited the governors and ranking
military officers of both Sonora and Chihuahua and found them not only
receptive to his crossing but eager to cooperate.

Another daunting priority was to find Charley McComas. In the last
stages of their foray, the Chatto-Bonito raiders had spotted a buckboard
parked beneath a tree on the road from Silver City to Lordsburg, New
Mexico. Its occupants had spread a picnic lunch on the ground and rested as
they ate. They were Judge Hamilton C. McComas, his wife, and their six-
year-old son, Charley. The family saw the approaching Indians, jumped back
in the buckboard, and turned back toward Silver City. The Apaches easily
gunned down the judge, smashed his wife's skull, and took Charley captive.
Bonito claimed the boy, and as the Indians rode away, Charley bounced behind Bonito on his mount, tied to his captor's belt with a piece of rope.[7]

More than any of the other depredations of Chatto and Bonito, the
slaughter of the McComas family enraged Arizonans and New Mexicans;
they knew nothing of Crook's impending expedition, but they demanded
that he find and liberate young Charley. The general and his officers felt deep
sympathy for the boy and determined to do all in their power to discover
his fate.

While Crook conferred with authorities in Mexico, a formidable force of
cavalry assembled at Willcox. Lieutenant Gatewood, who had been ordered
to enlist seventy more scouts at San Carlos (San Carlos Apaches, neither
Chiricahua nor White Mountain), arrived with the scouts. Captain Craw-

ford already had his scouts on the border. When Crook returned to Willcox, the command moved quickly to the boundary at San Bernardino Springs. Crawford and his scouts had arrived, as had more cavalry, affording Crook nine troops, with more expected. He distributed the cavalry along the boundary to block any attempt of the Chiricahuas to raid again in Arizona. He took with him into Mexico on May 1, 1883, one troop of cavalry (forty-two strong) under Captain Adna R. Chaffee and 193 Apache scouts under Captain Crawford and Lieutenant Gatewood. Crook considered the scouts, not the cavalry, the key to success, and his pack train of more than 350 mules and seventy-six packers the key to penetrating the heart of the Sierra Madre. Among others in Crook's entourage were his longtime aide, Lieutenant John G. Bourke; Chief of Scouts Al Sieber, aided by Archie McIntosh and Sam Bowman; and Interpreter Mickey Free (the youth Lieutenant Bascom accused Cochise of abducting, reared by Apaches).[8]

The route lay down the San Bernardino River, then up the eastern arm of the Bavispe River. The column made its way through riverside villages such as Bavispe, Bacerac, and Huachenera. Bourke described them as squalid and the inhabitants impoverished, victims of repeated Apache raids.

On May 7 the expedition turned east, toward the dark, forbidding heights pointed to by Peaches. Day after day, exhausted and dripping sweat, the men labored up and down in terrain nearly beyond endurance. One looming ridge after another, each separated by a deep canyon and each rising higher than the last, led into the heart of the Sierra Madre—country that more than one officer characterized as "indescribable." Mules slipped on narrow trails and plunged to their deaths far below, taking precious supplies with them. The Apache scouts put the whites to shame. They sprinted about the slopes and into the forests, hunting game, finding increasingly abundant Chiricahua sign, and enjoyed the evening dancing and singing.[9]

Peaches led them still farther up, to the sources of the Bavispe River and toward the place the Chiricahuas called Bugatseka. Crook advanced cautiously, basing his cavalry and packs at one site while Crawford and fifty of his scouts scoured the tangled ridges and gorges ahead. When Crawford sent word to move forward, Crook established another base as Crawford continued to scout. On May 15, a few eager young scouts came unexpectedly on two Chiricahuas and opened fire. They had uncovered the ranchería of Chatto and Bonito. All the fighting men had left on raids, but the scouts charged into the camp, firing as they went. They killed seven men (presumably, since they bore Winchester rifles) and captured two boys, one girl, and a young woman. The women had all fled, but the scouts burned twenty to thirty wickiups and brought back stock, provisions, and camp equipage.

The capture of the ranchería could hardly be characterized as a battle, or even a skirmish. But it put Crook on notice that further campaigning was useless. Once alerted, the Chiricahuas would scatter and not allow themselves to be surprised again. The general had to call off the campaign or find another means to round up the Indians. A possible solution lay in his captives.

The young woman claimed to be a daughter of Bonito. She said the Chiricahuas anxiously desired peace and had been talking of sending two emissaries to San Carlos to ask for terms. She added that her father had only recently returned from a raid. He had brought a little white boy, who was in the ranchería the scouts attacked. Crook gave the woman provisions and allowed her to take the older of the two boys and return to her people. He told her he would move camp to a place four miles distant, at the head of the Bavispe River, and wait for any overture the Apaches might make.[10]

As Crook climbed into the Sierra Madre, his scouts repeatedly assured him that the Chiricahuas had not discovered his approach. In fact, they had not. The fate of the ranchería stunned and demoralized the chiefs as they learned of it; they were widely scattered raiding. They had thought their strongholds impregnable. That American troops had found them seemed unbelievable. Moreover, Apache scouts—although not Chiricahuas—had found and seized the ranchería. The Chiricahuas proved receptive, some even eagerly, to the peace overture borne by Bonito's daughter.

All the leaders except one were absent on raids when the scouts fell on the ranchería. He was Chief Chihuahua, the independent-minded war leader with his own following. During the Victorio War he had served as an army scout. Women and even a few men made their way down to Crook's camp on the Bavispe. On May 17 a sister of Chihuahua appeared. She said Chihuahua would come in to talk if the general would send him a white horse that had been seized in the attack on the ranchería. Crook had the horse brought out and turned over to the woman. "Go to Chihuahua and tell him that we have only come to take his people back to San Carlos and not make war."[11]

Chihuahua appeared the next day, May 18, but in a spectacular manner. In the attack on the ranchería, a San Carlos Apache scout had shot and killed an old woman trying to surrender. She was Chihuahua's aunt. Scout John Rope described the scene:

> We could see someone riding that white horse over some rocky places at the foot of the mountain. It was Chihuahua, and he rode fast to our camp. On the end of his horse's tail was tied a strip of red cloth, and another strip of red cloth hung from under the bridle. In his belt he wore two pistols, and in his hand he carried a lance with a strip of red cloth tied around its end. He rode toward some of us scouts who were sitting under some oak trees. We all jumped up, not knowing what he intended to do. He asked where the head officer was, and we told him. Then he ran his horse right through us to Crook's tent. He rode through soldiers and scouts alike, and they had to get out of his way. Mickey Free and Si-bi-ya-na [Serviano], who were interpreters, followed him to Crook's place. Chihuahua got off his horse in front of the tent, and he shook hands with Crook. He said, "If you want me for a friend, why did you kill that old woman, my aunt? If I was trying to make friends with someone, I would not go and raid their camp and shoot their relatives. It seems to me that you are lying when you speak about being friends." Now they gave him some tobacco and some food to take back with him. He got on his horse and rode off fast, right through us, the way he had come.[12]

Unknown to Crook, the slaying of Chihuahua's aunt had another consequence. No Chiricahua ever admitted it, but at Carlisle Indian School Chihuahua's daughter, an eyewitness, told Jason Betzinez that the woman's son "was so enraged by this that he turned, and using rocks, brutally killed the small white captive Charley McComas. The Apaches of this group later told the soldiers that the little boy had run off into the brush and was never found." This finally emerged as the official conclusion, and it remained the standard belief until Betzinez told of the incident at Carlisle.[13]

Despite his blustery entrance into Crook's camp and his tough talk with the general, Chihuahua conceded that the discovery of the Chiricahua sanctuary by American soldiers and Apache scouts had convinced his people that returning to San Carlos was the best course of action. "It's no good, all these scouts and soldiers here," he had told his people. His decision, reached without consulting any other chiefs, had the desired effect. Chiricahua families began drifting into Crook's camp each day, while Chihuahua departed to round up his people.

The other chiefs had yet to appear. In fact, on the very day the scouts seized Chatto and Bonito's ranchería, Geronimo and his men raided in Chihuahua about 120 miles distant. That night, around a campfire, Geronimo demonstrated the Power that gave him much of his influence. As Betzinez related it, "Geronimo was sitting next to me with a knife in one hand and a chunk of beef which I had cooked for him in the other. All at once he dropped the knife, saying, 'Men, our people who we left at our base camp are now in the hands of U.S. troops! What shall we do?' . . . I cannot explain it to this day, but I was there and I saw it."[14]

On the morning of May 20 Geronimo and a large following appeared on a rocky bluff above Crook's camp. Unlike the blustery Chihuahua, who had galloped into Crook's camp and castigated him, Geronimo hung back. He sent word to Crook that he wanted to talk with him. Crook dispatched Peaches to say that they could come in without fear. Throughout the day Chiricahuas dribbled in, adding to the many who had already gathered. Not until evening, however, could Geronimo bring himself to descend from the bluff. He sat on a log near Crook's campfire as other leaders, a few at a time, seated themselves beside him. Finally Geronimo sidled up to Crook and, through Mickey Free, said he wanted to talk. Crook continued his meal without replying while Geronimo nervously waited. Finally, disdainfully, Crook pointed to all the Chiricahuas who had come in and invited Geronimo to observe how many of his own people had surrendered. He could do as he liked, "choose peace or war as you please." Seemingly chastened, Geronimo returned to the log and waited while the general went about his business. After about an hour Geronimo tried again, pleading to be returned to San Carlos. Crook again waved him off with the admonition to surrender unconditionally or fight.[15]

Early the next morning Geronimo tried again. Crook received him contemptuously and upbraided him for all the trouble and misery he had caused. Geronimo protested, but to no avail. Crook pointed out that he had allowed all the men to keep their rifles, to demonstrate that he had no fear of them. Now, he said, they wanted him to take them back to San Carlos and defend them against angry white people. At length, Geronimo resignedly concluded, "We give up, do with us as you please."[16]

How to account for Geronimo's submissive behavior? Crook had resolved to take a hard line with the Chiricahuas. Chihuahua did not even give him the chance. But Geronimo seemed thoroughly cowed, perhaps because he was still shocked that his own people had led the general to one of his hiding places. Or it may have registered another of his mood swings, from aggressive to intimidated. Or the knowledge that he now had to elude Apache scouts led him to permit Crook to bully him simply to gain return to the safety of the reservation. Geronimo's motives are rarely understandable.

Crook had to begin the return march at once. His supplies ran low, and he could not feed even the Chiricahuas who went with him. Some stolen cattle, however, eased the shortage. On June 11, 1883, Crook crossed the boundary with 325 Chiricahuas—fifty-two men and 273 women and children. About two hundred remained behind, including most of the fighting men. Geronimo, Naiche, Chihuahua, Chatto, and others explained that they had to round up their scattered people. They promised to follow quickly. Geronimo even gave assurance that he would overtake Crook at the boundary—a blatant falsehood. Of the leaders, Crook had with him only old Nana, Loco, and Bonito. Whether or not he believed it, for the record Crook predicted that the rest of the Chiricahuas would soon arrive at San Carlos.

Crook had barely crossed into Arizona when he confronted another crisis. On June 14, 1883, Secretary of the Interior Henry M. Teller informed Secretary of War Robert T. Lincoln that the Chiricahuas who had surrendered to Crook would not be received at San Carlos. They were a murderous crowd who would only make trouble with the peaceful Indians and eventually break out again. They ought to be turned over to civil authority and punished. Behind this emphatic decision lay the opposition of Agent Philip P. Wilcox. A Denver politician, he had received the San Carlos appointment solely because of his friendship with Secretary Teller (a former Colorado senator), and he made no secret of his motive: to enrich himself and his kin as fully as possible. He succeeded, even though the San Carlos summers drove him back to Denver for the season. He and his son-in-law, appointed agency trader and allied with corrupt contractors, harvested immense profits. Now Wilcox stirred up the reservation Indians with dire predictions of the trouble the returning Chiricahuas would cause. He refused to receive them, and Secretary Teller backed him.[17]

Secretary Lincoln stalled, protesting that Crook had not yet been heard from and had to be consulted. Crook, however, had read about the issue in the newspapers and on June 20 telegraphed his division commander, Major General John M. Schofield, of the consequences if even word of the order leaked to the Indians. Already deeply suspicious and distrustful, they would stampede back to Mexico, and the ones who had remained behind would not come in. A flurry of telegrams followed as Crook continued his march. Sending the Chiricahuas forward under Captain Crawford, Crook returned to his headquarters in Prescott. Crawford took four troops of cavalry and the Indian scouts and carried orders to hold the Chiricahuas together with the scouts until a solution could be worked out. With Wilcox protesting mightily from Denver, Crawford reached San Carlos on June 23.[18]

Summoned to Washington, on July 7, 1883, Crook sat at a table with the two cabinet secretaries and the commissioner of Indian affairs to work out an accommodation. Of course, no one dared challenge Crook. No ranking officer knew the Apaches as well, and none commanded their trust and respect. The entire army chain of command, especially General Schofield, solidly backed Crook. The conferees worked out a memorandum of agreement, which both Teller and Lincoln signed. All the Chiricahuas who came in with Crook, together with all who followed, would remain under control of the War Department and be placed on the White Mountain Reservation wherever Crook decided, except at the San Carlos Agency. This appeared to afford a workable solution, but the agreement went further. It also placed the police control of all the White Mountain Apaches under the War Department, which was also charged with protecting the agent in the discharge of all his usual duties except for police control. In other words, Crook would discipline, command, and punish the Indians while the agent would tend the books and take care of purely civil matters.[19]

The memorandum of July 7 provided an immediate resolution of the controversy. In the long term, it laid the groundwork for a severe conflict of authority between Captain Crawford, Crook's designee at San Carlos, and Wilcox and the agents who followed. Drawing a line between civil and military duties would prove impossible, especially when strong-minded men contended for supremacy.

The Chiricahua problem had hardly been solved. The principal leaders and fighting men had not yet crossed into Arizona. Geronimo had humbled himself before Crook and begged to be allowed to return to the reservation. Like other leaders, he had abjectly promised to come in as soon as he gathered all his people and stock. The promise quickly faded as soon as Crook marched down the mountain.

SEVENTEEN

RETURN TO SAN CARLOS, 1883–84

WHEN GENERAL CROOK LEFT Bugatseka early in June 1883 with Loco, Bonito, and their people, the chiefs who remained behind intended to keep their promise to follow. They had told the general they had to round up their scattered people before they could start, a sensible enough explanation. But they had other matters to attend to before the move to San Carlos, and that would take more time than simply gathering their people.[1]

Most pressing was the need for more horses and mules. Chatto had lost his herd when Crawford's scouts fell on his ranchería. "He knew it was hard to get stock at San Carlos," Captain Emmet Crawford later recalled him saying, "so that is why he remained out so long and stole stock from the Mexicans." Chatto's explanation glossed over raids lasting two weeks in June and targeting villages and ranches the length of the eastern branch of the Bavispe River, including Bavispe itself. Shortly after Chatto's return to Bugatseka, the Chiricahuas moved a short distance to the south and made camp. Here, late in June, Juh and his family appeared, thus uniting all the Chiricahuas in one place—190 people, including sixty fighting men.[2]

All the chiefs, now including Juh, reaffirmed their commitment to go to San Carlos. But as Zele recalled, "He saw Juh and all the chiefs all get together and said they had better see about their people [held captive] before they started for San Carlos." That meant another risky visit to Casas Grandes. First, though, they resolved on a sweeping raid into western Sonora, this time aiming at settlements on the Yaqui and Sonora Rivers. After days of summer storms, in July Geronimo, Chatto, Chihuahua, and Naiche led their men west. After crossing the Bavispe River, they divided into two parties. Geronimo led one. Moctezuma, Arispe, Nácori Chico, and other settlements bore the brunt of the rampage, taking Mexican lives as well as enough stock and plunder for the raiders to count the forays a resounding success. Reuniting, the two parties reached their base camp south of Bugatseka on August 9.[3]

Confirming the decision to go to Casas Grandes, soon after the return of the raiders in August, a woman named Mañanita, one of Geronimo's wives, appeared at the base camp. Taken prisoner by the Mexicans in the assault on Juh's ranchería the previous January, she had escaped from Chihuahua City. She had walked a perilous forty days into the Sierra Madre until instinct led her to the Chiricahua camp. She told of thirty-five other captives held in Chihuahua City. They included Chatto's wife and two children, Chihuahua's brother, and two wives of Geronimo (probably the one seized at Alisos Creek and the other taken in the attack on Juh's village). Bargaining with the Mexicans for the release of these people, hazardous as all knew it to be, had to be attempted before even thinking about San Carlos.[4]

By the end of August 1883 the Chiricahuas had made camp about fifteen miles from Casas Grandes. Indian women bore a message to a Mexican army camp outside the city saying that Geronimo, Naiche, Chatto, and Juh had come to make a treaty. A Mexican officer and four soldiers met with the chiefs near their ranchería. Juh stated that he wanted the grant of a huge section of land on which to plant seeds the government would provide along with agricultural training. Whether Juh actually thought the Mexicans would take this seriously may be doubted, but the Mexicans wanted to keep the Apaches nearby because, as always, they plotted a massacre.

Formal negotiations occurred twice during September. Geronimo spoke for the chiefs, demanding the return of their captives. The Mexicans stalled and tried to get all the leaders together at one time and place so they could spring an ambush. Meantime, the Apaches came and went in small groups or individually into the town to trade and usually to return with bottles of mescal generously provided by the Mexican officers.

The negotiations faltered because of Juh's sudden death. He drank copiously. As Zele recalled, "Juh was all the time drunk, and while on a spree ran his horse over a high bank and was killed." With slight variation, this is how all the Chiricahuas remembered it, although his son Daklugie later tried to revise the scene. Plainly, on September 21, 1883, a drunken Juh ran his horse off a steep trail and fell to his death in the Casas Grandes River. He either drowned or died in the fall.

The great Nednhi chief Juh, friend of Geronimo since youth and partner in war and peace since early manhood, had lost most of his influence after the Mexican troops surprised his ranchería in January 1883. He had been increasingly despondent ever since and drank more and more heavily. Some believed that he plotted his own death. Nonetheless, all the Chiricahuas mourned his passing.

Early in October the chiefs met a third time with Mexican officers. The officers had come prepared to exchange three Chiricahua captives for three Mexican captives. But the Mexicans had grown too impatient, and the Apaches, always suspicious, picked up on it at once. As Naiche remembered, "We found that about sixty soldiers had changed from their uniforms and put on old civilian citizens' clothes and had their guns hidden under their clothes." As they drifted in two bunches as if to surround the Indians, Geronimo turned to Kayatena and said, "We might as well go back, there are too many soldiers." He abruptly broke off the talks and, promising to return for another session in ten days, hastily withdrew. Although the Chiricahuas had no intention of returning, the Mexican commander still hoped at the next meeting to surround and wipe out the Apaches.[5]

Back at their camp after this near disaster, the chiefs to their surprise discovered Bonito and another man. After anxiously waiting for more than two months for the Chiricahuas who had remained in Mexico to show up at San Carlos, Captain Crawford obtained Crook's authorization to send Bonito and a companion to look for their tribesmen and find out why they had not come in. They left on August 25, 1883, and it was five weeks before they located their people near Casas Grandes. Bonito explained his mission to Naiche, who at once agreed to lead the way. About one hundred followed, including Chihuahua and Kayatena, while Ulzana (Chihuahua's brother), Chatto, and Zele hung back. That Geronimo sent his son Chappo to investigate conditions at San Carlos indicates that he was having second thoughts about honoring his promise to General Crook.[6]

Making their way through the Sierra Madre into Sonora, the group paused for long rests and headed toward San Bernardino Springs, where Bonito said soldiers would meet them with rations and provisions. Bonito sent his comrade forward to make contact. He found no soldiers there and made his way northwest to Fort Bowie, where he arrived on October 22. The next morning a troop of cavalry bearing rations rode out of Fort Bowie. On October 26, with troopers and scouts gathered from other points on the border, Lieutenant Britton Davis met the Chiricahuas at a designated rendezvous point ten miles north of the border. He counted seventy-nine men, women, and children. Others would follow in a few days, explained Naiche, especially Kayatena. In fact, Kayatena had joined Geronimo in another raid into Sonora. On November 16, the cavalry escort brought the people into San Carlos and turned them over to Captain Crawford. Two days later Kayatena crossed the border with a woman and ten men.[7]

Second Lieutenant Britton Davis, Third Cavalry, had graduated from West Point in 1881 and had already won the confidence of General Crook. He had not ranked high at the academy, but he had performed so admirably filling in for Captain Crawford at San Carlos during Crook's Mexican campaign that the general himself penned a special commendation. As commander of an Apache scout company at Fort Apache, he had learned quickly from the experienced Lieutenant Gatewood how to fit the mold artist Frederic Remington described as less "Indian fighter" than "Indian thinker." The epitome of a handsome, freshly commissioned young officer, Davis would serve Crook efficiently until, still a second lieutenant, he decided not to make a career in the army.[8]

None of the returning groups Davis met "surrendered." They had not surrendered to Crook, and now they retained their arms, traveled apart from the cavalry, and remained wary of treachery. Nor did they lay down their arms once arriving at San Carlos. As Crook and Crawford knew, these people had to be treated with respect and great caution.

Only the appearance of Geronimo and Chatto could quiet the scorn Crook continued to endure throughout Arizona or the impatience of his superiors in San Francisco and Washington. A report of the arrival of the two at the border turned out to be a mistake; it was Zele and his small following. Chatto would come soon and Geronimo would follow. For Chatto, "soon" turned out to be more than six weeks. On February 7, 1884, trailing a herd of eighty-nine stolen horses and mules, Chatto and fifteen men met Lieutenant Davis at San Bernardino Springs.[9]

Geronimo later declared that "he had remained in the mountains so long because he wanted to get some horses and cattle to bring here [San Carlos]." Although reports from Sonora in December and January confirmed this motive, it probably was not the principal reason. He had sent his son Chappo to see if he would be treated fairly at San Carlos and not, as Chappo expressed it to Crawford, "put in the calaboose." John P. Clum had done that to him, and he never forgot the humiliation. Almost certainly, Geronimo would return to San Carlos only if Chappo assured him he would be treated fairly. On December 11, 1883, Crawford dispatched Chappo with Chief Chihuahua to find Geronimo and bring him in.[10]

Finally, on February 26, 1884, Geronimo met Lieutenant Davis in New Mexico's Animas Valley, just east of Skeleton Canyon. He had left Bugatseka on January 26. Davis reported eight men and twenty-two women and children, with two more men expected the next day. Also with the party were Chihuahua, Chappo, and the other man who had been sent from San Carlos to look up Geronimo. His son's assurance that he would be well treated at San Carlos seems to have persuaded Geronimo to reach the difficult decision.

Like Chatto, Zele, and others who had already crossed the border, Geronimo trailed a herd of a hundred horses and mules. But he also herded 133 cattle stolen from Casa de Janos. Geronimo divided them among his men. Anxious to get back to San Carlos, Davis had planned a short route that could be traveled quickly. But the cattle needed grasslands, and Davis had to settle for a longer route around the southern tip of the Chiricahua Mountains and down the Sulphur Springs Valley. He made long daily marches. Geronimo protested that such haste wore fat off the cattle; he wanted to go slower. Since the abolition of the Chiricahua Reservation, the country had been occupied by ranchers, and Davis knew the journey to be full of risk.[11]

It was. The caravan—Davis's scouts and pack train, Geronimo's stock and cattle—reached Sulphur Springs Ranch on March 4. Davis's friend and West Point classmate, Lieutenant William "Bo" Blake, arrived from Fort Bowie with fifteen cavalrymen to help escort Geronimo to San Carlos. All made separate camps around the ranch building and the springs. Two civilians lingering at the ranch engaged Davis in friendly conversation, then revealed who they were and what they intended. John E. Clark, deputy collector of customs, and William P. Howard, special inspector of customs, had come to seize Geronimo's cattle, which they said had been illegally brought into the United States without paying duty. They had no official paper but had scribbled an explanation of how the law had been violated on a piece of notepaper.

Davis countered that Geronimo would fight before he would surrender the cattle. The customs officers stood firm, threatening to send to Willcox for a posse. Davis persuaded them to wait until the next day while he dispatched a courier to Willcox to telegraph for General Crook's instructions. Lieutenant Blake produced a quart of Scotch whiskey, and the military and civil officers spent a convivial evening until the customs agents walked off for a sound night's sleep.

Blake and Davis had already hatched a scheme for dealing with the crisis. They walked over to the Apache camp and tried to persuade Geronimo to steal away with his stock. No, he would fight, responded Geronimo. Davis observed that his plan probably would not work anyway, for the Apaches could not sneak away with the herd without waking the customs officers. What a great joke it would be if they could, though, he added. When Geronimo "almost smiled," the officers knew they had succeeded. Blake had a year's seniority on Davis, so he assumed command. Davis remained at the ranch to confront the civilians when they awoke. Blake and his cavalry accompanied Geronimo.

The next morning the surprised customs officers discovered that they had been tricked. They wanted to know where the Apaches and the stock had gone. Davis could only answer that he did not know. Moreover, nowhere they scanned with binoculars from the ranch roof could anyone spot a dust cloud. Accompanied by Blake, the Apaches had swung west into the San Pedro Valley and made their way north. Lieutenant Davis caught up with them, and on March 16, 1884, he and Blake turned the Apaches, and their stock and cattle, over to Captain Crawford at San Carlos.[12]

Nearly eight months after promising General Crook to settle again at San Carlos, Geronimo had kept his promise. "Honored" is too strong a word, for the eight months cost Mexicans dearly in life and property, caused continuing anxiety in the US military chain of command, and stirred Arizonans (and their newspapers) into frenzied abuse of General Crook.

Once more a "reservation Indian," Geronimo would lead what observers believed a cooperative and contented life. It would last little more than a year before the final breakout.

EIGHTEEN

THE LAST BREAKOUT, 1885

GERONIMO HAD BEEN ON at San Carlos only five days when he gave the customary statement of Chiricahua leaders arriving from Mexico. His opening sentence put Captain Emmet Crawford on notice that Geronimo would be likely to make trouble. After begging General Crook to receive him at San Carlos, he had passed nearly a year tearing up Mexico and apparently thinking little about returning to the reservation. He had shed his humbling experience with Crook and, speaking directly to Captain Crawford, set forth in great detail his expectations. "Geronimo said that he has come here with the understanding that everything he asked for was to be granted him."[1]

After a rambling discourse testifying to his pleasure at once more living at peace on the reservation, praising General Crook as God, and promising complete submission to authority, he repeated several times that Crook had promised him he could have anything he wanted and live wherever he wanted. The line around the reservation should be removed and his people allowed to settle on Eagle Creek and its tributaries. Whites who owned land there could be bought out. This country contained plenty of water, animals, and farming land. It would be ideal. He was "astonished"—he used the word repeatedly—that his wishes were not promptly granted (he had been at San Carlos only five days).

Geronimo also revealed a trait that had dogged him for years. He believed that "bad people" constantly conspired against him. He was gullible enough

149

to believe every rumor and "story" that reached his ears. He believed Chief George, he said, when he came among the Chiricahuas and told of soldiers coming to arrest the people, a story that triggered the outbreak of 1881. Twice he admonished Captain Crawford not to believe bad things told by bad people. "If in future some one tells anything bad about him, he wants to know right away who it is that is telling bad things about him." "If these Indians around San Carlos [that is, other Apache groups] come here after I leave and talk about me, I don't want you [Crawford] to believe them." This tendency, an element of the suspicion and distrust that had long ruled his relations with other Apaches and especially with all Mexicans and Americans, characterized his life on the reservation and played a significant part in his last breakout.[2]

Geronimo at once learned that he could not have all he wished. Captain Crawford confiscated his entire herd of cattle. All bore Mexican brands and became the subject of correspondence between the War and State Departments and the Mexican government. On July 26, 1884, Crawford held a public auction at San Carlos and disposed of the cattle. He turned the proceeds over to the Treasury Department for the State Department to draw on to meet claims of Mexican owners. Geronimo believed that his cattle were legitimate spoils of war, no different from horses and mules.[3]

The Chiricahuas camped across the San Carlos River from the agency, the same place Loco and his people had occupied before their abduction in 1882—supposedly the healthiest place on the Gila River. Nowhere on the Gila was healthy. Sandy, hot, infested with insects and thorny vegetation, malarial in places, almost unlivable in the summer, anywhere else seemed preferable. Even before Geronimo reached San Carlos, the chiefs favored Turkey Creek, in the White Mountains seventeen miles southwest of Fort Apache. Although Geronimo argued vehemently against this area in his interview with Crawford, the Chiricahuas decided on Turkey Creek. Early in May 1884 the move took place. This was White Mountain country. Lieutenant Britton Davis served as the Chiricahuas' military agent. At nearby Fort Apache, Lieutenant Charles Gatewood presided as agent over the White Mountain Apaches.

General Crook followed the procession of 520 Chiricahuas to their new home. En route, he held a council with all the leaders and concluded that "they are all satisfied and contented and will give no further trouble if fairly treated." Geronimo declared that he had stored in his head all Crook had told him in the Sierra Madre and would do so with what he said now. But he wanted Crook to remember what Geronimo said. In essence, this meant that Crook was now their Great Father, and he should guide them in their new life and treat them consistently and fairly. In these words, Geronimo probably spoke more sincerely than in his rant to Crawford in the first interview.

In his annual report in September, Crook remained optimistic, which reflected Crawford's optimism. The planting had gone well, he wrote with some exaggeration, and remarked that Geronimo and Chatto had made the most progress and maintained the best-tilled fields.[4]

Closer to the Chiricahuas than Crawford and Crook, Lieutenant Davis did not perceive the Apache leaders as contented. "The more suspicious and intractable" made their camps several miles away from where Davis pitched a large hospital tent to serve as his storehouse and a smaller tent next to it for his living quarters. He named these malcontents as Mangas, Chihuahua, and Geronimo. Kayatena, by contrast, located his people on a ridge just above Davis's camp, where he could watch everything that happened.[5]

Kayatena had been expected to cause trouble even before he came in. A fierce, independent war leader, he had never been on a reservation and never experienced any restraint by white officials. Before Geronimo arrived, while the Chiricahuas lived at San Carlos, Kayatena declared that he had lost all his horses and other property in gambling and that he was going on the warpath. Crawford dared not take severe action because it would likely stampede Geronimo and lead to another outbreak. The captain managed to smooth the affair over, although Kayatena continued to talk of war. After Geronimo had arrived, however, during a dance at Turkey Creek on June 21, Kayatena had some trouble with his wife and threatened to leave. Seeking an excuse to rid himself of Kayatena, Davis at once had him arrested by his scouts and sent to San Carlos.[6]

Official reports glossed over further proceedings by noting simply that he was tried by an Indian jury and banished to Alcatraz Prison in San Francisco Bay. In fact, Crawford acted as prosecutor and judge, and San Carlos Apache chiefs eager to please Crawford composed the jury. Of course the jury found him guilty of fomenting unrest. After some telegraphic exchanges between Crawford and Crook, Kayatena set forth under escort for Alcatraz. Both Crook and his division commander, Major General John Pope, began to have second thoughts about the legality of trying and imprisoning Kayatena. When Crook visited the Chiricahuas in the fall of 1884, he talked of freeing

Kayatena to return to his people. The chiefs objected, none more forcefully than Geronimo and Chatto. They had enjoyed the absence of the kind of turmoil Kayatena stirred. Crook left Kayatena at Alcatraz.

That General Crook had promised the Chiricahuas to do all in his power to secure the release of their people held in Mexico gained him their respect and friendship. The Chiricahuas may have looked to Crook, as they claimed, to guide them into the new way of life. But some of his guidance they abhorred. They regarded their traditional way of life as their own business, and any intrusive rules offended them. One was to forbid the custom of beating a wife for any offense and for cutting off her nose as punishment for adultery. Also, however, Crook insisted on banning tiswin: no more processing of corn by expert Apache women to produce the intoxicant that fueled tiswin drunks. Both had long been traditional in Apache culture, and the Indians strongly resented any interference with them. They emphatically informed Davis of their attitude. Yet he had the duty of enforcing these rules, by persuasion, reprimand, or even jail time. The Chiricahuas continued to do as they pleased. In less than a year, tiswin would produce a crisis.

To police his charges, Davis obtained authority to discharge his entire company of Apache scouts, mostly White Mountain. He then rebuilt a unit of thirty Chiricahuas, the very ones who had come in from Mexico. Most notably, he appointed Chatto as first sergeant.

Like Geronimo a Bedonkohe, but twenty years younger, a nephew of Mangas Coloradas, Chatto had grown up to wield great influence. He had a strong and cunning mind, a splendid physique, and the courage of a successful Apache fighting man. Kicked in the face by a mule, he acquired the name Chatto (Flat Nose). Before returning to the reservation, he ravaged Mexico as fiercely as any Chiricahua and led the most successful raid into Arizona. Now he abruptly concluded that the white man's way was best and switched sides to serve in the US Army, which he did competently and loyally. Chatto and Geronimo had fallen apart over some issue and remained hostile to each other for the rest of their lives. Into old age Chatto would disparage Geronimo.[7]

If Chatto and Geronimo had not collided already, Chatto's new role as first sergeant of scouts widened the gulf between them. Geronimo believed that Chatto and interpreter Mickey Free told "bad stories" about him. They may have. That such stories, whether false, true, or exaggerated, influenced Lieutenant Davis is possible.

Chief Chihuahua enlisted in the scout company, as did relatives of Geronimo, including his son Chappo, now twenty. He insisted on the post of Davis's "striker," the enlisted man assigned to every officer as a servant, because it paid an extra five dollars. "The hardest work he did," recalled Davis, "was saddling my mule, smoking my cigarettes, and loafing around Sam Bowman's cook tent."

From among the scouts, Davis selected three "secret agents." No one knew who they were. At night, if one had something to report, a pebble struck the canvas side of Davis's tent, and the agent quietly entered to report.[8]

Chihuahua later learned of the secret agents and also picked up tales that Chatto and Mickey Free tried to poison Davis's mind enough to get the chiefs sent to Alcatraz to join Kayatena—the "bad stories" Geronimo complained of for the rest of his life. Angry, Chihuahua barged into Davis's tent and announced, "I am quit." Davis remonstrated. Chihuahua threw down his scout uniform and equipment and declared, "Now, give them to your spies. I won't scout any longer."[9]

During their absence in Mexico, the predictable result of the memorandum of agreement of July 7, 1883, giving Crook police control of the White Mountain Reservation kept it in a state of turmoil. Captain Crawford and Agent Philip P. Wilcox repeatedly collided, with Wilcox accusing the rigid, dedicated captain of overstepping his authority. The conflict over one incident after another produced reams of official documents involving each level of authority up to the cabinet secretaries. Sometimes Crawford did interpret police control too liberally and irritated Secretary of War Robert T. Lincoln enough that he once suggested that Crawford be replaced. Finally, on April 21, 1884, less than a week after Geronimo's arrival, Crook responded to Crawford's formal application for a court of inquiry. The panel of three officers reviewed the voluminous records and took the testimony of most of the participants in the feud. Not surprisingly, on July 14, 1884, the court duly concluded that "the Crawford administration of affairs at San Carlos has been wise, just, and for the best interests of the Indians."[10]

The military finding resolved nothing. The quarrel continued with growing intensity until November 1884, when Wilcox resigned in despair. Charles D. Ford, an honest and competent agent, replaced the corrupt and incompetent Wilcox, only to face an escalating conflict with Crawford. Although Crook firmly backed Crawford, in February 1885 Secretary Lincoln overruled

Crawford in a major dispute. The captain asked to be relieved and returned to his regiment. Captain Francis E. Pierce replaced him early in March.

The long-running battle between Crawford and the two agents had its roots less in a highly competent officer determined to do his duty as he saw it than in the fundamental premise of the memorandum of agreement assigning him police control. Divided authority doomed it. Although Captain Pierce still held police powers, he proved much more flexible and less confrontational than Crawford. Distant in the mountains near Fort Apache, the Chiricahuas rarely felt the direct impact of any of the issues. Even so, the tumult at San Carlos added to the unrest already created by Lieutenant Davis's effort to stop wife-beating and tiswin-making.

The lieutenant's interference in Chiricahua customs did not reach crisis proportions at Turkey Creek. The people scattered among the forested creeks and valleys, farmed half-heartedly, and behaved much as they pleased, including regular tiswin drunks. Some of the leaders visited with Davis, First Sergeant Chatto daily. Nana and Loco came often to talk and relate their history and achievements to the young officer. Geronimo, Chihuahua, and Naiche never appeared.

Snow and freezing temperatures struck early in November 1884. Davis gathered the people and moved them to the lower elevation at Fort Apache. Three miles up White River, Davis pitched a comfortable walled tent while the Indians spread into the foothills and canyons along the river. Through a bitterly cold winter, they had nothing to occupy them. As the months passed, according to Davis, they "drew their rations, gambled, loafed, and quarreled." He might have added that they indulged in more tiswin drunks than they had on Turkey Creek. Davis informed Crawford, "We are having a great deal of trouble this winter with tiswin parties. The Apache calaboose has quite a number of Chiricahua and White Mountain Apaches in it under that charge." Scoldings were tolerable; jail time stoked increasing resentment.[11]

With the coming of spring 1885, the planting season began. Davis noted that women did most of the work. He regarded Geronimo's effort as typical. He invited Davis to see his farm in the White River bottom. Davis could not go that day, but he inspected the blister that Geronimo proudly displayed on his palm. The next morning Davis rode out to the farm. Geronimo "was sitting on a rail in the shade of a tree with one of his wives fanning him. The other two were hoeing a quarter-acre patch of partially cleared ground, in which a few sickly looking sprouts of corn were struggling for life." Davis pronounced no blame. The land was ill-suited for farming, and Apache women had always done the hard labor.[12] (The wives would have been Mañanita, Ziyeh, and another wife, Ith-tedda. She was a Mescalero residing at San Carlos when Geronimo married her, probably in 1884.)

Both at Turkey Creek and Fort Apache, Geronimo continued to evoke contradictory opinions. By the spring of 1885, about the time of visiting his farm, Davis judged him "a thoroughly vicious, intractable, and treacherous man." General Crook, who had praised his farming in the summer of 1884, regarded him as "vindictive, cruel, and crafty." On the other hand, Lieutenant James Parker, stationed at Fort Apache, recalled of that period that "Geronimo we saw constantly; he was friendly and good natured." He remembered an incident when the post surgeon, Dr. W. R. Fisher, tried to light a cigarette by rubbing two sticks together. He asked Geronimo how to do it. When "he came to understand what Fisher was driving at, he fell into paroxysms of laughter at the thought that a white man could hope to produce fire with two damp twigs."[13]

Dr. Fisher figured in another incident that suggested an enigmatic Geronimo. He commanded high distinction as a curing shaman and regarded himself as a traditional "medicine man" versed in Apache healing techniques. Nevertheless, in September and again in December 1884 he went into Fort Apache and, "suffering intensely," consulted Dr. Fisher. The doctor diagnosed him with "a *local* venereal disease," not with the type that led to syphilis. Fisher treated him regularly. Early in May 1885 Geronimo again visited Dr. Fisher, who pronounced him cured. Strangely, much as he believed in Apache ways and in his own powers, Geronimo sought treatment from an American doctor.[14]

In the early weeks of May 1885, as Geronimo learned from Dr. Fisher that American medicine had freed him of the painful venereal disease, the warming spring sun returned the Chiricahuas to their planting fields along White River east of Fort Apache. On May 11 Captain Pierce (Crawford's successor) came up from San Carlos to assess the farming efforts as well as the disposition of the Chiricahuas. The next morning, May 12, Pierce and Davis moved the Chiricahuas from the White River back to their old haunts at Turkey Creek, a much more congenial location now that the snows had melted. Apaches with farms near Fort Apache could periodically return to tend them. Pierce's visit, combined with the delight in returning to Turkey Creek, led to a grand feast in the afternoon.

The captain gathered the celebrants and told them how impressed he was with their behavior and promised to convey this sentiment to General Crook. Not to be outdone, the Indians responded. Naiche, always ready for a good time, "appeared in a long-tailed, senatorial 'jim-swinger' coat, and from the height of a new Studebaker wagon *he* made a speech about the blessings of peace. Even Geronimo talked along this line, if more briefly and with less enthusiasm." Pierce duly reported his heartening conclusion to Crook. These Indians could hardly be driven to the warpath.[15]

Only three days later events proved Captain Pierce wrong. On May 13, as Pierce made his way back to San Carlos and Davis returned to his base near Fort Apache, the Apache women at Turkey Creek began preparing tiswin for another party the next day. As often in the past, the wife of Mangas, Huera, concocted the tiswin; she was a renowned expert as well as a rabble-rouser. On May 14, before the party, Geronimo and Mangas began to feed each other's resentment of Lieutenant Davis and his acolytes, especially since Davis had lodged some of Geronimo's followers in jail for drinking tiswin. They decided the time had come to stand up to Davis, and they enlisted every chief in their cause. When the party got under way at the camp shared by Geronimo and Mangas, Naiche, Chihuahua, Loco, and Zele joined them in the conspiracy and in indulging in the usual tiswin drunk. They planned to confront Davis the next morning.

Conspicuously absent from the conspiracy was Chatto. In Mexico he had been one of the most aggressive raiders and had gained fame as a war leader. For thirty years, even though twenty years younger, he had been a close friend and companion of Geronimo's. Both Bedonkohes, both acolytes of Mangas Coloradas, they shared the common attitude toward Mexicans and whites— until the return to the reservation in 1884. Seemingly on his own, Chatto decided that the old ways would no longer work and that the future lay in casting his lot with the whites, especially General Crook. The general's promise to try to gain the release of the Chiricahuas held captive by the Mexicans, including Chatto's family, cemented his loyalty not only to Crook but to Davis. As first sergeant of Davis's scout company, he had clearly drawn the line. No longer could he be counted one of the leaders Geronimo and Mangas incited to defy Davis.[16]

As May 15 dawned, Davis awoke to find the Chiricahua leaders drawn up in front of his tent three miles from Fort Apache, most unarmed. About thirty Chiricahuas grouped behind them. Under Chatto, the scouts had gathered in knots of four or five, all armed. The chiefs said they had come for a talk.

First photograph of Geronimo, taken by A. Frank Randall at San Carlos in 1884, after Geronimo came in from Mexico following General Crook's campaign of 1883. (Courtesy Arizona Historical Society)

Chief Chihuahua, photographed at San Carlos by A. Frank Randall in 1884, after surrendering to General Crook in 1883. (Courtesy Arizona Historical Society)

First Lieutenant Charles B. Gatewood, Sixth Cavalry, in 1883. Stationed at Fort Apache, Gatewood commanded Apache Indian scouts and in 1886 played the critical role of putting two scouts in touch with Geronimo to help persuade him to surrender. (Courtesy Arizona Historical Society)

Apache scouts guarding a waterhole, 1886. (Courtesy Arizona Historical Society)

Brigadier General George Crook on his mule Apache, near Fort Bowie in 1886. He preferred to dress like his packers and carry a shotgun. (Courtesy Arizona Historical Society)

Fort Bowie, Arizona Territory, in 1886. Located near famed Apache Springs in Apache Pass, Fort Bowie was the nerve center for the operations of Generals Crook and Miles against Geronimo in 1885–86. It also figured importantly in Apache affairs from 1862 until 1886. The fort was abandoned in 1894. (Courtesy Arizona Historical Society)

Chief Chatto, one of the most accomplished and destructive Chiricahua raiders until he settled on the White Mountain Reservation following General Crook's Sierra Madre campaign of 1883. He chose the white man's way as the best and served as a skilled first sergeant of Apache scouts during the final campaigns against Geronimo. His reward was betrayal by the government and twenty-seven years as a prisoner of war. (Courtesy Arizona Historical Society)

Canyon de los Embudos, March 25, 1886. The first of three meetings between Crook and Geronimo. Uninvited Tombstone photographer C. S. Fly showed up and recorded a series of historic images. Geronimo is third from left, Crook second from right. Captain Bourke sits to Crook's right. All the officers have been identified. Among the Indians both seated and standing, those identified include Kayatena, Nana, Chihuahua, and Scout Sergeant Major Noche. (See Jay Van Orden, *Geronimo's Surrender* [Arizona Historical Society, 1991]; Courtesy Arizona Historical Society)

Geronimo at Canyon de los Embudos. He permitted C. S. Fly to wander among his followers and take a remarkable series of photographs. (Courtesy Arizona Historical Society)

Geronimo asked Fly to take this picture of him and Naiche on horseback. One of his foremost fighters, Perico, holds a baby. One of Geronimo's sons, Tisnah, stands beside Naiche. (Courtesy Arizona Historical Society)

Geronimo (center) and Naiche (far right) with some of their fighters. (Courtesy Arizona Historical Society)

Yahnoza, Geronimo's son Chappo, Fun, and Geronimo. (Courtesy Arizona Historical Society)

Geronimo (right) and Naiche on the parade ground of Fort Bowie, September 4, 1886, following their surrender to General Miles. (Courtesy Arizona Historical Society)

Brigadier General Nelson A. Miles.
(Courtesy National Anthropological
Archives)

Geronimo and Naiche with followers at trainside, headed for Florida captivity, September 8, 1886. Geronimo sits third from right, Naiche third from left. (Courtesy Arizona Historical Society)

Geronimo in captivity at Fort Pickens, Florida, 1887. (Courtesy Mark Sublette Medicine Man Gallery Tucson/Santa Fe)

Within the image: "The bent forms of former stalwart warriors, docile by compulsion." Left to right: Geronimo, Nachise, Mangus. Ft.Pickens, 1887.

Geronimo, Naiche, and Mangas in captivity at Fort Pickens, 1887. Note that Mangas wears an army officer's coat. (Courtesy Western History Collections, University of Oklahoma Libraries)

Chiricahua Apache camp at Mount Vernon Barracks, Alabama. (Courtesy Alabama Department of Archives and History)

Mount Vernon Barracks, 1889. Chihuahua, Naiche, Loco, Nana, Geronimo. The three in uniform were not in the army. (Courtesy Alabama Department of Archives and History)

Captain William W. Wotherspoon, Chiricahua overseer at Mount Vernon Barracks, 1898. (Courtesy US Army Military History Institute)

Captain Hugh L. Scott, Troop L, Seventh Cavalry, at Fort Sill, Oklahoma Territory, 1896. (Courtesy Fort Sill National Historic Landmark)

Naiche's village near Medicine Creek, Fort Sill, 1896. (Courtesy Fort Sill National Historic Landmark)

Geronimo and family in melon patch, Fort Sill, 1895. Wife Zi-yeh, Eva, Robert, unknown, Geronimo. (Courtesy Fort Sill National Historic Landmark)

Geronimo at Fort Sill, c. 1895–96. Note the Plains Indian feather war bonnet and fringed jacket. (Courtesy Mark Sublette Medicine Man Gallery Tucson/ Santa Fe)

Geronimo and Chiricahua delegation to Pan American Exposition, Buffalo, New York, 1901. (Courtesy Mark Sublette Medicine Man Gallery Tucson/Santa Fe)

Geronimo at Fort Sill, c. 1904, when he partici-
pated in the Louisiana Purchase Exposition in Saint
Louis. (Courtesy Mark Sublette Medicine Man
Gallery Tucson/Santa Fe)

Geronimo driving a 1904 Locomobile at the Miller Brothers Ranch, Oklahoma, for
a convention of the National Editorial Association, June 1905. (Courtesy Western
History Collections, University of Oklahoma Libraries)

Davis invited them inside. They squatted in a semicircle. Loco, Nana, Zele, and Bonito were badly hungover, while Mangas, Naiche, Geronimo, and Chihuahua were still intoxicated, Chihuahua especially so. Mickey Free interpreted. Loco, the least belligerent, began to set forth the complaints. Chihuahua, "palpably drunk and in an ugly humor," sprang to his feet and declared, "What I have to say can be said in a few words, then Loco can take all the rest of the day to talk if he wishes to do so."

Chihuahua directed his "few words" to a vigorous protest against the prohibition of wife-beating and tiswin drunks. They had never agreed to this in talks with General Crook, they had done it all their lives, and they had no intention of stopping now. In the midst of Davis's attempt to explain why Crook adopted the rules, old Nana jumped up and interrupted with an angry outburst, then stalked out of the tent. Mickey Free relayed what Nana had said: "Tell the *Nantan Enchau* [stout chief] that he can't advise me how to treat my women. He is only a boy. I killed *men* before he was born."

Chihuahua resumed, "We all drank tiswin last night, all of us in the tent and outside, except the scouts; and many more. What are you going to do about it? Are you going to put us all in jail. You have no jail big enough even if you could put us all in jail." Davis reasoned that the new defiance arose from the departure of Crawford and others well known to the Indians and their resulting conclusion that *Nantan Lupan* [Gray Wolf or Gray Fox, Crook] had also left.

Although he might have countered with several measures to avert a crisis, Davis decided to play for time. The issue was so grave, he explained, that only Crook could resolve it. He would seek the general's decision by telegraph and let them know, although several days might elapse. Seemingly mollified, the Chiricahuas returned to their camps on Turkey Creek. From Fort Apache, Davis telegraphed Captain Pierce at San Carlos, explaining the situation. He naturally assumed that Pierce, like Crawford, would at once recognize the gravity of Davis's dilemma and forward the telegram to Crook in Prescott. All Davis and the Indians could do was wait. Davis stood by the telegraph at Fort Apache; the Apaches at Turkey Creek simmered with growing anxiety.

As time passed with no word from Crook, Geronimo's suspicion of treachery drew support from rumors and false reports from other leaders. As so often in the past, he believed that bad people—Chatto, Davis, even Crook—prepared to do bad things to him. Huera, Mangas's wife, stoked the suspicions. By May 16 the impulse to flee to Mexico took control of both Geronimo and Mangas, restrained only by their failure to persuade more than fifteen men to join them. They needed the prestige of Chihuahua and Naiche to lend credibility to the plan, and they hung back.

Geronimo conceived a scheme for forcing their hand. During the day he sent a runner to the White River planting grounds east of Fort Apache to summon two cousins, members of Davis's scout company. They came and quickly returned, bearing orders from Geronimo to kill Davis and Chatto. Chihuahua and Naiche would then have to leave, for military retaliation would be swift. At Fort Apache, however, Davis received a tip that Apaches were preparing to bolt the reservation. He and Gatewood mobilized as many scouts as they could round up and headed for Turkey Creek to arrest Geronimo and Mangas. About six miles from camp, the officers met an Apache who told them Geronimo and Mangas had left and had forced Naiche, Chihuahua, and Nana to go. Loco, Zele, and Bonito refused, even though threatened with death.

In fact, Geronimo and Mangas did not "force" the other chiefs to break with them. As Davis learned only later, they told the others that his cousins had killed Davis and Chatto, or as Chihuahua later put it, Geronimo "tricked" them. Why the scouts failed to carry out Geronimo's orders was never explained. Meantime, the two cousins and two other scouts deserted and joined the people leaving the reservation.

Geronimo's stratagem had worked. He told Chihuahua and Naiche that Davis and Chatto had been killed. Alarmed, they mobilized their people and joined in the breakout. At dusk of May 17 thirty-four men, including the four deserters, eight adolescent boys, and ninety-two women and children fled Turkey Creek, headed southeast. Counting ten women and children of Naiche's following who later left, the total on the run numbered 144. The leaders of the outbreak were Geronimo, Mangas, Naiche, Chihuahua, and Nana. Remaining on the reservation were four hundred Chiricahuas, under Chatto, Zele, Bonito, and Loco.

Geronimo had broken away from the reservation for the third and last time.[17]

As Lieutenant Davis waited anxiously by the telegraph key at Fort Apache, he had no way of knowing that his telegram rested in an office pigeon hole at San Carlos. Crawford would instantly have forwarded it to Crook, but Pierce was new. He sought the advice of Chief of Scouts Al Sieber. He too might have urged sending it to Crook, but Sieber was sleeping off a hangover. Glancing at the telegram, he waved off Pierce with the comment that it was just another tiswin drunk, not to worry, Davis could handle it. Not for four months did Davis know what had happened, nor did Crook even know of the telegram's existence.[18]

General Crook remained convinced, probably correctly, that had he received the telegram he could have headed off an outbreak. Even so, Geronimo's chronic suspicion and readiness to believe any rumor, combined with the rivalries and politicking that constantly swept the Chiricahuas, made another outbreak inevitable.

NINETEEN

Back to the Sierra Madre, 1885

THE MOUNTAINS OF ARIZONA and New Mexico are high, steep, tangled, rocky, slashed by deep canyons and gorges, and for humans on foot or horseback, except the Apaches, virtually impossible to penetrate except at lower elevations and along the rivers and creeks that flow from their heights. South of the international boundary, similar ranges of mountains carpet both Chihuahua and Sonora, dominated by the towering Sierra Madre separating the two Mexican states. The mountains of Mexico resemble some of the most rugged north of the border, but the Sierra Madre dwarf all others in tortuous topography.

No Indian tribe mastered a hostile environment more perfectly than the Apaches. Trained from birth, they could live off the land or by plundering neighboring tribes or European newcomers. Man, woman, and child, they could move swiftly through desert and mountain, enduring long journeys without rest, food, or water, intimately familiar with the terrain and skilled in employing it as a weapon in warfare, hiding in mountain recesses unseen and unapproachable by anyone not welcomed. They could "read" the land in every aspect, from the meaning of the unnatural position of a stone or a twig to virtually invisible sign on boulders or rocky slopes. Ever on the alert, with acute vision, hearing, and smell, rarely could they be surprised.

Of all Apache tribes, the Chiricahuas excelled in these traits. The final two years of liberty from American oversight vividly illustrated Chiricahua command of the environment.

The Chiricahua breakout of May 17, 1885, demonstrated the incredible ability of Apaches to move fast, night and day, avoid troops except in ambush, wreak havoc on ranchers and their stock, and go where they wanted. All the Chiricahua leaders who led in the outbreak possessed these virtues. All moved in a body at times and divided into several bodies when pressed too closely. As he had shown in the abduction of Loco in 1882, Geronimo proved especially adept at confronting the challenges, exercising influence both when traveling with his own followers or when traveling with all the components.

Well aware that troops and scouts would take their trail quickly, the Chiricahuas journeyed swiftly through the night of May 17. Before reaching Eagle Creek on May 18, they glimpsed pursuers behind them. Descending to and crossing the creek, they scaled steep, canyon-scored mountains on the other side. Pushing through these mountains on May 19, the women and children scattered, to rejoin later. To slow soldiers behind them, the men took the most forbidding course possible through rocks and gorges, leaving a dim trail designed to prevent pursuit on horseback and exhaust pursuers on foot. White men they encountered they killed and robbed. After traveling all night, on May 20 they crossed Blue Creek and, coming on a cattle ranch, burned the house, killed two men, lanced the cattle, and made off with the horses and mules. Traveling up the San Francisco River on May 21, they entered a recently settled area and killed every white traveler they encountered.

Somewhere along this river, they paused to rest, Chihuahua's and Naiche's people in one group, those of Mangas and Geronimo in another. A raiding party returned with plunder, and one of the three Chiricahua scouts who had deserted told Chihuahua that Lieutenant Davis and Chatto had not been killed, as Geronimo had assured Chihuahua and Naiche on the evening of the breakout. Enraged over the deception, Chihuahua vowed to kill Geronimo. Rifles in hand, Chihuahua, his brother Ulzana, and the scout deserter headed for Geronimo's group. But someone had tipped off Geronimo, and by the time Chihuahua reached their resting place Geronimo and Mangas had gathered their following and fled, shortly turning east and south on Devils Creek. Chihuahua continued north up the San Francisco River, intending to hide in the mountains until the excitement quieted and he could slip back to the reservation. Naiche had traveled with Chihuahua but was in Mangas's group when they fled the wrath of Chihuahua and was forced to stay with it. He sent word to his wife to take their child and return to the reservation.[1]

Geronimo's role in the last outbreak reveals an unflattering element of his character. Because other chiefs refused to follow his lead, he deceived them. If Lieutenant Davis and Chatto had been assassinated, Chihuahua, Naiche, and others would be forced to join in Geronimo's outbreak or bear the consequences. Geronimo may have thought his scheme had been carried out when he told the other chiefs. He may simply have expected it to happen and told the other chiefs prematurely. In any event, such efforts to manipulate the other leaders show that Geronimo was willing to intrigue against his own people as well as white authority.

General Crook received his first intimation of an impending breakout at his Prescott headquarters on the afternoon of May 17, 1885, when Captain Pierce telegraphed from San Carlos that Lieutenant Davis, at Turkey Creek, feared that the Chiricahuas were preparing to bolt the reservation that evening. Of course, if Crook had received Davis's telegram of May 15, pigeonholed at San Carlos by Captain Pierce, Crook would have been alerted to brewing trouble two days earlier and probably could have headed it off. Because the telegraph line between Fort Apache and San Carlos had been cut, Crook did not learn until the afternoon of the May 18 of the breakout of the previous evening. With the Fort Apache garrison already in pursuit, the general began ordering troops from other Arizona forts into the field and warning citizens to the east. He also established contact with Colonel Luther Bradley, commanding the District of New Mexico.

Shortly after the Chiricahuas entered New Mexico and turned toward the Mogollon Mountains and the Black Range, General Crook moved his headquarters to Fort Bayard, New Mexico, the better to move his troops and cooperate with Colonel Bradley. During these days he learned once again what he would always preach—regular soldiers were no match for Apaches:

> The whole country north, east, and west of Fort Bayard was filled with troops. No less than twenty troops of cavalry and more than one hundred Indian scouts were moved in every direction either to intercept or follow the trails of the hostiles. But with the exception of the capture of a few animals by the Indian scouts under Chatto, and a slight skirmish with their rear guard by the troops from Apache under Captain Smith on May 22, in which three of his command were wounded, the Indians were not even caught sight of by the troops, and finally crossed into Mexico about June

10. . . . In the twenty-three days from the outbreak until the Indians crossed into Mexico, every possible effort was made by the troops, which were pushed to the limits of endurance of men and animals, but without result other than to drive the Indians out of the Black Range and the Mogollons, and also to save the lives, probably, of many ranchmen and prospectors.[2]

On June 5, 1885, Crook moved his headquarters from Fort Bayard to Deming, New Mexico, on the Southern Pacific Railroad. He knew that another campaign into Mexico such as he commanded in 1883 would be necessary. The railroad and telegraph line afforded the means of organizing and assembling the troops and scouts.

After confounding all the troops and scouts General Crook and Colonel Bradley could mobilize against them in New Mexico, Geronimo and the other leaders slipped across the boundary into Mexico. Geronimo and Mangas crossed at Lake Palomas, Chihuahua. Chihuahua, after surprising and destroying a cavalry supply base in Guadalupe Canyon, continued down the San Bernardino River to the Bavispe River. Naiche followed and joined Chihuahua. By mid-June 1885, all had hidden themselves in favorite refuges in the Sierra Madre. Chihuahua and Naiche made camp on a ridge at the junction of several deep canyons northeast of Oputo, although Naiche soon left to find Geronimo. Farther south, northeast of Nácori Chico, Geronimo and Mangas hid in their old haunt of Bugatseka.

Contrasting with their masterful evasion of troops and scouts in New Mexico's mountains after the breakout of May 17, 1885, once in Mexico the Apache leaders grew careless. They knew Crook would be after them once again, and soon. They knew he would use Apache scouts, recruited from the White Mountains if not their own Chiricahuas. They could not have forgotten how doggedly he ran them down in 1883. Yet twice in the summer of 1885 they allowed themselves to be surprised in their Sierra Madre bastions.

On June 23, little more than a month after the breakout, Chihuahua and his people went about their morning business at their ranchería laid out on a ridge northeast of Oputo. Heavy rain had fallen all night. About 9:00 a.m., as the sun broke through the overcast skies, volleys of gunfire from two directions swept the camp. The surprised Chiricahuas scattered. A man quickly hid the families in a cave, and then joined the other men in scrambling down the intersecting canyons with Indian scouts following and shooting at them.

After several miles, as the men scattered farther, the scouts called off the chase and returned to the ranchería. They easily found the hidden women and children. Among the fifteen were Chihuahua's entire family and Ulzana's wife and two children. Chihuahua and his men had left behind not only their families but the camp containing the horses, guns, and ammunition seized from the cavalry supply camp at Guadalupe Canyon.

Before this disaster, Chihuahua's men had raided for cattle on the Yaqui River. Likewise, Geronimo and Mangas had raided extensively along the Sonora River. But they happened to be in their stronghold at Bugatseka on August 7. Early in the afternoon they heard a mule bray and, too late, took alert. Indian scouts swept to the attack, dropping five to the ground dead (three men, one woman, and one boy about thirteen). Geronimo scooped up his young son and dashed into surrounding brush. Recognizing him, the scouts directed a heavy enough fire to cause him to drop the child, but he escaped. As with Chihuahua, the families were not so fortunate. Fifteen women and children fell captive to the scouts. They included three wives and five children of Geronimo's—two daughters wounded, one in an arm, the other in a lung. Among the captives also were Nana's wife and the wife of Mangas, Huera (the expert maker of tiswin whose provocative rhetoric caused much of the trouble that led to the outbreak of May 17). Horses, mules, and all the camp impedimenta had also been abandoned.[3]

The stock and other camp equipage forfeited in June by Chihuahua and in August by Geronimo and Mangas accounted for little loss. They could readily be replaced by another raid. But for all the leaders, the capture of their families represented a devastating blow. Apache families were very close, as illustrated time and again by the furor over Apache captives held by Mexico. Depending on where the families had been taken after their seizure, getting them back ranged from impossible to doubtful. At the same time, two such calamitous surprises instilled a new caution that would make the task of the Apache scouts more daunting.

By June 7, 1885, General Crook knew that he confronted another grueling campaign into Mexico and had moved from Fort Bayard, New Mexico, to Deming, where he could communicate quickly by telegraph. He had already summoned Captain Emmet Crawford from his regiment in Texas. He arrived at Deming on June 6, together with a train from the east bearing thirty Indian scouts and a troop of cavalry. Crook assigned Crawford to lead an immediate campaign into Mexico. He would move by rail to the west, then strike south and unite with Lieutenant Britton Davis. With Chatto and sixty scouts, Davis had been busy trying to flush the Chiricahuas out of New Mexico's mountains. Crawford and Davis merged as directed and with the cavalry troop and two pack trains crossed into Mexico, headed for the Sierra Madre.[4]

As Crook relocated his field headquarters west to Fort Bowie, he recognized that circumstances had changed since his 1883 campaign. The Southwest had been filled with even more stockmen and miners, and their newspapers unrelentingly blasted Crook for not stopping Apache outrages. Moreover, the election of 1884 had placed Democrat Grover Cleveland in the executive mansion. William C. Endicott held the position of secretary of war. General Sherman had retired and been succeeded as head of the army by Lieutenant General Philip H. Sheridan. Neither Cleveland nor Endicott knew anything about Indians. Sheridan knew nothing about Apaches, but he relied heavily on Crook, a West Point classmate. Even so, he was skeptical of Crook's use of Indian scouts, and he found both Cleveland and Endicott hard taskmasters as reports, most exaggerated, reached the president of Apaches running wild in the Southwest.

Crook's strategy in 1885 differed from that of 1883. Instead of personally leading an expedition into Mexico, he would send two columns of Indian scouts under experienced officers. Captain Crawford had crossed into Mexico on June 11, but the second column, under Captain Wirt Davis, did not leave Fort Bowie until July 7. Crook had sent Lieutenant Gatewood and his scouts into the mountains of New Mexico to make sure the Chiricahuas had all left. Wirt Davis needed Gatewood's scouts because they knew the Sierra Madre. When they finally arrived, he headed for Mexico with one hundred scouts, his own troop of cavalry, and a pack train. Gatewood returned to Fort Apache, exhausted and out of favor with Crook. He would remain there during this campaign.[5]

For the expeditions into Mexico, Crook relied almost exclusively on the Apache scouts. For this mission he had no confidence in regular cavalry. Only Apaches could find Apaches in the Sierra Madre. Crawford and Davis could use the regulars however they wanted, but the few who participated engaged primarily in escorting the mule pack trains on which Crook relied for transporting supplies from the base at Lang's Ranch, near the border at the southern end of the Animas Valley, New Mexico. If fact, the astute

Crawford ultimately dispensed with cavalry altogether, entrusting Chatto to employ the Apache scouts as he saw fit.

Crook hastened to assure his Washington superiors that he intended to make prominent use of the regulars. Indeed, he had to do all he could to bar the Chiricahuas from raiding back into the United States and further infuriating the public. He therefore stationed three lines of troops from the border to the railroad. In New Mexico Colonel Bradley did the same.[6]

Crook knew that the Apaches could slip through his border blockade whenever they wanted, so he placed his main reliance and attention on the ability of Captains Crawford and Davis to surprise the Chiricahuas in their mountain hideouts. Thus on June 23 Crawford's scouts, led by Chatto, surprised and attacked Chihuahua northeast of Oputo, and on August 7 Wirt Davis's seventy-eight scouts under Lieutenant Matthias W. Day surprised Geronimo at Bugatseka. Crook decided to hold the families and other relatives seized at both places in camp at Fort Bowie as a bargaining chip.[7]

Furious over the loss of his family in the attack led by Chatto on June 23, 1885, Chihuahua cut a bloody path west and northwest across Sonora, sometimes uniting with Naiche, sometimes separating from him. On July 23, Chihuahua even struck into Arizona southwest of Fort Huachuca, seizing cattle and horses but also testing whether he could break through to Fort Apache and look for his family. Almost at once troops struck his mountain camp and seized twenty-four horses. Chihuahua then discovered two scout units on his trail and, dropping all his stolen stock, veered back into Mexico, reuniting with Naiche in the mountains southwest of Cananea.[8]

Meantime, following their surprise at Bugatseka on August 7, the followers of Geronimo and Mangas spent several days rounding up their people. The two then parted, Mangas to lose himself in the Sierra Madre at Juh's old refuge of Guaynopa, across the summit in Chihuahua. Geronimo and Nana pushed directly east, into the Sierra Madre. Knowing that scouts would be on their trail, they chose the roughest mountain heights to cross the summit and descend into Chihuahua. Daily downpours soaked the Chiricahuas but made their trail harder to follow.

Geronimo had probably already decided to try to recover his family, whom he wrongly assumed had been taken to Fort Apache. Near San Buenaventura, Chihuahua, he turned southeast, crossed the Santa Clara River, and hid the women and children in the mountains to the east. His horses broken down, he raided around the town of Santa Clara and obtained fresh remounts. He then pushed directly north, toward New Mexico. Near Janos, Nana turned into the mountains to the northwest of the city.[9]

Once again, Geronimo would cross the border and race for the Mogollons, from which he could pounce quickly on the Chiricahua camp at Fort Apache and retrieve his family. General Crook had been astute in holding them at Fort Bowie.

TWENTY

CHASED BY CROOK'S SCOUTS, 1885–86

TWO DAYS AFTER THE attack on Geronimo's ranchería at Bugatseka on August 7, 1885, Captains Crawford and Wirt Davis met on the Bavispe River, and Crawford learned of the fight and the scattering of the Chiricahuas. By August 13 Crawford and his command had reached the site of the encounter and picked up Geronimo's trail to the east. With Lieutenant Britton Davis and fifty scouts ranging in advance, Crawford followed over the Sierra Madre and down into Chihuahua. At the crest, he sent word forward to Davis to take thirty-two picked scouts (including Chatto), three packers, and seven good mules, get on the trail, and not abandon it for any reason. If rations ran short, he could kill Mexican beef and give a receipt.

This is what Davis did. Alerted to the theft, a Mexican force of Tarahumari Indians set forth to find Davis. Unknown to him, Lieutenant Charles P. Elliott with pack mules bearing rations followed a day behind. The Mexicans cut Elliott's trail instead of Davis's and on August 23 set up an ambush in a canyon. Fortunately, with another rainfall threatening, Elliott bivouacked before riding into the trap. From the heights, the Mexicans opened fire. The Indian scouts fired back, but Elliott restrained them. With the packers, they took to the rocks on the canyon's side. Elliott walked out and tried to explain the identity of his command to the Mexican leader. The Mexican held a cocked rifle to Elliott's chest and demanded that he call the scouts out of the rocks, which he did. They dropped their rifles and cartridge belts as ordered. The Mexicans then tied their hands behind them and marched them to San Buenaventura. En route they met a command of Mexican regulars, whose commander, Lieutenant Colonel Pedro S. Marcías, doubted Elliott's explanation. In San Buenaventura, after parading through the town to the jeers of the citizens, all the scouts and packers were lodged in a military barracks.

Davis's Indian scouts had learned what had happened, and that night he moved them to the edge of San Buenaventura. The lieutenant, who spoke fluent Spanish, went into the town and found the *presidente.* In a conference with him and Colonel Marcías, Davis established his legitimacy. The colonel liberated the prisoners and returned all their arms and property. They went into camp to await the arrival of Captain Crawford. As instructed, Davis and his scouts got back on the Chiricahua trail and rode north.[1]

Elliott led his scouts on the back trail until meeting Crawford and his command. They joined and marched back to San Buenaventura. In the main street, a mob blocked the way, and two Mexicans came forth to demand that the officers enter a house for a conference. Outside, mounted soldiers surrounded the scouts. Whatever occurred inside, the scouts believed that an angry confrontation took place and that the Mexicans ordered the Americans to leave Mexico, an order repeated twice as Crawford's command moved north seeking Geronimo's trail. The scouts were angry and anxious to fight. In fact, Crawford had resolved to let Davis keep to the trail while he paused at a nearby ranch to refit.[2]

Meantime, after three days of hard work following the trail, in repeated downpours and glutinous mud, Britton Davis and his scouts halted for the night. A Mexican force rode into the camp. Colonel Marcías commanded. He informed Davis that two other Mexican commands had cut the Chiricahua trail in Davis's advance and were in pursuit. The treaty under which US forces operated in Mexico specified that, if a Mexican force got in advance of an American force, the Americans would have to call off the operation and return to the United States. If the Mexican officer consented, the Americans could continue, but Colonel Marcías refused to consent. Davis, his scouts and packers broken by days of negotiating precipitous mountains and canyons and plodding through mud under steady downpours, always short on rations, filthy and ragged, gladly accepted the colonel's decision.

One hundred miles of barren desert separated Davis from the nearest border crossing: El Paso, Texas. Davis's shabby command reached Fort Bliss, at El Paso, on September 5, 1885. In the city, Davis met a friend of his father's

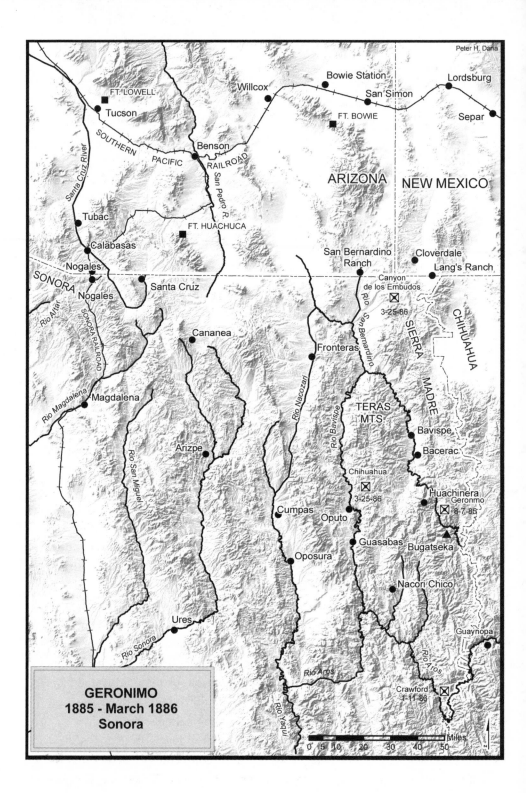

Peter H. Dana

Bowie Station
Lordsburg
Willcox
San Simon
FT. LOWELL
Separ
Tucson
FT. BOWIE
SOUTHERN
Benson
ARIZONA
NEW MEXICO
PACIFIC
RAILROAD
San Pedro R.
Santa Cruz River
Tubac
FT. HUACHUCA
Calabasas
San Bernardino
Ranch
Cloverdale
Nogales
Lang's Ranch
SONORA
Santa Cruz
Canyon
de los Embudos
3-25-86
CHIHUAHUA
Nogales
Rio Altar
SONORA RAILROAD
Cananea
Fronteras
SIERRA
Rio Magdalena
Magdalena
Rio Bavispe
TERAS
MTS
MADRE
Bavispe
Rio Nacozari
Bacerac
Rio San Bernardino
Arizpe
Chihuahua
3-25-86
Huachinera
Geronmo
8-7-85
Rio San Miguel
Cumpas
Oputo
Guasabas
Bugatseka
Oposura
Nacori Chico
Ures
Guaynopa
Rio Sonora
Rio Aros
Rio Aros
Crawford
1-11-86
Rio Yaqui

GERONIMO
1885 - March 1886
Sonora

Miles
0 5 10   20   30   40   50

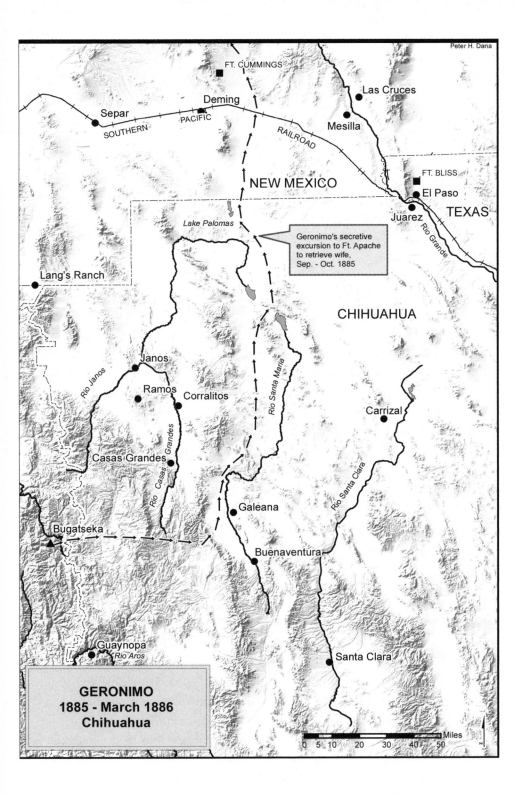

Peter H. Dana

FT. CUMMINGS

Las Cruces

Separ
SOUTHERN PACIFIC
Deming
Mesilla
RAILROAD

FT. BLISS
El Paso
Juarez
TEXAS
Rio Grande

NEW MEXICO

Lake Palomas

Geronimo's secretive
excursion to Ft. Apache
to retrieve wife,
Sep. - Oct. 1885

CHIHUAHUA

Lang's Ranch

Rio Janos

Janos

Ramos
Corralitos

Rio Santa Maria

Carrizal

Casas Grandes

Rio Casas Grandes

Galeana

Rio Santa Clara

Bugatseka

Buenaventura

Guaynopa
Rio Aros

Santa Clara

GERONIMO
1885 - March 1886
Chihuahua

Miles
0 5 10   20   30   40   50

who owned extensive ranching and mining properties in Chihuahua. His manager had just resigned, and he offered Davis the job. The ordeal through which he had just passed, combined with his hazardous service at Fort Apache, had persuaded him that the army wasn't for him. He accepted.[3]

As ordered by Crook, Davis and his scouts headed directly to Fort Bowie, arriving on September 12. Crook expressed disappointment with Davis's decision to leave the army, but his diary suggests that he was more interested in long talks with Chatto and others of Davis's scouts. He would have done better to have heeded Davis's report that Geronimo's trail pointed toward New Mexico.

Remaining with Geronimo after Nana's departure near Janos were five men and half a dozen women, those with family or relatives taken at Bugatseka and thought to be held at Fort Apache but actually at Fort Bowie. Geronimo crossed into New Mexico by the same route he had entered four months earlier, east of Lake Palomas. On September 11 the army picked up his trail and followed him across the Mimbres Mountains and River. He had already left a trail of murdered men. In Gallinas Canyon, the Chiricahuas fell on still another ranch and killed the inhabitants. Here, though, Geronimo himself took a captive, teenager James "Santiago" McKinn. Like Charley McComas two years earlier, Santiago McKinn would become the focus of an intense effort to liberate him. Swinging north across the Gila River, the little band climbed into the Mogollon Mountains. Among these peaks and canyons, Geronimo could easily evade any pursuers.[4]

None found him, so high and remote was his base. On September 18 he led his party down into Arizona, making for the east fork of White River, the Chiricahua planting grounds near Fort Apache. Shortly after midnight on September 22, Geronimo threaded his way through the White Mountain scouts patrolling the area. An old White Mountain woman informed him that Lieutenant Gatewood had drawn the Chiricahuas in close to Fort Apache. The woman also told him that only one of his wives and a child lived with the Chiricahuas. Her name was She-gha (Ith-tedda, the Mescalero), and she had not been taken captive in the attack on Bugatseka. Rather, soon after the breakout of May 17, Geronimo had sent her to the Mescalero Reservation to see if these Apaches might join in the outbreak. They refused and turned her, her child, and a companion over to the army, which sent them to Fort Apache. The White Mountain woman guided

Geronimo to the Chiricahua camp and pointed out his wife's wickiup. Without disturbing anyone, he quietly entered the wickiup and emerged with the woman, his child, and her companion.

By daybreak, the White Mountain people had been stirred up, angry that Geronimo had made off with some of their horses. The scouts combed the countryside looking for him. But he had swiftly ridden southeast across Black River and hastened back to the Mogollons. His foray a failure, he received unexpected help in his dash back to Mexico. In the Mogollons he found Nana and his people. And farther west, both Chihuahua and Naiche struck into Arizona, leaving trails north both east and west of the Chiricahua Mountains, uniting to find refuge from pursing Indian scouts in the Dragoon Mountains. Regular troops finally drove them back into Sonora. All this Apache activity confused the army and kept patrols in the field following false leads. By October 10 Geronimo was back in Mexico, and no Chiricahuas remained north of the border.[5]

Not for long, however, although Geronimo and Naiche remained to raid in Chihuahua. Late in October Ulzana and Chihuahua crossed into New Mexico near Lake Palomas. While Chihuahua remained in New Mexico to provide diversion, Ulzana and twelve men aimed for Fort Apache and San Carlos. Some had left their families with the Chiricahuas on Turkey Creek, and others thought their families captured at Bugatseka might be held at San Carlos. Throughout November 1885, Chihuahua's destructive raids among the ranches and settlements of southern New Mexico took a large toll in lives and stolen stock and property. A newsman listed the names of five people killed within two weeks and within twenty-five miles of Lake Valley, New Mexico. The newsman also wrote of ranchers who lost their cattle but escaped with their lives. Other newspapers named one after another citizen slain by the Apaches. Chihuahua's raid also set in motion a score of pursuing cavalry units, and as intended it diverted attention to New Mexico instead of Arizona.

Ulzana and his party killed many whites and angered the White Mountain Apaches around Fort Apache, who killed one of his men. No family members remained on Turkey Creek, but the angry Chiricahuas turned on the White Mountain rancherías and killed twenty-one people. With San Carlos now on guard, Ulzana circled to the east and headed for New Mexico. By December, Chihuahua and his followers had slipped back across the border.[6]

Throughout December, from hideouts in the Mogollon Mountains, Ulzana ravaged ranches in western New Mexico, north of Silver City and Fort Bayard. On December 9, while they burned a ranch and rounded up stock, a small detachment of cavalry attacked them. They abandoned their horses and scampered up a snow-covered mountainside. On December 19 the Chiricahuas exacted revenge on the same troopers, ambushing them as they left an overnight camp and killing the four horsemen in the lead. By the end of December 1885, Ulzana and his small band had traveled about twelve hundred miles, killed thirty-eight people, captured and wore out 250 horses and mules, and although twice dismounted crossed back into Mexico with the loss of the one man killed near Fort Apache.[7]

Geronimo, Chihuahua, and Ulzana had easily breached the elaborate lines of defense set up to keep the Chiricahuas south of the border, and Colonel Bradley already had troops in pursuit. With Bradley chasing these Indians in New Mexico, Crook turned to other matters. He burned the telegraph wires with the continuing battle over dual control of the White Mountain Reservation—a battle he won when the secretary of the interior agreed to turn over the reservation temporarily to Captain Pierce as Indian agent. Crook fended off criticisms of his archenemy, Brigadier General Nelson A. Miles, Bradley's superior at Fort Leavenworth. Miles made no secret of his contempt for Crook's reliance on Indian scouts and convinced New Mexico's governor that with Miles in command the Chiricahuas would quickly be conquered.[8]

Crook's hopes lay not with running the Chiricahuas down in New Mexico or Arizona but with the success of Captains Crawford and Davis in Mexico. In the event they succeeded, Crook needed a firm policy from Washington on how to handle the Apaches. On September 17 he began to force the issue by informing his superiors of his first intent to turn the Apaches over to civil authorities to be tried for their offenses. But lawyers advised him of the impossibility of obtaining evidence against individual Indians that could be used in a court of law (as Crook well knew). He then pointed out that killing all the Chiricahuas in the Sierra Madre would take years and that during this time their depredations could not be prevented. With a little more "hammering," he thought, they could be persuaded to surrender if assured that they would not be killed or turned over to the civil authorities. He asked for an immediate decision.

In Washington, General Sheridan observed that these Indians deserved no consideration at all. But "as a matter of policy," he believed Crook should be authorized to seek their surrender on the condition that they be regarded as prisoners of war and transported to a distant point. They should never be allowed to return to Arizona or New Mexico. Secretary Endicott approved Sheridan's endorsement and directed that as soon as the Apaches surrendered they be sent to Fort Marion, Florida, as were the chiefs of the Cheyennes, Kiowas, and Comanches who surrendered at the end of the Red River War in 1875.[9]

By October 11, Crook believed that none of the Chiricahuas remained north of the border, and he resolved on a new strategy to bring the Chiricahuas in Mexico into negotiations. The scouts and mules of both Crawford and Davis had endured such hard campaigning that they no longer possessed the vigor to embark on another expedition into Mexico. The general thought that the time needed to build new commands would lull the Chiricahuas into believing the army had called off the offensive. Crawford went to Fort Apache and Wirt Davis to San Carlos to begin discharging their scouts and enlisting fresh ones.[10]

New Mexicans had suffered death and destruction almost constantly since the outbreak from Turkey Creek on May 17, 1885, and they protested repeatedly and vociferously in their newspapers and in letters and telegrams to army commanders, members of Congress, and, increasingly, to President Cleveland. The raids of Chihuahua and Ulzana stirred the most intense outrage yet, and Secretary Endicott and General Sheridan repeatedly called on Crook to provide some reassurance that would relieve the pressures on the president. The reticent Crook would only reply that he and Colonel Bradley were doing the best they could.

That was not good enough for Washington, which had to keep New Mexicans from bedeviling the president. On November 20, 1885, Secretary Endicott and General Sheridan met to consider Crook's latest telegrams, which offered no encouragement. They discussed an idea that had been considered both in the Interior and War Departments for more than a year—a lasting solution to the Apache problem. It contemplated no less than the permanent removal to Florida of the entire Chiricahua tribe—not only the few who were in Mexico but the large majority living quietly on the White Mountain Reservation. The meeting ended with Endicott directing Sheridan to travel at once to Fort Bowie to broach this idea to Crook and resolve other problems.[11]

Sheridan and three members of his staff left Washington on November 22. He stopped in Chicago to talk with Major General John M. Schofield, who despite his assurances had failed to keep General Miles quiet. That was one of the issues Sheridan had to discuss with Crook. Because it involved Colonel Bradley, Miles's subordinate, Sheridan also stopped in Santa Fe to add him to his retinue. On November 29 the group disembarked at Bowie Station, where an escort conducted them to Fort Bowie and a seventeen-gun salute of welcome.

In conference, the officers readily resolved the problem of General Miles, except that it only provoked him to more interference. The solution was simple: temporarily transfer the District of New Mexico from Miles's department to Crook's. So far as the rest of the army knew, or the public, this was the purpose and the only outcome of Sheridan's visit. Except in a long report of Sheridan to Endicott from Albuquerque, the larger issue of Chiricahua removal escaped mention.

The topic probably overshadowed the easy restructuring of Crook's command. Sheridan broached removal to Crook, who objected but suggested that they seek the opinion of Captain Crawford. Only three days earlier, he and his battalion of two hundred White Mountain and Chiricahua Apache scouts had arrived at Fort Bowie, ready to head for Sonora. Crawford pointed out that such a mass removal would be likely to affect the conduct of his Chiricahua scouts. Crook had demurred on the same grounds. The phrasing was probably a polite way of making the point to the lieutenant general. Both had to know that the effect on the Chiricahua scouts would be disastrous. The argument had its desired result: Sheridan would drop the subject for the time being. The record does not reveal whether Crook or Crawford had any moral or other objections to the proposal; if so, they failed to voice them.

The meeting had another important consequence. For the first time, Sheridan gained an appreciation of the obstacles Crook faced, both in the Apaches and in the character of the country in which he had to operate. In his report to Endicott, Sheridan described them at great length and strongly supported Crook as the officer most likely to destroy or gain the surrender of the Chiricahuas in Mexico. Left unsaid was Sheridan's skepticism of Crook's heavy reliance on Apache scouts, which almost certainly the two talked about at Fort Bowie.[12]

Sheridan and his entourage left Fort Bowie the next day, November 30. His visit had fixed policy and turned Crook loose. But it had done nothing to relieve the pressure on President Cleveland. On December 23, Sheridan appealed almost plaintively for an immediate report of what steps Crook was taking to kill or capture the raiders in New Mexico. All Crook could do was detail the movement of troops seeking to catch them. Even Ulzana's return to Mexico at the end of December failed to end the stream of angry protests.[13]

Sheridan muted his doubts about the loyalty of the Apache scouts. Not so the newspapers in the areas of Arizona and New Mexico pounded by Geronimo and other leaders. One example of many, all employing the same language and tone, appeared in the *Tombstone Epitaph* early in 1886. The editor, reflecting public opinion, faulted Crook for "this most miserable campaign," attributable to his "incredible and criminal obstinacy, in continuing to employ the Chiricahua scouts." These "Indian hirelings . . . rob, ravish, and kill peaceful inhabitants of Sonora."

> When Geronimo is arraigned as murderer at the law of justice, General George Crook should stand by his side for upon his head lies the responsibility for the long consonance of this campaign for the deaths of scores of worthy men and women . . . and the damage done to this territory by the long series of outrages which his infamous system of employing these notoriously treacherous Chiricahua scouts has made possible.[14]

Crook ignored such inflammatory rhetoric, as political leaders could not, for as the editor correctly wrote: "Once General Crook gets a fixed idea in his head, nothing can remove it."[15] And his fixed idea was that only an Apache could catch an Apache.

After conferring with General Sheridan at Fort Bowie in November 1885, Crook turned his attention to the campaigns in Mexico. Captain Wirt Davis had crossed into Mexico at Guadalupe Canyon on November 21. He led a battalion of one hundred Apache scouts—none Chiricahua—a troop of cavalry, and three pack trains. His mission was to scour the eastern base of the Sierra Madre, in Chihuahua, while Crawford worked the western side, in Sonora. That is where the Chiricahuas were, as Crawford learned from villagers as he worked his way south along the Bavispe River. In two months of punishing campaigning, Wirt Davis learned that reality. He broke down his troops, scouts, and pack trains, together with his own health. Early in January, Crook allowed him to return to Fort Bowie for medical treatment. His command already had been in touch with Crawford's outfit. From the first, all the action had fallen to Crawford, whose command consisted entirely of Apache scouts. In his first campaign, Crawford had found the regulars an impediment. As in the first expedition, White Mountain and Chiricahua Apaches made up his command. Chatto had been discharged with the rest of the earlier scouts. The sergeant major was now Noche, equally accomplished if not enjoying the depth of Crawford's confidence in Chatto.[16]

Geronimo had not participated in the scourges of Chihuahua and Ulzana. In October 1885 Geronimo and Naiche based themselves in the Teras Mountains, in the great bend of the Bavispe River in Sonora. They raided settlements on both sides of the mountains, and then plunged far south to the Aros River for more raids. By December they had climbed into the mountain fastness called Espinosa del Diablo, between the Aros and Satachi Rivers. At the end of November Chihuahua had returned from his diversionary thrust into New Mexico and joined Geronimo and Naiche. Except for the handful with Ulzana, still north of the border, all the breakouts had gathered for the first time since fleeing Fort Apache in May. Only Mangas and his small party held back.

As usual, the Chiricahuas had watched for any army or scout units following their trail. They knew some were on the other side of the Sierra Madre, in Chihuahua; but since September none had been detected in Sonora. Feeling increasingly secure, they frequently failed even to post sentinels at night. Their ranchería—housing about eighty people, including twenty-four fighting men—perched on a high, rocky ridge a mile north of the Aros River and about fifty miles southeast of Nácori Chico. Before dawn on January 10, 1886, three men awoke to the braying of burros and walked out to investigate. From a higher slope shots aimed at the Chiricahuas sparked volleys from all around. Because the herd grazed about four hundred yards from the ranchería, the people had time to escape. Geronimo shouted for the women and children to run and scatter, and the men drew up to delay the attack. A running fight developed between army scouts and the fleeing Chiricahuas, but in the darkness no one was hurt on either side. The scouts took possession of a deserted camp, with all its contents and stock.

Rarely did the army with its Indian scouts succeed in finding a fugitive camp, much less in shooting down and capturing the inhabitants. That these

Indian scouts found and attacked Geronimo's camp on the Aros River only to find it deserted by all its people illustrates how skillfully the Apaches could detect an impending assault and scatter before the attack fell. The loss of all their stock and belongings meant little; raids could replenish what they had lost.

As the fleeing Chiricahuas discovered, they had been routed not only by White Mountain scouts but Chiricahuas, too. That their own tribesmen were army scouts who knew the country and their likely hiding places again proved highly unsettling. More immediately, their condition was perilous: high in the mountains in midwinter without food, stock, or any of the contents of their ranchería. Naiche spoke with one of the Chiricahua scouts and told him to tell the officer he wanted to come in and talk. If Naiche did not know who the officer was by now, the scout probably told him: Captain Emmet Crawford. The breakouts had known him at San Carlos as a fair, firm, and honest officer, and one who clearly had the confidence of General Crook.

That afternoon, Naiche sent a woman to the scouts' camp on the ridge line above the abandoned ranchería. The scouts had taken what they wanted and burned the rest. Now they rested or slept among the rocks as the woman made her way to Captain Crawford and relayed Naiche's request. The captain gave her some food and sent her back with word that he would meet with the chiefs the next morning on level ground about a mile from camp.

From a steep bluff across the Aros River where they had spent the night, the Chiricahuas awoke at daybreak of January 11, 1886, to the sound of gunfire. In the distance they could see the scout camp and rifle fire bursting from a rocky slope above. Some of the scouts briefly returned the fire, but it quickly ceased. The officers walked out to meet leaders of the attacking force, now discerned to be Mexican militia, including the hated Tarahumari Indians. The spectators heard more shots fired and then made out an officer, in his blue uniform, scaling a large rock and waving a white handkerchief. Another shot knocked him from the top of the rock. For several hours, the two sides maneuvered and periodically fired at each other. Geronimo, Naiche, Chihuahua, and Nana had never witnessed such a spectacle—a source of elation, possibly, but also concern over whether they could now arrange the talks they hoped for. As in the past, they had tired of life on the run, especially now that their own Chiricahua kin had joined the army. Once again, the security and rations of the reservation beckoned. Captain Crawford seemed their best chance for arranging to talk with General Crook and, as before, promise to return to life as it was before the breakout.[17]

Crawford's command awoke on the morning of January 11, 1886, to shouts from the scouts, scattered among the rocks, followed by a burst of rifle fire. The officers saw the attacking force as Mexicans, not in uniform, 154 in number. Crawford and First Lieutenant Marion P. Maus (Moss) rushed out waving their arms to stop: they were Americans. The firing stopped, and the officers turned back to camp. But the Mexicans opened fire again. Crawford climbed to the top of a large rock, his blue uniform clearly visible, and waved a white handkerchief. A bullet hit him in the head and knocked him to the ground. Maus turned to see his brains on the side of the rock.

As senior officer, Maus took command and tried to get the firing stopped. The scouts had returned fire and reluctantly stopped. With his interpreter, Concepcíon, Maus tried talking with the Mexican officer. The Mexican force, mostly Tarahumari Indians, were irregulars and plainly intent more on plunder than in attacking hostile Apaches. The determined scouts, positioned behind rocks, made further fighting an obviously costly effort. The Mexican officer took Maus prisoner, but he saw the excited scouts preparing for a fight and, after haggling over a bribe in mules, freed Maus and Concepcíon.

Maus worried that the Mexicans would try another scheme. The attack was clearly perfidious, as they at once knew they faced an American army force. Anxious to be away, and with ample grounds for a diplomatic protest, Maus gathered Crawford and the other wounded on litters and broke camp the next day, January 12. Slowed by the litter-borne wounded, the command moved only four miles before camping.

Geronimo held back, motivated by the proximity of Mexican Tarahumaris and the perennial suspicion of soldiers, even though he knew and trusted Captain Crawford. Only after the Americans had succeeded in separating themselves from their attackers did the chiefs cautiously venture forth. They watched the scouts begin the march toward Nácori Chico on January 12. In camp that night two Chiricahua women came in to ask permission for a council. They had to deal with an unknown officer because Captain Crawford lay on the ground with a bullet in his brain. Lieutenant Maus consented to a meeting. One occurred the next day, January 13, but still the chiefs hung back. Maus told the two men to say to the chiefs that if they would come in with their families and give up their arms, he would take them to General Crook. Finally, on January 14, Geronimo and Naiche appeared. Predictably, they refused to give up their weapons or bring in their families; even Crawford could not have accomplished that. They said they wanted to meet with Crook somewhere near the border in about a month, and meanwhile they would commit no depredations. They also agreed to yield some people as guarantees of good faith. By January 15, Maus had in his camp Nana and one of his men, a wife and child of both Geronimo's and Naiche's, and a sister of Geronimo's.

The Chiricahuas watched as Maus and his command crawled slowly toward Nácori Chico and the Bavispe River corridor to the north. They promptly broke their promise not to raid. They badly needed to replenish the stock and provisions lost when Crawford attacked their camp. For two months, in separate parties, all the chiefs led murderous raids on the ranches and settlements of Sonora. No communication passed between them and Lieutenant Maus, whom they expected to arrange the meeting with Crook. By the middle of March 1886, they had raided their way north toward the border, ready to meet with the general.[18]

Thus Geronimo and his comrades demonstrated their willingness to break agreements.

TWENTY-ONE

CANYON DE LOS EMBUDOS, 1886

SINCE THE MEETINGS BETWEEN the Chiricahua leaders and Lieutenant Marion P. Maus, following the killing of Captain Crawford on January 11, 1886, Sonora had borne the brunt of destructive raids on ranches and travelers. The raiders worked in two bodies, Geronimo and Naiche leading one, Chihuahua and his brother Ulzana the other. By early March 1886, two months after they had told Maus they needed time to collect their stock, they united in the Teras Mountains, nestled in the bend of the Bavispe River. Mexican troops had been combing Sonora trying to bring the raiders to battle, and the Apaches judged talks with Crook preferable to fighting the Mexicans.

Geronimo and Naiche sent four emissaries to the Pitachaiche Mountains, across the Bavispe to the north, to send up smoke to signal Maus that they stood ready to talk. Maus's scouts camped impatiently on the San Bernardino River eighteen miles north of the smokes. On March 14 Maus appeared with four Indian scouts, including the Chiricahua sergeant major, Noche. The messengers said that Geronimo and Naiche wanted to talk with Crook, as promised. Maus told them to return and bring them and their people to his camp. Reinforcing their anxiety, he warned them of the perils of an attack by Mexican troops.[1]

On March 19 Geronimo and Naiche, with twenty-two men and a herd of stolen cattle, appeared near the scouts' camp on the San Bernardino. Chihuahua and seven of his followers remained out. Mangas had no intention of coming in. Geronimo and Naiche held several talks with the lieutenant the next day. He wanted them to move closer to the boundary. They refused, declaring that Crook could meet them here. Warned repeatedly of the possibility of a Mexican attack, however, they reluctantly agreed. Selecting a shallow gorge named Canyon de los Embudos (Funnel Canyon), twenty-five miles south of the border, on March 22 Geronimo and Naiche moved twelve miles to this location. Maus and his scouts moved, too.

In their talks with Maus, and later with Crook, Geronimo and Naiche appear in the record as equal negotiators. These talks reaffirm the relationship between the two: Naiche the more pliable, Geronimo the firmly stubborn. Geronimo did most of the talking and displayed the stubbornness that Naiche lacked. Yet Geronimo always played the role of subordinate to Naiche because he was a chief, the son of Cochise, while Geronimo was never a chief. Naiche could speak his mind, but on important issues he rarely disagreed with Geronimo.

Brimming with distrust and anxiety, the Chiricahuas made camp half a mile from Maus's bivouac. They positioned themselves in an impregnable fortification, atop a small rocky hill amid a lava bed surrounded by deep ravines. Three steep gulches separated their fortress from the scouts' camp. They allowed no one from the military camp to enter their own. Heavily armed with rifles and abundant cartridges, they remained on the alert for treachery.[2]

Although expected daily, Crook had not arrived. Another white man had, a beef contractor named Charles Tribollet, who erected a small shanty near San Bernardino but below the border, where he dispensed whiskey and mescal. The scouts quickly discovered Tribollet, and even as the Chiricahuas settled into their positions, Maus's camp rocked with wild debauches. The Chiricahuas lost no time in discovering Tribollet, and for three days, until Crook belatedly appeared, both scouts and Chiricahuas indulged in raucous drunks. By this time, they were all badly hungover and the Chiricahuas in a foul mood.[3]

Late on the morning of March 25, 1886, Crook and his staff rode into Embudos Canyon, Crook in his canvas suit and astride his mule. He went at once to the camp of the packers and had lunch. Afterward, as Geronimo and Naiche stood by watching, Nana and Kayatena approached and shook hands with Crook. The sudden appearance of Kayatena took Geronimo by surprise and pleased him, too. The last he knew, Kayatena had been sent to Alcatraz

Prison. When Geronimo and Naiche walked to Crook, the three decided to begin the council at once.

While preparing for the meeting, a shout went up and in rode Chihuahua and Ulzana with six men trailing a herd of stolen horses. Chihuahua went at once to Crook and greeted him warmly. As the council proceeded, Chihuahua and Ulzana stood on the edge of the ravine and watched.

In a half circle Geronimo and Naiche, Crook, and a few officers and civilians sat on one side and at the bottom of a ravine shaded by cottonwoods and sycamores. Another surprise to the Indians, a photographer unpacked his rig and set up the camera for a picture of the participants.

Crook spoke gruffly, stating that he had come all the way from Fort Bowie, and asked what Geronimo had to say. After three nights of Tribollet's whiskey, Geronimo took offense at Crook's attitude and his refusal to say anything until Geronimo had finished talking. As an officer wrote words on paper, Geronimo launched into a long speech about how the "stories of bad people" at Turkey Creek had set him up for arrest and execution. He blamed Lieutenant Britton Davis, Chatto, and interpreter Mickey Free. Geronimo may truly have believed that he had been targeted for execution by the "stories of bad people." But he well knew that his denial of a plot to assassinate Chatto and Davis was a blatant lie because he himself had arranged it.

When he finally finished, Crook acidly replied by branding every one of his explanations a lie. Geronimo protested, but to no avail. At last, without ending the heated dispute, Crook interjected, addressing the interpreter. Everything Geronimo did on the reservation is known. No use for him to try to talk nonsense. Crook is no child. Geronimo must make up his own mind whether he will stay out on the warpath or surrender unconditionally. "If you stay out I'll keep after you and kill the last one, if it takes fifty years." The dispute raged on until Crook called a halt. During the night Geronimo should think over the issue, he said, and give his answer in the morning.[4]

Back in his stronghold, Geronimo felt angry and mortified by the attitude of Crook and his ultimatum to surrender unconditionally or fight to the end. He had come to the talks expecting to be allowed to return to the reservation and live as before. Crook's rude talk upset him. Two more Apaches figured in the talks that night: Alchise and Kayatena. Alchise, a White Mountain, had long been trusted by Crook as a willing agent. Kayatena had come back from Alcatraz a thoroughly transformed Apache, now committed to the white man's way.[5]

Alchise and Kayatena slipped into the Chiricahua camp that night. They found the Indians stirred up, suspicious, furious, and even straining to bolt once again. Geronimo stormed and ranted more than the others, directing all the men to keep guns in hand ready to shoot at a moment's notice. The chiefs argued all night. As the mood grew more rational, Alchise and Kayatena offered bits of advice, carefully ensuring that their words threw no more fuel on the fire. By morning the Chiricahuas felt calmer.

Later in the morning, Alchise and Kayatena left the Chiricahua camp with word that Geronimo, Naiche, and Chihuahua wanted to talk again with Crook. They came down to his camp. Chihuahua and Naiche seemed ready to accept Crook's ultimatum of unconditional surrender, but not Geronimo. Crook declared that under no circumstances could they return to the reservation, but they did agree to his next proposal: surrender on condition that they be transported to the East for two years, then allowed to come back to their homes.

The final formal meeting, again recorded, took place on March 27. The terms had been worked out the day before but not set to paper. No one repeated them here, only that they now surrendered to Crook. All knew the word meant the terms Crook had agreed to on March 26: transport to the East for two years, then return to the reservation. Chihuahua did most of the talking, much to Geronimo's irritation. Naiche simply declared that he surrendered. Last to speak was Geronimo, who said little beyond his decision to surrender. "Once I moved like the wind," he observed. "Now I surrender to you and that is all."[6]

The Chiricahuas remained in their fortress all night, except to ride to Tribollet's shanty. Returning at daylight on March 28, widely scattered and reeling drunkenly, Geronimo and a few others met Crook and his staff moving back to the boundary. Lieutenant Maus and his scouts remained in camp, waiting to escort the Chiricahuas to Fort Bowie. They had no intention of being escorted. They gathered in their defenses and continued to drink through the night, constantly firing their rifles. Naiche got so drunk that he shot and wounded his wife. On the morning of March 29 Scout Noche and Kayatena appeared in their camp to get them moving. They moved, but in a random, dispersed body, firing their rifles. Five miles up the valley they came together to meet Maus, all still drunk. They told him they would come in as soon as they were sober. By nightfall, five miles farther, they settled in a camp near Maus's.[7]

Among those in Chihuahua's camp was a white boy. He turned out to be
Santiago McKinn, the teenager taken prisoner by Geronimo in New Mexico
six months earlier. Unlike Charley McComas, who was killed when Crook's
scouts fell on Geronimo's camp in 1883, McKinn had been transformed into
an Apache, and as such he wanted to remain. He continued to live in Chihuahua's camp.

Although the army had destroyed Tribollet's shanty and all its contents,
Geronimo and Naiche had retained enough to get drunk during the night of
March 30. At 2:30 a.m. the next day, March 31, the two leaders gathered
eighteen men, fifteen women, and seven children and slipped away from the
camp, headed back for the Sierra Madre. They took only three horses from
the herd and made their way on foot. Knowing that the scouts would pursue
as soon as they discovered them gone, the Chiricahuas scattered and walked
only on rocks, thus leaving no trail.

Remaining in the camp next to Maus were Chihuahua, Ulzana, Nana,
ten other men, and forty-seven women and children. Later two of the escap-
ees returned to give up, making the total men fifteen. Even so, the two principal Chiricahua leaders and most of the men who surrendered to Crook at
Canyon de los Embudos had escaped. They made another war inevitable.[8]

Geronimo and Naiche did not bolt simply because they got drunk. Tribollet's whiskey may have brought to the surface thoughts suppressed after
the events at Canyon de los Embudos. Three years later Naiche explained to
Crook what went through his mind that night. He conceded that all were
drunk, but he said he worked it out himself. He didn't know how to do white-
man labor and didn't think he would like it. He feared being taken away to
some place he didn't know and wouldn't like it. And he concluded that all
who were taken away would die. For Naiche at least, and likely for Geronimo and the others, alcoholic fumes mixed with simple reality: they knew life
in the Sierra Madre, they did not know life in Florida. They chose the Sierra
Madre.[9]

While Geronimo raided in Sonora in the first months of 1886, General
Crook passed the weeks at Fort Bowie, hunting quail and playing whist
with the post officers. Except for a long report on military operations during the breakout from Turkey Creek, which dwelled more on the difficulties
of Apache warfare than on the campaigns in New Mexico, he retained his
usual reticence. He confined his reports to transmitting Lieutenant Maus's

dispatches. He expressed no reaction to the death of Crawford or even the perfidy of the Mexican attack. He received Maus's dispatches but never replied.[10]

Crook put on a show of reluctance to meet with the Indians, part of his strategy of taking a firm stance that admitted of no compromise. He knew of the plan to exile all the Chiricahuas from the reservation to Florida, but never alluded to it during these weeks or gave any hint that his opinion had changed since he and Crawford had met with Sheridan at Fort Bowie in November 1885. He would demand unconditional surrender, and if he could not get that he had the authority given him by the secretary of war on September 30, 1885, to accept their surrender as prisoners of war on condition of transport to the East. Above all, they could not be allowed to return to the reservation. If they insisted, war again.

When Crook received word from Maus on March 16 that he had established connection with the Chiricahuas, he telegraphed General Pope to release Kayatena from Alcatraz Prison and send him quickly by train to Bowie Station. He had learned from Pope that prison had entirely transformed Kayatena and believed that he might be a key to gaining a surrender. As Crook waited, at Canyon de los Embudos Maus and his scouts and the waiting Chiricahuas grew increasingly apprehensive. They had come this close to the border to talk with Crook, and he had not arrived. Maus appealed to Crook to hurry but received no reply. He delayed his departure for four days awaiting Kayatena. Finally, on March 22 Kayatena appeared, and Crook and his staff left for the talks. On the same day, at Canyon de los Embudos, both scouts and Chiricahuas launched their debauches with Tribollet's whiskey and mescal.[11]

Crook and his staff met with Geronimo and chiefs as soon as they arrived on March 25. His aide, Captain Bourke, transcribed the talks. This was the first of two formal talks. The second, also transcribed, took place on March 27. The crucial day was March 26, the day after the nighttime work of Alchise and Kayatena in the Chiricahua camp. Crook met privately with Geronimo and Naiche. Captain Bourke kept no record. Chihuahua had already accepted unconditional surrender, and perhaps Naiche could be persuaded. But not Geronimo. Faced by a long standoff with Geronimo, Crook invoked his fallback position: surrender as prisoners of war and accept exile in the East. Geronimo agreed to this with the added condition that their families accompany them east and all return home in two years. Crook accepted, although the two-year term and especially the return had not been authorized. In fact, the secretary of war had explicitly ruled that they never be permitted to return to Arizona.

The formal meeting of March 27 was just that, a formality that seemed to ratify the decision of the day before without actually recording it.

To the dismay of Lieutenant Maus, and especially packer Henry W. Daly, Crook insisted on starting back to Fort Bowie on the morning of March 28, leaving Maus to escort the newly designated POWs back to Fort Bowie. Soon after beginning the journey, Crook's party met Geronimo and others returning from Tribollet's shanty. Their drunken condition should have been a warning, but Crook was anxious to learn Sheridan's reaction to the reports he had already sent forward by courier.[12]

He got it soon enough, on March 30, the day after he reached Fort Bowie. A telegram from Sheridan relayed the president's decision: he would not assent to the surrender on Crook's terms. He instructed Crook to reopen negotiations on the basis of unconditional surrender, sparing only their lives. Later in the day Crook had to wire Sheridan the embarrassing news that Geronimo and Naiche and their followers had escaped.[13]

Before learning this distressing news, Crook had responded to the president's instructions by wiring that any attempt to renegotiate would result in an instant stampede by the Chiricahuas back to Mexico. Sheridan merely repeated the president's directive. Then, informed of the escape of Geronimo and Naiche and thoroughly exasperated, he declared that the only thing to be done now was to dispose the troops to protect the settlements and to request a plan of future operations. Instead of such a plan, Crook replied with another lecture on the difficulties of Apache warfare. He concluded by asserting that his plan of relying on scouts would ultimately prove successful but that perhaps he had become too wedded to his views. Therefore, since he had spent the hardest eight years of his life in Arizona, he asked to be relieved of command.[14]

Sheridan replied the next day, April 1. He transmitted General Orders No. 15, issued by the adjutant general, directing Brigadier General Nelson A. Miles to proceed at once to Fort Bowie and assume command of the Department of Arizona.

Crook still had to deal with Chihuahua's people, and he urged that they be sent away immediately. Once Maus arrived with Chihuahua and his people, arrangements had to be made to get them on a train headed east, which finally occurred on April 7. Only then could Santiago McKinn be taken away from his Apache friends. He was returned to his father and disappears from history. At Bowie Station, seventy-seven men, women, and children boarded the cars and, guarded by an armed escort, steamed eastward. Crook did not inform Chihuahua that the surrender terms had been rejected.[15]

On April 11, 1886, in what had to be a tense meeting, Crook turned over command of the Department of Arizona to General Miles and boarded a train for his new assignment, commanding the Department of the Platte, with headquarters in Omaha.

General Crook's time had run out; he was right to request relief. For nearly a year he had been caught in an unbreakable political vise. On the one hand, everyone conceded that he knew more about Apache warfare than any other senior officer. General Pope fully supported Crook's strategy. General Sheridan had reservations about the heavy reliance on Indian scouts, whose loyalty he had doubted since the Cibicue mutiny. But he, too, backed Crook until the final crisis.

On the other hand, despite Pope's support, the issue finally resolved itself into a collision of Crook's expert knowledge with the ignorance of President Grover Cleveland, Secretary of War William C. Endicott, and General Sheridan. Their knowledge of Apache warfare came only from Crook's descriptions, which failed to dilute their ignorance. They constantly complained of Crook's failure to end the Geronimo outbreaks or explain why to their satisfaction. Finally, they imposed conditions on Crook's negotiations that contradicted his expert knowledge.

Crook failed to handle his problem with much finesse. His unconcealed attitude of being the only know-it-all about Apaches irritated superiors and fellow officers alike. He hunted quail and played whist when he could have been thinking about how to deal more subtly with his superiors, how to convince them of his strategy without simply describing the difficulties of tracking Apaches in challenging country. Especially, he should have devoted more effort to explaining why only an Apache could catch an Apache, a doctrine hardly flattering to officers steeped in the traditions of the regular army. His characteristic reticence not only inhibited such an effort with his superiors but tormented his subordinates. His failure to keep Lieutenant Maus informed of his intentions diluted the effectiveness of that able officer.

Crook made three mistakes in conducting the talks, one deplorable. He waited too long to request the release of Kayatena from Alcatraz, which delayed his departure from Fort Bowie at a critical time when the Chiricahuas expected to talk but instead left them to indulge in Tribollet's whiskey for three days. The second mistake was his hasty departure from Canyon de los Embudos on the morning of March 28, leaving Lieutenant Maus to herd the drunken POWs to Fort Bowie. His presence on these pivotal days might have prevented the breakout of Geronimo and Naiche and their people.

His fatal error, however, was to concede terms of surrender that included return to Arizona. He had been enjoined by the secretary of war from promising a return to Arizona. Crook justified his departure from that command by declaring it the only terms he could get. And when the president rejected that, Crook rightly pointed out that reopening negotiations would stampede the entire band back to Mexico. He also knew that such a betrayal would violate his sense of honor, although he did not emphasize the point.

Whatever George Crook's mistakes and miscalculations in the final dealings with the Chiricahuas, history still awards him the distinction of the army's premier authority on Apaches and Apache warfare, a distinction demonstrated by his achievements and by the strategy that finally brought Geronimo to bay.

Geronimo would not be brought to bay for another five months. He went to Canyon de los Embudos simply because he was tired of life on the run and wanted to go back to the security of Turkey Creek. In the first meeting with Crook, hungover as he was, he understood that he would have to go back east. Chihuahua had readily agreed. Furious as Geronimo was the night after the first talk, he must have sensed that Alchise and Kayatena had been sent to calm him down and point him toward Crook's terms. He probably also puzzled over the huge change in Kayatena, who had made so much trouble that he had been sent to Alcatraz. The two emissaries of Crook may have influenced Geronimo to think about terms. But the general had "talked ugly" and Geronimo deeply resented it. If he had to leave Arizona for the East and trust the government to treat him well, he wanted to ensure that he could come back to Arizona. So the day after the first talk he haggled with Crook until he secured a promise to return from the East in two years—terms Crook had no authority to grant. Even those terms failed to prevent Geronimo and Naiche from breaking for the Sierra Madre. Whiskey may have been part of the motive, but distrust of Crook, mistrust of the government, and fear of the unknown doubtless proved stronger propellants.

Geronimo did not know it, but the terms he had wrung from Crook followed by his flight back to the Sierra Madre led to the downfall of the general who had treated him so insultingly ever since 1883.

TWENTY-TWO

MILES IN COMMAND, 1886

IN TWO AUTOBIOGRAPHIES GENERAL Nelson A. Miles denied any wish ever to serve in Apache country. When as commanding general of the Department of the Missouri he received orders on April 2, 1886, to replace General Crook as commanding general of the Department of Arizona, he later recalled that "it seemed a very undesirable duty and a most difficult undertaking." For two years, however, he had freely hurled criticisms at Crook and his methods and, within and outside of the army, strongly implied not only that he could do a better job but that he wanted to. Now he had his chance at what indeed was "a most difficult undertaking."[1]

Nelson A. Miles was ambitious, outspoken, pompous, arrogant, vain, and full of self-certitude. He had pushed his military career with every political stratagem he could muster. He believed that his best path to high rank lay with his wife's uncle, General William Tecumseh Sherman, and the general's brother, Senator John Sherman of Ohio. By bombarding General Sherman with personal missives, he probably did himself more harm than good, for that formidably ethical general granted no family favors, even when deserved.

By 1886 Nelson A. Miles had accumulated an impressive record, making him the most successful Indian-fighter in the army. As colonel of the Fifth Infantry, his role in the Red River War of 1874–75 was outstanding. His part in the Sioux Wars that followed Custer's disaster at the Little Bighorn, 1876–81, was decisive. In the same operations, General Crook seemed unable to do anything right, even though fresh from triumphs over the Apaches in Arizona. Crook and Miles harbored an intense dislike of each other; it did not amount to a feud but certainly was seen throughout the army as rivalry—rivalry that spawned Crook v. Miles factions in the army.

In ordering Miles to Arizona, Sheridan gently emphasized the "necessity of making active and prominent use of the regular troops" of his command. This "suggestion" of course reflected Sheridan's distrust of the Apache scouts, as well as his wish for the credit of ending the Geronimo outbreak to fall to the regulars. In their annual reports late in 1886 both Sheridan and Secretary of War Endicott bluntly stated their views: the scouts could be trusted only to capture or induce their kinsmen to surrender, not to fight or kill them.[2]

Miles needed no encouragement, for these coincided with his own views. He assigned the mission of running down and destroying or capturing Geronimo and Naiche to regular units. He did not abolish the Apache scouts altogether but retained some as auxiliaries (none Chiricahua or White Mountain), seeking enemy sign and following trails.[3]

After bolting back to the Sierra Madre on March 31, 1886, Geronimo and Naiche pushed rapidly westward, intent on launching another devastating raid against old adversaries. The first blow fell on April 2 west of Fronteras, only three days after the nighttime escape from Lieutenant Maus. They crossed the Sonora River and embarked on three weeks of death and destruction both east and west of the Magdalena River. The Sonora Railroad extended north along this river into Arizona to link with the Southern Pacific Railroad at Benson. On April 27 Geronimo and Naiche crossed into Arizona and put General Miles's new strategy to the test.[4]

Cavalry units proved active and aggressive enough to force Geronimo and Naiche, after three days of plundering on the Santa Cruz River near Calabasas, to withdraw into Mexico. American troops followed. On May 3, on the west side of the Piñito Mountains about thirty miles southeast of Nogales, Sonora, the Chiricahua leaders decided to throw off their determined pursuers. Securing their women and children, they set up an ambush on the rocky side of a canyon. They watched a troop of black soldiers halt and dismount rather than venture into the canyon. They then carefully advanced in a skirmish line on foot. When within range, the Apaches opened fire, dropping two soldiers and driving the rest back to safety. The troopers took formidable positions and returned the fire. The firing lasted more than an hour, with neither side achieving any advantage. One of the two soldiers who had fallen

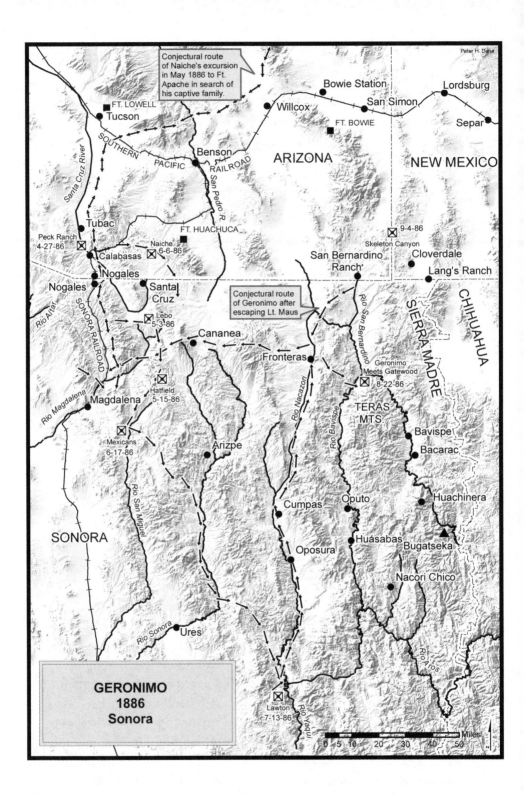

Peter H. Dana

Conjectural route of Naiche's excursion in May 1886 to Ft. Apache in search of his captive family.

Lordsburg

Bowie Station

San Simon

Separ

FT. LOWELL

Tucson

Willcox

FT. BOWIE

ARIZONA

NEW MEXICO

SOUTHERN

Benson

PACIFIC

RAILROAD

Santa Cruz River

San Pedro R.

FT. HUACHUCA

Tubac

Peck Ranch 4-27-86

9-4-86

Skeleton Canyon

Cloverdale

Calabasas

Naiche 6-6-86

San Bernardino Ranch

Lang's Ranch

Nogales

Nogales

Santa Cruz

Conjectural route of Geronimo after escaping Lt. Maus

Rio San Bernardino

SIERRA MADRE

CHIHUAHUA

Rio Altar

SONORA RAILROAD

Lebo 5-3-86

Cananea

Fronteras

Geronimo Meets Gatewood 8-22-86

Rio Nacazon

Rio Bavispe

TERAS MTS.

Bavispe

Rio Magdalena

Magdalena

Hatfield 5-15-86

Bacarac

Mexicans 6-17-86

Arizpe

Huachinera

Rio San Miguel

Cumpas

Oputo

Huásabas

Bugatseka

SONORA

Oposura

Nacori Chico

Rio Sonora

Ures

Rio Yaqui

Rio Aros

GERONIMO
1886
Sonora

Lawton 7-13-86

Miles

0 5 10   20   30   40   50

in the first fire lay wounded. Suddenly a bluecoat ran into the open and, dodging a withering fire, dragged him to safety. As dusk came on, both sides withdrew from their positions.[5]

Rarely had Geronimo and Naiche encountered such aggressive and persistent American soldiers. Twisting and turning back and forth across the Sonora Railroad, the Apaches also spotted Mexican troops trying to find them. Twice on May 11 the Indians took station among rocks on a hillside and engineered a classic ambush, sending the Mexicans flying in retreat. The Americans proved more formidable, "trailing us and skirmishing with us almost every day," remembered Geronimo. On May 15, camped on the summit of the Santa Cruz Mountains, "They surprised us about nine o'clock in the morning, and captured all our horses (nineteen in number) and secured our store of dried meat. We lost three Indians in this encounter." That afternoon they struck back. "We attacked them from the rear as they were passing through a prairie—killed one soldier, but lost none ourselves. In this skirmish, we recovered all our horses except three that belonged to me." That these fights loomed so large in Geronimo's memory reveals the impact of the newly energized regular soldiers.[6]

The next day, May 17, moments before a troop of cavalry charged their camp, the Apaches gathered their possessions and fled. After this close call, Geronimo and Naiche decided to divide. Naiche wanted to scout the situation at Fort Apache, check on his family, and perhaps put out peace feelers to General Crook (who was in Omaha by this time). Trailed closely by a cavalry column, the entire band crossed into Arizona and raided a ranch before Geronimo turned back to Sonora with two women and a child and the young girl captured in the first raid. Naiche and the rest of the Chiricahuas, twenty-seven in all, thrust down the Santa Cruz River, killing anyone who got in their way. He hid the women and children in the Rincon Mountains east of Tucson and later sent four men to escort them back to the border. With seven fighting men, he wended his way among the mountain chains northeast toward Fort Apache. Soldiers got on their trail and others tried to block the advance, but Naiche eluded them all.

After crossing the Gila and Black Rivers, on May 25 the little band concealed their horses and equipage in a wooded glen near the head of Bonito Creek, southeast of Fort Apache. At night, on foot, they made their way across seven miles of broken terrain to the Chiricahua camp on the edge of Fort Apache. Naiche snuck into the lodge of his mother, learned that his family was not there, and slipped out. He and his men hid in the vicinity for a day as his mother came out bearing an invitation from the soldier chief to give up. Rejecting such a dangerous proposition, Naiche and his men returned to gather their horses and equipment. Descending the trail at dawn on May 27, Naiche suddenly spotted some warning sign, shouted, and raced with his men back into the hills. A harmless volley of fire signaled a failed ambush set up by soldiers.

Naiche and his men hastened back toward the Rincon Mountains, killing two ranchers en route and avoiding the troops trying to head them off. In the Rincons, they discovered that their women and children had already left for Sonora. The little band followed, killing as they went, until they turned east into the Patagonia Mountains. At dusk on June 6, a troop of cavalry surprised them. Abandoning their horses and everything else, they scattered. By the next morning they had crossed into Sonora, leaving behind thirteen dead whites. On June 9, at the summit of the Sierra Azul, Geronimo and Naiche reunited, bringing together all the Chiricahuas who remained at large.

Two days later, forty strong, the Chiricahuas left the Sierra Azul. To confuse pursuing American soldiers, they split into three groups and headed in three directions. They planned to come together far to the south, near the confluence of the Aros and Yaqui Rivers, where they would decide where to take refuge.[7]

General Miles knew the Chiricahuas were raiding extensively in Sonora throughout April 1886. He conceived a strategy of organizing a light column to campaign against them south of the border. It would be commanded by Captain Henry W. Lawton, who would organize it at Fort Huachuca. Orders for the formation of this command did not reach the fort until May 4. Before that, on April 27, Geronimo had crossed into Arizona and begun his destructive raids down the Santa Cruz River.

The first blow fell the next day on the family of rancher Artisan L. Peck. He was working cattle two miles up the canyon when the raiders struck his home, killing his wife and baby daughter and taking captive his wife's ten-year-old niece, Trinidad Verdin. After discovering Peck himself, the Apaches beat and robbed him of his clothing. For an unknown reason, Geronimo told him he was free. Peck walked back to his home and viewed his dead family and ransacked house. Peck later identified the leader of the band as Geronimo.[8]

Three days of marauding along the Santa Cruz River threw Miles's strategy into disarray. As he traveled by rail between Benson, Calabasas, and Nogales, his troops in the region took the initiative, and Geronimo turned back to Sonora. The first to take up the pursuit, as soon as Peck told his story, was a troop of the black Tenth Cavalry under Captain Thomas C. Lebo. He followed the trail of the Apaches so persistently that Geronimo set up an ambush southwest of Nogales, in Sonora. On May 3 Lebo's troop reached the mouth of the deadly canyon. The captain did not ride into the trap. He dismounted his men, formed a skirmish line, and cautiously advanced into the canyon. From the cliffs the Apaches opened fire, hitting two men. One lay dead, but the other, Corporal Edward Scott, had fallen with a shattered kneecap and lay in the open exposed to the Indians' fire. Lieutenant Powhatan Clarke dashed out into a heavy fire and dragged Scott to safety. For this deed he was awarded the Medal of Honor.

Reinforced by another cavalry troop, Lebo continued the chase over punishing terrain. After five brutal days, they lost the trail and returned to Calabasas. But another unit, a troop of the Fourth Cavalry under Captain Charles A. P. Hatfield, had been alerted by a Mexican vaquero to the location of the Apaches. He hastened to take up Lebo's mission.[9]

On the morning of May 15, Hatfield surprised the Chiricahuas high in the Sierra Azul southeast of Nogales, Sonora. Geronimo took alert before the troopers could attack but abandoned the camp and its contents and fell back to high, rocky bluffs. The soldiers assailed these positions and drove the Apaches out, scattering them beyond hope of pursuit. The cavalry descended the mountains toward the Mexican town of Santa Cruz. Aware of the possibility of ambush, Hatfield disposed his command to avoid a trap. Even so, while halted to water the stock, the rear of the command came under fire from Apaches concealed in bluffs. Hatfield gathered his disorganized troopers and attacked the bluffs, driving the Apaches out. Nevertheless, he lost two soldiers killed and two wounded and had part of his horses stampeded.

The next morning, however, another troop of the Fourth Cavalry, under Lieutenant Robert A. Brown, struck Geronimo's camp in the western foothills of the Cananea Mountains, seized the camp, and recovered two of Hatfield's horses. The cavalry, largely acting on their own initiative, had kept the Indians stirred up. At this point, much to the army's confusion, a large group of Apaches ascended the Santa Cruz River and turned east into the Patagonia Mountains. On June 6 elements of Captain Lawton's command under Lieutenant Robert D. Walsh struck the camp and, joined by Lawton the next day, chased them into Mexico. This was Naiche returning from Fort Apache seeking to reunite with Geronimo, which he did. For his part, Miles had largely lost control of the conflict.[10]

Meantime, Captain Lawton had taken to the field pursuant to orders of May 4. A tall, strapping veteran of the Civil and Indian Wars, the senior troop commander of the Fourth Cavalry, he led his own troop of thirty-five, twenty infantrymen, twenty Indian scouts (none Chiricahua), and two pack trains. Three lieutenants served Lawton as well as Assistant Surgeon Leonard Wood. The doctor had more than medical ambitions: he wanted to be a line officer. Under Lawton, he would get that chance.[11]

Geronimo's raid into the United States threw Lawton's assignment into disorder. Parts of his command joined with other units in trying to run down the raiders, both in Arizona and in Sonora. Several times Lawton conferred with Miles, in Calabasas, Nogales, and even on a train. With the quarry now all in Mexico, Lawton could take up his assignment. The composition of his command had changed, but it remained essentially at the same strength.[12]

Lawton's command marched 120 miles down the Sonora River, enduring heat, rain, fever, and a tangle of ridges and canyons. At a point on the San Miguel River, they had a nearly violent confrontation with a Mexican command in a rough canyon. The Mexicans had battled a band of Apaches here on June 17, lost some men but recovered Trinidad Verdin, the girl seized by Geronimo in the raid on the Peck Ranch. The Mexicans took Lawton's advance guard of Indian scouts as the enemy returning for their dead and hastily withdrew. On June 18, with great difficulty, Lawton managed to establish relations with the Mexican troops. They turned over Trinidad Verdin, who was badly bruised. Mexican fire had killed the Apache carrying her, and she fell among the rocks. She related to Lawton all the atrocities Geronimo and his people had inflicted since her capture at the Peck Ranch on April 28. Of more immediate importance, she said the Apaches had become separated in the turmoil of fleeing the American troops, and those she was with were looking for the rest of their people. By June 30 the Americans had crossed the Sonora to the Yaqui River and camped near Cumpas.[13]

Geronimo led one of the bands seeking the rendezvous with the other two. He led them south and then turned east into a canyon in the mountains bordering the San Miguel River. As they camped, someone spotted a Mexican force approaching from behind with intent to attack. Geronimo ordered the people to flee farther into the canyon. Quickly mounting, he placed Trinidad Verdin on the horse behind him. The Mexicans loosed a heavy fire on the fleeing Apaches. Geronimo saw his wife hit. She climbed off her horse and fired a pistol at the Mexicans, but a hail of bullets cut her down. Geronimo's horse stumbled on a rock and threw both him and Trinidad among the rocks. Calling on her to follow, he ran on foot. Badly bruised by the fall, she did not follow but instead ran to the Mexicans. Geronimo barricaded himself in a cave and opened fire. The Mexicans advanced on the cave, but his rifle blasted three and the rest quickly backed off. Geronimo's scattered Chiricahuas came together and, still seeking the other two bands, left their stock and possessions in the hands of the Mexicans and continued their trek to the east and then south, down the Sonora River. This was not a raid, although they killed and robbed any Mexicans they met. Rather, Geronimo sought the other Chiricahuas and a hiding place from the solders they knew were looking for them. After he found the other two groups of Chiricahuas, Geronimo nestled into a secluded camp between two buttes on the Yaqui River six miles below its confluence with the Aros River.[14]

On July 13, one of the Chiricahuas returning from a hunt discovered the trail of a body of horses descending the slopes toward the Indian camp. He gave the alarm, and Geronimo quickly led all the people up a trail between the river and a steep cliff, leaving everything in the camp except their arms. On their heels, a force of infantry and Indian scouts charged into the camp. Once more, Geronimo had demonstrated his amazing skill at getting his people all out of a camp about to be attacked. Losing the camp and all its contents meant nothing compared with the lives of his people.

Geronimo and his little band continued up the Yaqui River, then turned up the Aros River.[15]

In May and June 1886, General Miles's troops had driven Geronimo and Naiche out of Arizona, and Captain Lawton had embarked on his struggle against almost overwhelming conditions of weather and terrain to find them. Miles turned to other concerns, traveling to Fort Apache to check on the reservation Chiricahuas. Under Chatto, they had led a peaceful and productive life, cultivating their crops and tending their stock. They detested their kinsmen in Mexico because they were likely to bring trouble on all the Chiricahuas. Moreover, Chatto and others had recently served General Crook as

enlisted scouts. Later, Miles portrayed the reservation Chiricahuas as forming a recruiting and supply depot for Geronimo and Naiche. Now, however,
their true condition suited his purpose.

In telegrams of July 3 and 7, Miles declared that the strongest military
reasons dictated that all the reservation Chiricahuas be relocated somewhere
east of New Mexico, and in view of their loyalty and good behavior, that
they be "allowed" to settle in the Indian Territory at the southeast base of the
Wichita Mountains, near Fort Sill. He knew that Congress had barred the
Apaches from ever moving to the Indian Territory, but he thought his rec-
ommendations could persuade Congress to lift the ban. Until Congress
acted, the Apaches might be placed near Fort Riley, Kansas. He proposed to
send a delegation of ten Chiricahuas to Washington to discuss the matter
and then be shown such land as the government might be willing to grant.[16]

Miles seemed unaware that this idea had been seriously discussed for two
years. General Sheridan had gone to Fort Bowie in November 1885 specifically to sound out General Crook on the propriety of such a move. Curiously, Sheridan now opposed Miles's scheme on the grounds that moving
Indians from their established homes had always proved mistaken because it
made them "bad Indians." Inconsistently, Sheridan did approve the dispatch
of a delegation of Chiricahuas to Washington to discuss such a move.[17]

Even before advancing his plan to relocate the reservation Chiricahuas,
Miles came to another decision, which he did not share with Washington. For
a month Lawton had toiled southward in Mexico but, so far as he knew, had
accomplished nothing but break down men and horses. Now Miles mulled
the unthinkable: Crook's formula of Chiricahua scouts. A former sergeant
major of scouts, George Noche, lived among the reservation Apaches. He
knew all of Geronimo's hiding places in Mexico and how to find them.

Miles sent for Noche and asked him to organize scouts to run down
Geronimo and Naiche. Two days later he again conferred with Noche, asking him the best way to catch the quarry. Noche suggested Tanitoe, who had
ridden with Geronimo until his horse was shot from under him in the fight
with Captain Hatfield on May 15. He had returned to the reservation and
now quietly tended his fields. But Tanitoe refused to go back to Mexico to
try to contact Geronimo. Noche therefore turned to Kayitah and Martine,
introducing the two to Miles. Kayitah told Miles that Geronimo and his
following, constantly hounded by Americans and Mexicans, were growing
increasingly exhausted and insecure. Both men had close relatives with

Geronimo. They could safely approach him without getting shot. Miles had Kayitah and Martine signed as scouts, issued them uniforms, equipment, and mules, and told them their assignment was to find Geronimo and persuade him to surrender.[18]

The two had to be supervised. The death of Crawford and resignation of Britton Davis left only one officer who knew the Apaches intimately and enjoyed their confidence: Lieutenant Charles B. Gatewood. The tall, lean officer who had served so long at Fort Apache had fallen out of favor with Crook, had endured eighteen months of tortuous litigation stemming from his arrest of an intruder on the reservation, and now commanded a company of Navajo scouts at Fort Wingate. Thoroughly disillusioned with scout duty, contemptuous of Navajos as scouts, weakened by recurring bouts of rheumatism and other ailments, Gatewood wanted out of the Southwest. Instead, while in Albuquerque on an official assignment, he was summoned by Miles, also in Albuquerque, and received orders to accompany the two scouts into Mexico. Both regarded it as futile, and Gatewood believed that his health would not hold through another trek in Mexico. As an inducement, Miles promised him a position on his staff, which appealed to the lieutenant as more agreeable duty than he had performed for years. Before leaving Albuquerque, he accidentally met George Wrattan, now heading a body of Indian scouts. Formerly a trader at San Carlos, Wrattan knew Apaches as well as Gatewood and spoke their language; he agreed to accompany Gatewood.

On July 15, at Fort Bowie, Gatewood, Wrattan, Kayitah, and Martine headed for the border at San Bernardino. They carried orders to join Lieutenant James Parker, whose troop of the Fourth Cavalry had followed a trail of six Apaches into Mexico. Parker received orders to halt and await Gatewood, then put him on the trail.[19]

When Gatewood and his small party arrived on July 21, Parker announced that there was no trail. Rain had washed it out. Gatewood, never keen on the assignment, replied that therefore he would go back and report the absence of a trail. No, declared Parker, if Miles wanted Gatewood on a trail, Parker would find one, or at least put him in touch with Lawton, who could surely find a trail. Gatewood balked. He said he was too sick to go on. Parker answered that they would remain in camp until Gatewood was well enough to continue. Six days later Gatewood had recovered enough to set forth.[20]

By July 1886 General Miles pushed three efforts he hoped would end the crisis: Lawton might run down the Chiricahuas and either destroy them or induce them to surrender; Gatewood might find them and Kayitah and Martine might persuade Geronimo to surrender; the delegation of reservation Chiricahuas dispatched to Washington might agree on a place to resettle all their people.

Permission to send the delegation rested on the assumption, which Miles did nothing to disabuse, that the reservation Chiricahuas wanted to move to a location far from their homeland and that the only question was where. He would have a hard time dissembling his way through that.

Never receptive to "surrender," only to a return to the old life on the reservation, Geronimo and Naiche and their handful of followers knew that their only choice was to keep moving or yield to the army and go back east. The soldiers had kept them on the run, tired, constantly insecure, enduring heat and rain, suddenly stampeded out of their camp with the loss of all their possessions, morale sinking, too distrustful of their pursuers even to consider any course other than to keep running. They knew the soldiers could not catch them but feared that they would not stop trying. So the chase continued, through July and August 1886, with no end in sight.

TWENTY-THREE

GERONIMO MEETS GATEWOOD, 1886

CAPTAIN LAWTON'S FORCE OF cavalry and Indian scouts had not succeeded in his mission of destroying the Chiricahuas or inducing them to surrender. Nor had Lieutenant Gatewood and his two Chiricahuas succeeded in talking with Geronimo.

Meanwhile, General Miles had other problems to address. On July 13, 1886, he received authority to send a ten-man delegation under Chatto to Washington. In charge of Captain Joseph M. Dorst, they entrained for the capital as Miles urged that Congress be asked to lift the ban on Apaches in the Indian Territory. On July 15 General Sheridan wired Miles that this was wholly impracticable. Even so, Miles asked that the delegation be allowed to visit the Indian Territory. Informed that these Indians would not be settled anywhere west of the Missouri River, he continued to advocate the Indian Territory, now settling on the portion known as the Cherokee Strip, bordering the Kansas boundary. By the end of July Miles had been informed in no uncertain terms that President Cleveland wanted all these Indians relocated in the East. Sheridan favored Fort Marion, Florida, where Chihuahua and the Chiricahuas who surrendered to General Crook had been sent.[1]

As this exchange proceeded, on July 26 Captain Dorst ushered Chatto and his companions into talks with the secretaries of war and the interior. The secretaries grasped that the Indians had not come to Washington to decide on a new home but to declare that they wanted to remain where they were. To try to put Chatto in a more receptive frame of mind, Secretary

L. Q. C. Lamar presented him with a presidential medal (it bore the likeness of former President Chester Arthur), and Secretary William C. Endicott presented an elaborate certificate. Dorst thought they had been mollified, and he once more put them on a train headed for home. Stalling for time, the authorities kept them for several days at Carlisle Indian School in Pennsylvania before letting them continue. On August 11, at Emporia, Kansas, Dorst received a telegram directing him to take the delegation to Fort Leavenworth, Kansas, and hold them for further orders.[2]

The confusion reflected the uncertainty not only over where to settle the Chiricahuas but also over when and how to gather them for deportation. On August 20, Lieutenant Colonel James F. Wade, at Fort Apache, assured his superiors that he could easily manage their deportation, by train from Holbrook. Doubtless exasperated by the continuing arguments between Miles and his superiors, on August 23 President Cleveland decreed that the destination be Fort Marion, Florida, and that Colonel Wade proceed at once.[3]

Even before the Chatto group had left Washington, Miles had prompted Sheridan to begin worrying about the effect of letting these dissatisfied Indians return home just as Colonel Wade arranged to deport them. This led to the diversion of the delegation to Fort Leavenworth. While there, on September 13 Colonel Wade succeeded in his assignment, and all the reservation Chiricahuas embarked from Holbrook for Fort Marion. At Fort Leavenworth, convinced they had been betrayed, the Chatto Indians grew increasingly "turbulent," which led Sheridan to order them sent directly to Fort Marion.[4]

Chatto, once a vicious raider, had turned himself into the most skilled Chiricahua scout. His service during Captain Crawford's operations in Sonora was indispensable; Crawford relied on him and his scouts to the exclusion of regulars, and they performed superbly. At Fort Apache, Sergeant Chatto had also served Lieutenant Britton Davis loyally. He excelled at farming and stock-tending. Now, two months after leading the Chiricahua delegation to Washington, he suddenly and inexplicably found himself labeled a prisoner of war and hastened to Fort Marion, Florida.

Three and a half years later Chatto gave his version of this experience in an interview with General Crook. He had been working his farm near Fort Apache. He grew wheat and barley. He had a wagon and made good money hauling hay and supplies. He tended about thirty sheep and made money shearing wool. He had horses and mules. The crops had just begun to ripen when he was called to Washington. He went, not of his own accord. Later, when the government sold all his possessions, he received not nearly their value.

When Chatto reached Washington, "they talked good to him" and said he could make a living. On the way back to Fort Apache, however, he was turned back and taken to a place where there were soldiers. He didn't know why. A letter from General Miles came to the Apache delegation at Fort Leavenworth. It was very long, and a lieutenant read it to them. It said that Fort Apache was a bad place for Indians. All the whites were down on them and other Indians, too. The letter said that one part of the country belonged to Washington and the other to Arizona. Miles wanted to put them on the Washington side, where there were good people. They "touched the pen" to a paper that promised a reservation where all the Chiricahuas would be gathered and provided stock and plenty of room for them.

As he described the paper they "signed," Chatto ripped the Arthur presidential medal from his chest. "Why did you give me that," he asked, "to wear in the guardhouse? I thought something good would come to me when they gave me that, but I have been in confinement ever since I have had it."

Thus George Wrattan interpreted Chatto's words, General Crook's loyal first sergeant of Apache scouts, US Army, now a prisoner of war.[5]

While General Miles distracted an elusive Washington officialdom, Captain Lawton kept an elusive Geronimo on the run. His cavalry ruined by heat, rain, and rugged terrain, the command in July consisted only of an infantry company and an Indian scout company (none Chiricahua) under Lieutenant Robert A. Brown. Brown was Lawton's only officer. A sergeant led the infantry. Assistant Surgeon Leonard Wood asked to command the infantry, which Lawton approved. Wood had taken the first step toward ending his career as army chief of staff.

In July Lawton's little command combed the mountains, ridges, and canyons in the region centering on the confluence of the Yaqui and Aros Rivers. Attired only in drawers and undershirts because of the heat and humidity, they stumbled from one trail to another, only to have it disappear or be rained out. They hurried from one murder reported by Mexicans to another and found new trails to follow. On July 13 a trail led Brown's scouts to the top of a mountain, from which they looked down into a canyon of the Yaqui River and sighted the Chiricahua camp, on a plateau tucked between two ridges, the stock grazing, cook fires burning, and people going about their daily lives. He sent a courier running back to Lawton, urging him to bring up the infantry as fast as possible. Lawton did, so rapidly that twenty fell out from exhaustion.

Lawton and Brown fixed on a plan to catch the quarry from two directions, Brown and his scouts from upstream and Lawton and the infantry from downstream. Before the infantry reached its position, the scouts opened fire. "Captured everything in the camp except the Indians," Wood wrote in his journal. The command had all of Geronimo's stock, food, and camp equipage, but once again the Chiricahuas had slipped out of the trap. "Everyone bitterly disappointed," Wood wrote, as they cooled themselves in the river and welcomed the pack train, which finally arrived at midnight.[6]

Although the Chiricahuas seemed uninterested in hiding their trail, Lawton made little progress in following it. His cavalry, under Lieutenant Robert D. Walsh, had rejoined, but Lawton thought him in such bad shape from an infected centipede sting on a foot that he could hardly perform any duty. As for Lieutenant Brown, he was a good and energetic officer but inexperienced. "The infantry, poor orphans, have to get along the best they can with no one. But for Dr. Wood, lord knows what would have become of them." The heat was so bad that Lawton thought operations should be suspended during July and August. Although discouraged, he tried to keep to the trail but was thwarted by the swollen Aros River.[7]

On August 3, Lieutenant Parker reported to Lawton, as he tried to cross the Aros River. He had not found Lieutenant Gatewood a trail, but he had found Lawton. When informed of Gatewood's mission, Lawton strongly objected. "I get my orders from President Cleveland direct. I am ordered to hunt Geronimo down and kill him. I cannot treat with him." Parker stayed three days with Lawton, arguing that General Miles had changed his strategy and that Lawton should act accordingly. Finally Lawton agreed to take Gatewood under his command. "But if I find Geronimo I will attack him; I refuse to have anything to do with this plan to treat with him. If Gatewood wants to treat with him he can do it on his own hook." Meantime, Gatewood had his own talks with Lawton, who stuck to the position he presented to Parker. Gatewood protested that he could not get his two Chiricahua Apache scouts, Kayitah and Martine, near Geronimo if Lawton insisted on fighting him.[8]

Talking with Dr. Wood, Gatewood revealed his own thoughts. He said that he had no faith in his plan and was disgusted with it. He was in bad health, suffering from an old bladder inflammation that made riding difficult. Later he repeated his misgivings and applied for a medical certificate that would allow him to give up the mission and return to Fort Bowie. Wood refused—possibly because he believed that Gatewood offered the only hope.[9]

The best clue to the Chiricahuas' whereabouts came from none other than General Miles. A dispatch from the governor of Sonora on August 18 alerted Miles that the fugitives were trying to make peace with the Mexicans at Fronteras. One of Lawton's Apache scouts en route to Fort Huachuca confirmed the report: he had encountered Geronimo and Naiche with a dozen other Chiricahuas on their way to Fronteras. They looked worn and hungry and told him they wanted to make peace. Geronimo carried his right arm bandaged in a sling. The scout described this incident to Miles at Fort Huachuca.[10]

Working his way north on the Nacozari River, Lawton learned the same news from a Mexican burro train traveling downstream. He judged the time right for sending Gatewood on his mission. Fitting him out with a pack train and a ten-man escort, he ordered the lieutenant to take his two Indians and George Wrattan and push rapidly ahead to Fronteras, get on the trail, and try to open communication with Geronimo. Still sick, Gatewood procrastinated all afternoon on the eighteenth. Late that night, discovering that Gatewood had not left, Lawton went to Wood's tent, furious and inclined to place Gatewood under arrest and send another officer. Wood talked him out of that. Not until after midnight did Gatewood and his contingent get under way.[11]

Mutual suspicion clouded the peace overtures in Fronteras. Lawton worked his way toward Fronteras. Nearing the town on August 22, he, Wood, and another officer went into the settlement. Before arriving, they ran into George Wrattan. Gatewood and his Indians were in Fronteras and had not taken the trail. Angry, Lawton sent for Gatewood. When he arrived, Wood met him and said that Lawton was busy and had directed him to order Gatewood to take the trail at once and to express his "extreme annoyance" that Gatewood had yet to begin his mission. In fact, Wood was covering for Lawton, who was too drunk to do anything. Gatewood got on the trail at once.[12]

Geronimo and Naiche had posted themselves atop a hill on the outskirts of Fronteras. They shouted that they wanted to make peace. Later, they sent two women into the town to buy supplies and mescal. In fact, as Lawton's scout had reported, the Chiricahuas were worn down and hungry. Since surprised and stampeded out of their camp on the Yaqui River by Lawton on July 13, they had been kept on the run and always insecure by the soldiers and scouts. They were tired. If the Mexicans would make peace, the Indians could regain their strength by raids into Arizona and New Mexico. But like all previous peace overtures to the Mexicans, this one failed. Fronteras was filled with Mexican soldiers. Geronimo and Naiche suspected trickery. They sent two men into Fronteras to get the women and needed supplies, including mescal. Then they broke camp and headed east, toward the Teras Mountains.[13]

Geronimo laid out the Chiricahua ranchería atop a steep ridge in the Teras Mountains overlooking the great bend of the Bavispe River. For two days they relieved their hunger from the supplies acquired by the two women in Fronteras and indulged in a prolonged mescal drunk. Sentinels kept watch for the Americans they knew to be looking for them. Sentiment for surrender began to rise, but the people and conditions had to be right. Geronimo in particular remained almost as suspicious of American officers as of Mexican soldiers. Yet he and Naiche longed to be reunited with their families, shipped east with Chihuahua's people who had surrendered to General Crook. (These were the women and children taken in the attacks of June and August 1885 and held at Fort Bowie by Crook.)

On August 24 the youthful Kanseah had posted himself on the slope overlooking the river and scanned the valley below with field glasses. Soon he detected two horsemen approaching. As they came closer into view, he saw one holding aloft the long stalk of a century plant, from which "something white" fluttered. He recognized them as army scouts. Geronimo and other men gathered. Geronimo instructed Kanseah that when the two got close enough, he should shoot them. By now they were recognized as Kayitah and Martine. Yahnosha, Kayitah's cousin and one of Geronimo's best and most loyal fighters, jumped atop a rock and asked what the two scouts wanted. Kayitah replied they had been sent by General Miles and Lieutenant Gatewood to talk peace with Geronimo. "Come on up," said Yahnosha, "nobody is going to hurt you." On the ridgetop Kayitah and Martine sat with Geronimo and Naiche.[14]

Kayitah did the talking. He described the pathetic condition of Geronimo and his people and the increasing likelihood that soldiers would find and attack them. He also described his agreeable life on the White Mountain Reservation and urged Geronimo to return there. Geronimo responded: "I don't want to go to San Carlos. They chop my neck off. This my home. I stay here, right here. You chase me. You kill me. Alright. I die right here. I got to die sometime." "You don't have to die now," answered Kayitah. "You come down and talk to soldiers. You come under white flag—they not hurt you." To which Geronimo declared, "Mangas Coloradas come under white flag. What they do to him?" These officers would do no such thing, said Kayitah. They could be trusted. After further argument, even pleading, Geronimo gave in. "Well we go, make talk. I will go with you."[15]

Kayitah stayed in the camp all night as the men sat in council debating what to do. Martine went back down the mountain to meet with Lieutenant Gatewood, whom the Chiricahuas knew well and trusted, and tell him that Naiche guaranteed his safety and that he and Geronimo would meet with him the next morning—with him, and no other officer. The next morning, sighting a troop of Apache scouts moving up the trail toward their camp, Naiche sent three men to meet Gatewood and tell him to return to the valley and move to a canebrake in the river's bend, where talks could be held in the comfort of wood, water, and shade. Also, the scouts had to return to their bivouac of the night before, and no other soldiers could come closer.[16]

On the morning of August 25, Gatewood and his small party, including George Wrattan and two other interpreters, had settled into the designated spot, as the Chiricahuas observed from patches of brush. In small groups, men rode in and later women and children, in all numbering about forty. Kayitah had also appeared. Everyone unsaddled, laid aside their arms, and threw the saddles over logs as seats. After many smokes, Geronimo slipped in and at once greeted Gatewood warmly, asking why he looked so thin and unwell. Then Naiche appeared. He, too, embraced Gatewood. After a hasty breakfast, the talks began, George Wrattan interpreting and two others confirming his words. Geronimo sat on a log so close to Gatewood that they touched, and the rest seated themselves on the ground in a semicircle.

Geronimo stated that all had now assembled and would listen to what Gatewood had to say. He replied at once and bluntly: "Surrender, and you will be sent to join the rest of your people in Florida, there to await the decision of the President of the United States as to your final disposition. Accept these terms, or fight it out to the bitter end."

After a long silence and a request by Geronimo for mescal, which Gatewood denied because he had none, Geronimo spoke. All the men had made medicine during the night before and discussed the issue. Their conclusion: the war would end only if they could return to the reservation, occupy their previous farms, receive the usual rations and other issues, and be guaranteed exemption from punishment for what they had done.

Gatewood replied that he had been ordered by General Miles to say what he had said and no more. This would probably be their last chance to surrender. If the war continued, they would all eventually be killed, or if captured the terms would not be as generous.

The impasse set the stage for hours of talk. Geronimo explained all the wrongs the whites had inflicted on his people. The Apaches would give up part of their homeland, but not all. He then led the men into a canebrake for an hour's private discussion. Returning at noon, they joined in a brief lunch with coffee. Then Geronimo looked Gatewood directly in the eye and declared, "Take us to the reservation, or fight."

Gatewood then startled all the Apaches with a revelation. General Miles had rounded up all the Chiricahuas on the reservation and sent them to Florida. If Geronimo and his people went back to the reservation, they would live among their hereditary enemies, the White Mountain Apaches. Again Geronimo fixed the lieutenant with an intense stare and asked if he told the truth or made up the story to get them to surrender. He quizzed Gatewood at length about how such a thing could happen to a people always on the alert. Finally, Geronimo led the men back to the canebrake for another conference. They returned in an hour, and Geronimo announced that they stood by their original terms. But he also said he wanted Gatewood to get on his mule, ride to the nearest army post, get in touch with Miles, and try to persuade him to modify his terms, at least to allow them all to be collected and settled somewhere in the West. Gatewood explained that he did not know where Miles was, and anyway Miles had made up his mind. Furthermore, Gatewood was sick, and he could not do more hard riding.

More talk ensued, until once again the Chiricahuas retired to the canebrake. They emerged an hour later to repeat that they would not surrender on Miles's terms. Geronimo thought they ought to talk all night, and he asked Gatewood to find a beef to eat. Gatewood declined. The argument continued late into the afternoon.

Then Geronimo turned the talks to General Miles. They didn't know him. What kind of a man was he? How old? How large? What color eyes and hair? Did he talk ugly or nice? Is he liked? Large or small heart? Gatewood answered all the questions. Then Geronimo said, "He must be a good man, since the Great Father sent him from Washington, and he sent you all this distance to us."

At sundown Gatewood gathered his gear and said he would return to his bivouac, that the Indians should discuss the matter all night. As he prepared to leave, Geronimo asked him to stay a few minutes, then said: "We want your advice. Consider yourself one of us and not a white man. Remember all that has been said today, and as an Apache, what would you advise us to do? Should we surrender, or should we fight it out?"

"I would trust General Miles and take him at his word."

Geronimo said they would return to their mountain camp, make medicine, hold a council, and reach a decision. He would let Gatewood know the result the next morning, August 26. He did. Geronimo and five men appeared near the army bivouac and shouted for Gatewood by his Apache name, Bay-chen-daysen (Long Nose). A few hundred yards from the camp, Gatewood and Geronimo shook hands. The night's council had produced a decision. He and all his people would meet with General Miles north of the border and talk the matter over with him. They would keep their arms and travel separately, but the American force would accompany them and protect them from any Mexican attack.

Geronimo then asked to meet the American commander. Gatewood escorted him into the bivouac and introduced him to Captain Lawton. Geronimo hugged him, and all sat down for a smoke. Lawton agreed to Geronimo's proposal. They selected as a place of meeting Skeleton Canyon, in the Peloncillo Mountains about sixty miles southeast of Fort Bowie. All the Chiricahuas came down and relaxed for the rest of the day.

On August 27 they remained in camp, waiting for Lawton's pack train to find its way to them. Geronimo dictated to George Wrattan a letter to General Miles. He began by demanding that he be allowed to go back to Turkey Creek, and he expected the government to have his family there when he arrived. After naming the exiles in Florida he wanted brought back, he stated that he wanted to meet the general in person, not talk on paper. He and his people would meet Miles north of the border. Captain Lawton's command and his people would move north separately and freely visit each other. Gatewood could travel with whom he wished. Geronimo made his mark, and Lawton signed as witness.

In a month, Geronimo had allowed his mind to drift from the adamant refusal even to use the word "surrender" to an agreement in which the word "surrender" was at least being talked about. He had not decided to surrender, only to keep his arms and meet with General Miles. But the talks with Gatewood and the nightly councils and medicine-making in the cane brake had wrought an unprecedented softening of his attitude. A number of observers, as far back as Fronteras, had commented on how worn down and emaciated Geronimo and his followers looked. As Gatewood had made explicit, the choice was war to the death or surrender. The exhaustion of July and August 1886 at least made Geronimo more receptive to an alternative to continued flight, although the prospect of "surrender" probably had yet to lodge in his mind.

He himself would decide whether General Miles could be persuaded to change his mind and whether he could be trusted any more than General Crook.

TWENTY-FOUR

GERONIMO SURRENDERS, 1886

FOR CAPTAIN HENRY W. LAWTON, the crucial day was August 26, 1886. Gatewood and his two Apache scouts, Kayitah and Martine, had accomplished their mission. Geronimo and Naiche came to Lawton's bivouac and met with him. They all stayed in his camp the rest of the day and the next. Geronimo continued to talk both days, including dictating his letter to General Miles. Lawton felt certain the war would soon be over if only Miles would consent to meet personally with Geronimo and Naiche.[1]

But Miles did not want to meet with them. Preoccupied with getting the reservation Chiricahuas off to Florida, he wanted Lawton to handle the surrender. (They had not been moved when Gatewood told Geronimo they had.) On August 29, Miles's adjutant acknowledged receipt of Lawton's dispatch reporting the talks and said that the general directed Lawton to inform the Apaches that their best course was to surrender to him as prisoners of war and trust the government to do the right thing. If they were acting in good faith, they would place hostages in Lawton's control. Pressed again by Lawton, Miles responded that if the Apaches could give any guarantee that they would surrender, such as hostages, he would meet with them. Otherwise Lawton should use his best judgment.[2]

Stressful as Miles's evasion proved for Lawton, he dealt with even more severe stress. Moving up the San Bernardino on August 28, both the Chiricahuas and the troops spotted a skirmish line of Mexicans, uniformed in white, advancing over a ridge. Both camps began throwing up defenses.

Lawton ordered Wood, Lieutenant Abiel L. Smith, and interpreter Tom Horn to hurry down to the Mexicans. Wood took the lead, the other two following when ready. He met them coming single file out of a canebrake. Wood told the leader to halt, that if he came farther a fight would take place. Both the troops and the Apaches were united and prepared for battle. Smith went back to get Lawton while Wood and Horn stalled by keeping the talks going. Lawton arrived and said the Indians had surrendered to the United States and he would not allow them to be interfered with.

Both Lawton and Wood knew the Mexican leader, the belligerent prefect of Arispe, Jesús Aguirre, with whom they had talked in Fronteras. He had almost two hundred infantrymen. He clearly did not want a fight, but they were all in a foul temper, and he wanted to take the Apaches back to Fronteras for punishment.[3]

The Chiricahua camp boiled with excitement. An agitated Geronimo told Gatewood that he and his people would run with him north toward the border. Lawton's men could stand off the Mexicans. Hastily the women packed up the camp, and the run began. They ran fast, crawling up and over ridges and down in gulches. Naiche and a rear guard of skirmishers brought up the rear. After an hour, having traveled about ten miles, the group halted. They wanted to remain close enough to Lawton to help him fight the Mexicans if necessary. Geronimo had sent a messenger with this assurance.

Soon Leonard Wood galloped into the group. He brought word that Aguirre would not be satisfied until he heard from Geronimo himself that he intended to surrender to the Americans. Lawton had arranged a meeting place, distant from the body of Mexican troops. The Mexican leader and seven men would meet with Geronimo and seven men, all armed. Geronimo saw treachery in such a scheme, and he yielded only after lengthy persuasion by Gatewood.

The Mexican leader and his officers lounged under a cottonwood when Geronimo and Naiche emerged from the brush, Geronimo dragging his Winchester by the muzzle and carrying a holstered pistol in front of his left hip. Aguirre jumped up and, introduced by Lawton, shook hands with Geronimo. But he also grasped his own holstered pistol and partially withdrew it. Geronimo, with a look of burning hatred on his face, began to pull his. Behind, the Mexican officers fidgeted with their weapons. All the Apaches leveled their Winchesters. Lawton and his officers jumped between the two sides. The Mexican prefect returned his pistol to behind his back, and Geronimo relaxed.

The prefect asked why Geronimo had not surrendered at Fronteras. Geronimo replied that was because he did not want to be murdered. "Are you going to surrender to the Americans?" asked the prefect. "I am," said Geronimo, "because I can trust them. Whatever happens, they will not murder me and my people. I have nothing further to say." "Then I shall go along and see that you do surrender," declared Aguirre. "No," answered Geronimo, "you are going south and I am going north. I'll have nothing to do with you or with any of your people." Except for one soldier left to keep watch, Aguirre and his command did as Geronimo demanded.[4]

With troops of both nations roaming the area, the Chiricahuas broke camp early on August 29 and moved warily up the San Bernardino. Lawton's command lagged behind. Lawton, Wood, and Lieutenant Thomas Clay caught up with them and asked them to wait for Lawton's command. But it did not come. Throughout the day, one after another, including Lawton, went in search but did not return. Near nightfall, Geronimo moved another eight miles and found a defensible position for the camp. At daybreak on August 30, the Apaches moved another eight miles and found a creek on which to wait for the command. It finally arrived that morning.

The next day, August 31, both parties crossed the border and paused in Guadalupe Canyon, near the head of the San Bernardino River. The Chiricahuas grew restive. They had overheard remarks made by some of the officers that aroused their suspicion. Leaving the troops behind, they hurried forward, out of the canyon.

Gatewood rode hard to overtake Geronimo. The pace slowed, and the two talked. Geronimo asked Gatewood what he would do if fired on by the American troops. He replied that he would rush out and try to have the firing stopped. If he failed, he would run away with the Apaches. Naiche had joined and advised Gatewood to stay with him and Geronimo because some of the young men, suspecting treachery, might try to kill the lieutenant.[5]

The danger, however, lay not with suspicious Apaches. It lay with the American soldiers themselves.

When the troops finally caught up with Geronimo, Lieutenant Abiel L. Smith, not Lawton, commanded. A strong-minded officer of twelve years' service, he had done nothing to distinguish himself but was known to believe that the best course of action was simply to kill Geronimo. Lawton had left the command to him after he found it six miles south of the San Bernardino Ranch. Lawton had decided to ride into the ranch and try to communicate with Miles by heliograph (mirrors flashing from peak to peak), and Smith was the next ranking officer.[6] Before leaving, Lawton confided to Smith his fear that he might fail to keep his promise to Miles and deliver the Chiricahuas safely. Ominously, Smith replied, "I haven't promised them [the Apaches] anything. You . . . communicate with Miles, and I'll take command."

Guided by Leonard Wood, Smith led the command to the Chiricahua camp, and on August 31 both Apaches and troops crossed the border and made their way into Guadalupe Canyon. The Apaches traveled in advance, and after several miles a lieutenant caught up with them. Almost certainly he brought copies of dispatches Lawton had received from Miles, by heliograph, instructing him to do anything necessary, including "any other measures," to end the standoff. Plainly, Miles did not want to meet with Geronimo, and Lawton could use his own judgment. Smith, and even Wood, took that to justify aggressive measures, as Miles intended. Some of this talk found its way to the Apaches and set off the flight from Guadalupe Canyon.

Learning of the belligerent attitude of Smith, Wood, and other officers, Gatewood took Wrattan and Geronimo back to confront them. They approached in single file. Smith said he wanted to meet with the Chiricahuas. Gatewood refused. Smith pointed out that he ranked Gatewood (both were first lieutenants, but Smith had seniority) and demanded a meeting. An angry exchange followed, but Gatewood stood his ground and declared that he knew what Smith intended and would "blow off the first man if they didn't stop." Both Smith and Wood backed down, but Wood sent his orderly galloping back to bring Lawton to the scene. His arrival later that night calmed the situation. With Wood and their orderlies, Lawton went forward to the Indian camp, took supper with them, and calmed them, too.[7]

But Gatewood would not be mollified. He had lost faith in himself—if he ever had it. He had voiced doubts about the mission from its inception. Gatewood went to Lawton and proposed to take his baggage and join some other column. He had been ordered to put Kayitah and Martine in touch with Geronimo. He had done that. His mission was completed. Lawton argued that Gatewood was indispensable to completing the surrender. If the

Indians escaped, both would be in trouble. If necessary, Lawton would use force to keep Gatewood. Pressure was applied and Gatewood stayed.[8]

The Apaches and Lawton's command reached their destination on the afternoon of September 2. Skeleton Canyon opened on the west side of the Peloncillo Mountains. Venturing into the narrow entrance, the Apaches noted that it widened and divided into two branches. But they also noted that several army units had already bivouacked, and more arrived before they could go into camp. The numerous soldiers, together with the many couriers who came and went, made all the Chiricahuas more nervous and suspicious than they already were. They informed Lawton that they would move deeper into the canyon and camp alone. Like Crook at Canyon de los Embudos, the absence of General Miles further upset them. With his usual acute eye for topography, Geronimo selected a plateau at the confluence of the two canyons. From here they could watch the soldiers below and scan the San Bernardino Valley beyond, as well as defend themselves if it became necessary. Gatewood and Wrattan stayed with them.

The agitation persisted through the night and into September 3. Finally, from their elevated perch, the Apaches sighted dust arising from the approach of vehicles. They assumed that at last the general had come. They could talk with him and "look him in the eye." Geronimo pressed Gatewood to take him to meet Miles. Near the mouth of the canyon, the great Apache leader and the great American general stood face to face. It was a more dramatic and meaningful encounter than Geronimo's with Crook at Canyon de los Embudos. For both Geronimo and Miles, the outcome would be momentous. It could mean Apache surrender, in the full sense of the word that Geronimo had never entertained, or an immediate exchange of fire between Apaches and soldiers and a stampede of Apaches back to Mexico. The two warily shook hands and then talked briefly. Gatewood, sitting to the rear, recalled that Miles simply told them to surrender and be sent to Florida to await the action of the president. Then Geronimo turned to Gatewood and said, "Good, you told the truth," shook hands with Miles, and declared he would go with him regardless of what the rest decided.

Naiche had neither accompanied Geronimo nor decided to surrender. Naiche's brother had gone to Mexico looking for a lost pony and perhaps been killed by Mexicans. Naiche had gone into the hills to mourn. After meeting with Miles, Geronimo went in search of Naiche and persuaded him to meet the general. They met with him on the morning of September 4. Naiche remained suspicious of the good intentions of Miles, and he had not yet surrendered his following, which was much larger than Geronimo's. Miles explained in more detail his plan for the Chiricahuas. Somewhat reassured and encouraged by Geronimo, Naiche surrendered his following. All laid down their arms.[9]

According to Geronimo, Miles's explanation took place before Naiche and the band as a whole had agreed to surrender or laid down their arms; only Geronimo himself had yielded. Doctor Wood and Lieutenant Clay were present. Miles said, "You go with me to Fort Bowie and at a certain time you will go to see your relatives in Florida." He drew a line on the ground and said it represented the ocean. Placing a stone beside it, he said, "This represents the place where Chihuahua is with his band [Fort Marion]." He then picked up another stone and placed it a short distance from the first. "This represents you, Geronimo." He then picked up a third stone and placed it a short distance from the others. "This represents the Indians at Fort Apache. The President wants to take you and put you with Chihuahua." He moved the Geronimo stone, and then he moved the Fort Apache stone next to the Chihuahua stone. "That is what the President wants to do, get all of you together."

Accompanied in an army ambulance by Geronimo and Naiche and three men and a woman, Miles and Lieutenant Clay pushed forward on the morning of September 5, moving hastily to reach Fort Bowie the same day. Lawton followed with the rest of the Chiricahuas, traveling at a more leisurely pace. They arrived at the fort early on September 8.

While waiting at Fort Bowie, Miles again explained his idea of the future to Geronimo and Naiche. He said, "From now on we want to begin a new life." He held up one of his hands with the palm open and marked lines across it with a finger of the other hand. "This represents the past; it is all covered with hollows and ridges." He rubbed the other palm over it and said, "That represents the wiping out of the past, which will be considered smooth and forgotten."

On the day Lawton arrived with the people, September 8, all were packed into wagons as the Fourth Cavalry Band drew up on the parade ground and played "Auld Lang Syne." The wagons moved north down the road to Bowie Station, where a train awaited them. After a photographer took pictures, they boarded the cars—fifteen Chiricahua men (including Gatewood's scouts

Kayitah and Martine), nine women, and three children, twenty-seven in all. Captain Lawton took charge with an escort of twenty cavalrymen. Miles and his staff rode as far as the Rio Grande, in New Mexico, then changed trains for Albuquerque. The special train steamed on east, headed for Florida.[10]

Although a man of periodic mood swings, Geronimo had provided exceptional leadership in the days following his extended discussions with Lieutenant Gatewood on the Bavispe River. He never relaxed his inbred suspicion, never let his guard down, and remained always alert for treachery. He forced the Mexican prefect, Aguirre, to back down and return to Mexico. He followed the wise counsel of Gatewood and appeared, or pretended, to accept Captain Lawton as trustworthy. Traveling north to Skeleton Canyon in tandem with an American command posed dangers, as the murderous intent of Lieutenant Smith demonstrated, but Geronimo negotiated this journey with skill. Naiche remained in the background, letting Geronimo plot the daily course of action. In the end, Geronimo probably had more influence than Miles in persuading Naiche to surrender his following.

When he met General Miles on September 3, Geronimo discovered a general who did not "talk ugly" like Crook and gave in to him. Putting his trust in Miles proved a mistake with lifelong consequences. But by now, surrounded and outnumbered by troops, an attempt to break free would be costly and leave his people as destitute as ever. Besides, Miles seemed like a trustworthy man, and his talk about getting all the Chiricahuas together held strong appeal. Geronimo did not understand how little control Miles had over their future.

Geronimo had the good sense to recognize the truth of what Kayitah and Martine said when they finally met with him in Mexico. They described the pitiful condition of the Chiricahuas, which Geronimo could plainly see around him as the two emissaries talked. Overcoming his stubborn reluctance to meet with soldiers, he consented to go down and talk with Lieutenant Gatewood. He had long known and trusted this officer. From this point forward, his strategy was to bargain for the best terms possible, ideally a return to the old life on the reservation. When this proved impossible, he held forth the prospect of continuing the war but also gradually accepted the inevitable.

As a matter of fact, although raiding occurred repeatedly, only two clashes with the US cavalry occurred during the last two years of Geronimo's freedom, with only minor skirmishes. Occasionally his camp was seized by scouts or soldiers, but not before Geronimo took alarm and scattered his people into the hills. The army and the scouts tried to find and destroy the Chiricahuas, without success. Geronimo and Naiche led their people through the tortuous Mexican defiles they knew so well and constantly eluded their pursuers. That in itself reflects creditably on Geronimo, whose leadership in avoiding the enemy and also providing subsistence for his people by raids on the Mexicans demonstrates superior leadership.

During the two-year period ending at Skeleton Canyon, Geronimo's name appeared almost daily in the national press. That he became the best known of all Indian leaders sprang largely from this two-year period. For vulnerable citizens in both Mexico and the United States, he personified the Apache menace. Ironically, despite the atrocities committed during raids on civilians, his fame grew not from war but from his uncanny avoidance of war.

Although 1885–86 marked Geronimo's preeminence as a war leader, his success in avoiding war and finally in working through the tortuous process of surrender marked his finest period as a fighting Apache.

TWENTY-FIVE

PRISONERS OF WAR, 1886–87

AS THE TRAIN RATTLED across Arizona and New Mexico on September 8, 1886, the twenty-seven Apaches pondered their future. As Naiche later explained his last breakout to General Crook, he didn't know anything about Florida, but he didn't think he would like it. All the travelers probably thought the same thing. Most painful, they knew they were leaving their mountain-and-desert homeland. But they had tired of running. They had looked into General Miles's eyes and liked what they saw. He did not "talk ugly" to them like General Crook. They decided to trust his promise eventually to put all the Chiricahuas together on a reservation. (At this time, the reservation Chiricahuas were struggling through rain and mud to reach Holbrook, where on September 13 they finally boarded railroad cars that would take them to Florida, too.) Geronimo and the others lamented leaving behind their homeland for the unknown in Florida, but the promise of a reservation only for Chiricahuas held appeal. As always, they remained suspicious, but submissive instead of defiant.

This last band of holdouts consisted of some of the Chiricahuas' finest fighting men. Naiche, Chokonen head chief since the death of Taza, had achieved the respect and confidence of his people since taking to the Sierra Madre. He was no longer the uncertain youth whose status as son of Cochise conferred legitimacy for which he was unprepared. He usually let Geronimo take the lead but did not hesitate to voice his opinions and exert his influence.

Geronimo, never a chief and recognizing Naiche's birthright, consistently put him forward even when making the decisions.

Among the rest, at thirty-seven Perico had long been considered the best of the fighting men, always loyal to his cousin Geronimo and with the courage, bravery, and determination that enabled him to carry out any mission. Not far behind was another of Geronimo's cousins, Fun. Geronimo's son Chappo, now twenty-two, had grown up an accomplished, intelligent, and brave young man, skilled in meeting the wishes of his father. Ahwandia, Napi, Yahnozha, Bishi, Motaos, Kilthdigai, Zhone, and Lonah bore reputations that testified to the success of the little band in eluding troops and scouts in the months before the surrender. Also on board were Kayitah and Martine, still army scouts and thus not warmly embraced by the others.[1]

President Cleveland having determined that all the Chiricahuas must be settled in the East, they all became prisoners of war. The War Department had exercised "police control" over the reservation Chiricahuas since 1883. In truth, the War Department now "owned" all the Chiricahuas. Chihuahua and others who surrendered to General Crook in March 1886 had been shipped to Florida as prisoners of war. The War Department decided that all the reservation Chiricahuas must go to Florida. No other category fit but prisoner of war, and they all picked up that label. These included every man who had faithfully served the US Army as a scout, taking the lead in running down Geronimo in Mexico. Chatto and his delegation held at Fort Leavenworth joined their brethren in Florida as prisoners of war. Ultimately, even Kayitah and Martine became prisoners of war.

The War Department repeatedly tried to get the Indian Bureau to assume responsibility for the Chiricahuas, find them a reservation, and administer them like all the other tribes under its jurisdiction. The bureau and its parent, the Interior Department, either flatly refused or stalled the question. These agencies had no place to put them, and Congress seemed unlikely to establish a new reservation.

Actually, the Chiricahuas fared better under the War Department than they would have under the Indian Bureau. Neither corruption nor theft dogged the army officers who cared for them, and the War Department ensured that appropriations usually provided sufficient rations and other necessities. Yet the label prisoner of war carried a humiliating stigma that could not be erased until the label itself was erased.

Both in Mexico and the United States, the Chiricahuas had committed horrid atrocities for many years, but as General Miles assured Geronimo, the slate had been wiped clean. Southwesterners passionately believed otherwise. They wanted Geronimo and his followers kept in Arizona, tried by civil authority, and hanged. So did President Cleveland. General Miles got them out of the territory before that could happen.

The train steamed through El Paso and then southeast across West Texas toward San Antonio, new country to the Apaches. Much to their surprise, on September 10 at San Antonio the train stopped and they were ordered off. An escort conducted them to a large, high-walled enclosure with iron gates. Herded inside, they were directed to tents even then being put up. This was clearly not Florida. Probably George Wrattan told them that it was an army supply depot for the soldiers in Texas.

"As soon as the Indians were within the depot enclosure," stated Brigadier General David S. Stanley, department commander, "all San Antonio turned loose, crazy to see them, and the same afternoon a mob, ill-mannered, insolent, and clamorous, pressed against the iron gates demanding to rush in and see the prisoners." The Apaches had never seen such throngs of white people, all trying to get close to them. They remained stoic behind the locked gates, although puzzled by what Wrattan probably explained to them were simply curious, not menacing, people. In fact, Geronimo's renown, the frequent appearance of his name in newspapers all over the country during the past two years, had aroused intense curiosity among the American people. At San Antonio, some had a chance to see the "bloodthirsty red savages." They were the first Geronimo confronted, but they would not be the last. When the throng grew calmer, the soldiers let small groups enter under escort to look at the Apaches.[2]

Geronimo had another serious worry. Would any of his people be killed? "They are not going to kill me," he assured Wrattan. "I have the promise of Usen [the Apache deity], but my warriors are not so protected. Usen promised that neither my sister nor Daklugie [Juh's son] would die, and he promised that I should live to be an old man and have a natural death. But he made no stipulations regarding the braves. It is for them I fear."[3]

Three weeks later, on September 29, Geronimo and Naiche were conducted into the presence of an army general, who met with them separately. Wrattan probably introduced the officer as General Stanley. Another officer was also present. The general quizzed each in turn about their understanding of the terms, if any, on which they had surrendered. Both gave the same account. At Skeleton Canyon, Miles said, "Lay down your arms and come with me to Fort Bowie, and in five days you will see your families, now in Florida with Chihuahua, and no harm with be done you." Later, at Fort Bowie, Miles said, "We are all brothers; don't fear anyone, no one will hurt you; you will meet all the Chiricahuas; . . . you will have a separate reservation with your tribes, with horses and wagons, and no one will hurt you." In his interview, Geronimo leaned over and cleared a piece of ground with his hand, then stated that at Fort Bowie Miles did the same thing and said, "Everything you have done up to this time will be wiped out like that and forgotten, and you will begin a new life."[4]

The Chiricahuas remained in their tents, with nothing to do but play cards, chew and smoke tobacco, and talk. On the day after the interview with General Stanley, Wrattan read a synopsis of General Miles's report to Washington. Geronimo repeatedly interrupted with grunts of approval. Every morning Geronimo inquired of the officer in charge whether any word had been received from the Great Father and also asked frequently about his wives in Florida, whom he wanted very much to see as well as others of his family.[5]

Day after day, however, the officer's answer was the same: no word from the Great Father in Washington. As time passed and boredom deepened, the officer took two of the Chiricahuas and the two scouts, Kayitah and Martine, for walks around San Antonio. The Apaches saw large numbers of white people and many buildings; whether they registered any reaction is unrecorded.

At last, on October 22, forty-two days after entering the compound at San Antonio, General Stanley informed the Chiricahuas that in a few hours they would be placed on railroad cars, the men in one, the women and children and the two scouts in another. The men would be taken off at a place called Fort Pickens, while the women and children would go on to Fort Marion, where Chihuahua and his people had been for more than six months and where the reservation Chiricahuas had arrived on September 20.

At once Geronimo and Naiche requested an interview with General Stanley. With two other officers standing by and Wrattan interpreting, the two Chiricahuas protested vociferously that this was contrary to what General Miles had promised. He had positively guaranteed that they would be united with their families at Fort Marion. They repeated what they had already told Stanley about the surrender but added that Miles had placed three stones on the ground—Geronimo, Chihuahua, and the reservation Indians—and put them one on top of the other. "That is what the President wants to do," Miles concluded, "get all of you together." Wrattan had not interpreted at Skeleton Canyon, but he vouched for the truth of the Apache account of what happened at Fort Bowie.[6]

At trainside the men were separated from the women and children and placed on separate cars, Kayitah and Martine on the car destined for Fort Marion. The train pulled out of San Antonio full of disgruntled, betrayed Apaches.

The long detention in San Antonio sprang from two circumstances. First, President Cleveland and General Sheridan wanted the Apaches turned over to the civil authorities in Arizona and tried for murder. Second, General Miles, who knew that his superiors expected the surrender to be unconditional, was a master at dissembling—at composing wordy dispatches that avoided the central question and kept the telegraph wires humming as the chain of command tried to discover if he had in fact granted terms.

Complicating this effort was the custom of high officials to escape Washington's summer heat in more agreeable climes: President Cleveland vacationed at a resort in New York's mountains, while Secretary of War Endicott took refuge in New Hampshire's mountains. Another complication centered in San Francisco, where General O. O. Howard failed to receive all the telegraphic exchanges between Miles and Washington.

Still another issue got tangled in the verbiage and met with the obfuscation at which Miles was so talented. What messages did Miles receive and when? On September 6 he issued field orders directing Captain Lawton, in obedience to telegraphic instructions of September 4 from the acting secretary of war, to take charge of the Chiricahua prisoners and proceed with them to Fort Marion. But the War Department denied that any such instructions had been sent on September 4 or any other date. The issue became further clouded on September 7, as telegrams sang back and forth among Miles, Howard, Sheridan, the secretary of war, and the president. The president wanted the prisoners held at Fort Bowie, but Miles pointed out that it was not secure enough. A telegram on the eighth informed Miles that the president therefore had directed that the prisoners be taken to the nearest fort or prison where they could be securely confined. Miles did not receive this before entraining, but his aide telegraphed it to him as the train crossed New Mexico. Miles replied to this on the ninth from Engle, New Mexico: He was carrying out the president's wishes. No fort in Arizona could securely confine the Indians, and they were now traveling between El Paso and San Antonio. As directed by the acting secretary of war (the lost or nonexistent dispatch of September 4), they would be taken directly to Fort Marion, Florida. If stopped, they could be confined in the Quartermaster Depot at San Antonio or the military prison at Fort Leavenworth. From Miles's perspective, most importantly they were out of his department; at Engle he was on his way to Albuquerque to get the reservation Apaches through to Florida.[7]

President Cleveland knew no more than that Miles had promised to get the Chiricahuas out of the country. That meant the surrender had not been unconditional. But exactly what more, if anything, had been promised he could not get a clear answer from Miles. Therefore, on September 10 he had orders issued to Brigadier General David S. Stanley, commanding the Department of Texas, to take the prisoners off the train at San Antonio and confine them in the Quartermaster corral until more answers could be obtained. Frustrated by Miles's wordy dispatches that provided no more answers, he directed that General Stanley interview Geronimo and Naiche to obtain their understanding of what had been promised.[8]

On October 25, 1886, the train stopped and the cars containing Geronimo and his men were uncoupled. George Wrattan probably explained that they had halted at Pensacola, Florida. Fort Pickens, where General Stanley had explained Geronimo and his men would be imprisoned, stood on a sandy island at the mouth of a large bay.

Of more interest to the Indians was a mob such as had greeted them at San Antonio, some two thousand citizens swarming around the railroad coaches. The cars were run down to the railroad wharf to place the Apaches on the excursion boat *Twin,* which would take them across the bay to the island. There another crowd had gathered, surging closer to see the Indians. "Dozens of small boats, filled with people, bobbed about in the choppy waters of Pensacola Bay," wrote a newsman. "The press of the large crowd forced the soldiers to form a double file to the *Twin.* The Apaches alighted and marched between the double file to the steamer. They moved quickly and without fear." The experience at San Antonio, and Wrattan's counsel, had taught them not to fear such throngs. They may have enjoyed the attention.[9]

Wrattan went with the men to the old fort and explained all he could of what they saw and experienced. The massive fortification, long abandoned by the army, presented a dismal scene. Weeds, brush, and even trees choked the masonry walls, the parade ground, and a surrounding ditch. Inside, sol-

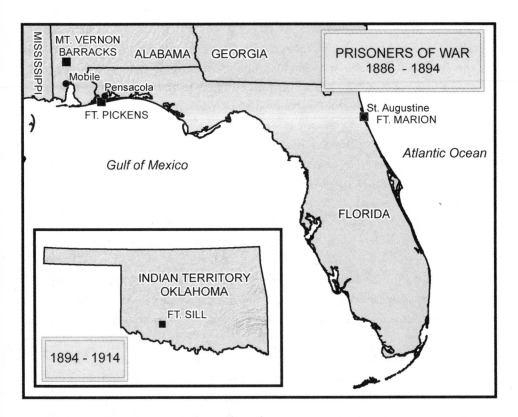

diers conducted the men to strange damp rooms Wrattan called casemates, where cannon had once been mounted to command the ocean approaches. Two rooms had been cleaned and bedding laid out on rough wooden bunks. Soldiers issued brown canvas suits such as they wore on work details, together with underclothing, shoes, and socks. In each casemate, one man served as cook, preparing food at a fireplace. They received army rations that at first seemed inadequate. Geronimo complained, but Naiche silenced him. Later the rations were increased. At once the men were put to work, clearing brush, cleaning the parade ground, and doing other manual chores. They worked six hours a day except Sunday and performed without complaint.[10]

To the officers who had charge of them, the men seemed satisfied, cheerful, and contented, possibly a pose to get their families returned. But Geronimo appeared to contradict that theory when he had Wrattan write a letter to his two wives, son, and daughter at Fort Marion. He declared that everyone at Pickens was happy and contented. "I am very satisfied here, but if I only had you with me I would be more so." Talking by paper was good, but when one saw lips move and heard the voice, it was much better. "I saw Gen. Miles, heard him speak, and looked into his eyes, and believed what he told me, and I still think he will keep his word. He told me I would see you soon; also a fine country and lots of people. The people and the country I have seen, but not you." Geronimo wanted the Great Father to let them be together again. "If the government would give us a reservation, so we could support ourselves—Oh! wouldn't it be fine?"[11]

On November 6 the fifteen men at Fort Pickens gained two more prisoners—Chief Mangas, son of Mangas Coloradas, and a companion. Mangas, so instrumental in the breakout of May 1885, had separated from Geronimo and Naiche and taken no part in the events that led to their surrender. In mid-October a cavalry patrol had trailed Mangas and two men with several women and children from Chihuahua through the Black Range and into the Mogollon Mountains of New Mexico. Twenty cavalrymen from Fort Apache got on the trail and captured the party. The men (one died en route) were sent to Fort Pickens, the women and children to Fort Marion.[12]

Only a week after Mangas arrived, a three-day convention of shipping magnates met in Pensacola and, when not conducting shipping business, flooded the fort with sightseers—459 on the last day of the convention. The parade continued for months, as visitors and townspeople by the hundreds trooped through the fort each day. Many journeyed to Pensacola for the sole purpose of glimpsing Geronimo and his "red-handed butchers."[13]

Geronimo and his cohorts made the best of the situation by selling craftwork to the visitors. Wratten had taught Geronimo to print his name, and he sold many autographs. In early June 1887 the Apaches consented to stage an all-night dance for visitors. An excursion boat towing barges full of people, who had paid twenty-five cents each, flew a banner proclaiming GRAND INDIAN WAR DANCE. Actually, it was a medicine dance, but it served the same purpose. Four to five hundred people crowded around as Chappo, painted entirely white and wearing only a breechclout, led off. Other painted men joined him, and to the beat of drums they chanted wildly and gyrated in contortions that greatly entertained the crowd and probably recalled earlier times to the dancers. Geronimo sat quietly watching. Not until dawn did the festivities end.[14]

"Excursionists" would continue to form an important part of the prisoners' lives so long as they remained in the East. Many of the visitors were newspaper editors, and they returned home to give national publicity to Geronimo and the celebrity prisoners of war.

For Geronimo and his little band, Fort Pickens provided more than ample space. It was one of a series of masonry coastal forts built before the Civil War, one of two erected to command the gateway from the Gulf of Mexico to Pensacola Bay and its navy yard. It occupied the tip of Santa Rosa Island facing Fort Barrancas across the entry to the bay on the mainland, also commanding the entrance to the bay. Barrancas fell to the Confederates at the beginning of the Civil War, but the Union garrison took refuge in Fort Pickens and held it throughout the war. After the war, artillery units garrisoned Barrancas but abandoned Pickens.

Fort Marion, on the east coast of Florida at Saint Augustine, did not provide such spacious accommodations for the prisoners. It, too, had been a coastal fortification, a classic Vauban star-fort design, erected of coquina (seashells compressed into stone) by Spaniards as Castillo de San Marcos and renamed Fort Marion in 1821. Like Fort Pickens, it had not been regarrisoned; the troops occupied nearby Saint Francis Barracks in Saint Augustine. Originally a Franciscan monastery, the barracks had been rebuilt as a US military installation and headquarters.

By the time Geronimo and his comrades arrived at Fort Pickens in October 1886, the officers who commanded on the Gulf Coast had ample experience with Apache prisoners. Brevet Major General Romeyn B. Ayres, colonel of the Second Artillery, ably assisted by his executive officer, Lieutenant Colonel Loomis Langdon, viewed their charges with compassion and treated them as well as the limited space and stocks of food, clothing, and other necessities permitted.

Chihuahua and his people, seventy-seven in all, had reached Saint Augustine on March 31, 1886, five months before Geronimo surrendered. They were immediately confined in the casemates of Fort Marion, which Colonel Ayres had tried to rid of dampness by maintaining fires in the stoves. By the end of the month, he had erected floored tents on the fort's upper deck, or terreplein.

Throughout the summer, with Colonel Ayers on leave, Colonel Langdon made many improvements for Chihuahua's people, in wall tents rather than A-tents, in sufficient rations, in better clothing, and in more freedom. They could walk at will outside the fort, play ball games in the surrounding ditch, and under escort a few at a time visit shops in Saint Augustine. The city's Sisters of Charity began a school for the children at the fort. Langdon consistently reported the Indians cheerful and obedient and seemingly satisfied. But by August 23 he began to worry about how long they were to be kept as prisoners, crowded and with almost nothing to occupy them. He urged that they be given a more permanent abode and even suggested Captain Richard H. Pratt's Indian school at Carlisle Barracks, Pennsylvania. Langdon's superior, Major General John M. Schofield, agreed, although without mentioning Carlisle. General Sheridan's blunt response: where and when they went would be decided by the Interior Department; meantime, hold them as prisoners of war.[15]

In September crowding at Fort Marion became worse. On the twentieth Captain Dorst arrived from Fort Leavenworth with Chatto's delegation of sixteen. On the same day Colonel Wade showed up with the reservation Chiricahuas, 381 men, women, and children. On September 29 Langdon received a list of seventeen Indian scouts transferred to his care. Only fifteen came because the other two, Kayitah and Martine, were now in San Antonio with Geronimo. What should be done with the scouts? Again Sheridan demonstrated his disdain for the scouts: muster them out and keep them at Fort Marion. In other words, make prisoners of war scouts who had loyally served the United States in chasing Geronimo. When Kayitah and Martine arrived, they suffered the same fate. The reservation Chiricahuas, of course, had committed no offense that justified the label of prisoner of war.[16]

Throughout the winter of 1886–87, with Geronimo and his men now at Fort Pickens, Colonel Ayres (back on duty) reported favorably each month on the condition and disposition of the Indians at Fort Marion. Colonel Langdon, at Fort Barrancas, did the same for Geronimo and his men at Fort Pickens; their only complaint was their wish to have their families sent from Fort Marion. Meantime, the Interior Department seemed to give no thought to what to do with the Indians, other than to send as many as possible to Captain Pratt's school at Carlisle. By March 1887, forty-four Chiricahua youths had been enrolled at Carlisle.

In March 1887 Secretary Endicott had reason to become alarmed over the issue of the Indian prisoners. Eastern states contained a number of reform groups dedicated to securing justice for the Indians. They wielded great political power with public opinion and with the Congress. None exerted more influence than the Indian Rights Association, based in Philadelphia, and its leader, Herbert Welsh. In March 1887 Welsh applied to Secretary Endicott for permission to visit Fort Marion and even requested that an army officer accompany him. Endicott acquiesced. The officer was Captain John G. Bourke.

At Fort Marion the two talked with Colonel Ayres as well as the principal Apache leaders, including Chatto. Welsh pronounced the fort entirely unsuitable for imprisoning nearly five hundred Apaches, and he published a widely circulated report in which he demanded the immediate removal of the Apaches to a more healthful place where they could engage in agriculture. But he reserved his harshest denunciation for the betrayal of the Apache scouts who had served the United States only to end as prisoners of war. The most conspicuous fact he had reported, Welsh wrote, was "the injustice with which the good behavior, the fidelity and, in some instances, the distinguished services of these imprisoned Chiricahua Indians have been rewarded by the government of the United States. I hold that in this case a fundamental principle of just and wise policy in the treatment of the Indians, has been violated, for not only have the innocent been condemned unheard, but the meritorious have received the punishment of the guilty."[17]

Welsh's publication in March 1887 provoked a burst of public criticism. It even brought Senator Henry M. Teller (secretary of the interior in the Arthur administration) to Saint Augustine. He confirmed all that Welsh had reported.[18] President Cleveland, however, remained unrepentant. According to the Washington agent of the Indian Rights Association, the president had told him that "there was no way to separate the guilty from the innocent before taking them down there. There was an urgency that would not admit of delay. He did not think they were so crowded as to endanger health."[19]

Welsh's accusations prompted General Sheridan to ask Colonel Ayres to count the scouts. The answer had to disturb the army's chief if for no other reason than the impact on public opinion if it became known. Of the eighty-two adult males at Fort Marion, sixty-five had served the government as scouts during the two years of the last breakout. Of the remaining seventeen, four were friendly during the entire time but too old to enlist. They were subchiefs and influential in keeping their people quiet. Loco and Chatto were scouts and also influential in keeping the reservation Apaches friendly. Captain Crawford had fifty of these men with him when he was killed. Of the 365 women and children at Fort Marion, 284 were families of the scouts and the four friendlies named.[20]

Even though Ayres's numbers did not reach the public, they confirmed Welsh's report, which prompted other Indian reform groups to join the chorus, along with leading citizens. Although he had no sympathy for Geronimo and his cohorts at Fort Pickens, Sheridan began to look for a place to settle the people at Fort Marion.

For Geronimo and his group at Fort Pickens, the irritant remained the same: the absence of their families. On April 17, 1887, as Herbert Welsh's report centered public and official attention on Fort Marion, at Fort Pickens Naiche, Mangas, and Geronimo sat with George Wrattan and dictated a letter to General Miles. All three made their marks, but clearly Geronimo did the speaking. He recited the scene at Skeleton Canyon when Miles arranged three stones to represent how all the Chiricahuas would be put together. Geronimo asked when they were to see their people. Miles told them they would be with their people and not separated. "Put us all together on some reservation and put George in charge of us and you will soon see what an Indian can do when treated right." He concluded, "Dear General please send us to our families soon." The tone suggested a continuing respectful trust in Miles or was framed to seem that way.

On the same day, Wrattan wrote his own letter to Miles, reporting on the conduct of the Apaches since leaving Fort Bowie. They had enough to make them discontented, he wrote, but they had not uttered even a murmur. They were easily handled. They worked every day without complaint. These people should be given a fair chance. If handled right, they could be civilized and made self-supporting. They thought of Miles all the time, had great faith in him, and believed that in time he would do as he had said.[21]

Miles did not answer the letters of Geronimo and Wrattan, but the furor stirred by Herbert Welsh would soon bring relief. Secretary Endicott sent Captain Bourke to Mount Vernon Barracks to investigate its suitability as a home for the Apaches. The post lay near Mount Vernon, Alabama, thirty miles up the Alabama River from Mobile. It was said to be one of the healthiest in the army. In a telegram of April 13, from Mobile, Bourke confirmed this but added that lack of arable land made agriculture unpromising. Back in Washington, he wrote a lengthy report for the secretary in which he described the post as surrounded by pine barrens, sand, and swamps. Hardly anything could be grown. If moved, the Apaches might be taught how to prepare pine and cypress lumber and clear land to raise cotton. They could cut and sell firewood, keep a few chickens, and raise a few vegetables if provided ample fertilizer. Most promising, they could be enlisted in the army as scouts and even be incorporated into the regular army.[22]

Aside from the health issue, Captain Bourke had set forth a bleak description of Mount Vernon Barracks as a suitable place to settle the Chiricahuas. It made no difference. General Sheridan had already acted. On April 18, 1887, the day before Bourke submitted his report, he directed that orders be issued to move the Chiricahuas from Fort Marion to Mount Vernon, eligible children to Carlisle, and the families of Geronimo and his band to Fort Pickens. As counted by Colonel Ayers in his final report, 354 went to Mount Vernon, sixty-two to Carlisle, and thirty (twenty women and ten children) to Fort Pickens.[23]

The 354 who went to Mount Vernon consisted of Chihuahua's people who had surrendered to General Crook in March 1886 and the Chiricahuas who had been moved from their reservation in September 1886. Also among them were Chatto and the other scouts, including Kayitah and Martine. The only remaining Chiricahuas were Geronimo's men at Fort Pickens, now joined by their families.

General Miles had not kept his promise to place all three stones together—one remained at Fort Pickens—but his promise to keep the families together had been honored. Miles deserved none of the credit. Geronimo and the others at Fort Pickens could thank Herbert Welsh.

The arrival at Fort Pickens of their families delighted Geronimo and the other men, although no hint of their reaction crept into official reports. Nor did the almost daily groups of tourists that the army gladly conducted into the fort to see the prisoners. For the men, life went on as it had for nearly a year. They ignored the "excursionists" as they went about their light work policing the fort and pulling weeds and brush from the masonry and ditch. Their living quarters, however, had deteriorated over the twenty years since soldiers occupied the fort. All the men and families occupied casemates that had once mounted guns. Doors, windows, floors, and fireplaces were dilapidated; even some doors had come unhinged. The Apaches may have wondered why they worked at so many tasks outside but never on their own quarters.

Naiche grew in stature. He impressed Colonel Langdon as having more influence than Geronimo over the other prisoners. He was "very manly, respectful, and patient. He never asks for anything nor complains of anything himself, and he discourages others who might. He sets a good example for the others, who are not slow to imitate it." However cheerful and obedient Naiche and the others appeared, discontent still ran beneath the surface. Several asked Wrattan to approach the colonel and tell him they wanted badly to go to permanent homes where they could till the soil. Langdon reacted with uncharacteristic gruffness. They had acted badly, and they had come here with their lives spared, which was all they deserved. They ought to allow the government to forget them for awhile, for they might prompt a reminder that they had not been punished for their crimes.[24]

George Wrattan, however, did not readily drop the issue. In October, at the request of the Apaches, he wrote to General Stanley in Texas asking when they would see the good land and farms Miles told them about. They had behaved well, and with their wives present life was more pleasant. But they would like to hear from Stanley about their talks in San Antonio. Wrattan also addressed Miles once more, telling of the Apaches' good behavior. Geronimo and Naiche, he wrote, wanted to know if Miles meant all he told them. They had been here a year, and Miles had told them all would be on a good reservation in six months. Wrattan repeated Geronimo's account of the three stones, even illustrating it with three dots on the paper. He ended by asking Miles to write him some encouraging words that he could pass on to the Apaches.

Miles did not, of course, but Stanley felt more of an obligation. He held Wrattan's letter for three months before endorsing it to Washington with the recommendation that these Indians be united with their people at Mount Vernon Barracks. He added his conviction that they had surrendered on promises that were "afterward so modified to amount to bad faith." Four days later General Sheridan wrote his own endorsement forwarding the document to the adjutant general—to be filed.[25]

On May 22, 1888, General Sheridan suffered the first of a series of heart attacks that in August would take his life. On May 10, 1888, probably reflecting the general's declining health and the impatience of Secretary Endicott with the issue, the War Department directed that the commanding officer at Fort Barrancas send Geronimo and the other prisoners at Fort Pickens to Mount Vernon Barracks. Pensacolans were dismayed by the loss of their prime tourist attraction.

For Geronimo, no thanks to Miles or Sheridan, the three stones had finally ended in a single stack. But despite the furor kicked up by Herbert Welsh, all the Chiricahuas continued to bear the label "prisoner of war."

GERONIMO AT MOUNT VERNON
BARRACKS, 1888–94

ON MAY 13, 1888, the train bearing Geronimo and the men and their families who had been incarcerated at Fort Pickens, forty-six in all, steamed to a stop at the railroad platform two miles west of Mount Vernon Barracks, Alabama. Not a person stood on the platform, even though the rest of the Chiricahua tribe had lived in a camp outside the post for a year, since moving from Fort Marion, Florida. The post surgeon watched the drama unfold and two years later described the appearance of Geronimo in a magazine article. He overdramatized the scene and got some of it wrong. But he was an eyewitness and a man of integrity who would become famous for identifying mosquitos as the cause of yellow fever: Captain Walter Reed.

The arrival of the great chief, on whom the Apaches had so implicitly relied in their war against the whites, was an event of importance. One would have supposed that the whole Indian camp would have turned out to greet the incoming train. But not an Indian appeared, and when the veteran of a hundred fights led his little band up the hill to the northern gate of the barrack wall and reached a spot where he could survey the [Apache] camp, not a living soul was in sight. Leaving his small party seated on their baggage, the old chief advanced some paces, paused, and calmly surveyed the scene. No sound broke the stillness. This camp of 350 souls seemed instinctively to realize that they were again under the burning gaze of the great warrior and priest. What thoughts passed through the warrior's mind as he beheld all that remained of his once powerful tribe transported from their native mountains to the pine lands of Alabama can only be imagined. While he gazed intently a woman emerged from a distant tent to advance slowly and with bowed head. Hesitantly she advanced and then hurried to the chief, threw her arms around his neck, and wept as if her heart would break. During this trying ordeal, not a muscle of the old warrior's face relaxed, nor did he show any outward sign of recognition that his only daughter was twining her arms around him.

She was not his daughter. All his immediate family had come with him from Fort Pickens. She may have been a relative left behind at Fort Marion and brought to Mount Vernon with the rest a year earlier. Other sources confirm this incident, but also indicate that a few people emerged from their homes to greet (or simply observe) Geronimo. That all did not welcome him enthusiastically may be attributed to their knowledge that, but for him and his final breakout from Fort Apache, none would be in this dismal pine forest as prisoners of war. He and his handful of followers bore the blame. Or the explanation may have been as simple as that they did not know he was coming on this day.[1]

Even so, Geronimo was assigned a dwelling in the center of the expanding Indian community. It was a two-room log cabin with the rooms separated by a breezeway. One of his two wives, Zi-yeh, occupied one room with her daughter, Eva, and son, Fenton, while Ith-tedda and her daughter, Lena, lived in the other. Son Chappo, now twenty-two, had been sent to Carlisle Indian School, but his wife and child lived elsewhere in the village.[2]

Geronimo now faced the challenge of integrating his family and followers into the Chiricahua community that had been living at Mount Vernon since May 1887. The addition of the forty-six prisoners from Fort Pickens—fifteen men, twenty-one women, six boys, and four girls—brought the total at Mount Vernon to 389.[3]

The main body of Chiricahuas, the reservation Apaches and Chihuahua's band that had surrendered unconditionally to General Crook, had lived in a camp outside Mount Vernon Barracks for a year when Geronimo arrived in May 1888. Spurred by Herbert Welsh and the Indian Rights Association, in the spring of 1887 the War Department had to remove the Chiricahuas from Fort Marion. Reputed to be the healthiest post in the army, Mount Vernon

Barracks seemed ideal. General Sheridan made the decision even before he read Captain John G. Bourke's inspection report, in which he described the sand, swamps, and pine barrens in the best light possible and concluded, "Justice, honesty, kindness, directed by firmness and good sense, will promptly effect wonders in them."[4]

"Wonders" is too strong a word, but all the Chiricahuas, including Geronimo and his followers when they arrived, did undergo changes. Doctor Walter Reed's monthly reports described ailments, mainly a predisposition to "consumption" (tuberculosis), but not for several years did he reveal the truth about the health of these Indians.

In the year before the arrival of Geronimo, the Chiricahuas from Fort Marion learned that the army's view of this healthy post did not accord with their own. Chihuahua's son remembered their reaction.

> We had thought that anything would be better than Fort Marion with its rain, mosquitos, and malaria, but we were to find out that it was good in comparison with Mt. Vernon Barracks. We didn't know what misery was until they dumped us in those swamps. . . .
>
> The married couples were placed in tumbledown houses with dirt floors. The unmarried men were housed together. It rained nearly all the time and the roofs leaked. On top of that the mosquitoes almost ate us alive. Babies died from their bites. It was hot and steamy. We had been accustomed to the dry heat of Arizona and could take that, but that humidity! It was worse than at St. Augustine; it was terrible. Everything molded—food, clothes, moccasins, everything.
>
> But we took it without complaining. If the children could stand it, so could the older people. And Nana went about telling us to remember that we were Apaches and that we were trained to suffer.[5]

As at Saint Augustine and Pensacola, the Apaches discovered themselves objects of intense curiosity. The old brick-walled arsenal, dating from 1828, had long been the scene of "outings" sponsored by school, church, social, and other groups in Mobile. "Excursionists" from Mobile found the new railroad eager to take them the thirty miles to Mount Vernon for a picnic and a glimpse of Geronimo and the Apaches. Major William Sinclair commanded, and while the army searched for a young officer to take charge of the Apaches he inherited the role. He seems to have delighted in the experience of wining and dining high officials from Mobile and welcoming any other group from there or elsewhere that wanted to look at Apaches.[6]

The Apaches, especially Geronimo, quickly took advantage of their re-nown, demonstrating their adaptability to new circumstances. They made bows and arrows, head gear, and other crafts to sell to the tourists. George Wrattan had come with the group from Fort Pickens. Although listed as in-terpreter, he continued to teach not only the Geronimo group but all the Apaches the mysterious ways of the white people and serve as superintendent of Apache activities. He became indispensable both to Indians and to the military, and he took an Apache wife.

At Fort Pickens, Wrattan had taught Geronimo how to print his name. Now he showed him how to make walking sticks. Geronimo inscribed them with his name and sold them to tourists for one dollar. He also fashioned other craftwork that readily sold. As Eugene Chihuahua observed, however, the people "soon learned that anything made by Geronimo was in demand and for a higher price than of others. So many put their products in his keep-ing. He did not tell anyone that he had made the articles he sold, though few of them were really his products. Thus many bows and articles purchasers thought were made by Geronimo are distributed over the country." The man who had surrendered at Skeleton Canyon only two years earlier had begun to evolve as a capitalist entrepreneur.[7]

The reservation Chiricahuas and Chihuahua and his people, confined at Fort Marion for a year, had been at Mount Vernon since March 1886. After a month of sickness due to vaccinations, they went to work. They couldn't farm, as they hoped, but Major Sinclair prevented idleness. He employed the men six days a week repairing roads, hauling bricks and mortar, cutting and hauling poles, and beginning to erect huts in which the families could reside. Women gathered firewood and attended to camp duties. All complained of hunger and pawned most of the articles they had brought from Saint Augus-tine to buy food. Both Major Sinclair and Dr. Reed considered the complaints valid. Within weeks, the ration had been increased to the full army size.[8]

As both men and women labored to erect log huts for their homes and perform other tasks for the military post, Dr. Reed reported monthly on their health. Besides diarrhea (which he blamed on "indiscretion" in the diet), he found "chronic lung diseases" (consumption) and "intermittent fever." He did not name the fever malaria, but it was, if Eugene Chihuahua can be credited:

> Our people got the shaking sickness. We burned one minute and froze the next. No matter how hot and muggy it was, no pile of blankets would keep us warm. We chilled and shook—not all the time, but every afternoon or every other day. There was an army doctor who gave us medicine, nasty bitter medicine [quinine]. I don't know whether or not it did us any good. We had our own Medicine Men, but none of them had the Power over this malaria.[9]

By the time Geronimo and his group arrived at Mount Vernon in May 1888, Major Sinclair's work program had produced twenty log cabins into which families had moved, and the work continued on more. A month later, once again Herbert Welsh and the Indian Rights Association took up the Chiricahua issue. Addressing Secretary of War Endicott, Welsh wrote that the Chiricahuas should be made self-supporting, and this could be done only by moving them to a reservation with arable land. Ideally, since they could not be returned to Arizona, a reservation should be given them in the Indian Territory. Furthermore, all those Chiricahuas who had been serving as army scouts, as well as all those who had not been engaged in hostilities when uprooted from their homes and sent to Fort Marion, should be compensated for the lands and property of which they had been deprived. During a recent visit to Chicago, Welsh added, he had talked with General Crook, who agreed with this plan.[10]

The letter sparked a conversation between Welsh and President Cleveland, who said that the Apaches could not be located west of the Mississippi River. Welsh then inspected a plot of farmland in Virginia near Hampton Industrial Institute, which he thought suitable. If Congress would not purchase it, friends of the Indian would call on their philanthropists for the money. The Boston Indian Citizenship Committee stood ready to help in purchasing a new location.[11]

Welsh's proposal set off a prolonged debate within the Cleveland administration, in which Welsh participated. This ended when Cleveland decreed that the Chiricahuas would remain at Mount Vernon. Another debate began when Benjamin Harrison moved into the executive mansion in the spring of

1889. Unlike Cleveland's war secretary, who could muster little interest in the plight of the Apaches, Harrison's appointee, Redfield Proctor, played an active and influential role. So did the army's new commanding general, Major General John M. Schofield. Captain Bourke and Herbert Welsh and his assistant inspected one proposed reservation after another, in Virginia, North Carolina, and even Florida. Neither within nor outside the army could agreement be reached. The argument condemned the Chiricahuas to Mount Vernon for an indefinite period.[12]

Ever since Fort Marion, the white man's school had troubled the Chiricahuas. When Captain Pratt removed almost a hundred youths from Fort Marion to his Carlisle Indian School in Pennsylvania, the people mourned the loss of their children. Similar fears plagued them at Mount Vernon when, late in 1888, they watched the army build a schoolhouse. Two dedicated young ladies (paid by the Boston philanthropists) opened the school in February 1889. As Eugene Chihuahua remembered:

> Teachers came and started a school. We were afraid that they wanted to take the children away from their parents as had been done in Florida. Some of the men believed they were there to help us, but Nana never did. Still, he advised us to be courteous and not to show our distrust. We also thought that Geronimo would oppose the school, but he was wise enough to know that we needed to know that we needed the white man's weapons in skulduggery just as we did for fighting. He acted as disciplinarian for the boys and was very strict, just as he had been back home.[13]

When General O. O. Howard (now commanding the Division of the Atlantic) visited Mount Vernon in April 1889, he assured the Indians that the school was not a ploy to remove the children to Carlisle, from which many returned to die of consumption. Geronimo, seeking to regain some of his former prestige, took an active role in encouraging the children and disciplining them—harshly. He also counseled them on the benefits of learning the white man's way, which seems to have been sincere. He wrote a letter to his son Chappo at Carlisle extolling education and consenting that Chappo's brother Fenton join him. Geronimo's role even earned favorable mention in a report of the post commander. Chihuahua showed his confidence by serving as the school janitor. By the end of 1889, the school had filled with children and some adults.[14]

Many of the changes that took place at Mount Vernon—school, white man's medicine, living in cabins, men working at unaccustomed tasks, entertaining and exploiting white excursionists, and more—seem inconsistent with the old ways and beliefs. Did Usen and all associated with the deity fade as change took place, or did the old beliefs survive, or were the new ways regarded as consistent with the old?

The declining health of the Indians remained a central concern even as the controversy raged over where to move the Apaches. Captain Pratt made matters worse when he complained in May 1889 of the health of his Apache students. Of more than a hundred brought to Carlisle from Florida and Mount Vernon, twenty-seven had died, two more would die in a few days, and others would soon take their places on the deathbed. In all cases, he noted, consumption was the culprit. Carlisle ought not to have these deaths on its record, and although he phrased it more delicately, he wanted to send all the afflicted back to Mount Vernon to die. In stages, he got his wish. Medical experts debated the cause. Some said Apache predisposition; others said change of lifestyle; still others pointed to climate.[15]

Doctor Walter Reed believed climate the principal reason. In November 1889 he penned a scathing report on the health of the Apaches, focusing on the high mortality rate. Only a change of location would halt the ravages of consumption, he declared. The Indians had all grown increasingly depressed not only by disease but by the conviction that the government did not intend to move them to a healthier clime as promised by General Howard and other high-ranking visitors. Nowhere near the Atlantic or Gulf Coasts qualified, asserted Reed. The heat, rain, and humidity contrasted too sharply with the dry mountain climate of Arizona. Contradicting the monthly military reports on the condition of the Indians, he added that the Apaches were not content. "They do not desire nor have they ever desired to remain here during the past twelve months." Any contrary reports reaching General Howard "have no foundation in fact."[16]

Reacting to the health crisis, Howard sent his son and aide-de-camp, Lieutenant Guy Howard, to prepare an investigation of conditions at Mount Vernon, which would be used as the basis for a recommendation to Congress. Howard, Schofield, and Proctor endorsed it, and following a visit in December, so did General Crook. In January 1890 President Harrison sent it to Congress with the recommendation that the Chiricahuas be authorized to move to Fort Sill, Indian Territory, and funds be appropriated for the purpose. Thanks to the opposition of delegates from Arizona and New Mexico, the legislation died.[17]

The Chiricahuas knew nothing of the effort to get Congress to let them move west and its failure in the summer of 1890. They did finally receive a direct overseer, the officer the army had sought for three years: First Lieutenant William W. Wotherspoon, Twelfth Infantry—a talented young officer destined to rise to army chief of staff. He and his family arrived in June 1890. Immediately he confirmed what Dr. Reed had reported. "They are in a most depressed condition. Hope seems to have been crushed out by the long delays in the many promises made for their improvement." Aware that the prospects of a move appeared dim, he believed that incentive to work would improve the Indians' condition, and he urged Secretary Proctor to set aside a special fund from which to pay the men for their labor in building log cabins, working on other camp details, and performing tasks in the fort. The post commander heartily agreed, noting that "the former policy . . . has been to herd them as cheaply as possible under the belief that they would soon be sent away and be a good riddance to the post." Within less than a month, Secretary Proctor had acted.[18]

The Apaches continued to work as hard as ever, but now the reward was not hope but money. As they gained skills in carpentry, industrial pursuits, and farming their small patches, they won permission to work for civilians and contractors outside the reservation. They performed well and welcomed the money. Much to Wotherspoon's distress, they spent much of it in saloons sprouting outside the military reservation. The lieutenant teamed up with the US district attorney in Mobile and successfully prosecuted enough whiskey-sellers to lessen the problem but not to eradicate drunkenness altogether.[19]

Throughout the two years since his arrival, Geronimo had gradually made progress in restoring his old prestige. He performed well as school disciplinarian, and he introduced football and baseball, which he enjoyed watching if not playing. Gradually he won the confidence of Lieutenant Wotherspoon. In October 1891, in addressing the Lake Mohonk Conference of Friends of the Indian, the lieutenant told of a decision that he reached with difficulty. "Geronimo, that great terror, is now acting as Justice of the Peace in the village." Wotherspoon had debated this question in his mind for a long time, for now Geronimo would have to act against his people rather than for them.

After much thought, Wotherspoon gambled—and succeeded. He found Geronimo's decisions "eminently wise, acute, and to the point. He has an excellent influence over the other Indians, and more than fulfills Wotherspoon's expectations."[20]

Early in 1891, the army began to consider enlisting Indians as soldiers in the regular army. They had performed well as scouts for the army, and they would be kept busy while receiving the same pay and allowances of regular soldiers. Both General Schofield and Secretary Proctor thought it a good idea, and President Harrison approved. A General Order of March 9, 1891, launched the experiment. Each of the twenty-six regiments of cavalry and infantry serving in the West would gain one company composed of Indians. The one exception was Company I, Twelfth Infantry, at Mount Vernon Barracks. Lieutenant Wotherspoon took command and set about recruiting and training prisoners of war.[21]

Prisoners of war in army uniform, drawing army pay and allowance, created a glaring inconsistency that the army chose to overlook until it faced a dilemma. As the enlistments began to run out, an honorable discharge meant exactly that. It freed them to go where and do what they wanted. The top command admitted as much, but as nearly all rejoined their people, the issue of prisoner of war remained ambiguous.

The Apaches at Mount Vernon eagerly expressed a desire to join the army. By late May 1891, Wotherspoon had forty-six Chiricahuas inducted, in addition to eighteen Tontos, eleven San Carlos Apaches, and two White Mountains brought from San Carlos Agency. In September another contingent from San Carlos brought the total to seventy-six, the largest Indian company in the army. Among the Chiricahuas were Naiche, Sam Hauzous, Chatto, Dutchy, Fatty, Fun, Kayatena, Martine, and Perico. Three white sergeants drew assignment to the company. Geronimo wanted to enlist also, but Wotherspoon considered him too old to adapt and rejected him. This greatly offended Geronimo, but Wotherspoon thought he had placated him, and he continued to perform well as justice of the peace.[22]

Wotherspoon (promoted to captain in April 1893) performed wonders in transforming prisoners into regular soldiers. Uniformed, equipped, and paid the same as white soldiers, they began to drill, march, camp, learn weapons and fortifications, and take long practice marches. Soon they were drilling and parading with the white battalion at the barracks. Wotherspoon believed they compared with the best white soldiers. Only two events marred their excellence. In March 1892, convinced that his young wife was unfaithful, Corporal Fun shot and wounded her before turning his rifle fatally on himself. He had been one of Geronimo's relatives and best fighting men, and so impressive a soldier that Wotherspoon promoted him to corporal. A year later, in March 1893, two enlisted men (one the renowned Dutchy, recently court-martialed and dishonorably discharged) got into a drunken row with two white soldiers and beat them to death. The case clogged the courts in Mobile for months, but it further scarred the otherwise exceptional company of Indian soldiers.[23]

The Apache children looked up to the soldiers, as Sam Kenoi remembered:

> We played soldier all the time. The big boys used to work us plenty. Sam Hoazous and James Nichols were leaders. One would command one company and one another. We'd march to the swimming place. There were about forty of us. Sometimes one would fight the other, the two boys. Those two would make us fight. They'd have clubs and say they would club us if we didn't. They would make us fight with fists, one from one side and one from the other. But it was good. You didn't get lonesome with those boys. We were always having fun.[24]

Geronimo's roles as school disciplinarian and justice of the peace appeared to have satisfied his wish to regain prestige and authority. He impressed visitors as pleased with himself and the attention he had attracted and with his adaptation to white civilization. In 1893 a captain at Mount Vernon Barracks became well acquainted with him and invited him to his quarters. The officer "learned to like and respect the old warrior. I used to have him and the interpreter, Mr. Wrattan, at my house quite frequently, and over pipes and tobacco, for the old man scorned cigars and cigarettes, we had many chats. He told me much of his life as a boy and as a young man, but would have nothing to say of the later years."[25]

A couple visiting their daughter, the wife of an officer, had a similar favorable view. Writing a long description of the Apaches to his hometown newspaper in New York, Joseph Edgerton named Geronimo as the leading character, "no longer a savage in appearance or dress." During their two months' visit, the couple had met frequently with the Apache. A Sunday or two before, he had called on the Edgertons, "with his wife, a young woman, and their child. All had a holiday look, and Geronimo, a man of sixty or more, instead of making his wife carry the baby, a clean, good-looking one, in the usual papoose cradle or hamper on her back, was hauling it himself, in a child's little express wagon, and seemed quite proud of his employment. He is a large and well-formed man with a good head and strong Apache features, a certain dignity and bearing, indicating a man of authority and self-respect."[26]

"Authority and self-respect" is what he had appeared to receive, together with status (or fear) among the Chiricahuas and the confidence of Captain Wotherspoon. In February 1894, in ill health, the captain left Mount Vernon to take station on Governor's Island, New York, as aide-de-camp to General Howard. Daniel C. Lamont, secretary of war in the second Cleveland administration, visited Mount Vernon a month later. Contradicting the persona that seemed to have emerged, Geronimo directly approached the secretary and asked him to discharge George Wrattan—the man most responsible for guiding Geronimo and the Chiricahuas since their surrender, and probably the most influential man in lifting Geronimo to "authority and self-respect." He gave no reason, and Lamont ordered the post commander, Major George W. Russell, to conduct an investigation.

Major Russell took great care to ensure fairness. He held no council but called Geronimo, then each of his witnesses, into separate meetings. Geronimo's allegations: One night last winter Geronimo and his wife were at Wrattan's house. Geronimo said he told Wrattan that some of the Indian soldiers were misbehaving, and Wrattan refused to listen. Geronimo also informed Wrattan that his salary came from him, not the government. He claimed, moreover, that General Miles, in granting his request to allow Wrattan to come east with the surrendered Apaches, had told him that whenever he wanted Wrattan to go away, he would go away. To these allegations, Geronimo added rudeness and brutality to all the Chiricahuas, both men and women. Russell referred these charges to Wrattan, whose written reply refuted each one. Russell also interviewed each of Geronimo's witnesses, and none offered anything bearing on the case. Both Russell and Wotherspoon's successor declared that Wrattan's honesty, patience, and fidelity were beyond question and that his removal would be a gross injustice to him and a grave loss to the government. If the secretary needed further commentary, he should call on Captain Wotherspoon in New York.

He did, and in reply received a glowing testimonial to the abilities and achievements of George Wrattan. As for Geronimo, the captain reported that Geronimo forever wanted to hold "pow-wows" to enhance his prestige. Wotherspoon allowed this only once. Geronimo gathered about him as many Apaches as he could and declared that Wotherspoon had failed to stop the Indians from drinking and that he should employ Geronimo at a salary to do this. When Wotherspoon refused, the next day Geronimo got drunk and wound up in the guardhouse. Wotherspoon conceded that he made a big mistake in restoring Geronimo's stature. To demonstrate the absurdity of the affair, the captain added that, according to Geronimo, General Miles had promised that whenever he wanted to visit Washington or New York, he was to have his expenses paid and someone to show him around.

On May 14 Major Russell received Secretary Lamont's decision: tell Geronimo his complaints were frivolous and that Wrattan would be retained as long as his services were required.[27]

How to explain Geronimo's contradictory persona—based entirely on white sources? They may have existed within his psyche, one of his occasional mood swings, a streak of paranoia that had surfaced at times in the past. That he was acting one role and suppressing the other seems far-fetched. At root may have been a struggle to diminish Wrattan's power and influence among all the Indians. Geronimo may have been trying to enhance his own power. The incident again, as in the past, points to Geronimo's contradictory personality—feats of brilliance followed by flawed leadership.

Since the legislative failure in 1890, the drive to move the Chiricahuas had subsided, but not entirely. The health issue remained, especially as Dr. Reed left Mount Vernon for another station and the need arose for a replacement. In the summer of 1892, Lieutenant Wotherspoon received instructions to report on the health and mortality for the full year of 1891–92. He had to concede that mortality remained high, but he urged that the living conditions at Mount Vernon, including diet, exercise, and sanitation, be given a chance. He was so proud of his achievement that he "deprecates agitation to remove these people for the present. It would only make them discontented and uneasy." He failed to see how a change would be beneficial as long as they were well fed, clothed, comfortably housed, and making "steady progress." He wanted to see where this progress led.

Wotherspoon's lengthy analysis worked its way up the chain of command until it hit the desk of the surgeon general of the army, Doctor Charles Sutherland, a distinguished medical officer since the Civil War. His astute endorsement contradicted Wotherspoon and once more made a solid case for relocating the Chiricahuas.

> These excessive [death] rates are not due to climactic influences but to change of habits. The history of all Indian tribes that have come under white civilization is that they become decimated by consumption as soon as they give up their mode of life in the so-called wild state, and these Apaches are no exception to the rule. . . . If they were permitted to live at will on a larger reservation, preferably in mountain country, the death rate would probably fall to the normal of 40 or 50 per thousand. But so long as they are confined in close limits as now, they will continue to be more than decimated annually.[28]

Two years later the issue again arose, this time driven by the full force of the War Department. It wanted to abandon Mount Vernon Barracks as no longer needed for military purposes. General Howard seized the opportunity to urge the removal of the Chiricahuas to Fort Sill. All officers united on that place and no other—until General Miles once more inserted himself into the matter. This time his advice made political sense. In 1890 part of the Indian Territory had been carved into the Territory of Oklahoma, which had an elected delegate in the Congress. By naming Fort Sill, which he himself had first proposed in 1886, the measure to move the Apaches there might fail. The army appropriations bill thus provided that the secretary of war could locate the Chiricahuas at any military installation he chose. Debate raged from spring well into summer as the delegates from Arizona and Oklahoma fought fiercely to block any move to Fort Sill. Even so, the appropriations bill emerged with the provision intact, which effectively superseded the 1879 law against settling Apaches in the Indian Territory. Early in August 1894, President Cleveland signed the bill into law.

After seven years—six for Geronimo and his followers—the Chiricahuas finally gained liberation from the Alabama pine barrens. The secretary quickly selected Fort Sill. Although still prisoners of war, the Indians would live in a land combining mountains, arable soil, ample water, and dry climate, a land such as Surgeon General Sutherland had diagnosed as essential to reducing mortality.[29]

TWENTY-SEVEN

GERONIMO'S FINAL HOME, 1894–1909

AS THE CHIRICAHUAS LEFT Mount Vernon for a new life at Fort Sill, they did not know what to expect. They had led a miserable life in the Alabama pine barrens for seven years. Except for occasional drunkenness, they had apparently lived an exemplary life. Captain Wotherspoon had sought, like Captain Pratt at Carlisle Indian School, to "civilize" them. But could the transformation they and other officers sought be achieved in seven years or less—or ever? To what degree had the Indians surrendered their old traditions and way of life? What went through their minds as they did what they were told? The sources name only Nana as clinging to the old attitudes. The dances and other ceremonies that figured so crucially in the old way could not be performed without the officers knowing it. Could other Apache ways of thinking and believing have gone underground while the veneer of white ways concealed them? Did Usen, the supreme deity, still speak to the people? And what torment did they suffer when the white officers commanded thought and action that violated Usen's dictates or assurances?

A clue that confuses rather than clarifies may be discerned in a letter Geronimo wrote to his son Chappo, who had been at Carlisle for six years and was now thirty years old, when he asked his father to allow his brother Fenton to join him in school. George Wrattan would have written Geronimo's reply, June 6, 1894, here paraphrased. Chappo's letter found Geronimo well and also Chappo's brother and sister. Geronimo understands what Chappo said about Fenton going to school and is willing for him to go.

Geronimo wants him to learn something and be a smart man. He would not say no because he wants to do what is right, and he thanks Chappo. When is Chappo coming to get him? All are here still and belonging to the government, but we do not all think the same. Geronimo has talked until he is tired and so he does not talk to the Indians anymore. They are not his relations, so they do not mind [obey] what he says. They have a captain here, and what he says Geronimo does. He will not say no to him. He would be ashamed to do wrong after he has been treated so well. He thinks good all the time and always tries to do right. From his loving father.[1]

Geronimo's letter seems to reveal that he had come to terms with the reality of his new life. He would do whatever the captain said. Interviewed in September by his old antagonist, Captain Marion P. Maus, Geronimo expressed his resignation. He did not consider himself an Indian anymore. He was now a white man.[2] Still, according to Geronimo, the people thought in varying ways. Like Geronimo, almost all the people did whatever the captain said, even Nana, so much of the old thinking may have persisted despite their obedience.

Two months after Geronimo's letter, on August 7, 1894, Captain Pratt discharged Chappo for illness and returned him to Mount Vernon. During September, as the Apaches packed their belongings for the rail journey to Fort Sill, consumption wasted Chappo in the post hospital. The doctor listed him as "very sick." By the time the people boarded the cars for the new land, Chappo had died of tuberculosis.[3]

Escorted by Company I, Twelfth Infantry, 305 Chiricahuas—compared with 389 counted at Mount Vernon in 1888—reached Fort Sill, Oklahoma Territory, on October 4, 1894. They had traveled by rail as far as Rush Springs and ridden wagons west the final thirty miles. Second Lieutenant Allyn Capron had commanded the Indian company for a year, and the soldiers liked and respected him. The Indians now came under the supervision of another officer, who had interviewed them at Mount Vernon but otherwise was a stranger: First Lieutenant Hugh L. Scott, Seventh Cavalry. The usual crowds did not turn out to gawk at the Apaches as they had in Florida and Alabama. A throng of Kiowas and Comanches, curious to see their new neighbors, gathered to watch and try to converse, succeeding only when Carlisle students were brought forth. Whites had not settled this country yet, and the Kiowa-Comanche Indian Reservation entirely surrounded the Fort Sill Military Reservation, which itself belonged to these tribes.

With winter approaching, the Chiricahuas moved temporarily into canvas-covered wickiups sheltered by timber about a mile from the fort. They did not yet know what Lieutenant Scott had in mind for their future, but they could foresee the possibility of a better life in a land more to their liking. As the lieutenant reported, the Apaches seemed delighted with the change from Mount Vernon. Their conduct had been excellent, and their health was already improving.[4]

What Lieutenant Scott had in mind would unfold over the next three years.

The Chiricahuas had been fortunate in their new overseer, in January 1895 to be promoted to captain. Like Captain Wotherspoon, Captain Hugh L. Scott would rise to chief of staff of the army. Like Wotherspoon, he devoted himself to caring for the Apaches and leading them toward self-support—as farmers and cattlemen, however, rather than wage-earners in the white world. Unlike Wotherspoon, Scott did not believe in entirely suppressing old Apache ways. In 1890–91, when the Ghost Dance swept the western plains, he had charge of the Kiowas and gained credit for keeping them quiet as other tribes threatened war. By 1894, he had won the trust and friendship of the Kiowas and Comanches as well as a reputation as an expert on Indians and Indian ways, especially the sign language. Where Wotherspoon had dedicated himself to destroying Apache ways, Scott respected the Apaches as Apaches. Where Wotherspoon had sought to break the power and influence of traditional leaders such as Geronimo and Naiche, Scott saw the value of restoring their stature if not their influence.

Despite a cold, stormy winter, the Apaches worked six days a week plowing land for spring planting, cutting logs for permanent homes, quarrying stone for chimneys, and chopping firewood to ward off the freezing temperatures. Construction of houses—two rooms with a breezeway as in Alabama—began in January and proceeded slowly but steadily. In the summer of 1895, as the agricultural effort progressed, Scott bought a herd of five hundred cattle and began to train Apaches how to herd them. Except for skilled carpenters, George Wrattan taught the Indians most of their new work, especially cattle herding. They had never cared for cattle and knew only how to eat them. They made poor herders.[5]

Scott's most innovative plan in building homes was to scatter them in twelve villages around the reservation west of the fort, each to have sufficient acreage that every family had ten acres to cultivate as a vegetable garden. In a move Wotherspoon would not have approved, Scott appointed a headman for each village. Each was enlisted and paid as an army scout and issued an army uniform. They were given no authority, but they exerted their influence. Wrattan chose the men, and their names resonated in Chiricahua history from the old days of war and raiding: Geronimo, Naiche, Chihuahua, Chatto, Mangas, Perico, Noche, Kayatena, Martine, Toclanny, Loco, and Tom Chiricahua.

Such a reminder of the old days suggests that the old ways had not died entirely in Alabama. In truth, they had not. Scott never reported ceremonies and dances, but as Geronimo wrote in his autobiography, the people revived them. In his adult years, Sam Kenoi remembered the revival clearly:

> There were many ceremonies at this time, but the boys did not attend. It was too common to bother. They were familiar with the customs of the people and didn't pay much attention. It was pretty hard for the younger people to attend. There were always restrictions on whoever was there. For some ceremonies you couldn't scratch, for some you couldn't leave before it was all over, for some you couldn't sleep. So they didn't care much about being there. But they always went to the tepee ceremony, for you always had a good time there.[6]

As the Chiricahuas made a new and better life for themselves at Fort Sill, one pain continued to rankle: their relatives held captive in Chihuahua. At the end of December 1894, George Wrattan composed a letter to Captain Scott naming forty-two Chiricahuas captured by the Mexicans ten or fifteen years in the past and believed still to be held in Chihuahua City—as they probably were, as servants in family households. On the list were relatives of Geronimo, Chatto, Mangas, and Kayatena. The Apaches, wrote Wrattan, said this: "We are settled now, in a good country, where we would all like to be together, have our farms and stock, together and be happy." As many times in the past, this request crawled up the chain of command, leaped to the State Department, and came back from Mexico with the reply that Chihuahua held no Apache prisoners.[7]

Lieutenant Capron's Apache company had no military duties. They guarded the Chiricahua camp and, like their people, worked at building their homes and tilling their gardens. The policy of Indians as soldiers had come under increasing scrutiny, and the opinions of high army officers spelled its doom. In July 1895, Company I of the Twelfth Infantry was mustered out of the service and its members integrated into Troop L, Seventh Cavalry, commanded by Captain Scott at Fort Sill. This troop, composed of Kiowas and Comanches, had performed well under the sure hand of its captain, and the well-trained Apaches made it even better. The experiment ended on May 31, 1897, as Troop L paraded for the last time and turned in its equipment, the last Indian unit mustered out of the army. Many of the Apache soldiers formed a scout unit to keep order in the Chiricahua villages near the fort. All, though honorably discharged from the army, lived as prisoners of war.[8]

As the Chiricahuas went about their chores of building, gardening, and herding cattle, they felt secure in the repeated promises that they now occupied the reservation General Miles had promised them in 1886. Unknown to them, however, a combination of events unfolded that once again portended betrayal. On the one hand, reflecting the fervent demand of the politically powerful Indian rights organizations, the Dawes Act of 1887 provided for allotment of land in severalty to the Indians. On the other, the demand of land-hungry whites led to efforts to buy all "surplus" reservation land not needed for allotments—and to buy before allotments began.

The Kiowa-Comanche Reservation fell victim to a fraudulent agreement in 1892: the Jerome Commission had failed to secure the vote of three-fourths of adult males as required by the Medicine Lodge Treaty of 1867. The army intended, when it ultimately abandoned Fort Sill, that the Kiowas and Comanches would be paid for the military reservation and it would become the Chiricahua Reservation. The fort embraced only enough land for allotments of eighty acres. So in 1896 Captain Scott, joined by the acting agent of the Kiowas and Comanches, Captain Frank D. Baldwin, negotiated with the two tribes for the needed additional acreage. These Indians trusted Captain Scott and would do anything he advised: they agreed. The Chiricahua Reservation appeared secure.[9]

Geronimo toiled seemingly content in his garden. He delighted in the crops of melons and sweet corn that he grew and sold to the army, along with sweet potatoes and other vegetables. Sam Kenoi remembered Geronimo's pride in his garden. "Every now and then," said Kenoi, "he'd take a watermelon, cut it up under his arbor, and say, 'Come on boys.' He liked watermelon pretty well himself. He used to tell the boys, 'Don't smoke until you have caught a coyote on foot boys. That's an old Apache custom.' "[10]

Seventy-one when he arrived at Fort Sill, Geronimo was regarded by officers as too old and worn-out to perform the duties of scout, or leader of his village. He loved his uniform and proudly wore it. He was hardly worn-out, as his future years demonstrated. His name still roused curiosity throughout the nation, although at Fort Sill the mobs such as in Florida and Alabama could not reach him. Special visitors, such as artist E. A. Burbank and Indians Rights officer Francis Leupp (a future commissioner of Indian affairs) readily gained military permission.

Burbank's visit, in 1897, belied the common belief. Geronimo "was short, but well built and muscular. His keen, shrewd face was deeply furrowed with strong lines. His small black eyes were watery, but in them there burned a fierce light. It was a wonderful study—that face, so gnarled and furrowed"—so wonderful, in fact, that Burbank won the permission of Geronimo and Captain Scott to paint it. "As we worked day after day, my idea of Geronimo, the Apache, changed. I became so attracted to the old Indian that eventually I painted seven portraits of him." He also painted Naiche and other Chiricahuas.[11]

Leupp toured the Chiricahua villages in 1897 and described them in detail. He had just come from Arizona, where everyone told him that Geronimo was the "Apache arch-fiend." If he ever set foot in the territory, he would be hanged without the formality of a trial. Such talk, ten years after Geronimo left Arizona, impressed Leupp. "But to pass up into Oklahoma and find this same Geronimo putting in his honest eight hours of work daily as a farmer in the fields, and at intervals donning his uniform as a United States scout and presenting himself with the other scouts for inspection," was even more impressive.[12]

Soon, however, Geronimo was to discover that the attitudes of Arizonans had not entirely died out among the melon fields of Fort Sill. In February 1898 newspapers carried the story of the sinking of the battleship *Maine* in Havana Harbor. The Chiricahuas learned of the coming war, and a number of the former soldiers came to Lieutenant Capron (who had succeeded Captain Scott in January 1898) and told him they would like to go with him and whip the Spaniards.[13]

In mid-April 1898, as the Apaches watched the Fort Sill garrison march away to Rush Springs to board a train for the war zone, Geronimo and other

Apaches gathered around a fire and joked about how easy it would be, with the soldiers all gone, to make a break for Arizona. A young girl, graduate of Carlisle who had forgotten some of her native language, took alarm. She worked as a servant for one of the officers at the fort and hastened to alert the women that Geronimo and the others were holding war dances and plotting an uprising. At the Apache villages, the people probably failed to note the frantic scampering of the women around the fort but took note of the arrival of cavalry units.

The captain of one of the cavalry troops summoned Geronimo, Naiche, and other headmen to the fort and questioned them. Expressing sadness at being mistrusted, the Apaches declared their innocence; the tale lacked any truth. Geronimo spoke up: "I am a U.S. soldier. I wear the uniform, and it makes my heart sore to be thus suspected." And suspected they were for a week or more.[14]

Geronimo would have been amused had he known what a stir, approaching panic, the rumor of an impending uprising caused in the army—from department commanders to the secretary of war. Even before Lieutenant Colonel Edgar R. Kellogg marched his battalion of the Tenth Infantry out of Fort Sill on April 19, the army's commanding general, Major General Nelson A. Miles, worried enough to order a troop of the Seventh Cavalry to hasten by rail to the fort. As Kellogg waited for transportation at Rush Springs, a telegram and a galloping courier reached him with word of the threatened outbreak. He sent Captain William C. Brown and his troop of the First Cavalry galloping back to Fort Sill to quell the uprising. After interviewing Geronimo and Naiche, and with the impending arrival of the troop of the Seventh Cavalry, Brown hastened back to Rush Springs to rejoin Kellogg. Even then, generals believed that Fort Sill needed more cavalry to stand guard over the Apaches. Within a week, all was calm at Fort Sill.[15]

The furor over a Chiricahua outbreak, which alarmed the people of the Southwest as well as the army high command, demonstrated that Geronimo, despite his seventy-five years, still aroused fear as well as public notoriety.

TWENTY-EIGHT

GERONIMO'S LAST YEARS

FORT SILL HAD DENIED Geronimo the chance to pose before the public and sell his craftwork, as he had done at Mount Vernon. That changed only a few weeks after the scare of an Apache uprising swept Fort Sill as the garrison marched off for the Spanish American War. The Trans-Mississippi International Exposition of 1898 opened in Omaha, Nebraska. A major segment of the exposition was the "Indian Congress," which drew five hundred Indians from thirty-five tribes and opened in August. Over the objections of their overseer, Lieutenant Francis H. Beach, Geronimo and Naiche headed a Chiricahua delegation of twenty-two from Fort Sill. They lived in tents, guarded by soldiers since they were still prisoners of war, displayed themselves to the public, and sold their craftwork to eager fairgoers. Most of the fair attendees demanded Indians in their native state, contrary to the attitude of those who pushed the "civilization" agenda. But the fair managers ensured that all the tribes engaged in war dances, ceremonials, and sham battles. Geronimo was the star attraction. "Whenever he appears in the procession," noted a reporter, "the beholders cheer him wildly."[1]

Geronimo rewarded another reporter with an account of the past and future as he conceived it. "For years I fought the white man," he began,

> thinking that with my few braves I could kill them all and that we would again have the land that our Great Father [Spirit] gave us and which he covered with game. I thought the Great Spirit would be with us, and after

we had killed the whites then the buffalo, deer, and antelope would come back. After I fought and lost and after I traveled over the country in which the white man lives and saw his cities and the work that he had done, my heart was ready to burst. I knew that the race of the Indian was run.

The newsman then asked about the future. "The sun rises and shines for a time," Geronimo replied, "and then it goes down, sinking out of sight and is lost. So it will be with the Indians."[2]

The Omaha exposition launched Geronimo to new heights of fame. For the rest of his life, he was in constant demand as an attraction at fairs large and small.

The two largest were the Pan American Exposition at Buffalo, New York, in 1901, and the Louisiana Purchase Exposition at Saint Louis in 1904. At both, Geronimo played his usual role, dressed in his traditional bonnet and a mix of civilian and Apache clothing. He posed for photographs and sold his craftwork. At Buffalo the assassination of President William McKinley overshadowed Geronimo and other celebrities. Even so, at seventy-eight and still under guard, Geronimo participated in mock skirmishes between Indians and cavalry. The *New York Times* commented that the Buffalo exposition presented an imposing array of Indian chieftains, "but among them all will hardly be found a more imposing figure than that of old GERONIMO."[3]

At the exposition in Saint Louis in 1904, Geronimo played his customary role. There, however, he was introduced to a feature of the Palace of Agriculture—the motion picture. With 150 other Indians, Geronimo was escorted into the Nebraska Theater and shown a film promoting agriculture. "While interested in the general farm scenes that show planting, cultivation and harvesting, the cattle scenes and especially those depicting the wild life on the range are most to his liking." This experience cultivated in Geronimo a "special fondness for the Nebraska Theater."[4]

Saint Louis also provided an opportunity for Geronimo to demonstrate his Power as a medicine man and healer. In a contest between Apaches and whites over whose medicine was more effective, Geronimo performed many of the incantations and gyrations that formed part of his healing ceremony. When the hats were passed, however, the whites had more dimes and pennies than the Apaches.[5]

Dimes and pennies had nothing to do with healing powers. Although Geronimo had once turned to an army doctor to treat him for incipient syphilis, he never in his own mind and the eyes of his people lost his healing Power. A better example of a "contest" had taken place in 1901 in the army hospital at Fort Sill. Geronimo took his daughter Eva to the hospital with a large boil on the back of her neck. Geronimo told the doctor that the boil should be opened. The doctor said that it should not. When the doctor turned his back, Geronimo pulled out his jackknife and lanced the boil. For this offense he was thrown in the guardhouse for three days. But the boil speedily healed. "Among the Apaches Geronimo is called an excellent doctor," concluded this account, "and they will have no other."[6]

The Saint Louis exposition provided the stepping-stone to Geronimo's next triumph as a celebrity. The assassination of President William McKinley elevated to the presidency Vice President Theodore Roosevelt. He won the election of 1904, and he ensured that his inauguration would showcase American Indians.

As the parade of marching bands, West Point cadets, and army regiments made their way past the presidential reviewing stand on March 4, 1905, the hyperactive president applauded, waved his hat, and vigorously pumped his arms. Then suddenly, around the corner, came a spectacle that brought the people in the stand to their feet—a rank of six mounted Indian chiefs riding side by side in front of the next band. They represented six tribes: Ute, Comanche, Blackfeet, two tribes of Lakota Sioux, and the Chiricahua Apaches. Next to Geronimo rode his neighbor, the Comanche chief Quanah Parker. Geronimo stood out among the six because the others sported colorful feather bonnets and traditional native paint and garb. Geronimo wore a broad-brimmed hat and dark clothing with no ornamentation. White horses flanked Geronimo's dark horse. The chiefs created a sensation, eclipsing the intended symbolism of a formation of 350 uniformed Carlisle students led by a marching band in which Colonel Richard H. Pratt took inordinate pride.[7]

As a newsman noted, the Indians seemed to interest the president more than any other parade feature except the cowboys. "When old Geronimo, as if carried away by the cheers which he and his companions received, brandished his spear and gave a wild whoop, the President acknowledged it by waving his hat."[8]

For Geronimo, the inauguration was not all triumph. On March 9, Commissioner of Indian Affairs Francis E. Leupp escorted Geronimo and the other chiefs into the president's office in the White House. After exchanging greetings, a tearful Geronimo begged President Roosevelt to "take the ropes from the hands" of his people. "The ropes have been on my hands for many years and we want to go back to our home in Arizona."

Through the interpreter, the president replied: "When you lived in Arizona you had a bad heart and killed many of my people. I have appointed Mr. Leupp the Indian Commissioner to watch you. I cannot grant the request you make for yet awhile. We will have to wait and see how you act."

As the group left the president's office, Geronimo told Commissioner Leupp he wanted to go back "and speak again to the father." Leupp denied the request and said that anything further Geronimo had to say would have to be submitted in writing.[9]

Geronimo returned home more bitter than elated. But his appearance in the inaugural parade may be considered his "Last Hurrah."

As Geronimo traveled about the country appearing at local celebrations, fairs, and other public events, the relentless opening of Indian reservations to white settlement continued. The Chiricahuas had little to worry about as the Territory of Oklahoma took shape after repeated land rushes beginning in 1889. The Fort Sill Military Reservation would become the Chiricahua Indian Reservation once the army abandoned the fort. In 1901, as Geronimo appeared at the Buffalo exposition, the sale by lottery of "surplus" lands of the Kiowa-Comanche Reservation added still another chunk of Indian land to the Territory of Oklahoma. It also produced the seat of Comanche County, Lawton, only five miles from Fort Sill. The white people who for seven years had been kept distant from the Chiricahuas now surrounded them. The Apaches had flourished under the care of the army and the fruits of their own labor. Their children attended an Indian school at Anadarko, thirty miles distant. Their health had recovered from the torments of Alabama. Dutch Reformed missionaries ministered to the Chiricahuas and converted some. Except for an occasional soldier bootlegging whiskey, the Indians had been relatively free of the old scourge of drunkenness. Now they could easily obtain whiskey, and they did.[10]

The Dutch Reformed missionaries made a special effort to convert Geronimo. Late in 1902 two missionaries invited him to attend a service. Usen's "religion" was good enough for him, but he went. After a sermon on the atonement, Geronimo declared, "The Jesus Road is best and I would like my people to travel it. Now we begin to think the Christian white people love us." Throughout his life Geronimo had frequently been impulsive, and for such a sudden transformation of belief, impulse seems to have governed.

Impulse governed for a year as Geronimo tried to make up his mind: cling to the old beliefs or embrace Christianity. In 1903, limping from a fall from his horse, he made his way into the church to listen to a sermon on Jesus. Geronimo then begged the pastors to give him a new heart. They did; they baptized him into the Dutch Reformed Church.

Geronimo influenced many of his people to take the Jesus Road, including Naiche. After Geronimo's baptism, he faithfully attended the weekly sermons. He asked the pastors to pray for him, and he told them, "You may hear of my doing wrong, but my heart is right."

Knowledge of Geronimo's drinking and gambling disturbed the church officials. He is said to have been "excommunicated" for his habits, but church records reveal nothing of the kind. He may have been censured or suspended for a time, and at least one missionary at Fort Sill declared it a mistake ever to have admitted him to membership.

The most plausible explanation of Geronimo's spiritual beliefs in his last years is a conflict between Usen and Jesus. Jesus may not have lost entirely, but despite periodic apostasy throughout Geronimo's life, Usen always prevailed.[11]

In the summer of 1904, Geronimo became acquainted with S. M. Barrett, the superintendent of schools in nearby Lawton. Geronimo needed an interpreter to help him sell a bonnet, Barrett translating between English and Spanish. When Barrett told Geronimo he had once been wounded by a Mexican, all the old hatred rose to the surface and cemented a friendship between the two. Each visited the other in their homes. Geronimo related to Barrett much of his life story as well as the history of the Chiricahuas. In the summer of 1905, shortly after Geronimo's return from the inauguration ceremony in Washington, Barrett asked Geronimo's permission to publish some of what the old man had told him. Geronimo at first refused, but ever on the alert for ways to make money, he said that if the army officer in charge consented he would tell the story of his life.

The officer was First Lieutenant George M. Purington, an enlisted man before the Spanish American War now commissioned in the Eighth Cavalry. He behaved in stark contrast to Captain Hugh Scott and all the previous officers who had charge of the Chiricahuas. He had no sympathy for them, and he promptly refused. The Apaches had been guilty of many depredations and cost many lives and much money to subdue. Geronimo deserved to be hanged rather than spoiled by all the attention he had been receiving. Undaunted, Barrett wrote directly to President Theodore Roosevelt, who had only a few months earlier met with Geronimo and other chiefs in the White House. Roosevelt quickly gave his consent, subject only to a final review by the War Department.[12]

In October 1905 Barrett secured an interpreter to translate what Geronimo said into English. He was Asa Daklugie, son of Chief Juh, second cousin to Geronimo, and Carlisle-educated. The first day Geronimo made clear that only he would talk. He would answer no questions. He had framed in his mind what he wanted to say at the session and would say no more nor answer any questions. When Barrett tried, Geronimo simply said, "Write what I have spoken." Later, when Barrett had set to paper what Daklugie had related, Geronimo met with the two and answered questions. This became the routine each day of the interviews.

As Barrett described the process: "He might prefer to talk at his tepee, at Asa Daklugie's house, in some mountain dell, or as he rode in a swinging gallop across the prairie, whenever his fancy led him, there he told whatever he wished to tell and no more."

Barrett mailed the manuscript to President Roosevelt. He approved, subject only to footnotes that clarified that any criticisms of individuals were those of Geronimo, together with a final review by the War Department. On June 2, 1906, Barrett mailed the completed manuscript to the War Department. Six weeks later an assistant to the army chief of staff advised the secretary of war that the manuscript contained five passages offensive to the army and that, even if those were eliminated, it should not receive the approval of the War Department. Barrett struck out the offending passages, and the president let the text go to publication.

Barrett included in his introduction examples of the War Department objections—such trivia as criticisms of Generals Crook and Miles. The officers who now ran the army, many of them veterans of the Indian wars, put both Geronimo and Barrett through a shameful process. The old Apache should have been allowed to tell his story unfettered by official restrictions. But the officers could tolerate no criticism, possibly because in retrospect Geronimo had made so many look foolish.

For the historian, Geronimo's autobiography, even without the excised passages, presents daunting problems. The most obvious are the perils of translation from one language to another. Daklugie's command of English may have been flawed. Barrett may have softened some of the content to avoid offending the army. At eighty-three, Geronimo's memory may have dimmed. Either because of memory loss or deliberate vagueness or exaggeration, much of his history is so confused that the historian is left to puzzle out what happened. Cultural differences, which were great, account for much confusion. Geronimo's chronology, for example, is severely flawed, reflecting the Apache focus on events rather than the white man's calendar. And what was important to Geronimo may not be of much interest to the historian. Even so, the autobiography is valuable for what it does contain and what the historian can infer from that.

Notably, the difficulties of making sense of parts of the book are largely in the period between the coming of the white people and the surrender at Skeleton Canyon. Geronimo's accounts of his youth, his culture and traditions, the ceremonies and dances, family relations, tribal relations, and the spiritual beliefs of the people contain little confusion or obscurity.

Uppermost in his mind, from Skeleton Canyon to Fort Sill, was the injustice of two decades as a prisoner of war and the intense yearning to go back to the Arizona mountains. His passion for that land emerges plainly at the end of the book:

> There is no climate or soil which, to my mind, is equal to that of Arizona. We could have plenty of good cultivating land, plenty of grass, plenty of timber and plenty of minerals in that land, my home, my fathers' land, to which I now ask to be allowed to return. I want to spend my last days there, and be buried among those mountains. If this could be I might die in peace, feeling that my people, placed in their native homes, would increase in numbers, rather than diminish as at present, and that our name would not become extinct.

Jason Betzinez, the most authoritative voice of the Chiricahua past, wrote that "Apaches possessed many virtues such as honesty, endurance, loyalty, love of children, and sense of humor. They also had at least two serious faults. One of these was drunkenness and the other was a fondness for fighting among themselves, these often going hand in hand."[13]

Drunkenness is a theme running throughout Apache history. No less than other Chiricahuas, Geronimo loved liquor, no matter what kind, and at Fort Sill he often got drunk. Betzinez, who had been with Geronimo since the warpath, wrote that his "greatest weakness was liquor."[14]

On February 11, 1909, Geronimo rode into Lawton to sell some bows and arrows. With the proceeds, he asked Eugene Chihuahua to buy him whiskey. As was customary at a time when law barred Indians from purchasing liquor, Eugene asked a soldier to get it for him. He then turned it over to Geronimo. Late at night Geronimo mounted his horse and rode back to Fort Sill. When almost there, he fell off his horse and lay there in the freezing weather until discovered the next morning. For three days his family cared for him in his home before one of the scouts reported his worsening cold to the Fort Sill surgeon, who had him brought to the hospital. The cold had developed into pneumonia.

The surgeon expected death to come quickly. Geronimo, however, insisted that Eva and Robert, his daughter and son, be brought to his bedside from the Chilocco Indian School. Typically, Lieutenant Purington wrote a letter instead of sending a telegram. Eugene Chihuahua sat with Geronimo during the day, Asa Daklugie during the night. Geronimo died at 6:15 a.m. on February 17, 1909. The funeral the next day had to be delayed until Eva and Robert arrived from Chilocco.

A prisoner of war for twenty-three years, Geronimo was buried in the Apache graveyard on Cache Creek at Fort Sill.[15]

EPILOGUE

A QUART OF WHISKEY, a fall from his horse, and pneumonia killed only the mortal Geronimo. The immortal Geronimo lives on, one of the enduring icons of American and Native American history.

Neither Geronimo's persona nor the legend explains why his name continues to resonate so vividly in the public mind. The reason is simple. The white citizens of Arizona and New Mexico endured a decade of Apache depredations, 1876–86. Hundreds died as Apache raiders swept down on farms, ranches, villages, mining claims, and travelers to exact an appalling toll of plunder, destruction, mutilation, and death. Their bursts of anguish and outrage, reported, embellished, and falsified by Southwestern newspapers and expressed in appeals to presidents, members of Congress, governors, and others of prominence, attracted the notice of all Americans. As the name Geronimo emerged from obscurity in the late 1870s, he came to personify all the Apache raiders, both in the minds of victims and in newspapers throughout the nation. Americans everywhere almost daily read of atrocities attributed to him. After his surrender in 1886, Geronimo became a prisoner of war for the rest of his life, but his name remained bright in the public memory. After 1898, he became a celebrity for other reasons, his name still in the forefront of Indian leaders.

So it remained until Geronimo's death in 1909. Afterward, the name endured, his years as a celebrity forgotten, his years as a murderous butcher remembered. This incarnation buried Geronimo in legend. By the late twentieth century, however, with fresh public attitudes shaped by the "Bury My Heart at Wounded Knee" syndrome, the Geronimo legend began to morph into the more congenial image that encompassed all American Indians: the Apache daredevil fighting for his homeland. Such remains the legend of Geronimo, even though he spent his adult life raiding and plundering in Mexico and the American Southwest or on a reservation. He did not fight for his homeland. He did fight for his values and life-way, which perhaps contained an element of homeland.

If a "real" Geronimo has emerged from the preceding chapters, how should he be characterized? Only two words apply universally: complex and contradictory. Dozens of other words and phrases describe him at various times and in various episodes of his life, but only a few continuously trace a pattern. They can be reconciled only under two words of generalization—complex and contradictory.

Most prominently, Geronimo repeatedly demonstrated courage and bravery, especially in clashes with Mexican troops. Pozo Hediondo in 1851 revealed him at his best. Teamed with Mangas Coloradas and Cochise, he fought viciously and contributed significantly to the almost complete obliteration of the Mexican foe. Yet at Alisos Creek in 1882 many tribesmen accused him of cowardice—sneaking out of the deadly ravine to save himself while leaving others to their fate. Although the belief is almost certainly wrong, that it existed at all reveals a contradiction that planted itself in the opinion of many Chiricahuas.

In the rush to the Sierra Madres that preceded and followed Alisos Creek, Geronimo exhibited exceptional leadership, especially in the fight in Horseshoe Canyon and in bringing the survivors of Alisos Creek to safety in mountain refuges. Jason Betzinez testified to Geronimo's critical leadership in eluding vigorous pursuit by US cavalry and Apache scouts. The flight involved women and children as well as the fighting men.

Even so, detracting from his superior leadership, he relaxed his vigilance after crossing the boundary and allowed his camp to be surprised and attacked by American cavalry and Indian scouts. Only the skillful flanking movement of some of his fighters opened the way to escape.

In both Mexico and the United States, he lived up to his reputation as a ruthless butcher. Especially in Mexico, he shot, slashed, tortured, and murdered almost anyone he came across. Yet, inexplicably, he occasionally spared the life of a victim or took him or her captive, sometimes under brutal circumstances. In 1886 he slaughtered the whole family of rancher Artisan Peck and then left Peck to look down on his dead and mutilated family. (Apaches neither raped nor scalped.)

A glaring contradiction is his skill at arranging ambushes of pursuers or travelers, taking full advantage of the terrain. He achieved this with the troops of Captains Lebo and Hatfield in 1886, in the final weeks of the military offensive. At the same time, Geronimo could grow lax in posting security and suddenly find soldiers and scouts charging into his ranchería. Like all

Apaches, however, he knew how to escape such an attack with his life, if little or nothing else. Both Captains Crawford and Lawton surprised him in hideaways he thought beyond discovery. But as Surgeon Leonard Wood observed of one such incident, the attackers were left with the camp and all its contents but no Apaches.

That his camps were so expertly concealed that such attacks occurred infrequently testifies to Geronimo's ability to secrete his people in rugged mountain hideouts thought impenetrable. Yet they were not, as both Mexican and American soldiers and Apache scouts occasionally found them.

For all his strategic or tactical lapses during the final two years of freedom, he merits admiration for outwitting five thousand American soldiers and keeping them on the run with few shots fired in anger. His skill at evading pursuit, at hiding in mountainous enclaves, at avoiding any semblance of battle, reveal his finest period of leadership.

These years also find him both defiant and submissive. Most dramatic was the day in August 1886 that Lieutenant Gatewood finally put Kayitah and Martine in touch with Geronimo. In only one day Geronimo's defiant refusal even to talk about giving up turned to submissive agreement to parley.

In 1883 Geronimo defiantly roamed Sonora butchering and plundering, but when General Crook penetrated his mountain bases, he turned so submissive that he humiliated himself by groveling and begging Crook to talk to him. Such servile behavior seems uncharacteristic of any Chiricahua, much less the renowned Geronimo.

As a prisoner of war at Mount Vernon Barracks, Geronimo exhibited erratic behavior that defies explanation. He appeared to have adapted well to the new circumstances of his life. He caused little trouble and behaved as his military overseers wanted. His visits to white officers at the post earned him high praise. He claimed that he now considered himself a white man. He served credibly as justice of the peace and encouraged the Chiricahua youth to go to the white man's school. He even reinforced his son Chappo's commitment to education at the Carlisle Indian School and readily consented to Chappo's request that his brother Fenton be sent to Carlisle.

Suddenly, however, he turned on George Wrattan, the one white man to whom he owed the largest debt in the transition from freedom to captivity, a betrayal as grievous as any that victimized him. He not only lied about a promise of General Miles to send Wrattan away any time Geronimo wanted. He also strung together the most unconscionable prevarications about other promises Miles had made him. A thorough investigation led the secretary of war to brand the accusations as frivolous.

Yet Geronimo told his son that he would do anything Captain Wotherspoon wanted because the captain had shown him the right way and treated him so well. He then turned on Wotherspoon and demanded to be paid to eliminate drunkenness. When refused, he got drunk himself.

Geronimo also professed undying devotion to the spiritual beliefs of his tribe. Usen, traditional ceremonies, and all Apache cosmology marked his path through life. The devotion, however, lapsed on occasion. If he followed the path during the years at Mount Vernon, he did it in secret. It may have been a matter of convenience. As a striking example, while at Fort Sill in the last years of his life, at the same time that the old ceremonies were being revived he allowed himself to be baptized in the Dutch Reformed Church. Perhaps this amounted to a pragmatic adaptation to the two sides of his life at Fort Sill.

Reverence for the old ways manifested itself in Geronimo's stature as a medicine man. He dispensed herbal remedies, made generous use of sacred pollen, and performed healing rituals in full view of onlookers. Yet when stricken with a mild form of syphilis, he turned to an American army doctor for treatment. If he attempted his own cure, it failed. The white man's medicine cured the great medicine man.

Like many other Chiricahuas, Geronimo liked strong drink. At times drunkenness affected his behavior, while well-documented incidents show him in control when drunk or hungover. His first breakout from the reservation, for instance, arose from a drunken tirade against a nephew that so shamed the young man that he killed himself. The addiction was so strong that Geronimo and his cohorts let the Mexicans lure them into situations where they drank to oblivion and opened themselves to massacre. They knew the stratagem, but they fell for it over and over. It was the stratagem that cost Geronimo his first family in 1851. In the end, in 1909, drunkenness cost him his life.

Certain traits of character, however, find little or no contradiction in the record.

One was deeply ingrained suspicion. He suspected all Americans and Mexicans of plotting treachery, as indeed they often were, and he suspected his own people of trying to get him into trouble. Suspicion led him to withhold trust from any official, or any other Apache, trying to accommodate him. Suspicion and distrust match his utter gullibility, his willingness to believe any "bad story" or any hint of "bad stories," or any other rumor or gossip that might affect his life. He fully displayed these tendencies in the drama that led to the last breakout in 1885.

Another persistent trait was lying. He told one lie after another to General Crook at Canyon de los Embudos. Unforgivably, he blatantly lied to Naiche and Chihuahua to force them to flee with him and his few followers in the breakout of May 1885. He assured them that he had caused Lieutenant Davis and Sergeant Chatto to be assassinated, which meant that the government would pounce on all the Chiricahuas who did not go with Geronimo. They went. Far more untruthful were the lies Geronimo told about George Wrattan at Mount Vernon Barracks and the lies about what General Miles had promised him.

Another consistency: From his first marriage through his last, Geronimo proved a deeply committed family man. The massacre of his first family in 1851 shaped a lifetime of bitter loathing and revenge against Mexicans. He mourned the death of any family member, and he never gave up trying to recover wives who had been captured. Eight named wives can be accounted for, but the record reveals several more unnamed.

Another conspicuous characteristic of Geronimo's was the mystical "Power." Outside his personal following, he commanded respect or fear because of his Power. Although Jason Betzinez witnessed a display of Geronimo's Power, no other credible event found its way into the record. The range and intensity of Geronimo's Power depended less on what people observed than on what they thought they observed or had been told by others that they had observed. These widespread beliefs, however, created a substantial enough foundation for Geronimo's Power to be taken seriously.

The contradictions in Geronimo's character and behavior are conspicuous, accounting for a major segment of his persona. At the same time, a few lifelong beliefs and practices, unrelieved by any exceptions, contrast with his contradictions. Together, these themes, resonating through his long life, stamp him as a man of complexity.

Stripped of legend, Geronimo was a blend of contradiction and complexity. Legend buries the blend, and he has come down in recent history as the valiant Apache fighting for his homeland. Although plainly false, motion pictures, television, popular literature, current Apache beliefs, and even museum exhibits reinforce the legend. For a public entranced by American

Indian history, the legend easily obscures contradiction and complexity and dominates the American memory.

How does Geronimo compare with the Indian chiefs whose names he has overshadowed? For non-Apaches, the answer lies largely in the vast difference in cultures. Sioux, Cheyenne, Arapaho, Nez Perce, Cheyenne, Kiowa, Comanche, Ute, and other plains and mountain tribes that confronted the white westward movement embraced a culture that mandated fending off enemy encroachment or warring with enemy tribes. Chief Joseph, Sitting Bull, Crazy Horse, Dull Knife, Quanah Parker, Satanta, and others who inscribed their names in the history of the American West contended with white people and their army until overwhelmed.

Apache culture emphasized war and raid—war for revenge and raid for subsistence and other supplies when the land's natural bounty could not sustain the people. The mission of the US Army was not to make war on the Apaches but to protect the settlers in their lives and property from Apache raiders. When that policy repeatedly failed, the army's mission broadened to attempting to destroy the Apaches or force them to surrender and settle on a reservation. Geronimo made his name as a raider and as a talented expert in eluding pursuing soldiers and Apache scouts.

Because of the cultural difference, therefore, Geronimo is hard to compare with other prominent chiefs. Two examples are notable.

Sitting Bull of the Lakota Sioux enjoys name recognition approaching Geronimo's. Sitting Bull was not a man of complexity and contradiction. He was an undeviating product of his culture. He steered a narrow path within the boundaries of his culture and excelled in every aspect. He never wavered, even when overcome by the white man.

Geronimo's culture gave him a wider margin within which to act. He deviated time and again. Unlike Sitting Bull, he often behaved selfishly, impulsively, deviously, mercilessly, egotistically, and at variance with the dictates of his culture. With Sitting Bull, his people came first. With Geronimo, he came first.

At Fort Sill, Geronimo's neighbor was the Comanche chief Quanah Parker. They rode together in Theodore Roosevelt's inaugural parade. Before his surrender at the end of the Red River War of 1874–75, Quanah Parker was a great warrior. Afterward, he accepted the reality and transformed himself into the image of the white man. In his last years, Geronimo cultivated the soil and proudly raised melons and other crops. Quanah Parker, however, acquired status as a successful and prosperous cattle rancher. Both Geronimo and Quanah adapted to the new reality, but Quanah exhibited an adaptability far beyond Geronimo's.

Within the context of his own culture, Geronimo did not rise to levels of leadership of other Apaches whose names are not as well known. Mangas Coloradas, Cochise, Victorio, Nana, and Juh all led in war if not peace better than Geronimo. They also adhered more closely to their culture than Geronimo. Yet Geronimo's name has overwhelmed them all.

This happened because of the white man's newspapers. All the formidable leaders, both Apaches and all other tribes, had faded from the scene by the time Geronimo emerged as the great Apache holdout. With his name a household word and his deeds appalling newspaper readers, he overshadowed all the other great leaders. His long life after surrender kept his name before the public. In modern times, few of the public know the names of any but Geronimo.

Geronimo died a prisoner of war, leaving the other Chiricahuas as prisoners of war, although they lived much as other Indians interned on reservations. The opening of the Kiowa-Comanche Reservation to white settlement in 1900, however, clouded their future. The Fort Sill Military Reservation, owned by the Kiowas and Comanches and intended as the Chiricahua Reservation after the army abandoned the fort, became US property. Within two years, the army had second thoughts about abandoning the fort: better to retain the entire reservation for military purposes and let the Interior Department move the Chiricahuas to some other reservation. Interior did not want to be involved.

Even before Geronimo's death, the Chiricahuas began to sense another betrayal in the making. The army continued to insist on establishing an artillery school on the reservation, and that left no space for Chiricahua villages. So long as Geronimo lived, however, any scheme that moved the Chiricahuas farther west would encounter opposition. Such was the power the old man's name continued to evoke. His death in 1909 freed the policy-makers to work more seriously to break the impasse.

In 1911 an old friend showed up at Fort Sill with orders to resolve the dilemma: Colonel Hugh L. Scott, Third Cavalry. He investigated the Mescalero Apache Reservation of New Mexico and talked with the Mescaleros.

They would readily welcome the Chiricahuas. Scott discovered, however, that not all the Chiricahuas wanted to move. Some would rather remain at or near Fort Sill, taking land allotments the same as the white settlers. After much bickering in Washington, those few who wanted allotments in Oklahoma were allowed to file for them. Most had become more acculturated or had married outside the tribe. They became the Fort Sill Apaches.[1]

Beginning in 1913, most of the Chiricahuas moved to Mescalero and shed the label "prisoner of war." There most remain today, originally living separately from the Mescaleros but leading a decent life. The old separate Chiricahua settlement on the Mescalero Reservation, at Whitetail, is now largely abandoned. The Mescalero, Chiricahua, and Lipan Apache people are blended on the Mescalero reservation. The individuals all know their ancestors, but few if any are "pure" Chiricahua.

Two years after Geronimo's surrender, General Miles's pile of three stones finally took shape. The Chiricahuas remained as one people for sixteen years. Thanks to one government betrayal after another, the pile of stones had collapsed by 1914. But at long last, the Chiricahuas no longer bore the onus of being prisoners of war.

Of Geronimo's comrades, *Naiche* ultimately gained equal importance. As the second son of Cochise, he inherited the chieftainship of the Chokonen Chiricahuas. As he aged, he grew in stature and paired with Geronimo. In captivity Naiche often commanded more influence and respect than Geronimo. With three wives, fourteen children, and a bevy of well-connected relatives, Naiche lived a more contented and even-tempered life during the years of captivity. He remained the most influential leader in the last years at Fort Sill and led the faction that wanted to move to the Mescalero Reservation in New Mexico. In 1913, with his one surviving wife, his mother, and six children, he made his new home in New Mexico, living contentedly until his death in 1921 at the age of sixty-five.[2]

Chihuahua, independent and outspoken as ever, lived through all the years of captivity. At Mount Vernon, he lost two wives and two infant daughters to illness. At Fort Sill, he led one of the Chiricahua villages. Chihuahua died there in 1901 at the age of seventy-nine. His surviving wife, his son Eugene, and three grandchildren settled on the Mescalero reservation.

Of all the Chiricahuas, *Chatto* led the most checkered career. From superb raider and war leader to close ally of a government that unconscionably betrayed him, he lived through Fort Marion, Mount Vernon, and Fort Sill as a prisoner of war and somewhat of an outcast because of his service to the army. He married three wives, one of whom abandoned him to marry a son of Chief Loco. At Fort Sill he headed one of the twelve Chiricahua villages. One of his sons died at Carlisle, and three sons, one daughter, a sister, and a granddaughter at Fort Sill. With two wives, he joined the others at Mescalero and died there in an automobile crash in 1934, aged eighty.

Mangas, son of Mangas Coloradas and hereditary chief of the Warm Springs Chihennes, did not surrender with Geronimo but was caught and lodged with him at Fort Pickens. He, too, lived as a prisoner of war at Mount Vernon and Fort Sill, where he was leader of one of the Chiricahua villages. At Mount Vernon he married a daughter of Victorio, and together the two had six children. All had died before the end of the Fort Sill years, including Mangas. He died in 1901, fifty-five years old.

Nana appears throughout this narrative, aged, wise, and opposed to all things white. He also, even in his older years, was one of the greatest fighting men of the Chiricahuas. Neither a chief nor a subchief, Nana was born a Mimbres Chihenne and remained with Geronimo's followers until his death. He probably had an unknown number of wives before he married Geronimo's sister. He died at the age of ninety-six at Fort Sill in 1896.

Loco, peace chief of the Warm Springs Chihennes, and his people were forced by Geronimo's raiders to leave San Carlos in 1882 and join the Chiricahuas in Mexico. He refused to flee to Mexico when Geronimo broke out the last time and instead joined with Chatto in the trip to Washington and ultimately, via Fort Leavenworth, to Florida as prisoners of war. He lived quietly at Mount Vernon and Fort Sill. Married three times, he had children by each wife. He died at Fort Sill in 1905, at the age of eighty-two.

The two scouts who went with Lieutenant Gatewood to talk Geronimo into surrender, *Martine* and *Kayitah,* were rewarded with the status of prisoner of war and thus lived at Fort Marion, Mount Vernon, and Fort Sill. The two cousins each married and had children. At Fort Sill Martine first headed a village, and in 1900 Kayitah took over. They were regarded as equals, however, and the village was known as that of Kayitah and Martine. Both went to Mescalero. Kayitah died in 1934 at the age of seventy-eight. Martine's death is unrecorded, but he was interviewed by Morris Opler in the 1930s.

For all the trouble he caused on the reservation, *Kayatena* proved an important influence in persuading Geronimo to surrender to Crook in 1886.

Peacefully living on the reservation, he and all the Chiricahuas were transported to Fort Marion in 1886. There he acquired the status of prisoner of war and lived through the years of Mount Vernon and Fort Sill. He married twice and in 1913 went with many other Chiricahuas to the Mescalero Reservation. He died of pneumonia in 1918 at the age of fifty-seven.

Jason Betzinez did indeed, as a youth of fifteen, "ride with Geronimo." A Warm Springs/Bedonkohe, he was the great-grandson of the venerated chief Mahco. Although a prisoner of war, he was educated at Carlisle from 1887 to 1895 and acquired literacy that allowed him to write, in collaboration with Colonel W. S. Nye, his own book, an indispensable source for the early years. At Fort Sill, he was the last Apache scout mustered out before the move to Mescalero. In 1919 he married a missionary he had known at Fort Sill but fathered no children. Not until 1960, at the age of one hundred, did Betzinez die—in an auto accident. His book, *I Fought with Geronimo,* has been used frequently in this narrative.

Geronimo's move to Mount Vernon Barracks in May 1888 marked his waning association with the military figures who had been part of his past. Within a short time they had dropped from the story of his life. Aside from General George Crook's interview with Geronimo and others at Mount Vernon Barracks in January 1890, he never again saw or heard from most of the others; and Crook died only three months later, in March 1890.

General Nelson A. Miles periodically wrote more wordy dispatches when he objected to events at Mount Vernon Barracks, and several times he raised the Chiricahua issue. At the same time, he came under growing criticism for the way he continued to describe the last campaign. In particular, in report after report he exaggerated the roles of Lawton and Wood while hardly mentioning Lieutenant Gatewood and his Chiricahua scouts, Kayitah and Martine.

Captain Henry W. Lawton continued to enjoy Miles's favor. In 1893, thanks to the general, Lawton received a Medal of Honor for heroism in the Civil War. In the Spanish American War, promoted to major general of Volunteers, he served creditably in Cuba before transferring to the Philippines. Although a general, he fought valorously in battles with Philippine insurgents. In one, on December 18, 1899, he caught a fatal bullet—the only US general killed in the Philippine Insurrection.

Assistant Surgeon Leonard Wood also benefitted from Miles's patronage. Like Lawton, in 1898 he received the Medal of Honor for services in the

Apache campaign. In 1898 also, he finally achieved his ambition of abandoning the medical service for the line. The Spanish American War afforded him his chance. Long a friend of Theodore Roosevelt, he gained the colonelcy of the First US Volunteer Cavalry, the "Rough Riders," of which Roosevelt was lieutenant colonel. With service in Cuba and the Philippines, he emerged a major general of Volunteers and a brigadier general in the regular army. After the reorganization of the army, he served from 1910 to 1914 as army chief of staff. His military ambitions led to political ambitions, and he unsuccessfully sought the Republican nomination for president in 1920. He died in 1927.

Nelson A. Miles rose swiftly, promoted to major general in 1890, the same year in which his longtime nemesis George Crook died. The citizens of Tucson awarded him a ceremonial sword for ending the Apache Wars, and in 1892 he, too, received a Medal of Honor for Civil War gallantry. Named commanding general of the army in 1895, he held the position through the Spanish American War, in which he performed without much distinction. Awarded a third star by the Congress, he retired in 1903, the army's last commanding general. President Roosevelt called him a "brave peacock" and refused to attend his retirement ceremony. A heart attack struck down Miles while attending a circus in 1925.

The true loser among all these distinguished officers was First Lieutenant Charles B. Gatewood. While downplaying Gatewood's contribution to the surrender of Geronimo, Miles honored his promise to appoint him a member of his staff. As he had alienated Crook, so Gatewood alienated Miles. Relegated to the margins of the staff, he suffered from long years of service and illness. Badly injured by a gunpowder explosion, in 1892 he sought the promotion to captain to which his seniority entitled him. The promotion board denied him on the grounds of bad health. On May 20, 1896, a malignant tumor on his liver killed him.

Such were some of the people who affected the life of Geronimo in one way or another. But Geronimo's name drowned them all in the memory of the public.

On September 4, 1886, at Skeleton Canyon, Arizona Territory, four centuries of Indian warfare in North America drew to a close. The Ghost Dance troubles four years later were a religious movement, not a war. The character of the Apache conflict differed profoundly from all other Indian wars. Other tribes often engaged in combat, which was rare in Apache hostilities. Few

Apache conflicts merit the term "battle" or even "skirmish." In most encounters the Apaches fled without loss of life. Even so, Skeleton Canyon achieves significance as the end of four centuries of Indian hostilities in North America. As the last holdout, Geronimo acquired the most recent position in the American memory, one reason his legacy has so firmly endured.

Legend or reality, Geronimo remains the dominant Indian name in the American memory.

APPENDIX

APACHE INDIANS

Mescalero (Mess-*ka*-lero) Tribe. Sierra Blanca of southern New Mexico
Jicarilla (Hick-a-*reeya*) Tribe. Northern New Mexico
Western Apache Bands. Arizona north of Gila River
> **White Mountain Band.** Largest and easternmost band, White Mountains of northeast Arizona; aka Coyotero (Coy-*o*-tero) (although Coyotero may be a separate White Mountain group).
> **San Carlos Band.** Gila River southwest of White Mountains in Arizona.
> **Cibicue (Sib-a-*que*) Band.** Arizona northwest of White Mountain band.
> **Tonto Bands:**
>> **Southern.** Arizona west of Cibicue Band.
>> **Northern.** Arizona northwest of Southern Tonto Band.

Chiricahua Apache Tribe (No tribal chief)
> **Chihenne (Chee-*hennie*) Band.** New Mexico west of Rio Grande into Black Range and Mogollon Mountains.
>> **Chihenne Local Groups:** Warm Springs (Victorio, Loco, Nana); Mimbres; Coppermine; Mogollon (*Mug*-ee-yon) (may be another name for Bedonkohe).
> **Bedonkohe (Be-*don*-ko-hee) Band.** Geronimo's band. Mogollon Mountains of southwestern New Mexico. Expert Morris Opler does not recognize the Bedonkoke. It may be another name for his Mogollons. By 1850s Mangas Coloradas's Bedonkohe following began merging with Chihennes to form a hybrid group, mainly Bedonkohe, at Santa Lucía Springs, New Mexico.
> **Chokonen (Cho-*ko*-nen) Band.** Southeastern Arizona in Chiricahua and Dragoon Mountains. Cochise headed the dominant Local Group. Others not apparent. By 1858 Cochise became the chief of the entire Chokonen Band. After death of Mangas Coloradas, Cochise emerged as the dominant leader of the entire Chiricahua tribe.
> **Nednhi (*Ned*-nee) Band.** Northern Mexico ranging into Arizona. Juh dominant leader. Local groups not known.

ABBREVIATIONS

AAAG   Acting Assistant Adjutant General

AAG   Assistant Adjutant General

ADC   Aide-de-Camp

AG   Adjutant General

AGO   Adjutant General's Office

AGUSA   Adjutant General US Army

AHS   Arizona Historical Society

CIA   Commissioner of Indian Affairs

CO   Commanding Officer

DM   Department of the Missouri

GFO   General Field Order

GO   General Order

LR   Letters Received

LS   Letters Sent

MDM   Military Division of the Missouri

MDP   Military Division of the Pacific

NARA   National Archives and Records Administration

OAG   Office of the Adjutant General

OIA   Office of Indian Affairs

RG   Record Group

SO   Special Order

SS   Secretary of State

SW   Secretary of War

NOTES

CHAPTER 1. APACHE YOUTH

1. Originally published in 1906 as *Geronimo's Story of His Life,* the book has progressed through many printings. I have used the Penguin edition of 1996 and cite it as S. M. Barrett, *Geronimo, His Own Story: The Autobiography of a Great Patriot Warrior,* as told to S. M. Barrett, new edition revised and edited by Frank Turner (New York: Penguin, 1996). Pagination differs among the various editions. The narrative can be easily dismissed as the meanderings of an old man, but it contains much of value when checked with reliable sources. Geronimo dictated his story at Fort Sill, Oklahoma, in 1905, a prisoner of war ever since his surrender in 1886. He spoke in his own language to Asa Daklugie, a Carlisle Indian School graduate and son of Chief Juh. Daklugie in turn translated into English for S. M. Barrett, a Lawton school superintendent. What was lost or corrupted in translation, and what Barrett changed to accord more with the white calendar and understanding, cannot be known. In addition, the War Department objected to the manuscript as reflecting badly on an army that Geronimo had repeatedly eluded, and Barrett made some accommodating changes. Only by direction of President Theodore Roosevelt, however, did the manuscript finally see print. I treat in more detail the autobiography in chap. 28.

At the time of Geronimo's birth, New Mexico was part of the Mexican state of Chihuahua (Chee-*wah-wah*). Arizona was also part of Chihuahua and the bordering Mexican state of Sonora to the west. The Mexican War of 1846–48 gained the United States the present states of New Mexico and Arizona, and in 1850 they were organized as the Territory of New Mexico. The Gadsden Purchase of 1853 added the country south of the Gila River as far as the present international boundary. Following the collapse of the Confederate Territory of Arizona in 1863, Arizona was detached from the Territory of New Mexico and established as the US Territory of Arizona. Both territories became states in 1912. To avoid confusion, locations are identified as in Arizona or New Mexico regardless of jurisdiction at the time.

2. Barrett, *Geronimo, His Own Story,* 69. Asa Daklugie (Geronimo's interpreter for Barrett) had also heard stories of Mahco even though living with his family in Mexico. Eve Ball, with Nora Henn and Lynda Sánchez, *Indeh: An Apache Odyssey* (Provo, UT: Brigham Young University Press, 1980), 14. Eve Ball, a retired school

teacher in Rudiso, New Mexico, was the only white person ever to get close enough to the Chiricahuas who lived at the nearby Mescalero Reservation in the twentieth century to get them to talk of the early years.

3. Morris E. Opler is the preeminent authority on Apache culture. For his discussion of sibling-cousin relations, see *An Apache Life-Way: The Economic, Social, and Religious Institutions of the Chiricahua Indians* (New York: Cooper Square, 1965), 58–62. The genealogy of Mahco and his offspring is so tangled in the sparse sources as to rest on much speculation. The most recent standard biography of Geronimo is Angie Debo, *Geronimo: The Man, His Time, His Place* (Norman: University of Oklahoma Press, 1976). She devotes much of her first chapter to this speculation and reaches no firm conclusion. I have turned to other sources as well and stated my conclusions more firmly than she. They seem to be the most that will ever be known about the family origins of Geronimo. Each of those named in my narrative is the subject of a biographical sketch in a large document assembled by Gillett Griswold, longtime director of the Fort Sill Museum. The manuscript is entitled "The Fort Sill Apaches: Their Vital Statistics, Tribal Origins, Antecedents," and was compiled in 1958–61.

4. To avoid confusion, Mangas Coloradas's lasting name will be used throughout, even when he was known as Fuerte (Spanish for strong); for the same reason Geronimo will replace Goyahkla even during his youth.

5. Most of my treatment of Chiricahua tribal organization and culture is taken from Opler, *Apache Life-Way.* Opler divided the Chiricahua tribe into only three bands, ignoring the Bedonkohe altogether. I believe it probable that the Chihenne local group Opler called Mogollon is what is now recognized as Bedonkohe, a full if small band.

6. Mangas Coloradas commands an exceptional biography in Edwin R. Sweeney, *Mangas Coloradas: Chief of the Chiricahua Apaches* (Norman: University of Oklahoma Press, 1998). I have relied heavily on him, for he has scoured every possible archive in the United States and Mexico and presented details never before set forth. The physical description of Mangas Coloradas, of which there are many, is drawn largely from the army surgeon who examined his corpse a few hours after his death, xxi.

7. Barrett, *Geronimo, His Own Story,* 59.

8. All these beings, ceremonies, and rituals are treated, with not always consistent testimony of interviewees, throughout Opler, *Apache Life-Way,* 205–16.

9. Ibid., 436–38, describes preparation of tiswin and its role in social occasions. He does not, however, go beyond its benign part in such affairs. Nor do other ethnologists or historians. That they were common emerges from documentary records of particular events. Some old Apaches denied the reality of tiswin drunks, claiming that they were powered more by the white man's whiskey than tiswin. For an example, see Sherry Robinson, *Apache Voices: Their Stories of Survival as Told to Eve Ball* (Albuquerque: University of New Mexico Press, 2000), 168.

10. Barrett, *Geronimo, His Own Story,* 60–61. Ethnologists generally deny that Chiricahuas practiced agriculture, citing the prevalence of nomadic mobility and the pattern of plundering raids on Mexicans and other Indians. Some, however, concede that some Chihennes and Bedonkohes may have resorted to agriculture on a limited scale. This would have been during the longer intervals of peace such as prevailed during Geronimo's youth. His memory of youthful farming is too explicit to ignore. As warfare grew more intense and mobility increased, opportunities for agriculture shrank. For most of his adult life, Mangas Coloradas farmed at Santa Lucía Springs.

11. Opler, *Apache Life-Way,* describes the novitiate, 134–39. Geronimo and all other sources state simply that Taslishim died during the boy's youth. However, he told one interviewer that he was ten at the time, which fits the probable sequence of his early life. MS, Interview by Capt. W. H. C. Bowen with Geronimo at Mount Vernon Barracks AL, in 1893, Col. W. H. C. Bowen Papers, box 3, US Army Military History Institute, Carlisle Barracks, PA. This document was called to my attention by Senior Historian Richard Sommers.

12. Barrett, *Geronimo, His Own Story,* 66–68.

13. Ibid., 70. Geronimo gave the year as 1846, but his true birth year was 1823, so the accurate year would be 1840. My description of the novitiate is drawn from Opler, *Apache Life-Way,* 134–39.

14. Barrett, *Geronimo, His Own Story,* 70–71.

CHAPTER 2. APACHE MANHOOD

1. S. M. Barrett, *Geronimo, His Own Story,* 70. "Alope" does not sound like an Apache name, but Geronimo was so specific in recounting his marriage that his statement is accepted.

2. Griswold, "Fort Sill Apaches." A good character sketch is in Charles Collins, *The Great Escape: The Apache Outbreak of 1881* (Tucson: Westernlore, 1994).

3. Sweeney, *Mangas Coloradas,* 42–44.

4. Ibid., 71–72. See also Sweeney, *Cochise: Chiricahua Apache Chief* (Norman: University of Oklahoma Press, 1991), 32–35.

5. Ralph A. Smith, *Borderlander: The Life of James Kirker, 1793–1852* (Norman: University of Oklahoma Press, 1999), chaps. 7–8. See also Sweeney, *Mangas Coloradas,* 83–84.

6. Sweeney, *Mangas Coloradas,* 102–5, chap. 5.

7. E-mail, Edwin Sweeney to Utley, February 5, 2007, discloses the 1843 date. Sweeney examined Mexican records in preparing his biography of Mangas Coloradas. As for his name, Debo, *Geronimo,* 13, recounts a tale told by the son of a bombastic future Apache agent of a battle with Mexicans in which they uttered some words of alarm that sounded like Geronimo. This seems implausible to me.

8. Barrett, *Geronimo, His Own Story,* 110. Raids and war are recounted in chaps. 7–11.

9. Sweeney, *Cochise,* xii–xix.

10. Ibid., 120–24.

11. Smith, *Borderlander,* 162–68. Sweeney, *Mangas Coloradas,* 135–36.

12. Jason Betzinez, with Wilbur Sturtevant Nye, *I Fought with Geronimo* (New York: Bonanza Books, 1969), 4–9, is the principal source for the revenge expedition. Betzinez was born about 1860 and did indeed ride in the final campaigns of Geronimo. He collaborated with W. S. Nye in this book and is regarded as an unusually reliable Apache source. He died at the age of one hundred in 1960. See also Sweeney, *Mangas Coloradas,* 146–48.

13. In an interview with Eve Ball, August 10, 1954. Robinson, *Apache Voices,* 57. Eve Ball sometimes took liberties with her sources. Sherry Robinson examined the Ball papers at Brigham Young University and here set the record straight.

14. Leon Perico interview, box 37, folder 28, no. 14/25/3238, Morris Edward Opler Papers, Division of Rare Manuscript Collections, Cornell University, obtained by Opler from Sol Tax. Copy provided by Edwin Sweeney. See also partial quotation in Opler, *Apache Life-Way,* 216. A biographical sketch of Perico is in Griswold, "Fort Sill Apaches."

15. Morris E. Opler, "Some Implications of Culture Theory for Anthropology and Psychology," *American Journal of Orthopsychiatry* 18 (October 1948): 617.

16. Sweeney, *Mangas Coloradas,* xviii.

CHAPTER 3. BATTLE AND MASSACRE

1. The most detailed and authoritative account of what followed is in Sweeney, *Mangas Coloradas,* 209–12. His *Cochise,* 83–87, is less detailed. Barrett, *Geronimo, His Own Story,* 78–83, contains Geronimo's own detailed account. His chronology is flawed, and he depicts the offensive as a revenge expedition he himself organized in retaliation for a disaster that was yet to befall him, to be treated later in this chapter. He both supports and strays from Sweeney's narrative. Some of the episodes he recounts probably occurred, and he undoubtedly took part, but he should be read only within the context of the Sweeney accounts.

2. These quotations are selected from Barrett, *Geronimo, His Own Story,* 82, 83. Geronimo's account can only refer to Pozo Hediondo, but it is flawed by his assumption that this was a revenge fight for the disaster soon to befall him. He portrays himself as more a tactical leader than he probably was, but he assuredly fought ferociously and in hand-to-hand combat, and his stature rose accordingly.

3. Sweeney, *Mangas Coloradas,* 212.

4. Scarce and often contradictory sources abound in this episode. Sweeney deals authoritatively with it in *Mangas Coloradas,* 218–19; and in "'I Had Lost All':

Geronimo and the Carrasco Massacre of 1851," *Journal of Arizona History* 27 (Spring 1986): 35–52. Geronimo tells his story at length in Barrett, *Geronimo, His Own Story,* 75–78. Although his account is full of untruths, I accept some of his most important statements, as does Sweeney. The most notable untruths are that the Apaches had been and were at peace and his chronology that places this event before Pozo Hediondo and the latter as the revenge expedition. Betzinez, *I Fought with Geronimo,* 16–17, is the authority for Apaches drinking in town and also recounts the story of the massacre.

5. Barrett, *Geronimo, His Own Story,* 77.

6. E. A. Burbank, as told by Ernest Royce, *Burbank among the Indians,* ed. Frank J. Taylor (Caldwell, ID: Caxton, 1946), 33.

CHAPTER 4. "AMERICANS"

1. Sweeney, *Mangas Coloradas,* chap. 3, deals with the early relations around the copper mines. I have examined and cited most of the original sources in my *A Life Wild and Perilous: Mountain Men and the Paths to the Pacific* (New York: Henry Holt, 1997).

2. Lt. Delos B. Sackett to AAAG Santa Fe, Doña Ana, December 14, 1848, encl. to Washington to Jones, February 3, 1849, LR, Hq. of the Army, W-21, NARA.

3. Capt. Enoch Steen to AAAG Santa Fe, Doña Ana, September 1, 1849, RG 77, LR, Topographical Engineers, S478/1850, NARA. Steen to AAAG Santa Fe, Doña Ana, October 20, 1849, RG 98, LR, Dept. NM, S-12, NARA. I deduce that these were Bedonkohes from their retreat to the copper mines, Bedonkohe country. Also, a raiding party of one hundred was unusually large and may well have been led by Mangas himself.

4. Steen to AAAG Santa Fe, Doña Ana, March 24, 1850, encl. to Munroe to Jones, April 15, 1850, RG 94, AGO Doc. Files, box 464, doc. 269-M-1850, NARA. Steen to AAG Santa Fe, Doña Ana, September 3, 1850, RG 98, LR, Dept. NM, S23/1850, NARA.

5. Sweeney, *Mangas Coloradas,* 244. Sumner to AGUSA, Hq. 9th Military Dept., Fort Union, January 1, February 3, 1852, RG 98, LS, Fort Union, NARA. Sumner to Lt. Col. D. S. Miles at Fort Conrad, Hq. 9th Military Dept., Albuquerque, April 5, 1852, RG 98, LS, Dept. NM, NARA.

6. Sweeney, *Mangas Coloradas,* 258–62. Griener to Lea, July 31, 1852, RG 75, LR, OIA NM, G41/1852, NARA. Sumner to Secretary of the Interior, July 21, 1852, RG 75, OIA Treaty File, NARA. *(Saint Louis) Daily Missouri Republican,* August 28, 1852. For a copy of the treaty and associated documents, see Michael Steck Papers, University of New Mexico.

7. Sweeney, *Mangas Coloradas,* 263–80. Griener to Lea, Santa Fe, August 30, 1852, RG 75, LR, OIA NM, G50/1852, NARA. Wingfield to Lane, Fort Webster,

December 20, 1852, encl. to Wingfield to CIA, January 29, 1853, RG 75, LR, OIA NM, W307/1854, NARA. Wingfield to Lane, Fort Webster, May 4, 1853, encl. to Lane, "Report," May 21, 1853, RG 75, LR, OIA NM, N128/1853, NARA. "Articles of a Provisional Compact . . . ," April 7, 1853, encl. to Meriwether (Lane's replacement as governor) to Manypenny, August 31, 1853, RG 75, LR, OIA NM, N-153, NARA. Steen to Lane, Fort Webster, May 16, 28, 1853, encl. to Lane to Manypenny, May 28, 1853, RG 75, LR, OIA NM, N131/1853, NARA. Wingfield to Lane, Copper Mines, c. May 20, 1853, ibid. Steen to AGUSA, Fort Webster, June 17, 1853, RG 94, LR, AGO, S438/1853, NARA.

8. Lane to Wingfield, Fort Webster, May 28, 1853, Steck Papers.

9. Sweeney, *Mangas Coloradas,* 296–304. George Ruhlen, "Fort Thorn—An Historical Vignette," *Password* (El Paso Historical Society) 4 (October 1960): 127–37.

10. The Michael Steck Papers at the University of New Mexico Library are rich in his history as agent and later as superintendent of Indian affairs. The collection includes Steck's appointment papers of May 9 and July 24, 1854. Steck's activities in examining the Chiricahua lands and meeting with the chiefs are addressed to Governor Meriwether from Fort Thorn, August 31 and October (n.d.), 1854. That Steck's issues were substantial is recorded in a certificate of contractor Estevan Ochoa listing the items issued on September 10, Steck Papers.

11. Sweeney, *Mangas Coloradas,* 306–7.

12. Steck to CIA, Santa Fe, August 7, 1857, CIA, *Annual Report* (1857), 579.

13. I narrate and document the Bonneville campaign of 1857 in *Frontiersmen in Blue: The United States Army and the Indian, 1848–1865* (New York: Macmillan, 1967), 155–57.

14. For Mangas's turn to Cochise and factionalizing of his following, see Sweeney, *Mangas Coloradas,* 343–62.

15. Sweeney, *Mangas Coloradas,* 373ff. Collins to CIA C. E. Mix, Santa Fe, December 5, 1858, RG 75, LR, OIA NM, C1903/1859, NARA. Draft, Steck to Collins, Apache Agency, February 1, 1859, Steck Papers. CIA, *Annual Report* (1858), 184–99; (1859), 334–47.

16. Griswold, "Fort Sill Apaches," under these names, including Geronimo.

CHAPTER 5. WAR WITH THE AMERICANS

1. Sweeney, *Mangas Coloradas,* 384. R. S. Allen, "Pinos Altos, New Mexico," *New Mexico Historical Review* 23 (1948): 302–32.

2. Steck to CIA A. B. Greenwood, Washington, May 11, 1860, RG 75, LR, OIA NM FP, NARA. Greenwood to Steck, May 16, 1860, Steck Papers.

3. Collins to Greenwood, RG 75, LR, OIA NM, 0620/1860, NARA. Steck to Greenwood, Apache Agency, October 17, 1860, RG 75, LR, OIA NM, C795/1860, NARA. Greenwood to Collins, January 5, 1861, RG 75, LR, OIA NM FP, NARA.

4. Unless otherwise cited, my account is based largely on Sweeney, *Cochise,* chap. 8. Like his biography of Mangas Coloradas, Sweeney's biography of Cochise is the ultimate authority. Sweeney had consulted every source and assembled a day-by-day narrative of this episode from the viewpoint of both sides.

5. Geronimo's account is in Barrett, *Geronimo, His Own Story,* 114–16. Geronimo mixed up the chronology and got some facts wrong, but he recalled enough detail to establish that he was there and participated in some of what followed. The scene was witnessed from behind the line of tents by Sergeant Daniel Robinson, leading a train of supply wagons west to Fort Buchanan. His eyewitness account is critical to understanding the sequence of events. Douglas C. McChristian and Larry L. Ludwig, "Eyewitness to the Bascom Affair: An Account by Sergeant Daniel Robinson, Seventh Infantry," *Journal of Arizona History* 42 (Autumn 2001): 277–300. See also McChristian, *Fort Bowie, Arizona: Combat Post of the Southwest, 1858–1894* (Norman: University of Oklahoma Press, 2005), 21–35.

6. I recount this in greater detail in *Frontiersmen in Blue,* 157–61. For more, see Benjamin Sacks, "The Origins of Fort Buchanan, Myth and Fact," *Arizona and the West* 7 (1965): 207–26.

7. Sweeney, *Cochise,* chap. 8. Utley, *Frontiersmen in Blue,* 161–63.

8. Barrett, *Geronimo, His Own Story,* 117.

9. Sweeney, *Mangas Coloradas,* covers these events, chap. 16.

CHAPTER 6. RETURN OF THE BLUECOATS

1. Robinson, *Apache Voices,* 27–29. Griswold, "Fort Sill Apaches," under Nanatha-thtithl. Barrett, *Geronimo, His Own Story,* 86–89. Geronimo does not mention the loss of his third wife and their child, although his account closely follows the other two citations.

2. Sweeney, *Mangas Coloradas,* 423–25. R. S. Allen, "Pinos Altos, New Mexico," *New Mexico Historical Review* 23 (October 1948): 303–4.

3. For Victorio, see Eve Ball, *In the Days of Victorio: Recollections of a Warm Springs Apache* (Tucson: University of Arizona Press, 1972); and Dan L. Thrapp, *Victorio and the Mimbres Apaches* (Norman: University of Oklahoma Press, 1974). For Loco, see Bud Shapard, *Chief Loco: Apache Peacemaker* (Norman: University of Oklahoma Press, 2010).

4. Griswold, "Fort Sill Apaches," under Nana. Multiple sources chronicle Nana's career in later years, when he continued as a respected war leader into old age.

5. Aside from a few brief comments of Asa Daklugie in Ball, *Indeh: An Apache Odyssey,* 19–20, no sources record the Apache perspective. The sequence is thoroughly detailed in military records, from which Sweeney reconstructed it in *Mangas Coloradas,* 429–40, and *Cochise,* 198–202. I have recounted the Apache viewpoint in what may be plausibly inferred from the military accounts, which I have examined

numerous times in the past. Debo, *Geronimo,* 68, shares my assumption that Geronimo participated, alluding to Chiricahua tribal tradition. Geronimo's failure to leave any hint of his presence is consistent with his lifelong practice. Even his account of the Bascom affair focuses on the ambush of the freight train in Apache Pass, not the soldiers.

6. Larry Ludwig, longtime park ranger at Fort Bowie National Historic Site, conducted an archaeological survey of both sides of what is now called Overlook Hill. He found no artillery fragments among the Indian defenses but plenty on the other side of the hill. He also found the small hill used to elevate the howitzers, confirmed by the artillery fuses dug up at its base. Infantry, not trained artillerymen, manned these guns and cut the fuses too long for bursts above the Indian positions. The exploding shells, even though missing the target, frightened the Apaches into abandoning their positions.

7. An excellent history of Fort Bowie, including chapters on the Bascom affair and the Battle of Apache Pass, is McChristian, *Fort Bowie.*

8. Utley, *Frontiersmen in Blue,* 232–33.

9. Sweeney, *Mangas Coloradas,* chap. 18, recounts in detail all the following events involving Mangas and documents them thoroughly from the ample original sources. Geronimo provides a reasonably accurate account in Barrett, *Geronimo, His Own Story,* chap. 13. I have treated the story from the military perspective in *Frontiersmen in Blue,* 249–56.

10. Sweeney, *Mangas Coloradas,* presents the most detailed and thoroughly documented account of the slaying of Mangas. I have relied heavily on his reconstruction. See also Lee Myers, "The Enigma of Mangas Coloradas' Death," *New Mexico Historical Review* 41 (October 1966): 287–304. This article quotes from all the relevant sources but reaches no conclusion. My version, in addition to Sweeney, is taken from the same sources.

CHAPTER 7. COCHISE: WAR AND PEACE, 1863–72

1. Geronimo mentions a number of clashes with soldiers following the death of Mangas Coloradas, although the details do not coincide with the military reports. Barrett, *Geronimo, His Own Story,* 119–20. Sweeney, *Cochise,* 209–10.

2. Griswold, "Fort Sill Apaches," under named individuals.

3. Edwin R. Sweeney, *From Cochise to Geronimo: The Chiricahua Apaches, 1874–1886* (Norman: University of Oklahoma Press, 2010), 19. Sweeney to Utley, June 20, 2007.

4. Official correspondence documenting this series of campaigns may be found in *War of the Rebellion: Official Records of the Union and Confederate Armies,* ser. 1, vol. 34, part 3; and vol. 60, part 2. See also Sweeney, *Cochise,* 218–23; and Steck Papers.

5. Annual Report of Maj. Gen. Irvin McDowell, San Francisco, October 18, 1866, SW, *Annual Report* (1866), 34–36.

6. Griswold, "Fort Sill Apaches," under named individuals, including Geronimo.

7. These conflicts are detailed in McChristian, *Fort Bowie,* chap. 6.

8. Cochise's year of birth is speculative. After careful analysis of contemporary evidence, Sweeney, *Cochise,* 6–7, arrives at the year 1810.

9. The agent, Lt. Charles E. Drew, fought hard for rations but could not move superiors. They supported him but lacked the resources to back him. Appointed in May 1869, he was removed a year later and died of exposure pursuing Mescaleros across the Jornada del Muerto. The correspondence between Drew and his superiors is printed in CIA, *Annual Report* (1869), 104–9. The circumstances of his death are recounted in W. F. M. Arny, *Indian Agent in New Mexico: The Journal of Special Agent W. F. M. Arny, 1870,* ed. Lawrence R. Murphy (Santa Fe, NM: Stagecoach, 1967), 54–58. The tortuous story of attempts to establish a reservation is detailed in Shapard, *Loco,* chaps. 2–4.

10. Sweeney, *Cochise,* 281ff. The post was Camp Mogollon, soon to be named Fort Apache. The officer, Maj. John Green, was undoubtedly startled to meet with the renowned Cochise.

11. Arny, *Indian Agent in New Mexico,* 54–58. Sweeney, *Cochise,* 297.

12. Sweeney, *Cochise,* 315. Cochise's name for Jeffords had been learned by Gen. O. O. Howard (to be treated below), who related it to a reporter in Washington, DC. "Account of Gen'l Howard's Mission to the Apaches and Navajos," reprinted from *Washington Daily Morning Chronicle,* November 10, 1872, 10. Papers of the Order of the Indian Wars, US Army Military History Institute, Carlisle Barracks, PA.

13. Sweeney, *Cochise,* 324–25.

14. Ibid., 339–40.

15. Ibid., 343–44.

CHAPTER 8. COCHISE: PEACE AT LAST, 1872

1. I have tried to describe these scenes as the Indians would have experienced them. Of course, they have been reconstructed from white sources, the only sources that exist. I have drawn my narrative from Sweeney, *Cochise,* 356–66, based on thorough research in original sources; "Account of Gen'l Howard's Mission," the newspaper interview, which is far more informative than his official report; Howard's official report, November 7, 1872, RG 94, LR, OAG, 1871–80, M666, 2465 AGO 1871, roll 123, frames 474–85, NARA (reprinted in CIA, *Annual Report* [1872], 175–78); Sweeney, ed., *Making Peace with Cochise: The 1872 Journal of Captain Joseph Alton Sladen* (Norman: University of Oklahoma Press, 1997) (MS, Sladen Papers, US Army Military History Institute, Carlisle Barracks, PA); and (in an

edition for which I wrote the foreword) Oliver O. Howard, *My Life and Experiences among Our Hostile Indians* (1907; New York: Da Capo Press, 1972), chaps. 13, 14.

2. All the sources quote the exchange in English, which nonetheless conveys the essence of what the two said in halting Spanish.

3. Actually, Sladen was a "teniente"—a first lieutenant and aide-de-camp to Howard. He held a brevet of captain and was addressed as such as a courtesy.

4. Puzzled by how Cochise and Howard communicated, I queried Edwin Sweeney. In an e-mail of December 25, 2009, he replied that the Howard Papers at Bowdoin College contained a contract with Jacob May to serve as Spanish interpreter. Also, Howard wrote an article, also in his papers, that described the exchanges. Cochise spoke in Apache, and Ponce and Jeffords translated through Spanish into English. After May arrived, of course, he translated from Spanish into English for Howard.

5. Barrett, *Geronimo, His Own Story,* 124. His account is badly confused but establishes his presence. A letter in the Howard Papers, cited by Sweeney, *Cochise,* 362, attributes the confirmation to Capt. Samuel S. Sumner, who was present at the Sulphur Springs parley on October 12.

6. Pile to Secretary of State, Santa Fe, June 19, 1871; Safford to editor, Tucson, November 9, 1871; both in RG 94, LR, OAG, 1871–80, M666, 2465 AGO 1871, roll 24, NARA.

7. For a history of Grant's Peace Policy, see Francis Paul Prucha, *American Indian Policy in Crisis: Christian Reformers and the Indian, 1865–1900* (Norman: University of Oklahoma Press, 1976); and Henry E. Fritz, *The Movement for Indian Assimilation, 1860–1890* (Philadelphia: University of Pennsylvania Press, 1963). For the origins of the Colyer mission, see Grant to Secretary of the Interior Columbus Delano, Long Branch, NJ, July 18, 1871; Grant to SW W. W. Belknap, Long Branch, July 29, 1871; both in RG 94, LR, OAG, 1871–80, M666, 2465 AGO 1871, Correspondence Relating to Vincent Colyer, roll 123, frames 37–38, 40–41, NARA.

8. *Peace with the Apaches of New Mexico and Arizona: Report of Vincent Colyer* (Washington, DC: GPO, 1871), 9–11 (Reprint, Tucson: Territorial Press, 1964). Colyer to Superintendent of Indian Affairs Nathaniel Pope, Camp Tularosa, August 29, 1871, RG 94, LR, OAG, 1871–80, M666, 2465 AGO 1871, Correspondence Relating to Vincent Colyer, roll 123, frames 85–87, NARA. Secretary of the Interior Columbus Delano to SW W. W. Belknap, September 4, 1871, transmitting Colyer to Delano, Cañada Alamosa, August 18, 1871, and Colyer to Delano, Ojo Caliente, September 2, 1871, ibid., frames 66–70. Pope to Col. Gordon Granger, Camp Apache, AZ, September 6, 1871, ibid., frames 81–82. CIA, *Annual Report* (1872), 295–302.

9. An authoritative biography is Charles M. Robinson III, *General Crook and the Western Frontier* (Norman: University of Oklahoma Press, 2001). *General George Crook: His Autobiography,* edited by Martin F. Schmitt (Norman: University of

Oklahoma Press, 1946), contains much of value that does not appear in official reports. Crook's reputation rests in large part on the excellent hagiographic book by his longtime aide: John G. Bourke, *On the Border with Crook* (New York: Charles Scribner's Sons, 1891).

10. Exhaustive documentation of the handling of the Colyer mission by the Interior and War Departments, and the president's final approval of Colyer's reservations, is contained in RG 94, LR, OAG, 1871–80, M666, 2465 AGO 1871, Correspondence Relating to Vincent Colyer, roll 123, for August 1871 to February 1872. See also Crook, *Autobiography;* and Robinson, *Crook.*

11. Howard's lengthy report, dated June 1872, with attachments, is printed in CIA, *Annual Report* (1872), 148–75. His statement to Crook is in Crook, *Autobiography,* 169. Extensive official documentation leading to and during the Howard mission is in RG 94, LR, OAG, 1871–80, M666, 2465 AGO 1871, Correspondence Relating to Vincent Colyer, roll 123, NARA.

12. Howard to CIA, November 7, 1872; Pope to CIA, October 10, 1872; both in CIA, *Annual Report* (1872), 176, 295–302. Sladen, *Making Peace with Cochise,* 32–35. Appendix A reprints the transcript of the September 12 council. Sweeney, *Cochise,* 352–53. Howard, *My Life and Experiences,* relates his experiences at Tularosa and Cañada Alamosa, and the circumstances of his meeting with Jeffords, in a number of ways that are contradicted by contemporary evidence.

13. Sladen, *Making Peace with Cochise,* 89–93.

14. Barrett, *Geronimo, His Own Story,* 124.

15. Schofield to AGUSA, San Francisco, December 26, 1872, enclosing Crook to AAG San Francisco, Camp Grant, December 13, 1872; Crook to AAG San Francisco, Florence, AZ, February 11, 1873; Crook to AAG San Francisco, Prescott, April 12, 1873; GO 12, by command of Bvt. Maj. Gen. Crook, Prescott, April 7, 1873; GO 13, by command of Bvt. Maj. Gen. Crook, Prescott, April 8, 1873; all in RG 94, LR, OAG, 1871–80, M666, AGO 2465 1871, Correspondence Relating to Vincent Colyer, roll 123, frames 519–27, 570–72, 595–601, NARA.

CHAPTER 9. THE CHIRICAHUA RESERVATION, 1872–76

1. Sweeney, *Cochise,* 369.

2. Ibid., 374. Crook to AAG San Francisco, Hq. DA Camp Grant, December 13, 1872, RG 94, LR, OAG, 1871–80, M666, 3383 AGO 1873, roll 24, frames 523–27, NARA.

3. Sweeney covers these events in *Cochise,* 363. However, he narrates them in greater and somewhat different detail in *Cochise to Geronimo,* 24–25, based on a variety of Arizona newspapers. He prepared this account long after publication of *Cochise,* and it reflects further research. See also Jeffords to CIA, Chiricahua Agency, Sulphur Springs, August 31, 1873, CIA, *Annual Report* (1873), 291–93; and Jeffords

to CIA, Pinery Canyon (now agency headquarters), November 30, 1873, RG 94, LR, OAG, 1871–80, M666, 3383 AGO 1873, roll 24, frames 61–64, NARA.

4. Indian Inspector William Vandever to CIA, Washington, January 23, 1874 (repeating a report of October 18 gone astray), RG 94, LR, OAG, 1871–80, M666, 3383 AGO 1873, roll 24, frames 70–78, NARA.

5. Sweeney, *Cochise,* 386–87. Sweeney, *Cochise to Geronimo,* 39. The Chiricahua Agency was located at Sulphur Springs, in the valley of the same name, until August 1873. It then moved across the Chiricahua Mountains to San Simon, where sufficient arable land afforded agricultural potential. But this location proved so unhealthy that the agency was moved in November 1873 to Pinery Canyon.

6. Howard's report of June 1872, CIA, *Annual Report* (1872), 155.

7. Crook to AAG San Francisco, December 13, 1872, January 24, February 11, 1873, RG 94, LR, OAG, 1871–80, M666, 2465 AGO 1871, roll 123, frames 519–21, 557–58, 570–72, NARA. GO 10, Hq. Military Division of the Pacific, San Francisco, November 21, 1871, ibid., frames 209–10. Charles Robinson, *Crook,* 130–31. John G. Bourke, *The Diaries of John Gregory Bourke,* Vol. 1, *November 20, 1872–July 28, 1876,* ed. Charles M. Robinson III (Denton: University of North Texas Press, 2003), 63–64, 468–70.

8. Charles J. Kappler, comp., *Indian Affairs: Laws and Treaties,* 7 vols. (Washington, DC: GPO, 1902–3), 1:813–14.

9. Vandever to CIA, Washington, January 23, 1874.

10. Smith to Jeffords, December 29, 1873, RG 94, LR, OAG, 1871–80, M666, 3383 AGO 1873, roll 123, frames 56–59, NARA.

11. Jeffords to CIA, May 31, 1874, RG 75, BIA NM, 1849–89, MT-21, roll 23, 1874, NARA.

12. Dudley to CIA, Santa Fe, June 30, 1874, CIA, *Annual Report* (1874), 300–302.

13. Sweeney, *Cochise,* 395–97, deals with Cochise's last days and burial.

14. Sweeney, *Cochise to Geronimo,* 30.

15. Shapard, *Loco,* chaps. 4–10, deals with the tortuous events that led to this outcome.

16. CIA, *Annual Report* (1874), 59, 63, 302–4, 310–11. Jeffords's annual report, August 21, 1875, ibid., 209–10. Sweeney, *Cochise to Geronimo,* 39.

17. Jeffords to CIA, Apache Pass, August 21, 1875, CIA, *Annual Report* (1875), 209–10.

18. Clum's annual report, September 1, 1875, ibid., 215–20. Events on the White Mountain Reservation, which involved incessant feuding with the military, are traced in a lengthy series of official documents in RG 94, LR, OAG, 1871–80, M666, 2504 AGO 1875, roll 194, on frames starting at the beginning of the roll. The White Mountains (or Coyoteros) were mountain Indians, and their homes starkly contrasted with the low-lying Gila Valley in the Howard extension.

19. Sweeney, *Cochise to Geronimo,* 47, citing Arizona newspapers. Jeffords to CIA, Apache Pass, October 3, 1876, CIA, *Annual Report* (1876), 3–4.

20. Sweeney, *Cochise to Geronimo,* 47, citing Jeffords to CIA, April 27, 1876, RG 75, M234, R16, NARA, and Thomas E. Farish, *History of Arizona,* 8 vols. (San Francisco: Filmer Brothers, 1915–18), 2:238–39.

21. Sweeney, *Cochise to Geronimo,* 49–50, including citations.

22. *(Tucson) Arizona Citizen,* April 15, 1876.

CHAPTER 10. REMOVAL TO THE GILA RIVER

1. The threat to Jeffords's life is recounted only in his final report, which strangely has not turned up in official records. It was printed in the Silver City *Grant County Herald,* July 22, 1876.

2. Schofield to AGUSA, citing telegram from Kautz, Fort Bowie, June 7, 1876, RG 94, LR, OAG, 1871–80, 2576 AGO 1876, M666, Correspondence relating to the removal of the Chiricahua Apaches to San Carlos, roll 265, frame 338, NARA. Kautz to AAG San Francisco, Hq. DA Prescott, June 30, 1876, ibid., frames 363–71. John P. Clum annual report, San Carlos, October 1876, CIA, *Annual Report* (1876), 10–12. Jeffords to CIA, Apache Pass, October 3, 1876, ibid., 3–4. Jeffords's final report is in *Grant County Herald,* July 22, 1876. Sweeney, *Cochise to Geronimo,* 56–57.

3. *(Tucson) Arizona Weekly Citizen,* June 17, 24, 1876.

4. Kautz to AAG San Francisco, Hq. DA Prescott, June 30, 1876. Kautz annual report, September 15, 1876, SW, *Annual Report* (1876), 98–104. Clum annual report, San Carlos, October 1876. John P. Clum, "Geronimo," *New Mexico Historical Review* 3 (January 1928): 18–19. In the 1920s, Clum wrote a series of long articles for this journal, all designed to portray himself as hugely important. Because Clum exaggerated and sometimes fabricated, the articles must be used with extreme caution. Sweeney, *Cochise to Geronimo,* 57–59.

5. Sweeney, *Cochise to Geronimo,* 69, citing Mexican and Arizona newspapers and RG 75, NARA.

6. Ibid., 75–77, citing newspapers. Also Thrapp, *Victorio,* 183.

7. Geronimo, scrambling chronology and facts, describes this fight in Barrett, *Geronimo, His Own Story,* 121. Detailed military reports are cited below. Perico Interview, Sol Tax Papers, box 19, folder 15, University of Chicago Special Collections Research Center.

8. Barrett, *Geronimo, His Own Story,* 122. Balatchu Account, "Chiricahua Bands," Opler Papers, box 35, folder 3. Sam Haozous told Opler that the peace at Ojo Caliente was shattered by the presence of these fugitives. Ibid., box 37, folder 36.

9. Sweeney, *Cochise to Geronimo,* 78–79. *(Tucson) Arizona Weekly Citizen,* February 10, 17, March 17, 1877.

10. The charges and countercharges, and the articles in the Tucson newspapers, are treated in *Army and Navy Journal,* April 7, 1877, 563. See also Kautz annual report, August 15, 1877, SW, *Annual Report* (1877), 133–49. Kautz to Gen. W. T. Sherman, Prescott, April 9, 1877, Sherman Papers, Library of Congress.

11. *(Tucson) Arizona Daily Citizen,* January 6, 1877.

12. Rucker to Post Adjutant Fort Bowie, January 14, 1877, RG 94, LR, OAG, 1871–80, M666, roll 265, frames 507–10, NARA. Barrett, *Geronimo, His Own Story,* 121–22. Sweeney, *Cochise to Geronimo,* 76–77. Rucker counted ten dead men. Geronimo recalled five women, seven children, and four men.

13. *(Tucson) Arizona Weekly Citizen,* March 17, 1877.

14. Andrew Wallace, "General August V. Kautz in Arizona, 1874–1878," *Arizoniana* 4 (Winter 1963): 54–65. Kautz annual report, 135.

15. Telegram, CIA J. Q. Smith to Clum at Camp Grant via Tucson, March 20, 1877, RG 94, LR, OAG, 1871–89, M666, 1927 AGO 1877, roll 326, frame 252, NARA.

16. This seems the best version that can be recovered, and it coincides closely with the first account Clum penned, on April 24—not to his superiors but to his friend, the editor of the *(Tucson) Arizona Weekly Citizen;* it appeared in the edition of May 8, 1877; another version was published on May 19, 1877. In a chain of magazine and newspaper articles, together with speeches and a pamphlet, ending only in 1929, Clum exaggerated and fabricated an increasingly dramatic account of his courageous and dangerous encounter with Geronimo. He repeatedly labeled it "the first capture of Geronimo." Andrew Wallace, "General August V. Kautz in Arizona, 1974–1878," *Arizoniana* 4 (Winter 1963): 62, is a more reliable rendering, as is a collection of documents entitled "All about Courtesy," in "Documents of Arizona History, Selected from the Archives of the Society: 'All about Courtesy': In a Verbal War, John P. Clum Has a Parting Shot," *Arizoniana* 4 (Spring 1962): 11–18. Wallace's conclusion, which I share, is that Clay Beauford deserves most of the credit for subduing Geronimo. So abundant are Clum's vainglorious rants over half a century that they provide the basis for most accounts of Geronimo's arrest.

For typical samples of Clum's version of history, see his "Victorio," *New Mexico Historical Review* 4 (April 1929): 107–27; "Geronimo," ibid. 3 (January 1928): 1–40; and Woodworth Clum, *Apache Agent: The Story of John P. Clum* (1936; Lincoln: University of Nebraska Press, 1978), chaps. 28–33.

17. Thrapp, *Victorio,* citing official records, has the clearest account of this sequence, 187–90.

CHAPTER 11. GERONIMO'S FIRST BREAKOUT, 1878

1. Clum, *Apache Agent,* 195. Clum recounts the story of this misadventure in chaps. 26–27. Sweeney, *From Cochise to Geronimo,* 67–69.

2. Ralph H. Ogle, *Federal Control of the Western Apaches, 1848–1886* (Albuquerque: University of New Mexico Press, 1970), 178. Clum, *Apache Agent,* 250–56. John P. Clum, "The San Carlos Apache Police," *New Mexico Historical Review* 4 (July 1929): 203–19. Sweeney, *Cochise to Geronimo,* 87.

3. Abbott to AAG Prescott, San Carlos, August 21, 1877, RG 94, LR, OAG, 1871–80, M666, 5705 AGO 1877, roll 366, frames 96–116, NARA.

4. Vandever to CIA, July 16, 1877, RG 75, Records of Field Jurisdiction of the Office of Indian Affairs, 1873–90, M1070, R2, NARA.

5. RG 393, E204, "Brief of Action Taken in the Matter of Indian Affairs at San Carlos A.T.," items 12, 25, NARA.

6. Ibid., items 27ff. Although Victorio's break from San Carlos and the events that followed are documented by much official paper, for the story more succinctly told, see Thrapp, *Victorio,* chap. 16.

7. RG 393, E204, "Brief of Action," item 45. Sweeney, *Cochise to Geronimo,* 105, citing Mexican and Arizona newspapers.

8. Hart to Vandever, San Carlos, September 24, 1877, RG 75, M1070, R2, NARA.

9. This state of affairs can be traced throughout RG 393, E204, "Brief of Action."

10. Ibid., item 63. Acting Agent George Smerdon to Abbott, San Carlos, August 9, 1878, RG 93, Misc. Records, DA, 1875–79, NARA. Betzinez, *I Fought with Geronimo,* 47–48. Sweeney, *Cochise to Geronimo,* 118–19. E-mail, Sweeney to Utley, April 5, 2010.

CHAPTER 12. BACK TO SAN CARLOS, 1878–79

1. *(Tucson) Arizona Weekly Citizen,* October 12, 1879, citing *(Silver City, NM) Grant County Herald,* October 8, 1879.

2. Abbott to AAG DA, Fort Thomas, December 4, 1878, RG 393, LS, Fort Thomas, NARA. Two women and two children, en route to San Carlos from the Nednhis south of Janos, stopped at Fort Thomas and related these events to Lt. Abbott, including casualties and locations and the Nednhi division into three groups. The attack on Geronimo is reported in the Sonoran *Boletin Oficial,* January 3, 1879, printing a military document from Arizpe of November 16, 1878. Edwin Sweeney generously provided this document in e-mail, Sweeney to Utley, April 16, 2010. In Barrett, *Geronimo, His Own Story,* 105, Geronimo recounts this fight, although he got the date wrong and he did not kill all the Mexican soldiers. His location and admitted loss of twelve warriors coincides with the Mexican commander's report. Sweeney, *Cochise to Geronimo,* 123.

3. Shapard, *Loco,* 120–23.

4. I have treated the war in "Victorio's War," *MHQ: The Quarterly Journal of Military History* 21 (Autumn 2008): 20–29. The history of the events preceding has

been well chronicled in Thrapp, *Victorio,* chaps 16–22; and Shapard, *Loco,* chaps. 10–17. For involvement of Juh's Chiricahuas in the Victorio War, see Maj. A. P. Morrow to AAG Dist. NM, Fort Bayard, November 3, 1879; and U.S. Consul H. L. Scott to Second Assistant Secretary of State, Chihuahua City, November 29, 1879; both in M1495, roll 14, Special Files of Hq. Div. of the Missouri Relating to Military Operations and Administration, 1863–1885, NARA.

5. Robinson, *Apache Voices,* 103. These words were related to Eve Ball by Eustice Fatty, Gordo's son.

6. A thorough account of Haskell's little-known mission is Allan Radbourne, "The Juh-Geronimo Surrender of 1879," *English Westerners Brand Book* 21 (1983): 1–18. Sweeney, *Cochise to Geronimo,* 138–39, is more detailed and in places differs from Radbourne.

7. Sweeney, *Cochise to Geronimo,* 139–45, has the best account of these activities.

8. Haskell reported these and later events in great detail in two long telegrams from Camp Rucker to Willcox in Prescott, December 14, 21, 1879, RG 393, LR, DA, 3995 DA 1879, 8294 AGO 1879, NARA.

9. Tucson dispatch of May 24, 1880, in *New York Times,* June 4, 1880, contains the item about Geronimo killing the dissident leader. It is part of a long and surprisingly accurate account of Haskell's mission.

10. Telegram, Haskell to ADC DA, Fort Bowie, December 31, 1879, RG 393, LR, DA, NARA. The entire Haskell episode is treated in Sweeney, *Cochise to Geronimo,* 138–43.

CHAPTER 13. GERONIMO'S SECOND BREAKOUT, 1881

1. Sweeney, "In the Shadow of Geronimo: Chihuahua of the Chiricahuas," *Wild West* 13 (August 2000), 25–28, 67. For the views of Asa Daklugie (Juh's son) and Eugene Chihuahua (Chihuahua's son), see Ball, *Indeh,* 31, 43, 47.

2. This paragraph has been distilled from Collins, *Great Escape,* 21–34. Ample documentation in both Indian and white sources confirms this portrait.

3. Albert E. Wrattan, "George Wrattan: Chief Apache Scout and Interpreter [for] Geronimo and His Warriors," MS, n.d., intended as a book. Albert was George's son. MS loaned by Henrietta Stockel.

4. Affidavit by Chatto, Opler Papers, box 36, folder 23.

5. Daklugie made this point in Ball, *Indeh,* 11.

6. The Cibicue affair and its aftermath generated reams of official documentation, both civil and military, which I have examined. Relevant in this study is the effect of Cibicue on Geronimo and the Chiricahuas, and the details need not be laid out. An authoritative history of Cibicue is Charles Collins, *Apache Nightmare: The Battle at Cibicue Creek* (Norman: University of Oklahoma Press, 1999).

7. Ibid. chronicles the Cibicue story in well-documented detail.

8. Opler Papers, box 35, folder 4.

9. Chihuahua and Naiche throw some light on this council, although nothing we do not know from other sources. Statement of Naiche to Capt. Emmet Crawford at San Carlos, November 5, 1883; and Chihuahua, November 19, 1883, RG 393, Records of San Carlos, NARA.

10. The official military and civil reports are self-serving. Sweeney, *Cochise to Geronimo,* 182–83, presents the best interpretation. See also Collins, *Great Escape,* 26–28; and CIA, *Annual Report* (1881), vii–x.

11. Maj. George B. Sanford to AAG DA, Willcox, October 15, 1881, SW, *Annual Report* (1881), 146–47. John F. Finerty, "On Campaign after Cibicue Creek," *Chicago Times,* September 18–October 21, 1881, in Peter Cozzens, ed., *Eyewitnesses to the Indian Wars, 1865–1890,* Vol. 1, *The Struggle for Apacheria* (Mechanicsburg, PA: Stackpole, 2001), 256–59.

12. My account of the breakout is based mainly on Collins, *Great Escape,* chaps. 3–7; and Sweeney, *Cochise to Geronimo,* 182–83.

CHAPTER 14. GERONIMO ABDUCTS LOCO, 1882

1. James Kaywaykla, Nana's grandson, was present and described the conference. Ball, *In the Day of Victorio,* 123–28. Sweeney, *Cochise to Geronimo,* 192–93.

2. Shapard, *Loco,* 143, discusses motivations, including the traditions of Loco's descendants. Shapard is also a prime authority for the following narrative. Sweeney, *Cochise to Geronimo,* 195–96. Geronimo recalled that Mexican troops had grown stronger, creating a need for more men to fight them. Barrett, *Geronimo, His Own Story,* 107.

3. Shapard, *Loco,* 146–48. Sweeney, *Cochise to Geronimo,* 211–14. Willcox's annual report, August 31, 1882, SW, *Annual Report* (1882), 147.

4. Betzinez, *I Fought with Geronimo,* 56. Sam Hauzhous, another of Loco's people, identified the shouting leader as Geronimo. Sam Hauzhous interview, Opler Papers, box 37, folder 36.

5. Shapard, *Loco,* 158. His account, based on official records, differs from Sweeney's account, also drawing on official records. The officer, Lt. George Sands, puzzled his superiors over his readiness to give up the pursuit, but he contended that he expected reinforcements and was running short on rations.

6. Betzinez, *I Fought with Geronimo,* 58.

7. The literature of Horseshoe Canyon and its aftermath is extensive: RG 94, LR, OAG, 1881–89, M689, 1749 AGO 1882, Papers relating to the outbreaks of violence, including several murders in New Mexico and Arizona, by Chiricahua Apaches who escaped from the San Carlos Reservation and to their pacification, NARA. Rolls 96 and 97 contain this entire file of official records from the outbreak of April 1882 to the denouement in Mexico. Forsyth tells his version of Horseshoe

Canyon in *Thrilling Days of Army Life* (1900; Lincoln: University of Nebraska Press, 1994), 79–120. His account includes one by Lt. David N. McDonald recounting his own experience. A biography is David Dixon, *Hero of Beecher Island: The Life and Military Career of George A. Forsyth* (Lincoln: University of Nebraska Press, 1994.). "Record of Events during the Expedition under Lt. Col. G. A. Forsyth, 4th Cavalry, from Fort Cummings, N.M., on April 18, '82, against the Hostile Apache Indians," Papers of the Order of the Indian Wars, box 10, folder X18, US Army Military History Institute, Carlisle Barracks, PA. Scout Al Sieber tells his version, critical of Forsyth, in *(Prescott) Weekly Courier,* May 27, 1882, in Cozzens, *Eyewitnesses to the Indian Wars,* 290–94. Betzinez, *I Fought with Geronimo,* 62–66. Shapard, *Loco,* 159–63. Sweeney, *Cochise to Geronimo,* 215–17.

Neither Indian nor white accounts deal with McDonald's foray into the canyon, only with the following battle. McDonald himself told the story in detail in Forsyth's book, cited above. Much of the Apache actions during this phase must be inferred from this account. Betzinez recounts only the battle.

8. Betzinez, *I Fought with Geronimo,* 65.

9. Forsyth's official report to AAAG Dist. NM Santa Fe, Stein's Pass, April 25, 1882, RG 94, LR, OAG, 1881–89, M689, 1749 AGO 1882, roll 96, NARA. Reports of the troop commanders are appended.

10. Betzinez, *I Fought with Geronimo,* 63.

11. The Indian movements are traced both in Sweeney, *Cochise to Geronimo,* 217–18; and Shapard, *Loco,* 162–64.

12. Scout Sherman Curley was next to the sergeant of scouts who shot the young woman at the mescal pit. He also tells of the party that got behind the force of scouts blocking the way to the Enmedio Mountains. Grenville Goodwin Papers, autobiography of Sherman Curley. Hauzous interview. Betzinez, *I Fought with Geronimo,* 68–69. See also Shapard, *Loco,* chap. 13; and Sweeney, *Cochise to Geronimo,* 219–21.

13. Betzinez, *I Fought with Geronimo,* 79–71. See also Shapard, *Loco,* 176; and Sweeney, *Cochise to Geronimo,* 222.

14. Betzinez, *I Fought with Geronimo,* 72. Hauzous interview.

15. Shapard, *Loco,* 181–82, accepts this accusation. Sweeney, *Cochise to Geronimo,* 226–28, analyzes all the evidence and concludes that the charge is groundless. Sweeney also has details of the battle drawn from Mexican official sources.

16. The entire sequence recounted here is based on an extensive report of Maj. Perry to AAG DA, Willcox, May 16, 1882. The report annexes Tupper to Perry, Fort Huachuca, May 8, 1882, and Rafferty to Perry, Fort Bowie, May 15, 1882. Tupper's first dispatch, telegraphed to Perry from "East Side of Animas Mountains," on April 28, located the battle site only as thirty-five miles east of Galeyville, omitting any mention of crossing the border. The army's official list of engagements places the battle in the Hatchet Mountains, New Mexico. Interestingly, Capt. Rafferty in 1890 received a brevet of major for gallantry in the battle in the Hatchet Moun-

tains. These documents appear in RG 94, LR, OAG, 1881–89, M689, 1066 AGO 1883, roll 97, NARA. Rafferty kept a daily diary, the relevant part printed in the *(Tucson) Arizona Daily Star,* May 17, 1882, in Cozzens, *Eyewitnesses to the Indian Wars,* 286–89. Perhaps sanitized for public consumption, the journal concedes no mistake in the battle nor admits crossing into Mexico. Lt. Stephen C. Mills commanded a scout company. He described the battle in detail in a letter to his mother, Fort Huachuca, May 8, 1882, Stephen C. Mills Papers, US Army Military History Institute, Carlisle Barracks, PA. See also Al Sieber in *(Prescott) Weekly Courier,* May 27, 1882, ibid., 290–94.

17. Forsyth's penetration of Mexico is drawn from Record of Events during the expedition of Lt. Col. G. A. Forsyth, 4th Cavalry, from Fort Cummings, New Mexico, on April 18, 1882, against hostile Apache Indians, box 10, folder X18, US Army Military History Institute, Carlisle Barracks, PA; and from his autobiography, *Thrilling Days of Army Life,* 114–20. Colonel Mackenzie, who a decade earlier had led a similar American foray into Mexico, returned Forsyth's official report with the explanation that if the Mexicans made a big issue of the crossing into Mexico, Forsyth might find himself in trouble—"the result justified the end, but the less said about it the better."

CHAPTER 15. MEXICO: MASSACRES AND RAIDS, 1882–83

1. Griswold, "Fort Sill Apaches," under Geronimo.

2. Betzinez, *I Fought with Geronimo,* 75–77. Betzinez followed Geronimo for nearly a year. He had a remarkable memory, which is validated by Mexican military records examined by Sweeney and set forth in *Cochise to Geronimo,* 233–37. Much of what follows is based on these two sources.

3. Barrett, *Geronimo, His Own Story,* 106. Betzinez, *I Fought with Geronimo,* 78.

4. Sam Hauzous biography, Opler Papers, box 36, folder 37.

5. Sweeney, *Cochise to Geronimo,* 234–35, citing Mexican military sources.

6. Betzinez, *I Fought with Geronimo,* 81.

7. Betzinez went with Geronimo and chronicled his movements and actions in detail. Mexican sources examined by Sweeney, *Cochise to Geronimo,* 239–48, confirm Betzinez's narrative. Betzinez, *I Fought with Geronimo,* chap. 9.

8. Betzinez, *I Fought with Geronimo,* 90.

9. Ibid., 91.

10. Ibid., chap. 10. Sweeney, *Cochise to Geronimo,* 252–53, citing Mexican sources. *(Silver City) New Southwest and Grant County Herald,* December 2, 1882.

11. Interview of "Peaches" by Lt. John G. Bourke, in Bourke's diary, April 7, 1883, US Military Academy Library, West Point, NY. Peaches was the anglicized name for a Chiricahua who lived with Geronimo throughout the winter of 1882–83 and was familiar both with these Chiricahuas and the country in which they

roamed. He will appear later in this narrative. Betzinez accompanied the raiders into Sonora and described the victims as well as the route, again corroborated by Mexican sources. Betzinez, *I Fought with Geronimo,* 99–101, and map. Sweeney, *Cochise to Geronimo,* 284–85.

12. Daklugie, in Ball, *Indeh,* 70–73, 101–2. Peaches interview, Bourke diary. Sweeney, *Cochise to Geronimo,* 286–89.

13. Betzinez accompanied Geronimo and Chihuahua so does not describe the Chatto raid. The best source is Peaches interview, Bourke diary. Peaches, a Cibicue White Mountain Apache, wanted to return to San Carlos, so went with the raiders in hopes of slipping away. The best account of the raid is Marc Simmons, *Massacre on the Lordsburg Road: A Tragedy of the Apache Wars* (College Station: Texas A&M University Press, 1997).

14. Brig. Gen. George Crook to AG MDP, Hq. DA Whipple Barracks Prescott, September 27, 1883, SW, *Annual Report* (1883), 159–70ff. See also Brig. Gen. R. S. Mackenzie to AAG DM, Santa Fe, September 26, 1883, ibid., 137–45. RG 94, LR, OAG, 1881–89, M689, 1066 AGO 1883, roll 173, NARA, during March and April 1883 is laden with army reports of operations seeking the raiders.

CHAPTER 16. GERONIMO CONFRONTS CROOK IN THE SIERRA MADRE, 1883

1. The officer was retired Brig. Gen. James Parker. He wrote an informative book entitled *Old Army Memories* (Philadelphia: Dorrance, 1929).The observations in my text, however, are drawn from "Extracts from Personal Memoirs of Brig. Gen. James Parker," Papers of the Order of the Indian Wars, x38/2, box 11, folder X-40, US Army Military History Institute, Carlisle Barracks, PA. A competent recent biography is Robinson, *General Crook and the Western Frontier.* Other sources: Crook, *Autobiography;* Joseph C. Porter, *Paper Medicine Man: John Gregory Bourke and His American West* (Norman: University of Oklahoma Press, 1986); and especially Bourke, *On the Border with Crook.* This book, by Crook's longtime aide, has had more influence in shaping public perceptions of Crook than any other and has gone through many editions. Despite Bourke's hagiographic portrayal of the general, Crook treated his aide shabbily.

2. Crook to AG, MDP, Prescott, September 27, 1883, SW, *Annual Report* (1883), 160. He shared his thinking with all his subordinates in GO 43, Hq. DA, October 5, 1882, ibid., 170–71.

3. Ibid., 160–61.

4. Britton Davis, *The Truth about Geronimo* (New Haven: Yale University Press, 1929, 1963), 31–32.

5. Ibid., 32. M. Salzman Jr., "Geronimo, the Napoleon of Indians," *Journal of Arizona History* 8 (Winter 1967): 240.

6. Davis, *Truth about Geronimo,* 57–59. Crook to AAG MDP, Prescott, July 23, 1883, RG 94, LR, OAG, 1881–89, M689, roll 174, NARA. This is Crook's initial report after his return from Mexico. He expanded on it in his annual report. As soon as he crossed the border, on June 11, he telegraphed an abbreviated report to DA headquarters. As forwarded to MDP, it is contained in ibid. In Washington in July, Crook gave an interview to a correspondent that provided some details of the expedition. *New York Herald,* July 9, 1883, in Cozzens, *Eyewitnesses to the Indian Wars,* 396–404.

7. Simmons, *Massacre on the Lordsburg Road,* 109–12, describes the event in detail. This book also is the most authoritative treatment of not only the McComas story but also the Chatto-Bonito raid.

8. Crook to AAG MDP, July 23, 1883, as cited in note 4, describes the force he assembled. Lt. Bourke kept a daily diary, May 1–23, which is reprinted in Cozzens, *Eyewitnesses to the Indian Wars,* 346–85. Another officer, thought to be Lt. William Forsyth, kept a diary reprinted in the *(Tucson) Arizona Daily Star,* June 17, 1883, ibid., 391–93. Still another diary, by A. Frank Randall (a photographer whose equipment smashed when a mule fell off a trail), appeared in the *El Paso Times,* June 20, 1883, ibid., 394–95. See also Dan L. Thrapp, *Al Sieber, Chief of Scouts* (Norman: University of Oklahoma Press, 1964), chap. 17.

9. White Mountain Apache scout John Rope described the movement in long and exacting detail: "Experiences of an Indian Scout: Excerpts from the Life of John Rope, an 'Old Timer' of the White Mountain Apaches," as told to Grenville Goodwin, *Arizona Historical Review* 7 (January 1936): 31–68. Another scout's story is shorter and less useful: "The Life of Sherman Curley—Arivaipa Apache," Grenville Goodwin Papers, Arizona State Museum, Tucson.

10. Bourke diary, May 16, 1883. Crook to AG MDP, July 23, 1883. Bourke writes that the woman said the Apaches had talked of sending emissaries to San Carlos, while Crook reports that they had been dispatched a few days earlier. Bourke also wrote of the Crook expedition of 1883 in *An Apache Campaign in the Sierra Madre: An Account of the Expedition in Pursuit of Hostile Chiricahua Apaches in the Spring of 1883* (New York: Charles Scribner's Sons, 1886, 1958).

11. Bourke diary, May 17, 1883. Crook's report of July 23, 1883, as cited. Rope, "Experiences of an Indian Scout." Bourke and Crook give slightly different versions. Rope goes into great detail, although he confuses the horse episode with the captive woman first sent out rather than the sister of Chihuahua. For a profile of Chihuahua, see Sweeney, "Shadow of Geronimo," 25–28, 67.

12. Rope, "Experiences of an Indian Scout," 64–65.

13. Betzinez, *I Fought with Geronimo,* 118–19.

14. Ibid., 113–14.

15. An extended description of the exchange is in Thrapp, *Sieber,* 280–82. See also Bourke diary, May 20, 1883; Bourke, *Apache Campaign in the Sierra Madre,* 101–5; and Crook to AG MDP, July 23, 1883.

16. Source cited in note 4. The quotation is from the Crook July 23, 1883, report.

17. Teller to Lincoln, June 14, 1883, RG 94, LR, OAG, 1881–89, M689, roll 173, NARA. John Bret Harte, "Conflict at San Carlos: The Military-Civilian Struggle for Control, 1882–1885," *Arizona and the West* 15 (Spring 1973): 33, 36–37.

18. Lincoln to Teller, June 15, 1883; Telegram, Schofield to AGUSA (forwarding Crook telegram), Presidio, June 20, 1883; Wilcox to Teller, San Carlos, June 15, 1883; Teller to Lincoln, June 18, 1883; Schofield to AGUSA, June 22, 1883; Telegram, AGUSA to Crook, June 25, 1883; Telegram, Crook to AGUSA, Prescott, June 26, 1883; Telegram, Schofield to AGUSA, Presidio, June 28, 1883; all in RG 94, LR, OAG, 1881–89, M689, roll 173, NARA. Davis, *Truth about Geronimo,* 69–71. Harte, "Conflict at San Carlos," 36–37.

19. Memorandum of the result of a conference between the secretary of the interior, the commissioner of Indian affairs, the secretary of war, and Brig. Gen. George Crook, July 7, 1883, RG 94, LR, OAG, 1881–89, M689, 1066 AGO 1883, roll 174, NARA. The official transmittal to Crook, same date, added that the secretary of war directed that the Indians brought in by Crook and those to follow be subsisted by War Department appropriations.

CHAPTER 17. RETURN TO SAN CARLOS, 1883–84

1. The movements of the various Chiricahua groups in the summer and fall of 1883 are recounted by the following: Chihuahua, Naiche, Zele, Chatto, Kayatena, Geronimo, and one of his wives, Mañanita. All accounts basically agree with one another, although the chronology and sequence of occurrence is mixed. When buttressed by Mexican sources, however, the story of the Chiricahuas before they began arriving at San Carlos can be reconstructed. Sweeney, *Cochise to Geronimo,* chap. 15. Indian sources, all of which I have examined, are: Statement of Chihuahua to Capt. Crawford, November 19, 1883; Statement of Kayatena to Capt. Crawford, November 7, 1883; Statement of Naiche to Capt. Crawford, November 5, 1883; Statement of Mañanita, March 21, 1884; Statement of Geronimo, March 21, 1884; all in RG 393, Misc. Records, 1882–1900, Post of San Carlos, NARA. Statement of Zele to Capt. Crawford, December 31, 1883; Statement of Chatto to Capt. Crawford, March 3, 1884; both in RG 94, LR, OAG, 1881–89, M689, 1066 AGO 1883, rolls 175, 176, NARA. The Indian statements were generously provided me by Edwin Sweeney.

2. Chatto's statement. Sweeney, *Cochise to Geronimo,* 327.

3. Zele's statement quotes Juh. The statements made by the Chiricahuas to Capt. Crawford at San Carlos make no mention of Chatto's raid but turn at once to Casas Grandes. Mexican sources, however, amply document the murderous destruction in western Sonora during July 1883. Sweeney, *Cochise to Geronimo,* 327–29.

4. Mañanita statement. All the statements of Indian leaders to Crawford dwell on the Casas Grandes venture as if it happened soon after Crook's departure. Sweeney, *Cochise to Geronimo*, 329.

5. All the cited statements of leaders to Capt. Crawford deal with the Casas Grandes adventure. They are reconciled only by Mexican military reports cited by Sweeney, *Cochise to Geronimo*, 330–32. The quotations are from Zele's, Naiche's, and Kayatena's statements.

6. Naiche's statement. Allan Radbourne, "Geronimo's Contraband Cattle," *Missionaries, Indians, and Soldiers: Studies in Cultural Interaction* (1996): 3. Sweeney, *Cochise to Geronimo*, 336.

7. Radbourne, "Geronimo's Contraband Cattle," 3–4. Sweeney, *Cochise to Geronimo*, 339. The Sonoran raids during October were reported in a dispatch from Chihuahua printed in the *New York Times*, October 28, 1883.

8. A profile of Davis, including Crook's commendation, is in Radbourne, "Geronimo's Contraband Cattle," 3.

9. Radbourne, "Contraband Cattle," 5. Sweeney, *Cochise to Geronimo*, 354–55.

10. Geronimo statement. Sweeney, *Cochise to Geronimo*, 347–48. Radbourne, "Geronimo's Contraband Cattle," 5–7. Crook to AAG MDP, December 18, 1883, RG 94, LR, OAG, 1881–89, M689, 1066 AGO 1883, roll 175, NARA.

11. Telegram, Davis to AG DA, Camp near Skull Canyon, NM, February 26, 1884, RG 94, LR, OAG, 1881–89, M689, 1066 AGO 1883, roll 176, NARA. Davis does not name the three men sent from San Carlos, nor does any other source I have found. But the three men included Chihuahua and Chappo. Sweeney, *Cochise to Geronimo*, 355–56. Radbourne, "Geronimo's Contraband Cattle," 7–8. Davis, *Truth about Geronimo*, tells his version of the story, chap. 6; but he must be used with caution because of many errors and a tendency to enlarge his role.

12. Crook to AGUSA, through MDP, March 20, 1884, enclosing telegram; Davis to AG DA, Sulphur Springs, March 12, 1884; Davis to Crawford, San Carlos, March 16,1884; all in RG 94, LR, OAG, 1881–89, M689, 1066 AGO 1883, roll 175, NARA. Radbourne, "Geronimo's Contraband Cattle," 9–15, gives the most balanced account, drawn from official records of Treasury Department and the Bureau of Customs, as well as local newspapers. Davis, *Truth about Geronimo*, 85–101, recounts an essentially accurate but somewhat more colorful version. See also Sweeney, *Cochise to Geronimo*, 356–58.

CHAPTER 18. THE LAST BREAKOUT, 1885

1. Statement of Geronimo, March 21, 1884, RG 393, Misc. Records, 1882–1900, Post of San Carlos, NARA. This is the original. For the cleaner version transmitted to Crook, see Crawford to Crook, San Carlos, March 21, 1884 RG 94, LR, OAG, 1881–89, M689, 1066 AGO 1883, roll 176, NARA. Encloses statement of

Geronimo made to Crawford here on March 21, 1884, through J. M. Montoya and Antonio Díaz, interpreters.

2. This prominent feature of Geronimo's character emerges clearly in Edwin R. Sweeney, "Geronimo and Chatto: Alternative Apache Ways," *Wild West* 20 (August 2007): 30–39.

3. Crook to AGUSA, August 15, 1884, transmitting relevant documents, including Crawford to AAAG DA, July 24, 1884, RG 94, LR, OAG, 1881–89, M689, 1066 AGO 1883, roll 175, NARA.

4. Crook to AAG MDP, Prescott, May 17, 1884, RG 94, LR, OAG, 1881–89, M689, 1066 AGO 1883, roll 176, NARA. Crook to AAG MDP, Prescott, [c. September 1884], SW, *Annual Report* (1884), 131–34. Betzinez, *I Fought with Geronimo*, 125. Sweeney, *Cochise to Geronimo*, 368–69. Porter, *Paper Medicine Man*, 167.

5. Davis, *Truth about Geronimo*, 107. Davis writes that the Indians did no farming during the summer of 1884. Contemporary reports contradict this, although early winter storms reduced the yield.

6. Crook to AAG MDP, Fort Bowie, September 9, 1885, SW, *Annual Report* (1885), 175–76. Crawford to Morton, San Carlos, June 25, 1884, Charles Morton Papers, MS 564, folder 7, Arizona Historical Society, Tucson. Maj. Gen. John Pope to AGUSA, MDP, July 14, 1884, RG 94, LR, OAG, 1881–89, M689, 1066 AGO 1883, roll 176, NARA. Pope had replaced Schofield in command of the Military Division of the Pacific. Davis, *Truth about Geronimo*, 125–30, recounts the arrest in detail, but with a dramatic flair that calls its credibility into question, especially in view of his similar exaggeration of the incident at Sulphur Creek. The best account, drawing on official records, is Sweeney, *Cochise to Geronimo*, 376–79.

7. Sweeney, "Geronimo and Chatto."

8. Davis, *Truth about Geronimo*, 106. Sweeney names the agents, drawn from the official roster of scouts. *Cochise to Geronimo*, 371.

9. As related by Chihuahua's son Eugene in Ball, *Indeh*, 49–50.

10. SO 31, Hq. DA, April 21, 1884, convened the court, while GO 13, Hq. DA, July 14, 1884, set forth the findings and conclusions of the court. RG 94, LR, OAG, 1881–89, M689, 1066 AGO 1883, roll 175, NARA. Rolls 175 and 176 of this special file contain the documentation of the controversy. They are not cited individually because not central to the story of the Chiricahuas. A good synthesis is Harte, "Conflict at San Carlos," 27–44.

11. Britton Davis, "A Short History of the Chiricahua Tribe of Apache Indians and the Causes Leading to the Outbreak in May – 1885," [c. 1920s] MS, Papers of the Order of the Indian Wars, box 4, C-4, US Army Military History Institute, Carlisle Barracks, PA. Sweeney, *Cochise to Geronimo*, 375–87.

12. Davis, *Truth about Geronimo*, 136–37.

13. Ibid., 142. Crook in *Arizona Daily Star*, April 2, 1886. Parker, *Old Army Memories*, 152.

14. Fisher to Capt. C. S. Roberts, In the Field, October 22, 1885, RG 393, LR, DA, 1885, NARA. Fisher attributed the delay to active field duty.

15. Thomas Cruse, *Apache Days and After* (1941; Lincoln: University of Nebraska Press, 1987), 205–6. A highly successful young officer in Apache country at this time, Cruse was not present but obtained his information from men who were. Sweeney, *Cochise to Geronimo,* 396–97.

16. Sweeney, "Geronimo and Chatto," 33–34.

17. Davis, *Truth about Geronimo,* 149–51. Sweeney, *Cochise to Geronimo,* 400–405. Davis's book omits some critical details, but they are provided in a Davis report to Crook in Crook to AGUSA, May 21, 1885, RG 393, LS, DA, 1885, NARA; and in a subsequent lengthy report to Crook, Fort Bowie, September 15, 1885. The latter was published in the *Army and Navy Journal,* October 24, 1885, and as an appendix to the 1951 edition of Davis's book; this appendix was not included in the 1963 edition of *Truth about Geronimo.* See also Sweeney, "Shadow of Geronimo."

18. Thrapp, *Sieber,* 294.

CHAPTER 19. BACK TO THE SIERRA MADRE, 1885

1. The route, chronology, and actions of the Chiricahua breakouts must be inferred from the account of Lt. James Parker, an officer in the pursuing command, and from an account by Lt. Britton Davis. Davis is authority for the angry determination of Chihuahua to kill Geronimo, but he is vague about exactly where and when it happened. Davis treats it as a camp in the Mogollon Mountains. But that camp, on a rim of Devil's Canyon, was the first true camp the Indians made after leaving Fort Apache, it was on the western edge of the Mogollon Mountains, and it consisted only of the people of Geronimo and Mangas. So the Chihuahua episode had to have occurred before this camp was made. I have treated it as a brief pause to rest on the San Francisco River, the only plausible explanation I can arrive at. Parker, *Old Army Memories,* 152–56. More detailed, and the source I have used, is "Extracts from Personal Memoirs of Brigadier General James Parker, U.S. Army Retired," 113–16. For Davis, see his report to AG DA, Fort Bowie, September 15, 1885, RG 94, LR, OAG, 1881–89, M689, 1066 AGO 1883, roll 183.

2. Crook to AG MDP, Fort Bowie, April 10, 1886, SW, *Annual Report* (1886), 147. The telegraphic traffic ordering and describing these operations appears in RG 94, LR, OAG, 1881–89, M689, 1066 AGO 1883, roll 178, NARA. I have examined all these documents.

3. The assault on Chihuahua is described in Capt. Emmett Crawford to Crook, Camp on Bertchito River six miles above Oputo, June 25, 1885; the surprise of Geronimo in Capt. Wirt Davis to Crook, Camp ten miles southwest of Huachinera, August 14, 1885. Both are in RG 94, LR, OAG, 1881–89, M689, 1066 AGO 1883,

the first in roll 178, the second in roll 179, NARA. Sweeney, *Cochise to Geronimo,* 434–35, 444–45.

4. Crook to AG MDP Presidio, Fort Bowie, April 10, 1886, SW, *Annual Report* (1886), 148–49. Telegram, Crook to Sheridan, Deming, June 7, 1885, RG 94, LR, OAG, 1881–89, M689, 1066 AGO 1883, roll 178, NARA. Crawford to Morton, Camp Skeleton Canyon, June 10, 1885, Charles Morton Papers, MS 563, folder 7, Arizona Historical Society. Henry W. Daly, "The Geronimo Campaign," *Journal of the U.S. Cavalry Association* 18 (1908): 68. Charles P. Elliott, "The Geronimo Campaign of 1885–86," ibid. 21 (1910): 217. Lt. Robert Hanna, "With Crawford in Mexico," *Arizona Historical Review* 6 (April 1936): 56–58 (reprinted from *Clifton Clarion,* July 7, 14, 1886). Daly was a mule packer whose account is reliable. Hanna and Elliott were officers with Crawford. Morton was a member of Crook's staff in Prescott.

5. Crook to AG MDP Presidio, Fort Bowie, July 7, 1885, RG 94, LR, OAG, 1881–89, M689, 1066 AGO 1883, roll 178, NARA.

6. Ibid. Crook to AG MDP Presidio, Fort Bowie, April 10, 1886, SW, *Annual Report* (1886), 149.

7. Pope to Sheridan, MDP Presidio, July 8, 1885, transmits Crook's request to hold the women and children at Fort Bowie. Endorsements of Sheridan and Endicott approve but forbid transferring these people to the reservation under any circumstances. A Tucson dispatch of September 3 in the *New York Times,* September 4, 1885, reported the arrival at Fort Bowie of the captives taken at Bugatseka and the women's description of the fight. The official report is Capt. Wirt Davis to Crook, Camp ten miles southwest of Huachinera, August 14, 1885, RG 94, LR, OAG, 1881–89, M689, 1066 AGO 1883, roll 179, NARA.

8. Telegrams, Pope to AGUSA, MDP Presidio, July 27, 31, 1885, both transmitting Crook telegrams of same dates, RG 94, LR, OAG, 1881–89, M689, 1066 AGO 1883, roll 179, NARA. Sweeney, *Cochise to Geronimo,* 448.

9. Geronimo's movements are reconstructed from reports of the officers trying to run him down. Crawford to Crook, Camp near Casas Grandes, Chihuahua, August 30, 1885, RG 94, LR, OAG, 1881–89, M689, 1066 AGO 1883, roll 183, NARA. Telegram, Pope to AGUSA, MDP Presidio, September 6, 1885, repeating dispatch from Crook repeating telegram from CO Fort Bliss, ibid., roll 179. Lt. Britton Davis to Crook, Fort Bowie, September 15, 1885, ibid., roll 183. Sweeney, *Cochise to Geronimo,* 454–60.

CHAPTER 20. CHASED BY CROOK'S SCOUTS, 1885–86

1. Crawford to Crook at Fort Bowie, Casas Grandes, Chihuahua, August 30, 1885, attaching Elliott to Crawford, Buenaventura, August 24, 1885. Lt. Col. Pedro S. Marcías, to Commander in Chief 2nd Military Zone Chihuahua, San Buenaven-

tura, August 23, 1885. Pope to AGUSA, MDP Presidio, September 6, 1885, repeating dispatch from Crook repeating dispatch from CO Fort Bliss, September 5. Elliott to AGUSA, Fort Columbus, NY, June 22, 1886. Britton Davis to AG DA Prescott, Fort Bowie, September 15, 1885. All in RG 94, LR, OAG, 1881–89, M689, 1066 AGO 1883, rolls 179, 183, 184, NARA. Elliott, "Geronimo Campaign of 1885–1886," 217, 225–26. Davis, *Truth about Geronimo*, 184–88.

2. None of the official sources, including Crawford's August 30 report, refer to the confrontation in San Buenaventura. The only source is the account of scout Sherman Curley, which is specific enough to establish credibility. In his August 30 report, Crawford referred briefly to Elliott's experience but emphasized the cordial way in which it ended. Elliott wrote nothing about what may have happened after his release. See "The Life of Sherman Curley—Arivaipa Apache," Grenville Goodwin Papers, folder 32.

3. Davis, *Truth about Geronimo*, 190–95.

4. Col. Luther Bradley to AAG DA, Santa Fe, September 13, 1886, SW, *Annual Report* (1886), 182. Telegrams, Bradley to AG DM, Santa Fe, September 12, 13, 1885, RG 94, LR, OAG, 1881–89, M689, 1066 AGO 1883, roll 179, NARA. Daniel D. Aránda, "Santiago McKinn, Indian Captive," *Real West* 24 (June 1881): 41–43. Sweeney, *Cochise to Geronimo*, 462–63.

5. Sweeney, *Cochise to Geronimo*, 469–76. Louis Kraft, *Gatewood and Geronimo* (Albuquerque: University of New Mexico Press, 2000), 106–8. Telegram, Gatewood to Crook at Bowie, Fort Apache, September 22, 23 (4), 1885, RG 393, LR, DA, 1885, NARA. Telegram, Bradley to AG DM, Santa Fe, September 22, 24 (2), 26, 1885; telegram, Pope to AGUSA, MDP Presidio, September 30, October 2, 10, 1885; all in RG 94, LR, OAG, 1881–89, M689, 1066 AGO 1883, roll 179, NARA.

6. Telegrams, Bradley to AAG DM, Santa Fe, November 5, 7, 9, 16, 1885; telegram, Schofield to Sheridan, MDM Chicago, November 11, 1885 (repeating Miles from DM); telegram, Crook to AG MDP Presidio, Fort Bowie, November 17, 1885; all in RG 94, LR, OAG, 1881–89, M689, 1066 AGO 1883, roll 180, NARA. George Crook diary, 1885–87, entries through November 1885, Crook-Kennon Papers, US Army Military History Institute, Carlisle Barracks, PA. Sweeney, *Cochise to Geronimo*, 479–91. *Silver City Enterprise*, November 20, 1885.

7. Crook to AG MDP Presidio, Fort Bowie, April 10, 1886, SW, *Annual Report* (1886), 151. 1st Lt. S. W. Fountain to AG Dist. NM Santa Fe, Alma, NM, December 12, 21, 1885, RG 94, LR, OAG, 1881–89, M689, 1066 AGO 1883, roll 181, NARA. Crook to Sheridan, Fort Bowie, December 26, 30, 1885, ibid., roll 180. Sweeney, *Cochise to Geronimo*, 480–83, 487–91, 507–12.

8. For the Miles controversy, see telegram, Gov. Edmund Ross to President Cleveland, Santa Fe, September 18, 1885. This is followed by an exchange of telegrams up and down the chain of command, including between Crook and Miles, with a final blast by Crook to AG MDP Presidio, Fort Bowie, September 18, 1885.

On September 19, Gen. John M. Schofield, Miles's superior in Chicago, advised Washington that he had just given instructions to Miles that would remove all cause of conflict between him and Crook. RG 94, LR, OAG, 1881–89, M689, 1066 AGO 1883, roll 179, NARA.

9. Crook to AG MDP Presidio, Fort Bowie, September 17, 1885, with endorsements by Gens. Pope and Sheridan and SW Endicott, RG 94, LR, OAG, 1881–89, M689, 1066 AGO 1883, roll 179, NARA.

10. Crook to AG MDP Presidio, Fort Bowie, October 11, 1885. Crook diary, November 7, 11, 13, 14, 1885. Capt. Wirt Davis to Capt. Cyrus Roberts, AADC, at Fort Bowie, Fort Lowell, March 20, 1886, RG 94, LR, OAG, 1881–89, M689, 1066 AGO 1883, roll 183, NARA.

11. Telegram, Sheridan to Crook at Fort Bowie, November 19, 1885; Crook to Sheridan, November 19, 1885; Endicott to Sheridan, November 20, 1885; all in RG 94, LR, OAG, 1881–89, M689, 1066 AGO 1883, roll 180, NARA. Annual reports of the Lieutenant General and the Secretary of War: Sheridan to SW, October 10, 1886; Endicott's annual report, November 30, 1886, SW, *Annual Report* (1886), 7, 71.

12. Sheridan to Endicott, Albuquerque, December 3, 1885; telegram, Sheridan to SW, Fort Bowie, November 30, 1885 (2); telegram, Sheridan to SW, Deming, NM, December 1, 1885; GO 121, AGO, November 30, 1885 (transferring NM to AZ); GFO 1, Fort Bowie, December 1, 1885 (implementing transfer); all in RG 94, LR, OAG, 1881–89, M689, 1066 AGO 1883, roll 180, NARA. Annual reports of Sheridan and Endicott, SW, *Annual Report* (1886), 7, 71.

13. Telegram, Sheridan to Crook, December 23, 1885; telegrams, Crook to Sheridan, Fort Bowie, December 26, 30, 1885; all in RG 94, LR, OAG, 1881–89, M689, 1066 AGO 1883, roll 180, NARA.

14. *Tombstone Epitaph,* February 4, 1886.

15. Ibid., January 13, 1886.

16. Davis to Roberts, AADC, at Fort Bowie, Fort Lowell, March 20, 1886, chronicles in almost daily detail the fruitless movements of Davis's command. Crawford to Crook, Huasaras, Sonora, December 24, 1885, and from Camp near Nácori, Sonora, December 28, 1885, RG 94, LR, OAG, 1881–89, M689, 1066 AGO 1883, rolls 183 (Davis) and 181 (Crawford), NARA. An accurate and much more descriptive narrative than the official reports is Lt. W. E. Shipp, "Captain Crawford's Last Expedition," *Journal of the U.S. Cavalry Association* 5 (December 1892): 343–61, in Cozzens, *Eyewitnesses to the Indian Wars,* 516.

17. Chiricahua movements are inferred from a detailed report of 1st Lt. Marion P. Maus to Crook, February 23, 1886, RG 94, LR, OAG, 1881–89, M689, 1066 AGO 1883, roll 181, NARA. This and other military reports are cited in more detail in a subsequent section dealing with these operations from the military viewpoint. The events are detailed in Sweeney, *Cochise to Geronimo,* 494–507. See also Shipp, "Captain Crawford's Last Expedition," 9.

18. Maus dispatch of January 21, 1886, repeated in telegram, Crook to Sheridan, Fort Bowie, January 27, 1886, details the negotiations between Maus and the Chiricahua chiefs, RG 94, LR, OAG, 1881–89, M689, 1066 AGO 1883, roll 181, NARA. Sweeney, *Cochise to Geronimo,* 516–19, details the raids in Sonora, based on Mexican sources.

CHAPTER 21. CANYON DE LOS EMBUDOS, 1886

1. Maus to Capt. C. S. Roberts, aide to Crook at Fort Bowie, Camp 18 miles south of camp near San Bernardino, March 14, 1886, RG 94, LR, OAG, 1881–89, M689, 1066 AGO 1883, roll 182, NARA.

2. Maus to Roberts, Fort Bowie, April 8, 1886; Maus to Roberts, March 14, 1886; ibid., rolls 183, 182. Bourke, *On the Border with Crook,* 473–74. Sweeney, *Cochise to Geronimo,* 516–20.

3. Daly, "Geronimo Campaign," 94.

4. Crook's aide, Capt. John G. Bourke, kept a verbatim record of the council: RG 94, LR, OAG, 1881–89, M689, 1066 AGO 1883, roll 182, NARA. Daly, "Geronimo Campaign," 94–95. Bourke, *On the Border with Crook,* 474–76. Sweeney, *Cochise to Geronimo,* 521–23.

5. Daly, "Geronimo Campaign," 100–101, is the authority for the role of Chihuahua, Alchise, and Kayatena. Long interview with Crook in *Tucson Daily Citizen,* April 2, 1886, RG 94, LR, OAG, 1881–89, M689, 1066 AGO 1883, roll 182, NARA.

6. The two-year exile is hard to piece together from several documents. Crook's diary for March 26, 1886, concedes the terms, as does his report of the conference to Gen. Sheridan in telegram (confidential), Crook to Sheridan, Canyon de los Embudos (through Fort Bowie), March 27, 1886, RG 94, LR, OAG, 1881–89, M689, 1066 AGO 1883, roll 182, NARA. He briefly acknowledges the terms in the interview in the *Tucson Daily Citizen,* April 12, 1886, ibid. Capt. Bourke kept the transcript of the March 27 formal council, which includes nothing about terms, only "surrender." Ibid. Bourke, *On the Border with Crook,* 479. All these sources deal with the work of Alchise and Kayatena in the Chiricahua camp in the night of March 25.

7. Crook diary, March 28, 1886. Maus to Roberts, Fort Bowie, April 8, 1886.

8. Maus to Roberts, Fort Bowie, April 8, 1886. Bourke, *On the Border with Crook,* 481. Daly, "Geronimo Campaign," 100–103, 249–53. Sweeney, *Cochise to Geronimo,* 525–27.

9. Notes of an interview between Crook and Chatto, Kayatena, Naiche, and other Chiricahua Apaches, Mount Vernon Barracks, AL, January 20, 1890, RG 94, LR, OAG, 1881–89, M689, 1066 AGO 1883, roll 191, NARA.

10. Crook to AAG MDP Presidio, Fort Bowie, January 11, 1886, ibid., roll 181, is the long report on Apache warfare. For the Maus transmittals, see telegram,

Crook to Sheridan, Fort Bowie, January 17, 1886 (Maus's dispatch of January 21); telegram, Crook to Pope, Fort Bowie, February 10, 1886 (paraphrasing Maus's dispatch without giving date); Crook to AGUSA, Fort Bowie, February 28, 1886 (transmitting full Maus report of January 21); telegram, Crook to Sheridan, March 16, 1886 (reporting highly condensed version of Maus's dispatch of January 14). All in ibid. For the diplomatic protest to Mexico: Acting SS to US Minister Mexico City, February 2, 1886, ibid.

11. Telegram, Crook to Sheridan, March 16, 1886; telegram, AAG DA to AG MDP Presidio, March 22, 1886; both in RG 94, LR, OAG, 1881–89, M689, 1066 AGO 1883, roll 181, NARA. Sweeney, *Cochise to Geronimo,* 519–21.

12. Telegrams, Crook to Sheridan, Canyon de los Embudos, via Fort Bowie, March 28, 29, 1886, RG 94, LR, OAG, 1881–89, M689, 1066 AGO 1883, roll 179, NARA.

13. Telegram, Sheridan to Crook at Fort Bowie, March 30, 1886; telegram, Crook to Sheridan, March 30, 1886, ibid.

14. Telegram, Sheridan to Crook, April 1, 1886; telegram, Crook to Sheridan, April 1, 1886, ibid., roll 182.

15. Telegrams, Crook to Sheridan, Fort Bowie, April 2, 4, 7, 1886, ibid.

CHAPTER 22. MILES IN COMMAND, 1886

1. *Personal Recollections and Observations of General Nelson A. Miles* (Chicago: Werner, 1896), 476. Miles, *Serving the Republic: Memoirs of the Civil and Military Life of Nelson A. Miles* (New York: Harper and Brothers, 1911), 221. I have written the introduction to a reprint edition of the first autobiography (New York: Da Capo Press, 1969). Of several biographies, consult Robert Wooster, *Nelson A. Miles and the Twilight of the Frontier Army* (Lincoln: University of Nebraska Press, 1995).

2. Telegram, Sheridan to Miles, April 3, 1886, RG 94, LR, OAG, 1881–89, M689, 1066 AGO 1883, roll 182, NARA. SW, *Annual Report* (1886), 11, 72.

3. GO 7, DA, Fort Bowie, April 20–21, 1886, RG 94, LR, OAG, 1881–89, M689, 1066 AGO 1883, roll 186.

4. The Chiricahua movements and raids in Mexico are detailed in Sweeney, *Cochise to Geronimo,* 535–37. Miles alluded to these raids and reported the intrusion into Arizona in dispatches forwarded by Howard to AGUSA, MDP Presidio, April 28, 30, May 1, 1886, RG 94, LR, OAG, 1881–89, M689, 1066 AGO 1883, roll 182, NARA. A thorough account of this last raid by Geronimo and Naiche north of the border is Allan Radbourne, "Geronimo's Last Raid into Arizona," *True West* 41 (March 1994): 22–29.

5. Jack C. Gale, "Lebo in Pursuit," *Journal of Arizona History* 21 (Spring 1980): 13–24. Telegram, Howard to AGUSA, MDP Presidio, May 4, 1886, RG 94, LR, OAG, 1881–89, M689, 1066 AGO 1883, roll 182, NARA.

6. Barrett, *Geronimo, His Own Story,* 134.

7. The events narrated above are badly scrambled in military records, testimony to the agility and leadership of Naiche. For the story, consult Sweeney, *Cochise to Geronimo,* 531–51; Radbourne, "Geronimo's Last Raid into Arizona," 22–29; and Jack C. Gale, "An Ambush for Natchez," *True West* 27 (July–August 1980): 32–37.

8. The Peck affair is described in detail in Radbourne, "Geronimo's Last Raid into Arizona," 23.

9. Gale, "Lebo in Pursuit," 13–24.

10. Telegram, Howard to AGUSA, MDP Presidio (repeating telegram from Miles from Nogales, May 16, 17, and ibid., May 18, 1886, repeating telegram from Miles from Fort Huachuca, May 17); all in RG 94, LR, OAG, 1881–89, M689, 1066 AGO 1883, roll 183, NARA. Annual report of Miles, September 18, 1886, in SW, *Annual Report* (1886), 167–68. Officers of 4th Cavalry, Fort Huachuca, to editor, June 14, 1886, *Army and Navy Journal* 23 (June 26, 1887): 989 (defending Hatfield). Sweeney, *Cochise to Geronimo,* 541.

11. The order, GO 58, by order of Col. W. B. Royall, Fort Huachuca, May 4, 1886, is in SW, *Annual Report* (1886), 176–77.

12. Miles's annual report, September 18, 1886, 169. Telegram, AAG MDP Presidio to AGUSA, June 8, 1886, repeating telegram of June 7 from Miles at Calabasas, RG 94, LR, OAG, 1881–89, M689, 1066 OAG 1883, roll 184, NARA. Lawton to Mame (his wife), June 22, 1886, Lawton Papers, Indian Wars, Misc. Corres., box 1, folder Personal Letters, US Army Military History Institute, Carlisle Barracks, PA. Lawton's daily movements may be followed in the diary of Leonard Wood: Jack C. Lane, ed., *Chasing Geronimo: The Journal of Leonard Wood, May–September 1886* (Albuquerque: University of New Mexico Press, 1970).

13. Lawton to Mame, Camp at Cumpas, June 30, 1886, Lawton Papers. Telegram, Miles to AAG MDP Presidio, Deming, NM, June 23, 1886, RG 94, LR, OAG, 1881–89, M689, 1066 OAG 1883, roll 184, NARA. A detailed account of the confrontation with the Mexican troops and the recovery of Trinidad Verdin is in Wood, *Chasing Geronimo,* entry of June 18, 1886, 55–56.

14. Sweeney, *Cochise to Geronimo,* 549–53, assembles this account in detail from Mexican accounts and the story told by Trinidad Verdin.

15. Wood, *Chasing Geronimo,* entry of July 13, 1886, 69–72. Lawton to Mame, Camp south of Aros River, July 16, 1886, Lawton Papers. Sweeney, *Cochise to Geronimo,* 554–55. Miles's annual report in SW, *Annual Report* (1886), 170. Lawton's official report of September 9, 1886, RG 94, LR, OAG, 1881–89, M689, 1066 AGP 1883, roll 186, NARA.

16. Telegrams, Miles to AAG MDP Presidio, Fort Apache, July 3, 7, 1886; Lamar to Endicott, July 10, 1886; both in RG 94, LR, OAG, 1881–89, M689, 1066 AGO 1883, roll 184, NARA.

17. Endorsement of July 7 on telegram of July 3, ibid.

18. Morris E. Opler, "A Chiricahua Apache's Account of the Geronimo Campaign of 1886," *New Mexico Historical Review* 13 (October 1938): 371–73. The narrator is Sam Kenoi, a youth of eleven among the reservation Chiricahuas; his father was close to Noche, Kayitah, and Martine. Kraft, *Gatewood and Geronimo,* 133.

19. Kraft, *Gatewood and Geronimo,* 114–15. *Lt. Charles Gatewood and His Apache Wars Memoir,* ed. Louis Kraft (Lincoln: University of Nebraska Press, 2005), 122–24. Parker, *Old Army Memories,* 174.

20. Parker, *Old Army Memories,* 174–76. Kraft, *Gatewood and Geronimo,* 138–39.

CHAPTER 23. GERONIMO MEETS GATEWOOD, 1886

1. This whole story, involving dozens of telegrams, is told in condensed form by both SW Endicott and Gen. Sheridan in their annual reports, November 30, October 10, SW, *Annual Report* (1886), 36–48, 69–78.

2. A transcript of a July 26 meeting between Chatto and Secretary Endicott, kept by Capt. John G. Bourke, mostly concerns Chatto's continuing preoccupation with the fate of his family in Mexico and efforts of the government to get them back: RG 94, LR, OAG, 1881–89, M689, 1066 AGO 1883, roll 187, NARA. Transcripts have not been found of the substantive exchanges. Telegram, AGUSA to CG MDM, Chicago, August 11, 1886; telegram, Dorst to AGUSA, Fort Leavenworth, August 14, 1886; telegram, Miles to AGUSA, Albuquerque, August 20, 1886; all in ibid., roll 184.

3. Telegram, Cleveland to Acting SW R. C. Drum, Prospect House, NY, August 23, 1886, RG 94, LR, OAG, 1881–89, M689, 1066 AGO 1883, roll 186, NARA. Like most top officials, the president escaped Washington's summer heat by vacationing in more comfortable climes.

4. Miles to Sheridan, Willcox, August 2, 1886; telegram, Miles to AGUSA, Willcox, August 6, 1886; telegram, Acting SW R. C. Drum to CG MDA, September 12, 1886; all in RG 94, LR, OAG, 1881–89, M689, 1066 AGO 1883, roll 186, NARA. This telegram informs the commanding general, Division of the Atlantic, that General Terry in Chicago has been ordered to have Capt. Dorst escort the Chatto delegation directly to Florida. Fort Marion lay within the Atlantic Division.

5. Notes of interview between Gen. George Crook and Chatto, Kayatena, Naiche, and other Chiricahua Apaches, George Wrattan interpreting, Mount Vernon Barracks, Alabama, January 20, 1890, RG 94, LR, OAG, 1881–89, M689, 1066 AGO 1883, roll 191, NARA.

6. Lawton to Mame, July 7, 1886, Lawton Papers. He continued this letter through July 14. Lawton's official report to AG DA, September 9, 1886, RG 94, LR, OAG, 1881–89, M689, 1066 AGO 1883, roll 186, NARA. Lane, *Chasing Geronimo,* entry of July 13, 1886, 69–72. In several ways, Lawton and Wood describe this event differently. I have chosen the Wood version, a journal, as the more reliable.

7. Lawton to Mame, July 22, 1886, continued through July 25, 26, 27, 29, Lawton Papers.

8. James Parker, *Old Army Memories,* 177. Lawton to Mame, August 1, 1886, continued through August 3, 4, 5, Lawton Papers.

9. Wood, *Chasing Geronimo,* entries of August 3, 7, 88, 92. Kraft, *Gatewood and Geronimo,* 144–47. In his memoir, Gatewood does not mention the disagreement with Lawton; *Gatewood Memoir,* 127–28.

10. Telegram, Howard to AGUSA, MDP Presidio, August 19, 1886, repeating telegram from Miles, August 18, RG 94, LR, OAG, 1881–89, M689, 1066 AGO 1883, roll 184, NARA.

11. Lawton to Mame, August 19, 1886, Lawton Papers. Wood, *Chasing Geronimo,* entry of August 19, 1886, 98.

12. Lawton to Mame, San Bernardino River, August 2, 1886, Lawton Papers. Wood, *Chasing Geronimo,* entry of August 22, 1886, 99–100. Editor Jack Lane explains in a footnote (p. 136) that Wood failed in his journal to mention Lawton's condition. Lane later reconstructed the story of that night from the papers of officers who were there.

13. This paragraph has been assembled from bits of information included in the sources cited in note 12. See also telegram, Howard to AGUSA, MDP Presidio, August 24, 1886, repeating Miles telegram from Fort Huachuca, August 23; Miles to Lawton, n.p., August 25, 1886, Nelson A. Miles Papers, box 3, folder 6, US Army Military History Institute, Carlisle Barracks, PA; *New York Times,* August 25, 1886, carrying Tombstone dispatch of August 24. Kraft, *Gatewood and Geronimo,* 149, 151–53. Sweeney, *Cochise to Geronimo,* 559–64, drawing on Mexican sources, traces Geronimo's movements and raids leading to the Fronteras exchange.

14. Kraft, *Gatewood and Geronimo,* 158–59. Sweeney, *Cochise to Geronimo,* 562. Robinson, *Apache Voices,* 51–52, quoting interview with Martine's son George by Eve Ball. This includes testimony by Kanseah, who was there. Opler, "Chiricahua Apache's Account," 337–86. This is Sam Kenoi, who was never off the reservation but who grew up learning the details. He portrays Martine as a coward, lagging behind Kayitah and never reaching the top; Kanseah does not confirm this. This reflects an ongoing feud on the reservation between Martine and Kayitah factions. Kanseah related that Geronimo wanted to kill the two before they reached the top but was restrained by Yahnosha.

15. I have relied on Kanseah for this dialogue, which may not be accurate but represents the essence of the exchange. Kanseah was there. See Robinson, *Apache Voices,* 51–52. Eve Ball, *In the Days of Victorio,* 185–87, gives a longer version and different dialogue but substantially the same as Kanseah.

16. For the talks in the canebrake, I follow principally Kraft, *Gatewood and Geronimo,* chap. 12; and *Gatewood Memoir,* 134–35. Sweeney, *Cochise to Geronimo,* 563–65, details the meeting.

CHAPTER 24. GERONIMO SURRENDERS, 1886

1. Lawton to Mame, San Bernardino River, August 26 (continued into August 27), 1886, Lawton Papers. Wood, *Chasing Geronimo,* entry of August 26, 1886, 103.

2. Thompson to Lawton, Fort Bowie, April 29, 1886; Lawton to Miles, San Bernardino, August 30, 1886; Miles to Lawton, Fort Bowie, August 31, 1886, Miles Papers, box 3, folder A.

3. Wood, *Chasing Geronimo,* entry of August 28, 1886, 104–6.

4. *Gatewood Memoir,* 145–47. Wood, *Chasing Geronimo,* entry of August 28, 1886, 106–7.

5. This entire sequence is documented by Wood, *Chasing Geronimo,* entries of August 29, 30, 31, 107–8; and *Gatewood Memoir,* 148–52.

6. The ranch belonged to Texas cowman John Slaughter, whose ranch headquarters lay west of the San Bernardino River, at San Bernardino Springs, on the Mexican border. By 1886, with the Tombstone violence in the past, Slaughter was elected sheriff of Cochise County. San Bernardino is still a working ranch, open to the public as a historic site. It lies at the end of the "Geronimo Trail," twenty-five miles east of Douglas, Arizona.

7. *Gatewood Memoir,* 151. In his memoir, Gatewood slides over this incident, writing only that some of the officers talked of killing Geronimo. Editor Kraft, however, researched the matter in the Gatewood and other collections and found the testimony of other officers who were present. Wood, *Chasing Geronimo,* provides a daily chronicle of happenings, entries of August 30, 31, 1886, 107–8.

8. *Gatewood Memoir,* 151–52.

9. Who said what to whom and when differs from one participant and witness to another. In a sequence of lengthy reports, and in his autobiography, Miles describes long conversations. He had an interest, official and personal, in misrepresenting the exchange. Even Geronimo, in his autobiography, cannot be relied on. Other sources are vague. Secondary works draw on these sources and portray the surrender differently. I rely on *Gatewood Memoir,* 152–53; and Wood, *Chasing Geronimo,* entries of September 1–5, 1886, 109–10. My main reliance in the paragraphs that follow, however, is based on Geronimo's more contemporary version in two documents: one is Geronimo, Naiche, and Mangas to Miles (written by George Wrattan), Fort Pickens, FL, April 17, 1887, Miles Papers, box 3, folder 4. The second is Brig. Gen. David S. Stanley to AGUSA, San Antonio, TX, October 27, 1886, RG 94, LR, OAG, 1881–89, M689, 1066 AGO 1883, roll 186, NARA. Stanley commanded the Department of Texas. Because Naiche was present and had not surrendered, I infer that this explanation took place on September 4, a day after Geronimo gave in. As narrated later, Geronimo and his people were held in San Antonio while Miles argued with the president. When the decision had been made to send them on to Florida, Geronimo requested an interview with General Stanley. It is detailed, wit-

nessed by two other officers, and interpreted by George Wrattan. Stanley stated that he believed the interview credible. I accept these documents as authoritative.

10. Wood, *Chasing Geronimo,* entries of September 5, 8, 1886.

CHAPTER 25. PRISONERS OF WAR, 1886–87

1. The names, ages, and other details were furnished by Brig. Gen. David S. Stanley by orders of the War Department. Telegram, Stanley to AGUSA, San Antonio, October 11, 1886, RG 94, LR, OAG, 1881–89, M689, 1066 AGO 1883, roll 186, NARA.

2. Stanley endorsement on critical newspaper item, October 8, 1886, ibid.

3. Kanseah, in Ball, *Indeh,* 131.

4. Telegrams, Stanley to Acting SW, San Antonio, September 30, October 1, 1886, RG 94, LR, OAG, 1881–89, M689, 1066 AGO 1883, roll 186, NARA.

5. *New York Times,* October 3, 1886, printing dispatch from San Antonio October 2.

6. Stanley to AGUSA, October 27, 1886, RG 94, LR, OAG, 1881–89, M689, 1066 AGO 1883, roll 186, NARA.

7. All these telegram are available on microfilm in ibid., scattered through rolls 184, 185, and 186. Most are printed in Senate Executive Document 117, 49th Cong., 2nd sess., vol. 2, 1887, serial 2449. Leonard Wood's diary, normally reliable, contains a passage relating that on the way down to Bowie Station on September 8, he rode next to Miles's adjutant, Capt. William Thompson. Influenced by old friendship and perhaps a few drinks, Wood wrote, Thompson leaned over, patted his pocket, and said: "I have got something here which would stop this movement, but I am not going to let the old man see it until you are gone, then I will repeat it to him." The only telegram that could have stopped the movement was the directive to hold the prisoners at Fort Bowie, but Miles received and responded to this on September 7 or 8. I have found no other telegram that would have stopped the movement, the latest being the president's directive of September 8, overriding earlier directives, to confine the prisoners at the nearest secure fort or military prison. Thompson wired the message to Miles en route, and he answered it, typically fogging the language, from Engle, New Mexico, as the train bore the prisoners across Texas to San Antonio. Wood, *Chasing Geronimo,* entry of September 8, 1886, 112. Later a controversy arose between Miles and Howard over a dispatch that Miles claimed he did not see for forty-one days. The dispute extended well into 1887 before apparently ending with Howard's transfer to another assignment. I have been unable to locate this dispatch.

8. Telegrams, Acting SW to President, September 10, 1886, and to Stanley, September 29, 1886, both in RG 94, LR, OAG, 1881–89, M689, 1066 AGO 1883, roll 186, NARA.

9. The scene is described by a reporter for the *Pensacolan,* October 27, 1886, quoted in Woodward B. Skinner, *The Apache Rock Crumbles: The Captivity of Geronimo's People* (Pensacola, FL: Skinner, 1987), 106.

10. Details of life at Fort Pickens are taken from Capt. J. E. Wilson to AAG Division of the Atlantic, Fort Barrancas, FL, November 30, 1886; and Lt. Col. Loomis Langdon to AAG Division of the Atlantic, Fort Barrancas, January 7, 1887; both in RG 94, LR, OAG, 1881–89, M689, 1066 AGO 1883, roll 187, NARA.

11. Skinner, *Apache Rock Crumbles,* 151–52. Skinner had access to the Wrattan Papers but apparently found this undated letter in a newspaper.

12. Annual Report of Brig. Gen. Nelson A. Miles, September 3, 1887, SW, *Annual Report* (1887), 158.

13. Skinner, *Apache Rock Crumbles,* chaps. 11, 13, describes many of these visits, drawn from Pensacola newspapers.

14. Ibid., 184–87.

15. Langdon to AAG Division of the Atlantic, St. Francis Barracks, August 23, 1886; with endorsement of Schofield August 28 and Sheridan September 3, RG 94, LR, OAG, 1881–89, M689, 1066 AGO 1883, roll 184, NARA.

16. Telegram, Schofield to AGUSA, Governors Island, September 20, 1886; telegrams, Langdon to AAG Division of the Atlantic, St. Augustine, September 20, 29, 1886, the latter with string of endorsements decreeing disposition of scouts, ibid., roll 186.

17. Herbert Welsh, *The Apache Prisoners in Fort Marion, St. Augustine, Florida* (Philadelphia: Indian Rights Association, 1887), 20.

18. Teller to Endicott, March 21, 1887, RG 94, LR, OAG, 1881–89, M689, 1066 AGO 1883, roll 189, NARA.

19. Welsh, *Apache Prisoners,* 20n.

20. Ayres to Sheridan, St. Francis Barracks, March 25, 1887, RG 94, LR, OAG, 1881–89, M689, 1066 AGO 1883, roll 189, NARA.

21. Naiche, Mangas, and Geronimo to Miles, Fort Pickens, April 17, 1887, dictated to "G.W."; Wrattan to Miles, April 17, 1887; both in Miles Papers, box 3, folder W.

22. Telegram, Bourke to Endicott, Mobile, April 13, 1887; Bourke to Endicott, Washington, April 19, 1887; both in RG 94, LR, OAG, 1881–89, M689, 1066 AGO 1883, rolls 190, 189, NARA.

23. Telegrams from AGUSA to General Schofield, Colonels Ayers at St. Francis Barracks, Colonel Langdon at Fort Barrancas, and Maj. William Sinclair at Mount Vernon Barracks, April 18, 1887; Ayers to AAG Division of the Atlantic, St. Francis Barracks, April 27, 1887; all in ibid., roll 189.

24. Langdon to AAG Division of the Atlantic, Fort Barrancas, June 6, August 9, 1887, ibid., roll 190.

25. Wrattan to Miles, Fort Pickens, October 27, 1887, Miles Papers, box 3, folder W. Wrattan to Stanley, Fort Pickens, October 3, 1887, with Stanley endorsement of December 24 and Sheridan endorsement of December 28, RG 94, LR, OAG, 1881–89, M689, 1066 AGO 1883, roll 190, NARA.

CHAPTER 26. GERONIMO AT MOUNT VERNON BARRACKS, 1888–94

1. Walter Reed, "Geronimo and His Warriors in Captivity," *Illustrated American* 3 (August 16, 1890): 231–35, in Cozzens, *Eyewitnesses to the Indian Wars*, 627. Skinner, *Apache Rock Crumbles*, 223, drawing on Mobile newspaper accounts. He confirms Reed except that he has some people emerging from their habitations. Albert E. Wrattan, "George Wrattan, Friend of the Apaches," *Journal of Arizona History* 27 (Spring 1986): 106.

2. Skinner, *Apache Rock Crumbles*, 223.

3. Monthly report on prisoners, Maj. William Sinclair to AAG Division of the Atlantic, Mount Vernon Barracks, May 31, 1888, RG 94, LR, OAG, 1881–89, M689, 1066 AGO 1883, roll 190, NARA.

4. Bourke to AGUSA, Washington, April 19, 1887, ibid., roll 189.

5. Eugene Chihuahua in Ball, *Indeh*, 139, 152.

6. For example, see Skinner, *Apache Rock Crumbles*, 169–73, quoting from description by a reporter in the *Mobile Register*, June 26, 1887.

7. Eugene Chihuahua's quotation is from Ball, *Indeh*, 153. Skinner, *Apache Rock Crumbles*, describes many excursions from Mobile drawn in detail from Mobile newspaper accounts. See also Wrattan, "George Wrattan, Friend of the Apaches," 106.

8. Sinclair to AAG Division of the Atlantic, Mount Vernon Barracks, September 30, 1887, RG 94, LR, OAG, 1881–89, M689, 1066 AGO 1883, roll 190, NARA.

9. Ball, *Indeh*, 153. The War Department required a monthly report from the officer in charge of the Apaches; it annexed a detailed report by the post surgeon.

10. Welsh to SW William C. Endicott, Philadelphia, June 11, 1888, RG 94, LR, OAG, 1881–89, M689, 1066 AGO 1883, roll 190, NARA.

11. Welsh to President Cleveland, Indian Rights Association, Philadelphia, August 25, 1888, ibid.

12. Welsh to Secretary of the Interior William F. Vilas, November 27, 1888; Welsh to Endicott, December 13, 1888; Welsh to Cleveland, February 2, 1889; S. C. Armstrong (superintendent of Hampton Industrial Institute) to Maj. Gen. O. O. Howard, February 11, 1889; Bourke to SW Redfield Proctor, March 14, 1889; Extract of Report of an Inspection of Mount Vernon Barracks on April 7, 1889, by Inspector General Robert P. Hughes; three members of Boston Indian Citizenship Committee, Committee on Mount Vernon Apaches, to Maj. Gen. O. O. Howard,

Boston, May 16, 1889 (Howard commanded the Division of the Atlantic at Governors Island, NY); Howard to Proctor (following visit to Mount Vernon), July 1, 1889; Proctor to Welsh, July 7, 1889; Bourke to AGUSA, Washington, July 5, 1889; all in RG 94, LR, OAG, 1881–89, M689, 1066 AGO 1883, rolls 192, 193, NARA. These are only a sample of the correspondence that flew among all parties through 1888 and 1889. The controversy continued, and more sources are cited as needed.

13. Ball, *Indeh,* 154. See also Reed, "Geronimo and His Warriors in Captivity," 628.

14. Pratt to 1st Lt. C. C. Ballou at Mount Vernon Barracks, June 15, 1894, enclosing letter Geronimo to Chappo, June 6, 1894, RG 94, LR, OAG, 1881–89, M689, 1066 AGO 1883, roll 198, NARA.

15. Pratt to CIA, Carlisle, May 24, 1889; Howard to AGUSA, New York, May 31, 1889; both in bid., roll 192.

16. Reed to AAG Division of the Atlantic, Mount Vernon Barracks, November 18, 1889, ibid., roll 193.

17. President Harrison to Senate and House, January 20, 1889, attaching Proctor to President, January 13, 1890; Crook to Proctor, Washington, January 6, 1890; Guy Howard to Proctor, New York, December 23, 1889; Howard to Proctor, March 18, 1890; Herbert Welsh to Proctor, June 24, 1890; Sen. Henry Dawes to Proctor, June 28, 1890; all in ibid., rolls 193, 194. John Anthony Turcheneske Jr., *The Chiricahua Apache Prisoners of War: Fort Sill, 1894–1914* (Niwot: University Press of Colorado), 27–28, recounts the handling of the legislation in the House and Senate.

18. Wotherspoon to Post Adjutant, Mount Vernon Barracks, June 21, 1890, with endorsements of Howard, the Quartermaster General, and Secretary Proctor, RG 94, LR, OAG, 1881–89, M689, 1066 AGO 1883, roll 194, NARA.

19. Wotherspoon's monthly reports describe these events in detail, all in ibid.

20. Wotherspoon, "The Apache Prisoners of War," presentation to Lake Mohonk Conference, in *Proceedings of the Ninth Annual Meeting of the Lake Mohonk Conference of Friends of the Indian, 1891* (Lake Mohonk Conference, 1891), reprinted in House Reports, 52nd Cong., 1st sess., 1891–92, at 1159–80.

21. Eric Feaver, "Indian Soldiers, 1891–96: An Experiment on the Closing Frontier," *Prologue: The Journal of the National Archives* 7 (Summer 1975): 109–18. SW, *Annual Report* (1891), 14–16.

22. Wotherspoon to Post Adjutant, April 20, 1891; Wotherspoon to Proctor, May 16, 1891, RG 94, LR, OAG, 1881–89, M689, 1066 AGO 1883, roll 195, NARA. Michael L. Tate, "Soldiers of the Line: Apache Companies in the U.S. Army, 1891–97," *Arizona and the West* 16 (Winter 1974): 343–64. Skinner, *Apache Rock Crumbles,* 312, 316–17, 320.

23. Skinner, *Apache Rock Crumbles,* 324–25, chaps. 35–36. Wotherspoon's monthly reports in RG 94, LR, OAG, 1881–89, M689, 1066 AGO 1883, roll 196, NARA, recount in detail the activities of the company, as does Skinner.

24. Morris Opler, comp., "Autobiography of a Chiricahua Apache, Sam Kenoi," Opler Papers, no. 14/25/3238, part II, box 35, folder 4.

25. MS, "Interview by Capt. H. C. Bowen, 5th Infantry, with Geronimo at Mount Vernon Barracks, Alabama, beginning late summer 1893," Col. H. C. Bowen Papers, box 3, US Army Military History Institute, Carlisle Barracks, PA.

26. *Plattsburgh (NY) Republican,* February 15, 1893. RG 94, LR, OAG, 1881–89, M689, 1066 AGO 1883, roll 196, NARA.

27. Russell to Capt. George W. Davis (military secretary to SW), April 4, 1894; Wotherspoon to Davis, May 11, 1894; AGUSA to CO, Mount Vernon Barracks, May 14, 1894; all in RG 94, LR, OAG, 1881–89, M689, 1066 AGO 1883, roll 198, NARA. Wrattan, "George Wrattan," 111. Skinner, *Apache Rock Crumbles,* 372–77.

28. Wotherspoon to CO, Mount Vernon Barracks, July 25, 1892, with endorsements including Surgeon General's of August 28, 1892, RG 94, LR, OAG, 1881–89, M689, 1066 AGO 1883, roll 196, NARA. Sutherland retired a year later.

29. The trail of this bill through the Congress is complicated, convoluted, and laden with maneuver, deception, falsehood, and misunderstanding. It is recounted in detail in Turcheneske, *Chiricahua Apache Prisoners of War,* chap. 3.

CHAPTER 27. GERONIMO'S FINAL HOME, 1894–1909

1. Pratt to 1st Lt. C. C. Ballou (Wotherspoon's successor), Carlisle, June 15, 1894, enclosing letter of Geronimo to Chappo, June 6, 1894, RG 94, LR, OAG, 1881–89, M689, 1066 AGO 1883, roll 198, NARA.

2. Miles to Maj. George W. Davis in Office of SW, MDM Chicago, September 3, 1894, ibid., roll 197. This is a very long letter with informative attachments by 1st Lt. Hugh L. Scott and Capt. Marion P. Maus, both of whom General Miles sent to interview and assess all the adults at Mount Vernon.

3. Griswold, "Fort Sill Apaches," 43.

4. Scott to AAG MDM Chicago, Fort Sill, November 7, 1894, RG 94, LR, OAG, 1881–89, M689, 1066 AGO 1883, roll 198, NARA.

5. Ibid.

6. Sam Kenoi interview, Opler Papers, box 37.

7. Wrattan to Scott, December 29, 1894, with endorsements periodically until May 1895, RG 94, LR, OAG, 1881–89, M689, 1066 AGO 1883, roll 199, NARA.

8. Tate, "Soldiers of the Line," 343–64; Feaver, "Indian Soldiers, 1891–96," 109–18. Skinner, *Apache Rock Crumbles,* 397.

9. The history of the implementation of the Dawes Act on this and other reservations is too complex to detail here. As applied to the Chiricahuas, it is described by Brenda L. Haes, "Fort Sill, the Chiricahua Apaches, and the Government's Promise of Permanent Residence," *Chronicles of Oklahoma* 78 (Spring 2000): 28–43; and Turcheneske, *Chiricahua Apache Prisoners of War.* Scott to AG DM, February 2,

1897, RG 94, LR, OAG, 1881–89, M689, 1066 AGO 1883, roll 200, NARA, reports the Scott-Baldwin agreement with the Kiowas and Comanches.

10. Kenoi interview.

11. E. A. Burbank, *Burbank among the Indians,* as told by Ernest Royce, ed. Frank J. Taylor (Caldwell, ID: Caxton, 1946), 18–19, 21.

12. Francis E. Leupp, *Notes of a Summer Tour among the Indians of the Southwest* (Philadelphia: Indian Rights Association, 1897), 3.

13. Capron to AGUSA, Fort Sill, February 28, 1898, RG 94, LR, OAG, 1881–89, M689, 1066 AGO 1883, roll 200, NARA. Capron became a troop commander in Theodore Roosevelt's "Rough Riders" and was killed at San Juan Hill.

14. W. S. Nye, *Carbine and Lance: The Story of Old Fort Sill* (Norman: University of Oklahoma Press, 1937), 298–99. The officer was Capt. William C. Brown, from whom Nye obtained his information, as well as other facts from the post trader, W. H. Quinnette.

15. The telegrams that kept the wires humming April 16–20 are in RG 94, LR, OAG, 1881–89, M689, 1066 AGO 1883, roll 200, NARA. A more detailed account is in Turcheneske, *Chiricahua Apache Prisoners of War,* 68–20.

CHAPTER 28. GERONIMO'S LAST YEARS

1. *(Nebraska City) Conservative* September 29, 1898. The exposition and Indian Congress are described in http://digital.omahapubliclibrary.org/transmiss/congress /about.html and http://digital.omahapubliclibrary.org/transmiss/secretary/indcon gress.html. The second is a link from the first including a lengthy report by the Smithsonian's distinguished ethnologist James Mooney, who was brought in to assist in setting up the Indian Congress.

2. *New York Tribune,* October 11, 1898.

3. *New York Times,* July 4, 1904. Both Buffalo and Saint Louis are described at http://library.bfn.org/local/pan-am.html. http://lcweb2.loc.gov/papr/mckpanex.html. http://www.lib.udel.edu/ud/spec/exhibits/fairs/louis.htm. http://library.bfn.org/local/pan-am.html. http://lcweb2.loc.gov/papr/mckpanex.html. http://www.lib.udel .edu/ud/spec/exhibits/fairs/louis.htm.

4. *St. Louis Republic,* August 6, 1904.

5. *Guthrie (OK) Daily Leader,* June 20, 1904.

6. *(Woodstock, VA) Shenandoah Herald,* July 12, 1901.

7. *New York Times,* February 2, March 9, 1905. http://www.smithsonianmag .com/specialsections/heritage/Indians-on-the-Inaugural-March.html?c=y&page=1#.

8. *(Richmond, VA) Times Dispatch,* March 5, 1905.

9. *Alexandria (VA) Gazette,* March 9, 1905. Accounts also appear in *Washington (DC) Times,* March 10, 1905; and *New York Times,* March 10, 1905.

10. For the opening of the Kiowa-Comanche Reservation, see http://digital.library.okstate.edu/encyclopedia/entries/K/KI020.html. A long report on the condition and activities of the Indians for the year 1901–2 is Capt. Farrand Sayre to AG MDM, Fort Sill, June 30, 1902, RG 94, LR, OAG, 1881–89, M689, 1066 AGO 1883, roll 202, NARA. Sayre presents great detail on farming, herding, health, school, missionary work, sale of beef, hay, and other products, and the flow of whiskey from Lawton and other surrounding settlements.

11. Kate Uttinger, "Geronimo: A Study in Grace," *Leben: A Journal of Reformation Life* 5 (October–December 2009).

12. Barrett relates the story of the process of getting Geronimo's autobiography into print in the introduction to the book. It went through a number of editions, with different pagination. I have used Barrett, *Geronimo, His Own Story.*

13. Betzinez, *I Fought with Geronimo,* 38.

14. Ibid., 198. My account is drawn largely from this source, Betzinez, and Debo, *Geronimo,* chap. 23. She based her account on sources, largely the Lawton newspaper, that I have not been able to access. *New York Times,* February 17, 1909.

15. A stone monument now marks his grave, but controversy continues to question whether his bones are still there.

EPILOGUE

1. The Hugh Scott Papers, Library of Congress, contain most of the documents recording his assignment to the Chiricahua problem. I have relied on the complete history set forth by Turcheneske, *Chiricahua Prisoners of War.* See also Haes, "Fort Sill, the Chiricahua Apaches, and the Government's Promise of Permanent Residence," 28–43.

2. All the Indian sketches are taken from Griswold, "Fort Sill Apaches," which is alphabetized; and Dan L. Thrapp, ed., *Dictionary of Frontier Biography,* 3 vols. (Glendale, AZ: Arthur H. Clark, 1988).

BIBLIOGRAPHY

Adjutant General. *Chronological List of Actions, etc., with Indians from January 15, 1837, to January, 1891.* Introduction by Dale E. Floyd. Fort Collins, CO: Old Army Press, 1979.

Allen, R. S. "Pinos Altos, New Mexico." *New Mexico Historical Review* 23 (October 1948): 302–32.

Altshuler, Constance Wynn. *Cavalry Yellow and Infantry Blue: Army Officers in Arizona between 1851 and 1886.* Tucson: Arizona Historical Society, 1991.

———. *Chains of Command: Arizona and the Army, 1856–1875.* Tucson: Arizona Historical Society, 1981.

Anderson, Douglas F. "Protestantism, Progress, and Prosperity: John P. Clum and 'Civilizing' the U.S. Southwest, 1871–1886." *Western Historical Quarterly* 33 (Autumn 2002): 315–35.

Anderson, Hattie M. "Mining and Indian Fighting in Arizona and New Mexico, 1858–1861—Memoirs of Hank Smith." *Panhandle-Plains Historical Review* 1 (1920): 67–115.

Aránda, Daniel D. "Santiago McKinn, Indian Captive." *Real West* 24 (June 1981): 41–43.

Arny, W. F. M. *Indian Agent in New Mexico: The Journal of Special Agent W. F. M. Arny, 1870.* Edited by Lawrence R. Murphy. Santa Fe: Stagecoach, 1967.

Baldwin, Frank. Papers. Huntington Library, San Marino, CA.

Ball, Eve. *In the Days of Victorio: Recollections of a Warm Springs Apache.* Tucson: University of Arizona Press, 1970.

Ball, Eve, with Noran Henn and Lynda Sánchez. *Indeh: An Apache Odyssey.* Provo, UT: Brigham Young University Press, 1980.

Barnes, Will C. *Apaches and Longhorns: Reminiscences of Will C. Barnes.* Tucson: University of Arizona Press, 1982.

———. *Arizona Place Names.* Revised and enlarged by Byrd H. Granger. Tucson: University of Arizona Press, 1979.

———. "In the Apache Country." *Overland Monthly* 9 (February 1887): 172–80. In Cozzens, *Eyewitnesses to the Indian Wars,* 614–24.

Barrett, S. M. *Geronimo, His Own Story: The Autobiography of a Great Patriot Warrior.* New ed. Revised and edited by Frederick Turner. New York: Penguin, 1996.

Basso, Keith H. "Western Apache." In *Handbook of North American Indians,* Vol. 10, *Southwest,* edited by William C. Sturtevant, 462–88. Washington, DC: Smithsonian Institution, 1983.

———, ed. *Western Apache Raiding and Warfare, from the Notes of Grenville Goodwin.* Tucson: University of Arizona Press, 1971.

Basso, Keith H., and Morris E. Opler, eds. *Apachean Culture History and Ethnology.* Anthropological Papers of the University of Arizona, 21. Tucson: University of Arizona Press, 1971.

Bennett, James A. *Forts and Forays: A Dragoon in New Mexico, 1850–1856.* Edited by Clinton E. Brooks and Frank D. Reeve. Albuquerque: University of New Mexico Press, 1948.

Benson, H. B. "The Geronimo Campaign." MS, 1909. Papers of the Order of the Indian Wars, box 2, folder C-38. US Army Military Heritage Institute, Carlisle Barracks, PA. *Army and Navy Journal* (July 3, 1909): 1240–41, in Cozzens, *Eyewitnesses to the Indian Wars,* 552–56.

Betzinez, Jason, with Wilbur Sturtevant Nye. *I Fought with Geronimo.* New York: Bonanza Books, 1969.

Bourke, John G. *An Apache Campaign in the Sierra Madre: An Account of the Expedition in Pursuit of Hostile Chiricahua Apaches in the Spring of 1883.* New York: Charles Scribner's Sons, 1958.

———. "Apache Mythology." *Journal of American Folklore* 3 (July–September 1890): 209–12.

———. *The Diaries of John Gregory Bourke.* Edited by Charles M. Robinson III. Vol. 1, *November 20, 1872–July 28, 1876.* Denton: University of North Texas Press, 2003.

———. *On the Border with Crook.* New York: Charles Scribner's Sons, 1891.

———. "With Crook in the Sierra Madre." John G. Bourke Diary, 66–68, USMA Library, West Point, NY. Diary entries for May 3–26, 1883, in Cozzens, *Eyewitnesses to the Indian Wars,* 346–85.

Bowen, W. H. C. Papers. Box 3. US Army Military History Institute, Carlisle Barracks, PA.

Bret Harte, John. "Conflict at San Carlos: The Military-Civilian Struggle for Control, 1882–85." *Arizona and the West* 15 (Spring 1973): 27–44.

Burbank, E. A., as told by Ernest Royce. *Burbank among the Indians.* Edited by Frank J. Taylor. Caldwell, ID: Caxton, 1946.

Carpenter, John A. *Sword and Olive Branch: Oliver Otis Howard.* Pittsburgh: University of Pittsburgh Press, 1964.

Carroll, John M. *The Papers of the Order of Indian Wars.* Fort Collins, CO: Old Army Press, 1975.

Carter, William H. *The Life of Lieutenant General Chaffee.* Chicago: University of Chicago Press, 1917.

Clay, Thomas J. "Some Unwritten Incidents of the Geronimo Campaign." In Carroll, *Papers of the Order of Indian Wars,* 114–15.

Clum, John P. "Apache Misrule." *New Mexico Historical Review* 5 (April 1930): 138–239.

———. "The Apaches." *New Mexico Historical Review* 4 (April 1929): 107–27.

———. "Geronimo." *New Mexico Historical Review* 3 (January 1928): 1–40; (April 1928): 121–44; (July 1928): 217–64.

———. "The San Carlos Apache Police." *New Mexico Historical Review* 4 (July 1929): 203–19.

Clum, Woodworth. *Apache Agent: The Story of John P. Clum.* 1936. Lincoln: University of Nebraska Press, 1978.

Collins, Charles, *Apache Nightmare: The Battle at Cibicue Creek.* Norman: University of Oklahoma Press, 1999.

———. *The Great Escape: The Apache Outbreak of 1881.* Tucson: Westernlore Press, 1994.

Colyer, Vincent. *Peace with the Apaches of New Mexico and Arizona: Report of Vincent Colyer.* Washington, DC: GPO, 1871. Reprint, Tucson: Territorial Press, 1964.

———. Report of Western Trip, Board of Indian Commissioners, *First Annual Report, 1869,* 54–55. Washington, DC, 1870.

Conner, Daniel Ellis. *Joseph Reddeford Walker and the Arizona Adventure.* Edited by Donald J. Berthrong and Odessa Davenport. Norman: University of Oklahoma Press, 1956.

Cozzens, Peter, ed. *Eyewitnesses to the Indian Wars, 1865–1890.* Vol. 1, *The Struggle for Apacheria.* Mechanicsburg, PA: Stackpole, 2001.

Cremony, John C. *Life among the Apaches.* Tucson: Arizona Silhouettes, 1954.

Crook, George. "Apache Affairs: An Interview with General Crook." New York *Herald,* July 9, 1883. In Cozzens, *Eyewitnesses to the Indian Wars,* 396–404.

———. "The Apache Problem." *Journal of the Military Service Institution of the United States* 7 (September 1886): 257–69. In Cozzens, *Eyewitnesses to the Indian Wars,* 593–603.

———. "The Apache Troubles." *Army and Navy Register,* October 21, 1882. In Cozzens, *Eyewitnesses to the Indian Wars,* 311–13.

———. *Crook's Resume of Operations against Apache Indians, 1882–1886.* Introduction and notes by Barry C. Johnson. London: Johnson-Taunton Military Press, 1971.

———. "Diary, August 13, 1885–April 14, 1886, Geronimo Campaign." Crook-Kennon Papers. [This folder also contains typescript of excepts from Schmitt's autobiography of Crook, and photocopy of *New York Herald,* n.d., containing extensive coverage of Agreement of July 7, 1883, with emphasis on Crook interview.]

———. *General George Crook: His Autobiography.* Edited by Martin F. Schmitt. Norman: University of Oklahoma Press, 1946.

———. Interview with Washington correspondent, July 7, 1883. *New York Herald,* July 9, 1883; filed in folder Crook Diary, US Army Military History Institute, Carlisle Barracks, PA.

Crook-Kennon. Papers. US Army Military History Institute, Carlisle Barracks, PA.

Cruse, Thomas. *Apache Days and After.* 1941. Lincoln: University of Nebraska Press, 1987.

———. [Describes Cibicue, particularly conduct of Carr in connection with findings of court of inquiry.] January 1893. Papers of the Order of Indian Wars, box 3. US Army Military History Institute, Carlisle Barracks, PA.

———. "From Hembrillo Canyon to Chevelon's Fork." Tucson: Gatewood Collection, Arizona Historical Society. In Cozzens, *Eyewitnesses to the Indian Wars,* 262–66.

Curley, Sherman. "The Life of Sherman Curley—Arivaipa Apache." Grenville Goodwin Papers, Arizona State Museum, Tucson.

Daly, Henry W. "The Capture of Geronimo." *Winners of the West* 11 (December 1933): 1, 3. In Cozzens, *Eyewitnesses to the Indian Wars,* 447–73.

———. "The Geronimo Campaign." *Journal of the U.S. Cavalry Association* 19 (October 1908): 247–62. In Cozzens, *Eyewitnesses to the Indian Wars,* 473–84.

———. "Scouts Good and Bad." *American Legion Monthly* 5 (August 1928): 24–25, 66–70. In Cozzens, *Eyewitnesses to the Indian Wars,* 484–85.

Davis, Britton. "The Difficulties of Indian Warfare." *Army and Navy Journal* 33 (October 24, 1885): 242–44. In Cozzens, *Eyewitnesses to the Indian Wars,* 488–94.

———. "A Short Account of the Chiricahua Tribe of Apache Indians and the Causes Leading to the Outbreak in May – 1885." [c. 1920s] MS. Papers of the Order of Indian Wars, box 4, folder C-4. US Army Military Heritage Institute, Carlisle Barracks, PA.

———. *The Truth about Geronimo.* 1929. Edited by M. M. Quaife. Foreword by Robert M. Utley. New Haven: Yale University Press, 1963.

Debo, Angie. *Geronimo: The Man, His Time, His Place.* Norman: University of Oklahoma Press, 1976.

Dixon, David. *Hero of Beecher Island: The Life and Military Career of George A. Forsyth.* Lincoln: University of Nebraska Press, 1994.

"Documents of Arizona History Selected from the Archives of the Society: 'All about Courtesy': In a Verbal War, John P. Clum Has a Parting Shot." *Arizoniana* 4 (Spring 1962): 11–18.

Dunlay, Thomas W. *Wolves for the Blue Soldiers: Indian Scouts and Auxiliaries with the United States Army, 1860–90.* Lincoln: University of Nebraska Press, 1982.

Elliott, Charles P. "The Geronimo Campaign of 1885–1886." *Journal of the U.S. Cavalry Association* 21 (September 1910): 211–36. In Cozzens, *Eyewitnesses to the Indian Wars,* 427–46.

———. "An Indian Reservation under General George Crook." [c. 1901.] *Military Affairs* (Summer 1948): 91–102. In Cozzens, *Eyewitnesses to the Indian Wars,* 405–13.

Ellis, Richard N. *General Pope and U.S. Indian Policy.* Albuquerque: University of New Mexico Press, 1970.

Farish, Thomas E. *History of Arizona.* 8 vols. San Francisco: Filmer Brothers, 1915–18.

Faulk, Odie B. *Crimson Desert: Indian Wars of the American Southwest.* New York: Oxford University Press, 1974.

———. *The Geronimo Campaign.* New York: Oxford University Press, 1969.

Feaver, Eric. "Indian Soldiers, 1891–96: An Experiment on the Closing Frontier." *Prologue: Journal of the National Archives* 7 (Summer 1975): 109–18.

Fieberger, G. J. "General Crook's Campaign in Old Mexico in 1883: Events Leading up to It and Personal Experiences in the Campaign." In Carroll, *Papers of the Order of the Indian Wars,* 193–201.

Finerty, John F. "On Campaign after Cibicue Creek." *Chicago Times,* September 18–October 21, 1881." In Cozzens, *Eyewitnesses to the Indian Wars,* 236–61.

Forsyth, George A. "Record of Events during the Expedition under Lieut. Col. G. A. Forsyth, 4th Cavalry, from Fort Cummings, N.M., on April 18, '82, against the Hostile Apache Indians." Papers of the Order of Indian Wars, box 10, folder X18. US Army Military History Institute, Carlisle Barracks, PA.

———. *Thrilling Days of Army Life.* 1900. Introduction by David Dixon. Lincoln: University of Nebraska Press, 1994.

[Forsyth, William W.] "Diary of the Sierra Madre Campaign." *(Tucson) Daily Arizona Star,* June 17, 1883. In Cozzens, *Eyewitnesses to the Indian Wars,* 391–93. [Anonymous but probably Lieutenant William W. Forsyth, Sixth Cavalry. Covers May 1–30, 1883.]

Fountain, S. W. [Fight with Geronimo at Lillie's Ranch, NM, December 9, 1885.] MS 12/7/31. Papers of the Order of Indian Wars, box 10, folder X19. US Army Military Heritage Institute, Carlisle Barracks, PA.

Frazer, Robert W. *Forts of the West: Military Forts and Presidios and Posts Commonly Called Forts West of the Mississippi River to 1898.* Norman: University of Oklahoma Press, 1977.

Frelinghuysen, Frederick T., [Secretary of State]. "Mexico: Reciprocal Right to Pursue Savage Indians across the Boundary Line." Agreement between United States and Mexico, July 29, 1882. In Cozzens, *Eyewitnesses to the Indian Wars,* 343–45.

Fritz, Henry E. *The Movement for Indian Assimilation, 1860–1890.* Philadelphia: University of Pennsylvania Press, 1963.

Gale, Jack C. "An Ambush for Natchez." *True West* 27 (July–August 1980): 32–37.

———. "Lebo in Pursuit." *Journal of Arizona History* 21 (Spring 1980): 13–24.

Gardner, John P. "Escorting Chihuahua's Band to Florida." *National Tribune,* September 27, 1923. In Cozzens, *Eyewitnesses to the Indian Wars,* 567–68.

Gardner, Mark L. *Geronimo: A Biography.* Tucson: Western National Parks Association, 2006.

Gatewood, Charles. *Lt. Charles Gatewood and His Apache War Memoir.* Edited by Louis Kraft. Lincoln: University of Nebraska Press, 2005.

———. Papers. Arizona Historical Society, Tucson.

———. *The Social Organization of the Western Apache.* Preface by Keith H. Basso. Tucson: University of Arizona Press, 1969.

Grant, U. S., et al. "Where Is Crook?" *El Paso Times,* May 20, 1883. In Cozzens, *Eyewitnesses to the Indian Wars,* 386–90. [Newspaper items about Crook in the Sierra Madre.]

Gregg, Robert D. *The Influence of Border Troubles on Relations between the United States and Mexico, 1876–1910.* 1937. New York: Da Capo, 1970.

Griffen, William B. *Apaches at War and Peace: The Janos Presidio, 1750–1858.* Norman: University of Oklahoma Press, 1998.

———. "Apache Indians and the Northern Mexican Peace Establishments." In *Southwestern Culture History: Collected Papers in Honor of Albert Schroeder,* edited by Charles H. Lange. *Papers of the Archaeological Society of New Mexico* 10 (1985): 183–95.

———. "The Chiricahua Apache Population Resident at the Janos Presidio, 1792–1858." *Journal of the Southwest* 33 (Summer 1991): 151–99.

———. "The Compás: A Chiricahua Apache Family of the Late 18th and Early 19th Century." *American Indian Quarterly* 7 (Spring 1983): 21–49.

Griswold, Gillett. "The Fort Sill Apaches: Their Vital Statistics, Tribal Origins, Antecedents." 1961. MS, Field Artillery Museum, Fort Sill, OK.

Haes, Brenda L. "Fort Sill, the Chiricahua Apaches, and the Government's Promise of Permanent Residence." *Chronicles of Oklahoma* 78 (Spring 2000): 28–43.

Haley, James L. *Apaches: A History and Culture Portrait.* Norman: University of Oklahoma Press, 1981.

Hand, George. *The Civil War in Apacheland: Sergeant George Hand's Diary: California, Arizona, West Texas, New Mexico, 1861–64.* Edited by Neil B. Carmony. Silver City, AZ: High Lonesome Books, 1996.

Hanna, Robert. "With Crawford into Mexico." *Arizona Historical Review* 6 (April 1935): 56–65. *Overland Monthly* 8 (July 1886): 78–83. In Cozzens, *Eyewitnesses to the Indian Wars,* 509–15.

Horn, Tom. *The Life of Tom Horn: Government Scout and Interpreter.* Norman: University of Oklahoma Press, 1986.

Howard, O. O. "Account of Gen'l Howard's Mission to the Apaches and Navajos." Reprinted from *Washington Daily Morning Chronicle,* November 10, 1872. Papers of the Order of Indian Wars. US Army Military History Institute, Carlisle Barracks, PA.

———. *My Life and Experiences among Our Hostile Indians.* 1907. Introduction by Robert M. Utley. New York: Da Capo Press, 1972.

Jett, William B. "Engagement in Guadalupe Canyon." *Winners of the West* 14 (August 1937): 3, 5. In Cozzens, *Eyewitnesses to the Indian Wars,* 495–96.

———. "The Reluctant Corporal: The Autobiography of William Bladen Jett." Edited by Henry P. Walker. *Journal of Arizona History* 12 (Spring 1971): 1–50.

Jozhe, Benedict. "A Brief History of the Fort Sill Apache Tribe." *Chronicles of Oklahoma* 34 (Winter 1961): 427–32.

Kappler, Charles J., comp. *Indian Affairs: Laws and Treaties.* 7 vols. Washington, DC: GPO, 1902–3.

King, James T. *War Eagle: A Life of General Eugene A. Carr.* Lincoln: University of Nebraska Press, 1963.

Kraft, Louis. *Gatewood and Geronimo.* Albuquerque: University of New Mexico Press, 2000.

———, ed. *Lt. Charles Gatewood and His Apache Wars Memoir.* Lincoln: University of Nebraska Press, 2005.

Lake Mohonk Conference. *Proceedings of the Ninth Annual Meeting of the Lake Mohonk Conference of Friends of the Indian, 1891.* Lake Mohonk Conference, 1891.

Lawton, Henry W. Letters to wife Mame from Mexico. Papers of Order of the Indian Wars, Misc. Coll., box 1, folder Personal Letters, September 2, 1886. US Army Military History Institute, Carlisle Barracks, PA.

Leckson, Stephen H. *Nana's Raid: Apache Warfare in New Mexico, 1881.* El Paso: Texas Western Press, 1987.

Leupp, Francis E. *Notes of a Summer Tour among the Indians of the Southwest.* Philadelphia: Indian Rights Association, 1897.

Lister, Forcence C., and Robert H. Lister. *Chihuahua: Storehouse of Storms.* Albuquerque: University of New Mexico Press, 1966.

Lloyd, Frederick. "A Profile of San Carlos Agency." In Cozzens, *Eyewitnesses to the Indian Wars,* 324–31.

Lockwood, Frank C. *The Apache Indians.* New York: Macmillan, 1938.

Longstreet, David. Narrative. In Basso, *Western Apache Raiding and Warfare,* 187–203. [Apache scout interviewed in 1931, born c. 1855.]

Lummis, Charles F. *General Crook and the Apache Wars.* Foreword by Dudley Gordon. Edited by Turbese Lummis Fiske. Flagstaff, AZ: Northland, 1966.

Marion, Jeanie. "'As Long as the Stone Lasts': General O. O. Howard's 1872 Peace Conference." *Journal of Arizona History* 35 (Summer 1994): 109–40.

Masterson, Murat. "General Crook's Return." *(Prescott) Arizona Democrat,* November 25, 1882. In Cozzens, *Eyewitnesses to the Indian Wars,* 314–17.

Mazzanovich, Anton. "Life in Arizona Army Posts during the 1880s." *Arizona Daily Star,* Fiftieth Anniversary Edition, 1927. In Cozzens, *Eyewitnesses to the Indian Wars,* 332–39.

———.*Trailing Geronimo.* 1926. Revised ed., n.p., 1931.

McCarthy, Kiernan, and C. L. Sonnichsen. "Trina Verdin and the Truth of History." *Journal of Arizona History* 14 (Summer 1973): 149–64.

McChristian, Douglas C. *Fort Bowie, Arizona: Combat Post of the Southwest, 1858–1894.* Norman: University of Oklahoma Press, 2005.

———, and Larry L. Ludwig. "Eyewitness to the Bascom Affair: An Account by Sergeant Daniel Robinson, Seventh Infantry." *Journal of Arizona History* 42 (Autumn 2001): 277–300.

Meriwether, David. *My Life in the Mountains and on the Plains.* Edited by Robert A. Griffen. Norman: University of Oklahoma Press, 1965.

Miles, Nelson A. *Personal Recollections and Observations of General Nelson A. Miles.* Chicago: Werner, 1896. Reprint ed., with new introduction by Robert M. Utley, New York: Da Capo, 1969.

———. [Photocopies of correspondence and other papers relating to the Apache campaign of 1886.] Miles Papers, box 3, folder 6. US Army Military History Institute, Carlisle Barracks, PA.

———. *Serving the Republic: Memoirs of the Civil and Military Life of Nelson A. Miles.* New York: Harper and Brothers, 1911.

———. "On the Trail of Geronimo." *Cosmopolitan* 51 (June 1911): 249–62. In Cozzens, *Eyewitnesses to the Indian Wars,* 536–39.

Mills, Stephen C. Papers. US Army Military History Institute, Carlisle Barracks, PA.

Myers, Lee. "The Enigma of Mangas Coloradas' Death." *New Mexico Historical Review* 41 (January 1966): 287–304.

Nye, W. S. *Carbine and Lance: The Story of Old Fort Sill.* Norman: University of Oklahoma Press, 1937.

Official Records of the War of the Rebellion. Ser. 1, vol. 50, pts. 1 and 2.

Ogle, Ralph H. *Federal Control of the Western Apaches, 1848–1886.* 1940. Introduction by Oakah L. Jones, Jr. Albuquerque: University of New Mexico Press, 1970.

Opler, Morris E. "The Apachean Culture and Its Origins," in William C. Sturtevant, ed., *Handbook of North American Indians* 10, *Southwest* (Washington DC: Smithsonian Institution, 1983), 368–92.

———. *An Apache Life-Way: The Economic, Social, and Religious Institutions of the Chiricahua Apache Indians.* Chicago: Cooper Square, 1965.

———. *Apache Odyssey: A Journey between Two Worlds.* New York: Holt, Rinehart, and Winston, 1969. 2nd ed., introduction by Philip J. Greenfield. Lincoln: University of Nebraska Press, 2002.

———. "Chiricahua Apache." in William C. Sturtevant, ed., *Handbook of North American Indians,* vol. 10, *Southwest,* ed. Alfonso Ortiz, 401–18. Washington DC: Smithsonian Institution, 1983.

———. "A Chiricahua's Account of the Geronimo Campaign of 1886 [Samuel E. Kenoi]." *New Mexico Historical Review* 13 (October 1938): 337–86.

———. "The Identity of the Apache Mansos." *American Anthropologist* 44 (October–December 1942): 725.

———. "An Interpretation of Ambivalence of Two American Indian Tribes." *Journal of Social Psychology* 7 (1936): 32–116.

———. *Myths and Tales of the Chiricahua Apache Indians.* Memoirs of the American Folk-Lore Society, 1942. Menasha, WI: George Banta, 1942.

———. "An Outline of Chiricahua Apache Social Organization." In *Social Anthropology of North American Tribes: Essays in Social Organization, Law, and Religion,* Edited by Fred Eggan. Chicago: University of Chicago Press, 1937.

———. Papers. No. 14/25/3238. Division of Rare Manuscripts Collections, Cornell University Library.

———. "Some Implications of Culture Theory for Anthropology and Psychology." *American Journal of Orthopsychiatry* 18 (October 1948): 617.

———, ed. *Grenville Goodwin among the Western Apache: Letters from the Field.* Tucson: University of Arizona Press, 1973.

Opler, Morris E., and Harry Hoijer. "The Raid and War-Path Language of the Chiricahua Apache." *American Anthropologist* 42 (October–December 1942): 617–35.

Ove, Robert S., and Henrietta Stockel. *Geronimo's Kids: A Teacher's Lessons of the Apache Reservation.* College Station: Texas A&M University Press, 1997.

Park, Joseph F. "The Apaches in Mexican-American Relations." *Arizona and the West* 3 (Summer 1961): 129–46.

———. "Spanish Indian Policy in Northern Mexico, 1765–1910." *Arizona and the West* 4 (Winter 1962): 325–44.

Parker, James. "Extracts from Personal Memoirs of Brig. Gen. James Parker, U.S. Army Retired." Papers of the Order of Indian Wars, x38/2, box 11, folder X-40. US Army Military History Institute, Carlisle Barracks, PA. [Near duplicate of his book.]

———. "The Geronimo Campaign." *Proceedings of the Annual Meeting and Dinner of the Order of the Indian Wars of the United States* (January 26, 1929): 32–61. Papers of the Order of Indian Wars, box 3, folder G-6 (Gatewood). U.S. Army Military Heritage Institute, Carlisle Barracks, PA.

———. *The Old Army: Memories, 1872–1918.* Introduction by Major General Robert L. Bullard. Philadelphia: Dorrance, 1929.

Perry, Richard J. *Western Apache Heritage: People of the Mountain Corridor.* Austin: University of Texas Press, 1991.

Pettit, James S. [Fourth Cavalry; commanded supply camp at Lang's Ranch.] "Apache Campaign Notes—1886." *Journal of the Military Service Institution of the United States* 7 (September 1886): 331–38. In Cozzens, *Eyewitnesses to the Indian Wars,* 532–35.

Pierce, Michael D. *The Most Promising Young Officer: A Life of Ranald Slidell Mackenzie.* Norman: University of Oklahoma Press, 1993.

Porter, Joseph C. *Paper Medicine Man: John Gregory Bourke and His American West.* Norman: University of Oklahoma Press, 1986.

Prucha, Francis Paul. *American Indian Policy in Crisis: Christian Reformers and the Indian, 1865–1900.* Norman: University of Oklahoma Press, 1976.

Radbourne, Allan. "Geronimo's Contraband Cattle." *Missionaries, Indians and Soldiers: Studies in Cultural Interaction* (1996): 1–24.

———. "Geronimo's Last Raid into Arizona." *True West* 41 (March 1994): 22–29.

———. "The Juh-Geronimo Surrender of 1879." *English Westerners' Brand Book* 21 (1983): 1–18.

———. *Mickey Free: Apache Captive, Interpreter, and Indian Scout.* Tucson: Arizona Historical Society, 2005.

Rafferty, William A. "Rafferty's Trail." *(Tucson) Arizona Daily Star,* May 17, 1882. In Cozzens, *Eyewitnesses to the Indian Wars,* 286–89.

Randall, A. Frank. "In the Heart of the Sierra Madre." *El Paso Times,* June 20, 1883. In Cozzens, *Eyewitnesses to the Indian Wars,* 394–95. [Diary, May 14–22, 1883.]

Reed, Walter. "Geronimo and His Warriors in Captivity." *Illustrated American* 3 (August 16, 1890): 231–35. In Cozzens, *Eyewitnesses to the Indian Wars,* 625–29.

Reeve, Frank D., ed. "Puritan and Apache: A Diary." *New Mexico Historical Review* 23 (October 1948): 269–302; 24 (January 1949): 12–53.

Rippy, J. Fred. "The Indians of the Southwest in the Diplomacy of the United States and Mexico, 1848–1853." *Hispanic-American Historical Review* (August 1919): 363–96.

Roberts, Charles D. [Letters/diary, 1886.] Papers of the Order of Indian Wars, box 7, folder R-12 or A-15. US Army Military History Institute, Carlisle Barracks, PA. Diary. Arizona Historical Society, Tucson.

Roberts, David. *They Moved Like the Wind: Cochise, Geronimo, and the Apache Wars.* New York: Simon and Schuster, 1993.

Robinson, Charles M., III. *General Crook and the Western Frontier.* Norman: University of Oklahoma Press, 2001.

Robinson, Sherry. *Apache Voices: Their Stories of Survival as Told to Eve Ball.* Albuquerque: University of New Mexico Press, 2000.

Rolak, Bruno. "General Miles's Mirrors: The Heliograph in the Geronimo Campaign of 1886." *Journal of Arizona History* 16 (Summer 1975): 145–60.

Rope, John. "Experiences of an Indian Scout: Excerpts from the Life of John Rope, an 'Old Timer' of the White Mountain Apaches." As told to Grenville Goodwin. *Arizona Historical Review* 7 (January 1936): 31–68.

———. Narrative. In Basso, *Western Apache Raiding and Warfare*, 93–185. [Interviewed in 1932, born c. 1855; experiences as Apache scout.]

Ruhlen, George. "Fort Thorn—An Historical Vignette." *Password* (El Paso Historical Society) 4 (October 1960): 127–37.

Russell, Don. *Campaigning with King: Charles King, Chronicler of the Old Army.* Edited by Paul Hedren. Lincoln: University of Nebraska Press, 1991.

Sacks, Benjamin H. "The Origins of Fort Buchanan, Myth and Fact." *Arizona and the West* 7 (Autumn 1965): 207–26.

Salzman, M., Jr. "Geronimo, the Napoleon of the Indians." *Journal of Arizona History* 8 (Winter 1967): 215–47.

Santee, Ross. *Apache Land.* 1947. Lincoln: University of Nebraska Press, 1971.

Schroeder, Albert H. *Apache Indians.* Vol. 4, *A Study of the Apache Indians.* New York: Garland, 1974.

Schubert, Frank N. *Voices of the Buffalo Soldier: Records, Reports, and Recollections of Military Life and Service in the West.* Albuquerque: University of New Mexico Press, 2003.

Scott, Hugh L. Papers. Library of Congress, Washington, DC.

———. *Some Memories of a Soldier.* New York: Century, 1928.

Shapard, Bud. *Chief Loco: Apache Peacemaker.* Norman: University of Oklahoma Press, 2010.

Sherman, William T. Papers. Library of Congress, Washington, DC.

Shipp, W. E. "Captain Crawford's Last Expedition." Papers of the Order of Indian Wars, box 2. US Army Military History Institute, Carlisle Barracks, PA. *Journal of the U.S. Cavalry Association* 5 (December 1892): 343–61. In Cozzens, *Eyewitnesses to the Indian Wars,* 516–31.

Sieber, Al. "Military and Indians." *Prescott Weekly Courier,* May 27, 1882. In Cozzens, *Eyewitnesses to the Indian Wars,* 290–310.

Simmons, Mark. *Massacre on the Lordsburg Road: A Tragedy of the Apache Wars.* College Station: Texas A&M Press, 1997.

Skinner, Woodward R. (Woody). *The Apache Rock Crumbles: The Captivity of Geronimo's People.* Pensacola, FL: Skinner, 1987.

Smith, Ralph A. "Apache Plunder Trails Southward, 1831–1840." *New Mexico Historical Review* 87 (January 1962): 20–42.

———. *Borderlander: The Life of James Kirker, 1793–1852.* Norman: University of Oklahoma Press, 1999.

———. "Indians in American-Mexican Relations before the War of 1846." *Hispanic American Historical Review* 43 (February 1963): 33–64.

———. "The Scalp Hunt in Chihuahua—1849." *New Mexico Historical Review* 40 (April 1965): 116–40.

Sonnichsen, C. L., ed. *Geronimo and the End of the Apache Wars.* Lincoln: University of Nebraska Press, 1990.

Steck, Michael. Papers. University of New Mexico Library, Albuquerque.

Stevens, Robert C. "The Apache Menace in Sonora, 1831–1849." *Arizona and the West* 6 (Autumn 1964): 211–22.

Stockel, H. Henrietta. *Chiricahua Apache Women and Children: Safekeepers of the Heritage.* College Station: Texas A&M Press, 2000.

———. "Geronimo: Facts, Anecdotes, and Hearsay." *Journal of the West* 47 (Spring 2008): 3–11.

———. *Shame and Endurance: The Untold Story of the Chiricahua Apache Prisoners of War.* Tucson: University of Arizona Press, 2004.

Stout, Joe A., Jr. "Soldiering and Suffering in the Geronimo Campaign: Reminiscences of Lawrence R. Jerome." *Journal of the West* 11 (January 1972): 206–24.

Strickland, Rex W. "The Birth and Death of a Legend: The Johnson Massacre of 1837." *Arizona and the West* 18 (Autumn 1976): 257–86.

Summerhayes, Martha. *Vanished Arizona: Recollections of the Army Life of a New England Woman.* 1911. Lincoln: University of Nebraska Press, 1979.

Sweeney, Edwin R. "Cochise and the Prelude to the Bascom Affair: *New Mexico Historical Review* 64 (October 1989): 427–46.

———. *Cochise: Chiricahua Apache Chief.* Norman: University of Oklahoma Press, 1991.

———. *From Cochise to Geronimo: The Chiricahua Apaches, 1874–86.* Norman: University of Oklahoma Press, 2010.

———. "Geronimo and Chatto: Alternative Apache Ways." *Wild West* 20 (August 2007): 30–39.

———. "I Had Lost All: Geronimo and the Carrasco Massacre of 1851." *Journal of Arizona History* 27 (Spring 1986): 35–52.

———. "In the Shadow of Geronimo: Chihuahua of the Chiricahuas." *Wild West* 13 (August 2000): 25–28, 67.

———. *Mangas Coloradas: Chief of the Chiricahua Apaches.* Norman: University of Oklahoma Press, 1998.

———. *Merejildo Grivalva: Apache Captive, Army Scout.* El Paso: Texas Western Press, 1992.

———, ed. *Making Peace with Cochise: The 1872 Journal of Captain Joseph Alton Sladen.* Norman: University of Oklahoma Press, 1997.

Tate, Michael L. "Soldiers of the Line: Apache Companies in the U.S. Army, 1891–1897." *Arizona and the West* 16 (Winter 1974): 343–64.

Tax, Sol. Papers. University of Chicago Special Collections Research Center.

Tevis, James H. *Arizona in the '50's*. Albuquerque: University of New Mexico Press, 1954.

Thrapp, Dan L. *Al Sieber, Chief of Scouts*. Norman: University of Oklahoma Press, 1964.

———. *The Conquest of Apacheria*. Norman: University of Oklahoma Press, 1967.

———. *Dateline Fort Bowie: Charles Fletcher Lummis Reports on the Apache War*. Norman: University of Oklahoma Press, 1979.

———. *General Crook and the Sierra Madre Adventure*. Norman: University of Oklahoma Press, 1974.

———. *Juh, an Incredible Indian*. El Paso: Texas Western Press, 1973.

———. *Victorio and the Mimbres Apaches*. Norman: University of Oklahoma Press, 1974.

———, ed. *Dictionary of Frontier Biography*. 3 vols. Glendale, AZ: Arthur H. Clark, 1988.

Toole, James H. "Agent Tiffany Torn to Tatters." *(Tucson) Arizona Daily Star*, October 24, 1882. In Cozzens, *Eyewitnesses to the Indian Wars*, 318–20.

Turcheneske, John Anthony, Jr. *The Chiricahua Apache Prisoners of War: Fort Sill, 1894–1914*. Niwot: University Press of Colorado, 1997.

US Army Military History Institute, Carlisle Barracks, PA.

US Board of Indian Commissioners. *Second Annual Report, 1870*. Washington, DC: GPO, 1871.

US Bureau of Indian Affairs. Annual Reports, 1849–87.

US Congress. Senate Executive Document 117. 49th Cong., 2d sess., 1887.

———. Senate Executive Document 35. 51st Cong., 1st sess., 1890.

US National Archives and Records Administration. RG 75, OIA Treaty File; OIA NM LR.

———. RG 77, Topographical Engineers, Office of the Chief of Engineers, LR.

———. RG 98, Dept. NM, LR.

———. RG 108, Hq. Army, LR.

———. Microfilm. RG 94, LR, OAG, 1871–80, M666: roll 24, 2465 AGO 1871, Correspondence Relating to Vincent Colyer; roll 123, 3383 AGO 1873, Correspondence Relating to Howard's Mission to Cochise; roll 194, 1504 AGO 1875, Correspondence Relating to Ouster of James E. Roberts as agent at Fort Apache and removal of Apaches to San Carlos by Clum; roll 265, 2576 AGO 1875, Correspondence relating to removal of Chiricahuas to San Carlos; roll 326, 1927 AGO 1877, Correspondence relating to arrest and removal of Geronimo's band from Ojo Caliente to San Carlos; roll 366, 5705 AGO 1877, Correspondence relating to operations against Warm Springs Indians who fled San Carlos, 1877–79; rolls 526–28, 6058 AGO 1879, Papers relating to operations against Victorio, 1879–81.

————. Microfilm. RG 94, LR, OAG, 1881–89, M689: roll 44, 4746 AGO 1881, Correspondence concerning efforts to capture Chiricahuas terrorizing border region of District of NM, July–December 1881; rolls 96–97, 1749 AGO 1882, Papers relating to the outbreaks in NM and AZ by Chiricahuas who escaped from San Carlos; rolls 173–202, Papers relating to Chiricahua uprising under Geronimo et al.; roll 536, 3264 AGO 1887, Reports of Miles and others concerning operations in AZ against Apaches.

US War Department. Annual Reports of the Secretary of War, 1866–87.

Utley, Robert M. *Frontiersmen in Blue: The United States Army and the Indian, 1846–65.* New York: Macmillan, 1957.

————. *Life Wild and Perilous: Mountain Men and the Paths to the Pacific.* New York, Henry Holt, 1997.

————. "Victorio's War." *MHQ: The Quarterly Journal of Military History* 21 (Autumn 2008): 20–29.

Uttinger, Kate. "Geronimo: A Study in Grace." *Leben: A Journal of Reformation Life* 5 (October–December 2009).

Valor, Palmer. Narrative. In Basso, *Western Apache Raiding and Warfare,* 41–71. [Interviewed in 1932, when about ninety-five; White Mountain Apache, recounts raids into Mexico.]

Walker, Henry P., ed. "Colonel Bonneville's Report: The Department of New Mexico in 1859." *Arizona and the West* 22 (Autumn 1980): 343–62.

————. "Soldier in the California Column: The Diary of John W. Teal." *Arizona and the West* 13 (Spring 1971): 33–82.

Wallace, Andrew. "General August V. Kautz in Arizona, 1974–1878." *Arizoniana* 4 (Winter 1963): 54–65.

Welsh, Herbert. *The Apache Prisoners in Fort Marion, St. Augustine, Florida.* Philadelphia: Indian Rights Association, 1887.

Wilcox, Philip P. "An End to Indian Outbreaks." *(Denver) Tribune,* November 2, 1882. In Cozzens, *Eyewitnesses to the Indian Wars,* 321–23.

Willcox, Orlando B. Papers, box 9. US Army Military History Institute, Carlisle Barracks, PA.

Wood, Leonard. *Chasing Geronimo: The Journal of Leonard Wood, May–September 1886.* Edited and introduction by Jack C. Lane. Albuquerque: University of New Mexico Press, 1970.

Wooster, Robert. *Nelson A. Miles and the Twilight of the Frontier Army.* Lincoln: University of Nebraska Press, 1995.

Worcester, Donald E. *The Apaches: Eagles of the Southwest.* Norman: University of Oklahoma Press, 1979.

Wotherspoon, Lt. W. W. "The Apache Prisoners of War." Presentation to Lake Mohonk Conference. In *Proceedings of the Ninth Annual Meeting of the Lake Mohonk*

Conference of Friends of the Indian, 1891. Lake Mohonk Conference, 1891. Reprinted in HR, 52nd Cong., 1st sess., 1891–92, at 1159–60.

Wrattan, Albert E. "George Wrattan: Chief Apache Scout and Interpreter [for] Geronimo and His Warriors." MS, n.d., 27–36. [Intended as book. Albert was George's son. MS loaned by Henrietta Stockel.]

———. "George Wrattan, Friend of the Apaches." *Journal of Arizona History* 27 (Spring 1986): 91–124.

Wright, Harry R."In the Days of Geronimo." *Pearson's Magazine* 26 (February 1905): 196–200. In Cozzens, *Eyewitnesses to the Indian Wars,* 497–501.

INDEX